The Supermanagers

· The Supe

McGRAW-HILL BOOK COMPANY

ROBERT HELLER

managers

Managing for Success,
The Movers and The Doers, The Reasons Why

New York   St. Louis   San Francisco
Auckland   Bogotá   Guatemala
Hamburg   Johannesburg   Lisbon
London   Madrid   Mexico   Montreal
New Delhi   Panama   Paris   San Juan
São Paulo   Singapore   Sydney
Tokyo   Toronto

A Truman Talley Book, reprinted by permission of
E. P. Dutton, Inc.

First McGraw-Hill Paperback edition, 1985

1 2 3 4 5 6 7 8 9 F G R F G R 8 7 6 5

ISBN 0-07-028309-5

Library of Congress Cataloging in Publication Data

Heller, Robert, 1932–
The supermanagers: managing for success, the movers and
the doers, the reasons why.

Reprint. Originally published: New York: E. P. Dutton, © 1984.
1st ed.
Bibliography: p.
1. Management.   2. Industrial management.   I. Title.
HD31.H445   1985   658   85-164
ISBN 0-07-028309-5 (pbk.)

In memory of Roy Andries De Groot

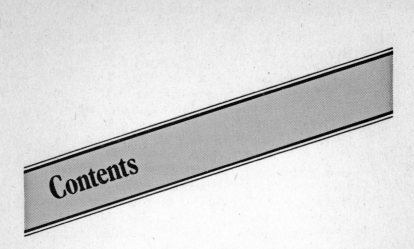

Contents

CONTENTS

CONTENTS

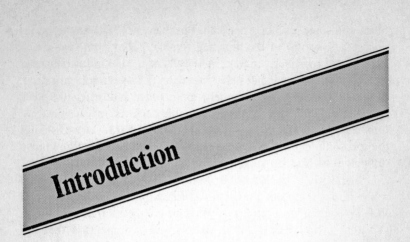

Introduction

Management is an American invention. With almost no exceptions, every significant advance in management has come from the States, and so has almost every management writer worth reading. The supercompanies which form the peaks of world business are also overwhelmingly American—and often overwhelming in their markets. So why have America's managers spent the last few years in self-flagellation and self-doubt? What's happened to the self-confidence that not only is essential to successful management, but was once as natural to the American businessman as glamour is to Hollywood?

To this observer, after years spent among the self-doubting, self-deprecating British, the answer is obvious. The world has changed, as change it must. New stars have risen, in business as in films, and some are not American. But many are. The new superindustries, above all in the amazing Silicon Valley complex, are as strongly led by American Supermanagers as the old industries were.

But the old businesses are sinking as fast as the new ones rise. Because America once absolutely commanded industries like steel, cars, tires, and chemicals, their inevitable declines, relative or absolute, were bound to strike America especially hard—and to shatter the self-confidence of managements which had never before known difficulty or defeat on such a scale.

The British commitment to yesterday's industries was shown up much earlier when the old Empire markets disappeared after World War I. America has been hit by the same competition in world markets that forced British backs to the wall—competition that has come mainly from the defeated countries of World War II, first West Germany, then Japan. But America wasn't prepared for the backlash. It should have been. For it was (and is) American managers who have provided, directly and indirectly, the examples, the know-how, and the methods which competitors are using so successfully.

In that sense, the rise of the new world economic powers is American-based. But America's management prowess has only been shared—not dissipated. In the Age of Competition, which stretches ahead to the end of the century, the United States has most of the advantages—by far the largest home markets, by far the largest number of trained managers, by far the best access to capital, by far the greatest body of applied scientific and technological expertise, by far the richest natural resources. If you've got the markets, the management, the money, the materials, and the magic, how can you lose?

For a country, as for a company, as for an individual, the answer is simple. You lose, even where you have all the cards, by playing them poorly. If that's what you want—to fail—it helps to start by believing in your failure. Self-doubt is as effective a weapon as self-confidence, but it works in the opposite, deadly direction.

This book is about and for the modern Supermanagers, the New Americans. They have confidently and sometimes stunningly applied the strong old virtues of American management to the enormous challenges of a changing world—and having exported their skills, they must now compete not only with each other, but with everybody, and in everything. They can win—if they want to. This book shows how.

What it describes is the beginning of a renaissance in American management. The good omens range all the way from the introduction of modern quality control methods (American by origin, of course) in U.S. factories to the runaway success of a management book (American, of course) which shows graphically how the world's leading companies in key industries (American, of course) conduct themselves *In Search of Excellence.*

The title of this book, by Thomas J. Peters and Robert H. Waterman, Jr., has rightly passed into the language of a country which is itself searching for the rediscovery of strengths that seemed lost, but were only waiting to be released. *The Supermanagers* is dedicated to the release of these energies. It follows Peters and Waterman right into the heart of the firm, where the day-to-day and week-to-week challenges facing the modern manager can be met and turned into success by the practical and effective methods, gleaned from today's live and active Supermanagers, which I have collected and collated over these last few extraordinary years.

The coming years will be no less remarkable, disturbing, and brilliant. The twenty-five-year-old manager who joined a company in 1980, remember, will still be shaping the U.S. economy when the twenty-first century is a decade old. Fortunately, the knowledge he will need for successful management in an age of turbulent competition and continuous change already exists—in the experience obtained, in both success and failure, by contemporary firms; and in works like those of Peter Drucker and Peters and Waterman. My objective has been to draw on all these sources available to the modern manager to guide him through every type of situation in a world of endless opportunity. For those managers who make it—and there's nothing to stop them but themselves—these opportunities will create, not just an American renaissance, but a personal Golden Age.

· The Supermanagers

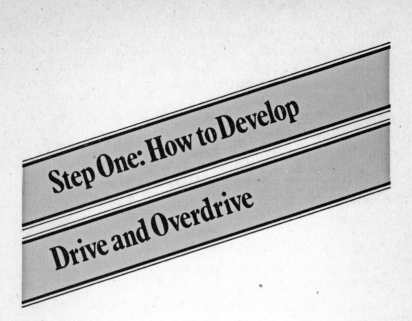

Step One: How to Develop Drive and Overdrive

1. THE WOULD-BE MILLIONAIRE

The businessman thought for a long time, staring out of the window at his suburban garden. He picked up his pen, put it down, picked it up again, and finally wrote this letter:

> Dear Robert Heller,
>
> With a strong urge to become a millionaire in the next five years, and $100,000 cash available, what would you suggest?

This book is the answer to that real-life letter—not the original reply, but the one that grew over years of investigating what really produces Supermanagement. My Would-Be Millionaire, I realized, had several things going for him—not least, $100,000. But he'd also chosen a realistic target that could be put into words and figures. He had set a realistic time horizon for reaching his target. He was thinking in highly personal terms, as you must, if you want to get anywhere. And he knew that he needed help from other people to get what he wanted.

Above all, though, the Would-Be Millionaire had one rare quality. He had ambition.

That's the first truth about Supermanagers. *Most people don't manage to the utmost of their ability because they don't want to.* You don't believe it? Then try this questionnaire based on a study in the *Harvard Business Review.*

Do you have:

◇ A high level of drive and energy?
◇ Enough self-confidence to take carefully calculated, moderate risks?
◇ A clear idea of money as a way of keeping score, and as a means of generating more money still?
◇ The ability to get other people to work with and for you productively?
◇ High but realistic, achievable goals?
◇ Belief that you can control your own destiny?
◇ Readiness to learn from your own mistakes and failures?
◇ A long-term vision of the future of your business?

If you have, in your opinion, half a dozen of the nine attributes, that's a higher score by far than that of the great majority of business executives who I've had answer the quiz. But unless you can score eight out of nine, you must be falling well short of your success potential. And unless you think you can get a perfect score, and want to, you're not truly ambitious.

That's the second truth about Supermanagement. *Every one of the qualities needed for executive success can be acquired, developed, or improved.*

You don't believe that, either? You think that some qualities are inborn, like "a high level of drive and energy"? True, some people are born supercharged: the nonstop hustler, the fellows who can stay out drinking until three in the morning, start work at seven, wear out three secretaries before lunch, who can fire a failure as soon as look at him, and who force their projects to succeed by sheer energy. You're not like them, and neither am I. We don't have to be.

I prefer the pattern of a man named Max. All the years I knew him, Max hardly ever worked more than four hours a day or more than four days a week. Inside a decade, though, Max parlayed a handful of obscure hotels into one of the largest chains in the world—and that wasn't all, not by any means. His empire owned bars and breweries, liquor and L & M cigarettes, gambling and milk, and much, much more. Max had a high level of energy and drive, true. But the energy and drive were in the proper place—his head.

Nobody can succeed on Max's fabulous scale by just deciding to. But that method—just deciding to—is the way for anybody to achieve great improvements in any of the nine steps which lead to business success. There's no magic involved—except the magical results of *making* things happen instead of letting them happen. That's what the Supermanagers do, whether their native language is American, English, French, German, Japanese—or anything else.

2. THE MEN WHO MADE IT

Energy and drive just as magnificent as Max's can thus be seen in the careers of Charles, Arnold, Royal, Ken, and Soichiro. They're five very different men from three different nations, but they have six shared characteristics—Six Highest Common Factors. And they also share a high, a very high, rating in the Supermanagement stakes.

The first, surnamed Forte, built up the largest European hotel and catering empire, with U.S. interests which include the Travelodge motel chain. The second, Arnold Weinstock, created the General Electric Company's amazing growth record. The third, Royal

D. Little, first the eccentric founder of the Textron conglomerate, later became the backer of innumerable management buy-outs. The fourth, Ken Olsen, is the computer engineer behind the phenomenal growth of Digital Equipment Corporation. The fifth, Soichiro Honda, is the motorbike and car tycoon whose story is maybe the most extraordinary fable of the Japanese miracle.

These men made happen what they wanted to happen by applying the following half-dozen Highest Common Factors:

1. Tenacity
2. Loyalty to long-lasting colleagues
3. Tightness with money, coupled with tight controls
4. The money-making drive
5. The urge to simplify and to build on simple foundations
6. The ability to admit and learn from mistakes (Little even wrote a book entitled *How to Lose $100 Million and Other Useful Information*).

Once I was running through this list of qualities (which by no coincidence bears a close resemblance to the nine in the questionnaire). I mentioned things like tenacity, with which Honda overcame setback after setback, Weinstock's reliance on right-hand men who came with him into GEC, Forte's development of key and simple business ratios when he owned one milk bar, Olsen's uncarpeted offices in New England—and Little's lovely book. When I'd done, a businessman-politician stood up and questioned the truth of what I'd been saying.

Why, he said, nobody could have been more tenacious than himself. He'd stuck to it through thick and thin, and after ten years his company was at last in profit. As for loyalty, he still had the same nincompoops he'd had around from the very beginning. Tightness with money? He was the meanest man in the land. As for money, he never thought of anything else. Over the years, too, he'd simplified and improved constantly—because he wasn't afraid to admit his errors, of which he'd made plenty, and to correct them. So why wasn't he a Forte or a Weinstock or a Honda?

Two questions solved the puzzle. How big was his company? It did two million dollars worth of turnover. What business was it in? Well, not one, actually, but five. They were unrelated, they were by definition small, and they gave away the game. Nobody who truly had the money-making drive would have stuck to such unrewarding divisions for a whole decade. Max, Royal, Arnold, Charles, Soichiro—any of them would either have found a way to make one of the businesses big and rich or moved on to lands of brighter promise.

The businessman-politician didn't know himself as he really was. His ambition actually lay elsewhere—in politics, or course. And that delusion—the cardinal one which explains why ambitious personal designs so often founder—was one error to which he couldn't confess and which he therefore couldn't correct.

Never make that same mistake. Instead, follow up the example of a Man Who Made It, a young entrepreneur named John Bray. He quit a family firm, despite his rapid rise and success in its employment. His reason? The family wouldn't give him a share in the business. The company he next joined, though also a family firm, did give him a stake. But far from being a red-hot success like his previous employer, this new one was ice-cold. The business was dying, and Bray was forced to find another market. He started from the once and future foundation of any business—what it does well. Bray searched for a product to which the firm's existing technical skills could be applied, preferably in a large market, one where he could find all the sales volume he needed, even if he took only a tiny bite from the pie.

The chosen big market, in home decoration, was dominated by a very big company, but Bray wasn't intimidated by that. He knew that the larger the share one firm has of any market, the more vulnerable it is to mismanagement—to complacency, incompetence, and the depressing effects of large fixed assets and lumpy fixed thinking. Because he knew all this, and could clearly see the symptoms in this particular giant's market and marketing, Bray wasn't even distressed by the fact that sales in his chosen market were actually declining. He could (and did) still double his sales every year merely by raising his market share from minute to small. He planned to achieve that by finding a product advantage, something that would single out his product from the pack and which would have market appeal.

But Bray was also an expert at selling. He looked for the weaknesses in his huge competitor's distribution system so that he could both avoid them and turn his alternative approach into a strength. He introduced a stronger fashion element into the product. He recruited the best people he could find and used their own selfish drives to motivate them—so that they served his selfish ends as well.

Above all, Bray sold—and made everybody else sell. His initiatives were not immediately successful; new departures rarely are. Bray, however, was thoroughly tenacious. He changed the entire technology and raw material base of the firm's original business, in paper bags, the one that was dying, and the new line of plastic bags also became a success. He invested up to the hilt in new machinery. No technical expert himself, he found the best technical adviser he could, and gave him full backing. And by those means he raised turnover from peanuts to $40 million, with profits up one hundred-fold to $5 million, in only a few hectic years.

Then, he turned over the management to one of those highly motivated, selfish people he'd hired—which left Bray free for pastures new. What separates the men who make it from those who don't isn't just the Highest Common Factors, important though they are, but the object to which they're applied and the will with which the aim is pursued. And, fortunately, getting clear—crystal clear—about the object helps wonderfully to create that all-conquering will.

3. BE YOUR OWN BUY-OUT

If you can provide the self with its selfish motive, you can transform human performance for nonselfish ends and, with it, corporate performance. This principle is the nonfinancial essence of the "leveraged buy-out" in which Royal D. Little specialized so successfully in his second career. When a group of managers "buys out" the operation managed by themselves from its owner—usually some benighted conglomerate—they get all the advantages of "le-veraging," since the larger part of the "buy-out" or purchase price is borrowed at fixed interest.

Levers are the oldest machines in the history of financial leger-demain. If you invest $100,000 of your own loot in a business and sell it a year later for $200,000, anybody can see that you've made a 100 percent profit. But if you supply just $10,000 yourself, borrow-ing the rest even at 20 percent interest, you make $82,000 profit on $10,000 investment—or 720 percent. The arithmetic is very seduc-tive, and it seduces even managers who by definition have brought no drive and no great success to a business (otherwise, why would it be for sale?).

One of the many buy-out mechanics who have swarmed onto the scene says that it's fascinating to find a sea change coming over managers with whom he discusses buy-outs. At first, they show the typical dumb-struck reaction of the typical dumb management in the typical dumb company to any bright new idea. But then he goes into that seductive arithmetic; they quickly discover that a 25 per-cent equity stake divided among themselves can very easily multiply their capital (obtained by mortgaging their houses, wives, and any-thing else they can lay their hands on) by ten times for every dou-bling of profits.

Once that amazing thought has sunk in, along with the fact that they would be their own masters, they become changed men. They will go to endless pains, burning up the midnight oil and the calcu-lator batteries to produce information and bring the deal to pass.

Just as mothers in all species fight ferociously only for their own young, so managers, in general, work most fiercely for their own direct benefit. The best advice to the would-be millionaire is to put his $100,000 into a leveraged buy-out—that is, on the assump-tion that he doesn't have, or can't start, a business of his own. The best investment is almost always the one you have gotten to know most intimately by working in it. If your own business can't produce the desired payoff (that aspiring Croesus wanted a tenfold gain in five years), then the chances of finding something else that will bear you fruit can't be good. But a buy-out must be the next best thing, for the following reasons:

1. You get an experienced team with a track record.

2. You can be reasonably sure that tolerable business systems exist.

3. You start with a substantial turnover, and an established position in the market—you don't face the inevitable horrors of building up from scratch.

4. You may very well be able to pick up the business cheap—the big company managers selling off the outfit won't be red-hot bargainers.

5. Making the management team put most of their money where their mouths are gives a much better incentive than buying into an operation that the entrepreneur started on a shoestring—and where his true stake is thus tiny.

6. Anyway, it's amazing what wonders of cost cutting and profit raising people can accomplish when they escape from big company overheads and have to run a business on their own—and with their own financial futures at stake.

Many entrepreneurs—none in more legendary style than the aforementioned Royal D. Little—have made fortunes out of demonstrating the apparently absurd proposition that the very same fuddy-duddy set of stumblebums who led the business nowhere can work wonders, *if* they are properly motivated by their perfectly proper selfish interests.

It's by no means entirely a matter of money. As noted above, the idea of being your own master is also powerfully attractive to those who work for other people. Indeed, the ideal situation for the hired hand is to feel that he is as much the master, as much in charge, as if he really did own the business lock, stock, and barrel.

Even the most illustrious of hired hands will tell you, though, that it's not quite the same thing—ownership does confer something other than property rights. But unless hired hands do feel they have an acceptable (to them) degree of control over their own destiny, unless they do feel that in some very real sense (real to them) the business is their own, their performance will remain stuck in the pre-buy-out syndrome. The fact of the matter is that all too many businesses are in that sad situation. The buy-out itself often rests on a *deus ex machina*, the Royal D. Little who appears from outer space to set the people free. The ambitious man or woman must learn to be his or her own Little—and it can be done.

4. THE WOULD-BE ROBERT REDFORDS

A hot-shot entrepreneur was asked by a friend to advise on the latter's money-losing business. The entrepreneur wanted to oblige, but didn't have much time to spend on the problem—especially for free. So he made a rush job of it. He went through the business at high speed, starting with goods inward, following them all the way through to goods outward. He could find no serious fault.

So he turned next to the office. A similar speedy search demonstrated that the financial and commercial systems, taking and making orders, were even better than the factory systems. So then he turned to the products; nothing wrong there, either. The next and last stop was the sales manager—and there the entrepreneur found his answer.

He called together the entire sales team and asked what their reaction would be if they were asked to study for the chance of a big part and a fat fee in a major Hollywood movie. Naturally they were all, as one man, ready to work every available hour in the evenings and on weekends. Given the opening he sought, the entrepreneur then suggested that the same effort and hours put into a really professional selling operation would pay dividends—as duly happened.

Up to then, under an undermotivated manager, these sales people, unmotivated themselves, hadn't harnessed their will, hadn't utilized the urge that would be stimulated by a chance to become a Robert Redford, and to earn a Robert Redford income. The will exists within most people. Without it you can achieve very little in management—and you certainly can't become a millionaire in five years.

5. WORK FOR ONLY ONE <u>SOB</u> AT A TIME

The would-be Robert Redfords who became better salesmen, and the bought-out managers who became rich, largely by doing what was within their reach and capacity all along, should have kicked themselves for not having seen and seized their opportunities far earlier. It's true that the previous regime may have laid dead and deadening hands on the bought-out firm. But the managers didn't have to stay there. Their duty to themselves included the obligation to ensure that they were in the right job and employed in the right way—"right" meaning what suits your wishes and abilities, and where both can be fully realized. Life is too short to be unhappy, uncommitted, or unsuccessful in your work, and there are always opportunities.

The likelihood is that, inside many great companies, businesses are underperforming because their managers are; and that the latter underperform because they are undermotivated. Money is the simplest way of committing them, though not the only one; nor is it necessarily effective on its own. It needs support from the way in which the whole organization operates. But unless the managers are motivated, the company has a large and growing problem, because the odds are that, having joined an organization, the person will stay there—very possibly underperforming all the way to the end of the line.

The tendency for the great majority of managers to stay put, despite the folklore of rapid and often violent changes of jobs, may be on the wane, judged by the latest statistics. Up to now, though, American managers have been no more likely to job-hop than those in West Germany, where youngsters still tend to join firms with the intention of resting (sometimes no doubt literally) there for life.

A good reason for staying put is that you love or like the job and the place so much that you simply don't want to leave, ever. A bad reason is fright, simple fear of the unknown. An unemotional reason is the calculation that in the key material respects, such as money or status, you will be unable to better yourself by change. The last sounds plausible, but is not likely to be true. Anybody who has ever had the misfortune to fire somebody else knows the feeling of blessed relief when, more often than not, the sacked person pops up in a visibly better job. If opportunities exist for failed managers, how many more must there be for those who are riding the crest of their own particular wave?

The difficulties are psychological. Change is traumatic, especially when it involves swapping a devil you've known for years for one you know not. Mostly, the only executives who take change in their stride are those who are forced to, like the executive inhabitants of multinationals, particularly those that are American-owned. Whether or not being shunted around the universe every three years is a good idea, it does instill into the executive the habit of moving—while the very mobility increases his outside value.

There is a school of thought, too, which holds that any period of service above three years is too long. Tex Thornton and Roy Ash, when riding high at the conglomerate Litton Industries, theorized that the first year is spent learning the job; in the second year the incumbent is at his peak; the third year sees the gradual onset of boredom, at the end of which it's time to move on.

The theory holds some truth (though Ash and Thornton at the time had held their jobs much longer than three years). The end of a three-year stint is a good time for taking stock. But the learning curve, the lovable process which improves performance with every repetition, continues after three years. There will come a point, too, where the position and the occupant are in perfect harmony. And that is the object of the personal quest—to find that point of near-maximum fulfillment—only *near*-maximum because human life isn't given to perfection.

At some point reasonably close to the summit, the ambitious executive is best advised to come to a rest, because three quarters of the very top appointments are made from within. Even at the approach to the summit, though, two questions still have to be answered. Is the organization, or what I can make of it, able to satisfy my personal objectives? Have I got the personal abilities to exploit the opportunity? Often the only way to find the second answer is to take the job. That may prove a painfully hard route to a resounding "No." But in the end the time is likely to come in any manager's life when he has to discover just how good or bad he truly is, and that means taking one of the calculated risks that are inseparable from all management.

But don't take any risks with the company. Always assess a potential employer with as much care as if you were buying the company, which in a sense you are. The investment of part of a human life, especially your own, is no small down payment.

The profile must cover:

1. The company's market position
2. Its current financial status
3. The consistency of its record
4. The future prospects for its sector
5. The return on investment.

In other words, you assess the upside potential and the downside risk as carefully as any buy-out backer looking at a possible candidate. It doesn't follow that a negative report on points like the above should put you off. Success in saving the day may do the executive far more personal good than joining a company in first-class fettle. That's because the corporate crisis provides both the compelling need to act and the urgent authority to do so—and many people in management do seem to require some abnormal outside stimulus, like a disaster, or the *deus ex machina* of the leveraged buy-out, to extract their best performance.

The chosen job should therefore be one where stimulus of one variety or another already exists, or where you can create it. But the most important pre-entry condition is the calibre of colleagues. Just as this determines the potential of a buy-out, so it profoundly affects the desirability of letting yourself be bought in.

That's especially the case where the company is dominated by a powerful individual. One middle-aged executive who had plunged from a dull, large corporation into the excitements of a millionaire entrepreneur's court found some aspects of the change, including the financial ones, very attractive—but not the fact that he was now working, in his own words, for "an SOB." There's only one SOB you should ever work for—and that's yourself. And you shouldn't be one.

6. THE SUPERMANAGER'S SERMON

The truly great leaders, in war or peace, are never bastards, anyway. They are intensely human and they treat other people in human and humane terms. Listen to these words from a boss whose smashing success turned him into a Supermanager. He arrived at a time when disaster after disaster, setback after setback, had demoralized the organization. Immediately on taking over he assembled his executives, many of them stuck deep in the mire of defeatism, and spoke to them as follows:

"You do not know me. I do not know you. But we have got to work together—therefore we must understand each other and we must have confidence in each other. I have been here only a few hours. But from what I have seen and heard since I arrived I am prepared to say, here and now, that I have confidence in you. We will then work together as a team. I believe that one of the first duties of [a boss] is to create what I call atmosphere. I do not like the general atmosphere I find here. It is an atmosphere of doubt, of looking back. All that must cease."

The Supermanager then made it absolutely clear that there was no alternative to success—it was win or nothing. "I want to impress on everyone that the bad times are over. And it will be done. If anyone here thinks it can't be done, let him go at once—I don't want any doubters. It can be done and it will be done; beyond any possibility of doubt." The Superboss rubbed home the lesson yet again. "I understand there has been a great deal of 'bellyaching.' By bellyaching I mean inventing poor reasons for not doing what one has been told to do. All this is to stop at once. If anyone objects to doing what he has been told, then he can get out of it—and at once."

After this stern stuff, the speaker lightened the tension by saying, "I have little more to say just at present. And some of you may think it is quite enough and may wonder if I am mad. I assure you I am quite sane." He stressed the "atmosphere" that he wanted to permeate right down through the organization. Everybody "must know what is wanted; when they see it coming to pass, there will be a surge of confidence throughout. . . . I ask you to give me your confidence and to have faith that what I have said will come to pass."

The short speech (compressed here) ended on an upbeat. Beating the arch-competitor "will be quite easy. There is no doubt about it. He is definitely a nuisance. Therefore we will hit him a crack and finish with him." The peremptory note gives away the game. This wasn't a civilian manager taking charge; it was General Montgomery laying down the law to his Eighth Army officers immediately on taking command in the fight against Hitler and the feared Field Marshal Rommel. Just two months later that demoralized and defeatist force won the decisive battle of El Alamein.

7. TEN PILLARS OF LEADERSHIP

Analogies between the conduct of war and that of business should be handled with care. But Montgomery's speech of only a few hundred words to his officer/executives struck every note of effective management, every chord of turning group potential into successful achievement by the group and by the individuals who form the group. What was the Supermanager trying to establish? What principles was he following?

First, trust is a two-way process. The boss earns the trust of others ("We must have confidence in each other") in part by trusting them—and telling them so ("I am prepared to say, here and now, that I have confidence in you"). The corollary is that if you can't trust 'em, you don't keep 'em ("If anyone thinks it can't be done, let him go at once").

Second, the work of management can only be done together ("We will then work together as a team"). The more genuine this togetherness, the better the performance will be. But, third, the chances of effective collaboration, like everything else in the management of men and women, depend on the "atmosphere," the climate, the culture; and that's one responsibility the boss can't evade ("one of the first duties . . . is to create what I call atmosphere"). He creates that atmosphere automatically, for good or ill, simply by being there, by being boss and by being what he is. With the very words "I do not like the general atmosphere I find here," Montgomery had changed it—decisively and for the better.

Fourth, the objective of the enterprise must be sharply defined and determined. Montgomery's aim was to beat Rommel, and he had no compunction in telling these officers that it was do or die. Businesses should never be reduced to those stark alternatives—and neither should armies. But a world of difference lies between desperation and determination. Montgomery had no intention of dying, of failing: "it will be done; beyond any possibility of doubt."

Fifth, that aim must be communicated with total clarity, and (sixth and equally important) with the total confidence of the speaker. The self-confidence of the leader or leaders and the confidence of the organization go hand in hand. Both are created and enhanced by clarity of communication and objective (Everybody "must know what is wanted; when they see it coming to pass, there will be a surge of confidence").

The confidence will be false, seventh, unless it has material backup, the resources required are provided, and unless actions always support words. To prove that "the bad times are over," Montgomery took pains to mention that four hundred new tanks had just been off-loaded at Cairo. Exhortation has nothing to do with good management. Leadership is rather a matter of inspiration—of encouraging people to achieve what is possible, and insisting that they do so.

Eighth, total emphasis has to be placed on performance—on getting things done as and when they should be willingly and without excuses ("poor reasons for not doing what one has been told to do. If anyone objects to doing what he has been told, then he can get out of it—and at once").

The ninth essential is to temper discipline with humanity: the touch and the attitude which communicate caring. Montgomery forcefully established this point by telling the underbosses (a) that he wasn't mad and (b) that they were being moved at once to more comfortable, fly-free HQ near the sea, where they could work properly. Physical moves, incidentally, are one of the most effective ways of producing swift organizational change—provided, that is, that they are moves for the better and are used for their symbolic value, as well as for the rut-breaking that always stimulates moribund mentalities.

The tenth and final principle is aggression of the controlled and rational type—the urge to out-achieve the competition by applying the simplest possible strategy in the most effective possible way ("we will hit him a crack and finish with him"). In this respect, Montgomery made it crystal clear to his audience that nothing and nobody would make him move before he was good and ready. Beating Rommel would be "quite easy"—but only when he had given his competitive, aggressive strategy the utmost chance of success by building up a massive superiority and by intensively training his forces to take full advantage of their greater strength.

Generals in war, of course, have advantages when it comes to being boss that are not shared by people managing in peacetime—or even by peacetime generals. Worldwide the trend has rightly been away from automatic, formal authority toward genuine cooperative, informal association. That increases the demands on the boss. But permissive, cooperative, nonauthoritarian ways are not an end in themselves. They are means to an end, and the achievement of objectives is as important today as it was to those officers in the desert, listening in astonishment and hope to this fiery, crisp commander who was to change all their lives. The glove can be as velvet as you wish. But within it the iron fist of determined management must make use of the Montgomery method: trust, teamwork, atmosphere, objectives, clarity, confidence, backup, performance, humanity, and aggression—the Ten Pillars of Leadership.

8. THE FATAL FOURTEEN

Do you have the tenfold qualities of true leadership? Are they reflected in the way your organization has operated down the years—and operates today? The answer lies in whether you or your company have ever been guilty of any (or all) of the following grievous management faults:

1. A serious wastage of human resources and failure to observe one of the first principles of management—economy of force. (This failure derives in part from an inability to implement plans swiftly; it also derives from certain attitudes of mind—as below.)

2. A fundamental conservatism and clinging to outworn tradition, an inability to profit from past experience (owing in part to a refusal to admit past mistakes and also involving a failure to use or tendency to misuse available technology).

3. A tendency to reject or ignore information which is unpalatable or which conflicts with preconceptions.

4. A tendency to underestimate the opposition and overestimate the capabilities of your own side.

5. Indecisiveness and a tendency to abdicate from the role of decision-maker.

6. Obstinate persistence in a given task despite strong contrary evidence.

7. Failure to exploit an advantage gained and a tendency to "pull punches" rather than push home an attack.

8. Failure to make adequate study of the market or industry.

9. A predilection for frontal assaults, often against the opposition's strongest point.

10. A belief in brute force rather than in using the clever strategy or tactic.

11. Failure to make use of surprise or deception.

12. Undue readiness to find scapegoats for setbacks.

13. Suppression or distortion of news from the sharp end, usually rationalized as necessary for morale or security.

14. A belief in mystical forces—fate, bad luck, etc.

It's a rare business and a rare executive that has never displayed one or more of these fourteen "aspects of incompetence"—as described in one of the best management books ever written. Only it's not a management book, ostensibly. The title is *The Psychology of Military Incompetence,* and that's what it deals with.

Many writers have pointed to the parallels between war and management, but largely to draw the lessons of success—as in the Alamein story just told. As the list of the Fatal Fourteen above shows, though, the aspects of incompetence isolated by author Norman F. Dixon are common to both generals and chief executives. But the list wouldn't be useful if it merely told you what's wrong; it's a marvelous guide, in reverse, to what's *right*.

Take the following very incomplete roll call of giant errors made by the giant of world manufacturing, General Motors. At one GM plant, output over the years fell by half while the labor force stayed the same—and losses became progressively more enormous (Fault One).

After inventing the automatic transmission in the 1930s, GM lagged behind its competitors on nearly all subsequent major advances, from power steering to disk brakes. As recently as 1976, its own Technical Center developed excellent robots for assembly work—but the project was allowed to run to waste (Fault Two).

As the world car market and car technology moved powerfully against GM, the management acted like Montgomery's men when informed that German tanks were in the Arnhem dropping zone. The adverse intelligence coming into GM from other companies and other countries was pooh-poohed by executives whose company, as *Fortune* writer Charles G. Burck puts it, tended "as a whole to resist ideas from outside" (Fault Three).

In its attitude to the rising threat from the East, GM reacted rather like the British at Singapore, whose commanding general, rather than take defensive action against the rapidly advancing Japanese, point-blank refused to do anything at all. Just as bad, for years GM also failed to react to Ford's far more successful surge into Europe (Fault Four).

The top management (mostly top-heavy with age) failed to provide decisive leadership—for example, on quality and even control of inventory, which was allowed to reach an appalling $9.7 billion in mid-1981. Sometimes, GM won the worst of both worlds by indecisive muddle. For instance, the development of new cars was removed from the decentralized divisions, which had to market them. With no one person or organization wholly responsible, inadequate results followed inevitably (Fault Five).

For years, GM clung obstinately to the belief that its huge U.S. lead with the so-called dominant design (front-engined, full-sized, rear-wheel drive, chassis-mounted) made it invulnerable to any threat. In the U.S. market that obstinate persistence reduced GM's share to a grisly 38 percent in 1974 (Fault Six).

After joining the other large U.S. car firms in their first counterattacking response to the small car (mainly the VW Beetle), GM (like the others) very soon played down and even abandoned the "compact" auto, giving the initiative back to the importers. GM's subsequent efforts, with Toyota *et al.* now on the scene, included best-forgotten episodes like the Vega (Fault Seven).

The failures described above arose in part because GM had a strange distaste for market research. It didn't ask questions because (a) its executives thought they knew all the answers; (b) they didn't want to hear unpalatable truths—witness their bizarre reaction when Ralph Nader blew the whistle on the unsafe-at-any-speed Corvair, GM's first, abortive attempt to break away from the "dominant design" (Fault Eight).

Forced by its sheer size and spread to be full-frontal, with no option but to compete across the board, GM allowed itself to be outflanked by others, to be undercut on cost and economy (Fault Nine). It failed to look for, find, or exploit the chinks in the armor of foes who were vastly weaker in wealth (Faults Ten and Eleven).

For its inability to compete, GM management was always ready to blame the UAW—and other unions in trouble spots like Britain. But the escalation of wage costs, coupled with inattention to cooperative methods of raising labor productivity, was management's responsibility above all—not just that of the unions it chose as scapegoats (Fault Twelve).

In all the above, the GM management displayed Fault Thirteen—the suppression or distortion of news from the sharp end to keep up their own courage and everybody else's. That was the awful excuse given by the British general in command at Singapore, when he refused, not for the first time, to authorize the building of physical defenses against the advancing Japanese. As his chief engineer observed, with despairing and futile indignation, "Sir, it will be a damned sight worse for morale to have Japanese running all over the island."

The generals in Detroit, though, finally did much, much better than that: they faced up to the harsh truth that, unless GM looked to its own defenses and offenses, the Japanese would be running all over the American and world car industry. The four years of auto recession only reinforced this new realism—and powerfully. "If anybody thought we had a charter to stay in business forever, that period showed it wasn't true," president F. James McDonald told *Business Week*. "We have to improve, consistently and constructively."

In not one of the faults previously displayed by General Motors did bad luck (Fourteen) have anything to do with the disaster. It wasn't fate that caused the Singapore or Arnhem disasters—or that produced the collapse of the great car giant's profits into loss. It was, just as the book says, incompetence springing from emotional blockages and hang-ups. What followed when GM took its own fate in its own hands proves that faith in yourself, based on fact, can move even the mightiest corporate mountain.

9. GENERAL MOTORS' GREATER GENERALS

Asked to name any past or present General Motors executive, most people will be hard-pressed to think of anybody except Harlow (Red) Curtice and John Z. DeLorean—the first because, when appointed Secretary of Defense by President Eisenhower, he allegedly remarked that "what's good for General Motors is good for America"; the second because of his scandalous attempts to create and preserve his very own car company. But today some relatively unsung (or unslanged) GM bosses really do deserve to enter the Hall of Supermanagement Fame.

These new motor generals of Detroit include Thomas A. Murphy and Elliott M. Estes, the chairman and president who launched the giant's Fifty Billion Dollar Fight-back; and Roger B. Smith and F. James McDonald, the pair who took that enormously costly drive into a new phase of dynamism in the 1980s. True, without the bad generalship of their predecessors, such Herculean labors would not have been needed. But on every one of the Fatal Fourteen, the fight-back has been strong enough to persuade one magazine, in 1983, to run an article titled "Will Success Spoil General Motors?" It won't—not if GM goes on relentlessly attacking its past and present failures, turning the Fourteen inside out.

The Psychology of Managerial Competence starts with the realism shown by McDonald's admission that the world doesn't owe even General Motors a living. Free from emotional blockages and hang-ups, or as free as effort can make him, the Supermanager commits himself to LIMO—the Least Input of human (and all other) resources for the Most Output. Conservatism and tradition are rejected in favor of learning the lessons of the past, including past mistakes, and of winning every possible advantage from the modern—especially modern technology.

Information, all information, is taken dead seriously—and neutrally. If it is unpalatable, or conflicts with preconceived views, that makes the data more welcome to the Supermanager—not less. He especially seeks to learn all there is to know about the true strengths (and weaknesses) of the opposition—and about those of his own company, neither underrating the former nor overrating the latter.

He acts decisively, and never shuns his responsibility for taking decisions and (most important) following them through. Perhaps the crucial display of decisive power is readiness to abandon any course of action, however dear to anybody's heart, if the contra-indications turn thumbs down. On the other hand, if the evidence turns thumbs up, the Supermanager presses home his advantage unceasingly.

The evidence comes from deep and continuing study of the market and those competing in it. The Supermanager uses this knowledge in planning a competitive strategy that will avoid the opposition's points of maximum strength, but rather, by intelligent use of tactical means, including surprise or even legitimate deception, will concentrate on outflanking the enemy and hitting him where he is weakest.

Above all, the starting position of fundamental realism is maintained, whatever happens. The Supermanager has no scapegoats for failure, only himself. If bad news arrives, he never conceals it or sugars the bitter pill (especially for his own benefit). For he knows that, whatever role good or bad luck may seem to play, his fate, and that of his organization, ultimately lies in his own hands.

How well have GM's new generals lived up to this competent psychology? First, they determined to use the giant's immense financial resources for massive, no-holds-barred investment so as to restore its competitive leadership in every aspect of automobile production and every market—a bold plan, but realistic, since, like Montgomery at Alamein, GM had all the resources required, both material and human.

But the LIMO philosophy has been applied worldwide to establish how many people the company truly needs, doing what is needed and doing it in the right way. In 1982 alone, GM's worldwide labor force was reduced from 741,000 to 657,000 (a fall of 11.5 percent), cutting the human input while raising its output. All the way down to making Buick water pumps (a 20 percent rise in output per man) and all the way up to final assembly times (a projected drop per large Buick from 47.8 hours to 19 hours), the story has been the same—LIMO.

The results of throwing conservatism out of the Detroit windows (which include those surges of productivity) are especially clear where they are most needed—in new technology and new methods. In the knowledge that these days anybody who sticks with the old technology gets stuck, GM poured billions into goodies that range from "mega-plants" like the $600 million, highly robotic complex at Orion Township, Michigan; to the Pontiac Fiero sports car, with its plastic body machined by a new, proprietary cost-cutting process; to big advances in computer-aided design (for everything from car bodies to connecting rods); to the Delco circuit-board technology that's made it possible to return auto radio manufacture from the Third World to Kokomo, Indiana.

As that demonstrates, "invented here" surged ahead at GM; at the same time, "not invented here," while still a heavy hangover from the past, came under strong attack. The mega-plant at Detroit /Hamtranck, for example, was designed to be notably simpler than Orion Township, says *Fortune,* because "as the company came to understand the Japanese production system better, it backed away from" more complex plans. Far from underrating the opposition, in other words, the GM management was striving, sometimes desperately, to match the Japanese point for point. As for Europe, GM outbid Ford by integrating its own vastly improved European cars with worldwide product development. The immediate result was a successful challenge to VW (the company whose all-conquering Beetle first exploited the gaping holes in GM's American defenses) on the German company's own ground.

Without a new decisiveness, none of this would have been possible. On new projects, too, chairman Smith and president McDonald took a different, far more decisive tack. Their new project teams (the Fiero one is formed entirely of Pontiac men, for example) were built to see the whole auto through from start to realization. On the crucial issue of quality, as well, firm decisions at last got firmly enforced. McDonald ordered every general manager to present one-year and five-year plans for improving quality—not by exhortation, but by properly designed schemes for imposing Japanese-style control over production. That self-same approach, applied to inventories, helped to reduce that disgraceful mid-1981 mountain by $2.2 billion in two years.

The no-win strategy of the old "dominant design" died, to be replaced by front-wheel drives, transverse engines, catalytic converters—any new design that would improve performance, economy, and sex appeal. This stable of advanced world car designs departed from the old dominant in almost every respect save one. It took GM to as great a dominance of the U.S. market (61 percent of domestically made cars) as ever. Far from pulling its punches, GM in fact got so fully committed to the compact and subcompact car that, when the U.S. market at last boomed in 1983, it found itself short of larger models as customer tastes switched. Not so in Europe; the British subsidiary, for instance, had been hamstrung by Detroit's long refusal to build small cars until the 1960s. From 1981, though, GM all but doubled its U.K. market share in only two years.

That was one golden prize for fully and finally committing itself to cars the customers wanted to buy, rather than those GM wanted to make; hardly a revolutionary marketing principle, but a practice in stark contrast to GM's past. But so was the fact that its development teams, according to *Fortune*, had been made to put "a premium on market research," which represented a real revolution in GM terms. Without research, though, you can only find the weak, soft points of the opposition by accident—and GM urgently needed to find those openings.

For Smith and McDonald recognized the real possibility that they might never be able to win a frontal assault on Japan's strongest bastion—a $1,500 to $2,000 cost advantage per car in 1983. Despite all GM's efforts to raise productivity, "We're not only not gaining, we're falling behind"—so vice-president Robert J. Eaton told *Business Week*. The facts left no answer but to seek that clever tactic or strategy, that surprise or deception, which gives the crucial advantage. The weak spot of the Japanese has always been automobile technology and design, a weakness that, judged by performance in other industries, may not last. But the 7,000 staff at the GM Technical Center, a uniquely large resource, were harnessed to an outflanking drive on plant automation, to leap-frogging design of the whole automobile, from power plant to overall concept, in a determined soft-spot assault.

Where it knows it can't beat 'em, GM has tried to join 'em. Witness a planned joint Toyota-GM car, made in America. One of the attractions of that project was to offer GM still more knowledge of how the Japanese manage their labor with such apparently miraculous results. There is no miracle, as GM discovered when it started, after all those years, to manage its labor force properly. The management got the UAW (after agreeing to massive wage and benefit concessions) to throw its full weight behind the Quality of Working Life (QWL) programs that increasingly enthusiastic executives set up all over the company. The scapegoat had gone.

What hadn't vanished was the specter of possible failure. For all the dramatic distance that GM had traveled between 1973 and 1983, nobody inside or outside the company could doubt that a long journey still lay ahead. Apart from anything else, 45,500 managers (more than the entire labor force at Germany's BMW) had to be swung behind the new policies. On costs and competition, bad news could be expected to arrive from the front line at any time.

But on the form of the early 1980s, bad news will act, not as an occasion for self-deception, but as a spur to renewed effort of the kind that enabled GM to cash in heavily on the boom market (and the restrictions on Japanese imports) prevailing in 1983. It wasn't luck that produced the resurgence of high profitability that year— with a $900 million of net income rolling in every quarter. It was competence based on the removal of emotional blockages and hang-ups, and the substitution of rational ambitions, rationally pursued with reasoned drive, determination, and energy. That's almost a definition of Supermanagement—and of the way in which companies infinitely smaller than GM can rise phoenix-like from the ashes of past incompetence.

10. THE MAN WHO MOVED MOTOROLA

Any hang-up can be overcome by determined Supermanagement. Notoriously, hung-up sons of famous fathers don't follow in their footsteps to famous effect—witness the sorry end to Robert W. Sarnoff's career, ousted as chairman of RCA, founded by General David Sarnoff. But the radio business (this time, automobile radios) has also thrown up an instructive contrast. At Motorola, Paul Galvin's son—another Robert W.—has proved his point in one very clear way. "A lot of companies that used to be competitors to Motorola aren't around anymore, because they haven't adapted to the environments—companies that used to be household names, like Admiral and Philco."

That's what the younger Galvin justly told writer John Thackray. But there's more, much more to Bob Galvin's achievement. The markets in which Motorola won its growth and glory— semiconductors, communications, and computery—are high on every corporate shopping list. Motorola not only got into the right game early, but maintained a leading position through thick and thin—once, very thin.

That skinniest moment came during the great semiconductor recession of 1974–75, when Motorola made massive losses on the devices. But Galvin's company fought back with the strongest weapon it could have found—technological excellence. "Ten years ago," he said in 1983, "we couldn't move this institution toward a really adequate commitment to R & D.... We're spending more consistently now, to get maximum advantage soonest." The performance when recession struck again in 1982 provided the payoff and demonstrated the policy. The decline in Motorola's corporate profits was kept to only 9 percent—but the R & D spend was boosted by 11 percent to $278 million.

Once a long way behind the leaders at third or fourth, Motorola moved up to challenge Texas Instruments strongly for the lead in world semiconductor markets. The formidable position Galvin has secured in the most advanced microcircuits promises brilliantly for a future that in the 1960s couldn't have been imagined. The turning point, the takeoff into technological leadership, dates back, according to Thackray, to the mid-1970s, when the company got out of domestic TVs and started to tighten up its management, dropping the old to get on with the new, and making decentralization work to true effect.

In such policies Motorola has followed a path well-trodden by the other excellent large companies that are its peers. Yet Galvin found one bothersome aspect of Motorola's success as a result of reading *In Search of Excellence*. Successful firms, on its authors' thesis, have a single essential theme. But, says Galvin, "if we do have an essence—for example, in IBM it's the concept of 'service'— it is not all that clear to me. We don't seem to have a projectable single value." What Galvin has noted, and Motorola's excellence exemplifies, is a single essential truth—that there is no such thing as a single essential truth in Supermanagement.

11. EXCELLENCE, TRUE AND FALSE

Should a business have a single theme to qualify in the Supermanagement stakes? What else does it need? Weigh the following propositions, just as Bob Galvin weighed the single-theme theory. Are they true or false?

TRUE   FALSE

1. Big is better because you can always get economies of scale. When in doubt, consolidate things—eliminate overlap, duplication, and waste. As you get big, you must make sure that everything is carefully and formally coordinated.

_____ _____

2. Low-cost producers are the only sure-fire winners. Customers will always focus on cost in the final analysis, and survivors always make it cheaper.

_____ _____

3. Analyze everything. Big foolish decisions can be avoided through good market research; discounted cash flow can and should be used in judging risky investments like research and development. Budgeting can and should be used as a model for long-range planning. Always insist on forecasts, setting hard numerical targets on the basis of those forecasts.

_____ _____

4. Fanatical product champions and other individualists are no substitute for effective planning and massive commitment of resources. One new product development activity is all that's required to produce the needed breakthrough, and the more skilled staff are put on the project, the better.

_____ _____

5. The manager's job is decision-making—making the right decisions and the tough ones, balancing the portfolio, buying into the attractive industries. Implementation, or execution, is of secondary importance. The whole management team can be replaced if necessary to get implementation right.

_____ _____

6. Control is everything. A manager's job is to keep things tidy and under control, to specify the organization structure in detail, write clear job descriptions, develop matrix organizations

to ensure that every possible contingency is accounted for, issue orders, make black and white
decisions, and realize that people are factors of
production.

7. Get the incentives right and productivity
will follow. If people have big, straightforward
monetary incentives to do things right and
work intelligently, the productivity problem
will go away. The right schemes will give very
large rewards for top performers and weed out
the 30 and 40 percent dead wood who don't
want to work.

8. Control of quality is vital and demands
efficient inspection. Quality, like everything
else, depends on discipline. Triple the quality
control department if necessary and make it report to the managing director. That will prove
to everybody that you mean business.

9. A business is a business is a business. A
manager who can read the financial statements
properly can manage anything. The people, the
products, and the services are those resources
he must align to get good financial results.

10. Top executives have a better view of
the company than the stock market. As long as
earnings quarter by quarter never stop growing,
the market will eventually come to the same
conclusions.

11. It's all over if the company ever stops
growing. When a firm runs out of opportunity
in its own industry, it should buy into other
ones to continue its growth.

If you've agreed with all eleven propositions, you're in tune
with conventional business thinking. But you're all (or mostly)
wrong, according to Thomas J. Peters and Robert H. Waterman, Jr.,
the authors of *In Search of Excellence,* from which the above is

taken. The "conventional business rationality," they say, simply does not explain most of what makes the excellent companies work. Why not?

First, economies aren't the only things in business life. If cost reduction becomes priority number one, with revenue enhancement taking a back seat, it leads to obsession with cost, not quality and value; to patching up old products rather than fooling with untidy new product or business development; and to fixing productivity through investment rather than revitalization of the workforce.

All really good companies, what's more, do things that analysis would rule out as uneconomic—like the overcommitment to reliability by Caterpillar Tractor ("Forty-eight-hour parts service anywhere in the world—or CAT pays"); the home-laundry company Maytag boasts "Ten years' trouble-free operation," which also makes no economic sense. On-purpose duplication of effort by IBM and 3M on product development, or cannibalization of one P & G brand by another P & G brand, or McDonald's fetish for cleanliness are also foolish quantitatively—but they make enormous sense in the real world.

Second, become too rigidly rational, and you rule out experimentation and abhor mistakes. "The IBM 360 is one of the grand product success stories in American business history, yet its development was sloppy," write the duo. Along the way, chairman Thomas Watson, Sr., asked vice-president Frank Cary to "design a system to ensure us against a repeat of this kind of problem." Cary did what he was told. Years later, when he became a chairman himself, one of his first acts was to get rid of the laborious product-development structure that he had created for Watson. "Mr. Watson was right," he conceded. "It [the product-development structure] will prevent a repeat of the 360 development turmoil. Unfortunately, it will also ensure that we don't ever invent another product like the 360."

The authors also point out that the rationalist approach dislikes internal competition—a company's not supposed to compete with itself. In fact, in excellent companies you find example after example of just that supposedly foolish phenomenon. General Motors pioneered the idea of internal competition sixty years ago; 3M, P & G, IBM, and Tupperware are among its masters today. Divisional overlap, product-line duplication, multiple new-product development teams, and vast flows of information to spur productivity comparison are wasteful in one sense, but pay off handsomely in another.

So what do you do? Plainly, you don't throw out the baby with the bathwater. Because too much control is bad, it doesn't mean that no control is good. In all the "false" answers to the eleven questions at the start, there's a strong element of truth—as long as it's understood that nothing in management happens automatically.

To turn it the other way around, there's a strong element of untruth in all the eleven "true" answers. It takes a very good management to get good results out of an organization that is full of overlaps, that doesn't bother its head about costs, and that allows individuals to head off hot-footed on their own hobbyhorses.

Also, don't be misled by the Peters-Waterman critique of analysis. Among the excellent companies of which they are fond, most analyze the hell out of everything. But you can't *manage* by analysis—the latter just helps vitally by showing you more clearly what you're doing, and if you're doing it well—which is the real objective.

To find out, recast the eleven true or false propositions as follows:

1. Does my company lead its market in cost-effective production—i.e., highest perceived value, highest prices, and highest margins?

2. Does it have timely and accurate numbers to support all its decisions and monitor their implementation?

3. Does it generate a flow of new ideas—and turn them into reality—with the speed and success I want?

4. Is the quality (and speed) of decisions good—and are they tied effectively into implementation?

5. Is the business under strict control, exercised by the simplest and least bureaucratic means possible?

6. Do you know if productivity has been improving and how it will be improved still more?

7. Is quality built into incentive systems, work organization, design, and everything else you can think of?

8. Are your people, products, and services each given at least as much weight in company thinking as the financial aspects of performance?

9. Do you have short-, medium-, and long-term objectives for the business that will blend together and achieve a worthwhile increase in its true, underlying value and strength?

10. If any of the answers to the nine questions above are "no," will the company immediately set about turning it to "yes"—and succeed?

Ten true affirmatives here, and it doesn't matter what anybody thinks of your firm. It's as fit as a fiddle.

12. THE HYPOKINETIC PITFALLS

A fit business needs fit Supermanagers. There's a personal questionnaire, parallel to the corporate one just given, in the book *Fit for Life,* by Donald Norfolk.

1. Do you walk more than two hours a week?	Yes	No
2. Do you normally go to bed when you are tired and wake up fully refreshed?	Yes	No
3. Can you bend down and touch your toes?	Yes	No
4. Have you made any radical changes in your hairstyle or dress in the last five years?	Yes	No
5. Are you a nonsmoker?	Yes	No
6. Have you an all-absorbing interest in music, stamp collecting, vintage cars, antiquarian books, pottery, or other similar subject?	Yes	No
7. Do you long for more time to accomplish all you want to achieve?	Yes	No
8. Do you frequently climb the stairs rather than use the elevator?	Yes	No

9. Do you get up in the morning feeling fit rather than aching and stiff? Yes No

10. When you go to the doctor are you most satisfied when you come away without a prescription for drugs? Yes No

11. Have you taken up a new hobby or sport in the last three years? Yes No

12. Are you currently living without the aid of sleeping pills, tranquilizers, and antidepressants? Yes No

13. Do you spend as much time as possible out of doors? Yes No

14. Do you sometimes vary the route you take to the office or shops, and read a different daily paper? Yes No

15. Can you grip your hands behind your back, left hand passing behind your left ear, right arm passing behind your back? Yes No

16. Do you take part at least twice a week in an active sport such as cycling, swimming, jogging, or tennis? Yes No

17. Do you make friends easily? Yes No

18. When you wake up in the morning do you normally look forward to the challenges that the day may bring? Yes No

19. Do you drink in moderation (less than two pints of beer a day, or half a bottle of wine, or three and a half measures of spirits)? Yes No

20. Can you sit for two hours in a car seat or easy chair without suffering backache? Yes No

21. Have you more than three intimate friends? Yes No

22. Do you live in the present rather than wishing you were back in the past? Yes No

23. Are you engaged at present in studying a new subject or learning a new skill? Yes No

24. When you're in pain do you always try to remedy the underlying cause of your discomfort before you resort to taking pain-killing drugs? Yes No

25. Can you squat down on your haunches with knees fully flexed and heels resting on the ground? Yes No

26. Have you in the last week exercised hard enough to
    get out of breath?   Yes No
27. Do you sometimes cry over a film, book, or piece of
    music?   Yes No

Now for the results. You score one point for every "Yes," no points for a "No."

Total Points		How You Rate
1–3	Extremely low	The life you lead at present is unhealthily inactive, monotonous, and dull.
4–7	Low	Your physical and mental well-being is suffering considerably from your hypokinetic life-style.
8–11	Below average	You follow a conventional sedentary existence and would benefit greatly by adopting a more dynamic approach to life.
12–15	Average	You have escaped the worst pitfalls of hypokinetic living, but would still derive marked gains in health and happiness by pursuing a more dynamic life-style.
16–19	Above average	Your life is more vigorous than most people's, but you are liable to suffer occasionally from the effects of sedentary living and should try to increase your vitality rating.
20–23	High	Your life is lively and stimulating, but could be enhanced by the injection of a little more vitality, novelty, and excitement.
24–27	Exceptionally high	You lead a life which is remarkably energetic, varied, and exciting.

13. FIVE FOUNDATIONS OF FITNESS

Get high. If you can, get exceptionally high. The work of an executive (and his play) puts a heavy tax on his physical and mental powers, and the strain gets no less with age. The case for regular exercise, supported by nearly all the evidence, is that it enhances the powers of body and mind—preferably not by self-torture. Exercise that's boring or painful does less good than it should. Suitable exercise that's enjoyable has a doubly therapeutic effect, providing a valuable contrast to the monotony of a desk, while still exerting the famous and important "training effect" on the heart and lungs.

The list is long and nourishing: badminton, basketball, fast canoeing, climbing, cycling, digging, gymnastics, hiking, trotting or galloping a horse, rowing, running, skating, skiing, squash, swimming, tennis, brisk walking, wrestling. Do any of these vigorously for half an hour and you'll earn what Donald Norfolk, the osteopath and author, calls an "activity unit" in his book *Fit for Life*.

The units are not the same, though, as the "aerobic" points of Dr. Kenneth H. Cooper, who measures the heart and lung (cardiovascular) benefit of different exercises. Of the above list, running is the most effective way for the average sedentary worker to get Cooper's basic thirty aerobic points per week. Cooper recommends this exercise diet as a minimum "fitness" standard; fifty points equates with excellent condition. To relate this to running, two miles in under twenty minutes four times a week (Cooper's recommended ration) gives thirty points with ease: two and a half miles in under twenty-five minutes five times a week takes you over fifty.

Activity units, of which Norfolk recommends ten a week, are designed to get the otherwise inactive person out and about, up and doing. Fitness doesn't mean passing an insurance medical or running for a bus without collapsing: it's a complex of attributes. Aerobic fitness ranks high among them, but improving strength, balance, and agility requires other physical activities. Mental "activity" levels also form part of general fitness; the questionnaire from Norfolk's book shows the great range of areas in which anybody's life is likely to set into a de-conditioning rut.

Of course, physical and mental performance is also determined by genetics. Wiry, short, lean men will outrun tall and rounded ones every time on much less training: some exceedingly effective people in all walks of life never seem to take any exercise more violent than standing up or sitting down. Oscar Wilde, a man of great physical strength, never walked—he always took a cab, for even the shortest distance. But there's no point in legislating for the exceptional. The average person can no more perform at his or her best without physical conditioning than the average person could survive and flourish on the enormously self-indulgent regimen of the brandy-swilling, cigar-smoking, and sleeping pill-popping Sir Winston Churchill.

Healthy exercise is far easier to describe than healthy diet. Followers of Nathan Pritikin cut protein (especially red meat) to a minimum; eliminate sugar, tea, and coffee; hardly touch any alcohol; and gorge themselves with fruit and mostly unrefined carbohydrates, including whole-meal bread and cereals. Others hearken to Dr. Richard McCandless (whose book on food allergies is titled *Not All in the Mind*) and adopt a "stone age" diet: masses of fat, red meat and no refined carbohydrates of any kind. Between those diametrically opposed extremes lies almost every possible variation; though, to tell the truth, most slimming diets, often with all manner of obfuscation on the way, do the necessary trick of cutting down total calories by economizing heavily on carbohydrates and fats.

Overweight is the obvious major reason for interest in diet. The small poundages by which most slimmers are overweight won't do them any harm. But if the slimming urge even temporarily cuts food intake, so much the better. Pritikin claims some remarkable results with old and physically pathetic patients at his clinic in California—and it's more than probable that a combination of physical exercise (he makes his patients walk for miles) and a restricted diet (any balanced one) will do wonders of rehabilitation for a sedentary, overeating senior—or junior, for that matter. Walk for half an hour after each main meal, and the effect of any diet will be enhanced.

Exercise and a controlled diet must be more effective, at any time of life, than inactivity and gluttony. It doesn't matter exactly what you eat and drink, provided that the body gets all the vitamins and protein required (quantities on which experts disagree, but never mind); enough calories to fuel the owner's drive through life; and no foods to which it has allergic reaction. It can safely include alcohol, the only hard or soft drug with a good track record—provided that its virtues are not turned into vices by abuse.

The force which drives abusing executives to the bottle works powerfully in other occupations, like politics and journalism, where deadlines and personal pressure dominate the day. Most managers, and most journalists, lead relatively easy lives, with plenty of time to relax (which is usually when the bottle gets hit). The pain which alcohol dulls is anxiety: the fear, predominantly that of failure, which can swamp internally the most externally superconfident of people.

The anxiety is made of the same cloth as the nervous drive and energy that are indispensable forces for success: and success is a better antidote than booze. The right course for the nervous, anxious, hard-driving executive is to recognize himself for what he is and to act accordingly.

1. Take as much time off as possible during the year—in several doses, rather than one large gulp.

2. Take plenty of exercise—at least two half-hour walks a day, or four weekly twenty-minute jogs (or the equivalent): some fairly convincing evidence shows that running is as effective as tranquilizers.

3. Learn one or two of the many relaxation routines that have come from the East via all too many gurus.

4. Don't overdo *anything*—especially as physical age marches inexorably onward; even moderate exercise carries risks of aches, pains, and strains. A good warm-up routine will help avoid them—even if you don't, once warmed, actually take any exercise.

5. Watch out for the physical and mental signs of excess: don't glory in them, but take a break, or deliberately slow down, if the signs, individual and probably well known to you, begin to appear. You ignore them at your literally deadly peril.

14. THE QUESTIONS WITH NO-NOS

So you're in good shape, and keeping yourself that way. What for? The answers to these questions will help you to find out.

1. (a) How do you want to spend your time in life? (b) What aspirations do you have? (c) Where do you want to be ten or twenty years from now?

2. (a) If an employee, what career prospects do you have in your present organization? (b) Do you hope for promotion, consolidation, or a gradual run-down to retirement? (c) Would you consider a highly paid but risky job, or do you prefer security?

3. What skills and personal attributes do you have? What can you do better than others?

4. On average, how many hours a week do you work?

5. What are your regular time commitments, e.g., on:
    (a) day-to-day staff management;
    (b) the professional part of your job;
    (c) contact with customers or clients;
    (d) the administrative part of your job?

6. (a) What is the pressure on your time? (b) Do you have any discretionary time available after meeting your regular time commitments?

7. (a) What is your overall flexibility? (b) Does your investment in keeping on top of your job and in streamlining procedures allow you to cope with unusual time pressures?

8. How much of your discretionary time do you invest, e.g., in:
    (a) studying and personal development;
    (b) learning new skills;
    (c) building personal relationships?

9. How do you review your activities and compare priorities? You should consider not only what the organization gains from each activity, but also what else you could be doing with that time.

The questions come from a booklet called *Time, the Essence*, published by the BIM Foundation. If you can't answer any of the questions now, get the answer—and soon. If you've answered "No" to questions 6 (b) and 7 (b) or "None" to 8 (a), (b), or (c), you are not managing your time properly—or yourself.

15. TIME IS MORE THAN MONEY

Executive crack-ups commonly occur to those who hide their anxiety behind the ferocious, unremitting activity of which they boast. One such manager was actually proud when his doctor pronounced him one of those men who had to press on at unremitting pace until they collapsed completely—the point when he had "to recharge my batteries." That man's hyperactivity became a poor substitute for thought. He dynamically led his company into one of the greatest commercial disasters of modern times. Far better not to allow the "batteries" (to continue with that slightly fatuous analogy) to run down to the stage where judgment and performance are bound to be affected.

The run-down battery produces a state of permanent jetlag. The jet is a major executive hazard. It removes a good excuse for staying at home, cuts heavily into time, and provides peculiar forms of stress all its own. Everybody knows the rules. (Get a good night's sleep before starting work after a transatlantic flight; a whole day's rest if it takes you to or from the West Coast; two whole days if you're going from the Atlantic countries to the Pacific, or vice versa.) But almost everybody breaks the rules—some with a manic passion. And some do it at other people's expense.

The jet-lagged dynamos can easily carry great bundles of stress and anxiety around as presents for their subordinates, making it difficult, if not impossible, for the latter to gain control over the most critical element in their lives, working or not: time.

Time is more than money to the manager. It is the ability to manage. Of all the resources available to a manager, time is the most personal, and the most commonly wasted. It isn't wasted in the sense of being frittered away on, say, practicing golf on the executive carpet. Indeed, efficient use of time demands, among other things, leaving brief spaces in the day for total idleness and lessening of tension. The waste comes rather in the hours when the manager is actually trying to manage.

Bane number one is interruption. According to a consultant in these matters, Bruce Austin, nearly half the managers who tested out a new time diary for him recorded a hundred interruptions in a single week. Allow three minutes wasted by the act of interruption (which doesn't count the time occupied by the interruption itself), and five valuable hours a week disappear in this way—and there's a further significant loss in terms of disturbed concentration.

Any more effective use of time must therefore start with a time diary or log—to show exactly how time is spent at present. The cure continues with eliminating the unnecessarily wasted stretches, starting with the interruptions. The latter are far more likely to come from subordinates than superiors, so the research shows; the interruptions should be that much easier to eliminate.

The principles of removing interruptions are much the same as those of reorganizing the whole of your time.

1. Take some time to plan the day in advance, doing work where concentration is less important during the periods when you expect to be interrupted.

2. Delegate work you don't have to do yourself—and delegate it properly: give the delegate full day-to-day responsibility.

3. Include in delegation a screen (probably a secretary) who can handle some interruptions for you and (by returning phone calls, say) concentrate other break-ins into times set apart for the purpose.

4. Give subordinates fixed times for meeting you, and ensure, by planning, that you cover all outstanding matters at the meeting.

5. Be mean with your time—and even Machiavellian. Austin recommends the ploy of meeting in other people's offices rather than your own (it's easier to end the discussion, by saying good-bye); in your own office, there's always the time-honored subterfuge of having your secretary remind you of some fictitious but desperately urgent next appointment.

6. Always take along some reading or work on your travels, so that time in transit or waiting can be used.

7. Arrange interdepartmental, management, committee meetings, etc., only as and when needed—and only have people there who are needed.

A good sign that either the meeting or some of the people are superfluous is when they try to get out of coming. Max Taylor of the Coverdale consultancy suggests that you should review the usefulness of a meeting every six months—and hold a secret ballot on whether it should continue.

He cites several common time hazards, like the meeting that

drifts on and on. The suggested remedies hinge around the chairman. If it isn't you, there isn't much you can do about the drift. If it is, be stern: allow information, but cut out discussion. Set a maximum time to the meeting—and don't let too many items get on the agenda. If all else fails, make people stand up. Just don't provide any chairs. If an individual hogs the meeting with his pet subject, hope and pray that the chairman will invite him to discuss the point later—outside the meeting. If it's the chairman who's the hog, rotate the chairmanship, elect him into an observing role, or stop turning up yourself.

If you're not wasting other people's time, the least you can ask is that they shouldn't waste yours. The object of the exercise is not only to use your time in operating effectively, but also to allow time to rest and to *think*. Management is essentially a cerebral activity, although the irresistible force of harnessed emotion comes into it. That run-down battery hasn't enough power to activate thought or control emotion: a sure recipe for personal and corporate disaster.

16. THE RUSSIAN WHO COULDN'T FORGET

There's a sure sign, as well, when the run-down is beginning. People start to notice signs of failing powers: most commonly, memory. They tend to blame these lapses on advancing age. That's because they don't want to blame themselves—and don't know about the man called "S."

In the 1920s, a Russian editor noticed something most unusual about one of his journalists. The man never took notes at briefings—but he never forgot. The brain expert Professor Alexander Luria subjected the journalist "S" to innumerable tests which demonstrated that his recall was virtually total and perfect.

As Tony Buzan describes it in his book *The Evolving Brain,*

> "S" had always had a phenomenal memory. . . . He could even remember his emotional reactions while in his pram. In addition to a phenomenal memory, his senses also tended to

blend things. . . . Whenever he heard words he would not only have a mental picture of the word, but would associate with each word a different sound, a different smell, "feel," "movement" and so on.

"S" also reported that he was often able to eliminate pain by forming a perfect image of the pain in his mind, and then imagining that the image was gradually disappearing to the horizon. When the image finally disappeared over the horizon, the pain disappeared with it! "S" was further able to change his temperature, once again by making mental images in his mind of the kind of temperature he wanted to be in.

The powers of this journalist are far beyond those of less gifted people (though otherwise his mind was apparently average). But anybody can use the same approach to improving memory; and that single improvement makes it possible to perform many other feats of mental agility. Buzan lists, among the common problems about which everybody (especially managers) complains, all these mind-linked phenomena:

1. concentration
2. organization
3. logic
4. retention
5. time pressure
6. recall
7. studying
8. thinking
9. note taking
10. problem solving
11. creating.

To test the theory, see how many of those eleven you can remember by rote; then try again by making associations like that Russian journalist of long, long ago. If you can still remember all eleven problems on one associative read-through, after you've finished the next chapter, you're well on the way to solving the lot.

17. INTELLIGENT PEOPLE ARE LAZY

The brain responds to exercise, in fact, as rewardingly as the muscles. Even the foundation of mental prowess, involved in all the activities of the mind, can be much improved: memory itself. Memory is the key component of learning, and as author Peter Russell points out in *The Brain Book,* the eight rules of learning will also guide the mind through any sustained intellectual activity—like reading or studying a long report.

1. When learning anything, or concentrating on papers, the beginning and end of the session are remembered better; so are outstanding or highlighted items.

2. Taking regular breaks during any study or learning increases overall recall. Breaks take maximum advantage of "primacy, recency, and reminiscence," the technical terms for the strongest periods of recall. Break once every forty minutes, at least, and for about five to ten minutes each time. During the breaks, rest, relax, take some fresh air, and so on.

3. After a break, have a quick review of what you've been doing in the previous session or sessions. This warms you up mentally and also gets you mentally "set" for the subject. Even when work seems to be going superbly, it's still good to take a break. Understanding is not necessarily remembering.

4. Immediate memory is limited to about seven "chunks" of information. Most people can remember about seven numbers in a row, seven colors, seven shapes, or seven of any other item. If you need to remember more than seven items, it's better to organize them into a smaller number of chunks.

5. Organization is also very important in memory. Unconsciously, the mind organizes any new material into groups and patterns. The greater the subjective organization, the better the memory. Consciously looking for underlying patterns and principles is more effective than learning by rote. It's the ordering of the material that the mind remembers. Chess masters, for example, remember the configurations on a board, not the individual positions.

6. The more consciously you are involved with anything, and with its meaning and significance, the greater the depth of pro-

cessing, the greater the organization, and the better the memory—that's why your memory, however bad you wrongly think it is, functions so superbly in matters of special interest or concern to you.

7. Memory of visual images is essentially perfect. Shown ten thousand pictures, people can recognize 99.6 percent correctly. Your memory can be improved by making a greater use of imagery. When two images are associated, make them connect and interact as directly and vividly as possible. In fact, the basic principle underlying all mnemonics is to make a strong association with the thing to be remembered. As much as possible, the associations should be unique, exaggerated, sensory, simple, creative, and outstanding. A little vulgarity often helps.

8. There's a simple system for remembering lists—the number-rhyme system, in which the numbers one to ten are given rhyming images, such as one-gun, two-shoe, etc. (itself an easy mnemonic), and each element of the list is associated with one of the images. A technique like this is invaluable for remembering odd things when you haven't got pencil or paper handy, or when you want to stun an audience by speaking without notes. Mnemonic principles can be used for learning both the vocabulary and grammar of foreign languages, for remembering faces, and for remedying absentmindedness in general.

Without the power of memory, bane number two of executive time becomes even worse: reading. The problem here doesn't arise because executives do too much reading, but because they don't do enough. Inability to read more than a fraction of the printed material that hits their desks is the single most common managerial complaint. Reading is information; reading coupled with efficient memory is knowledge; management is applied knowledge—*not* reading is thus a serious deficiency.

The answer is to set aside reading time in your diary or time plan, and to use it more effectively by mastering the techniques for reading faster, or for scanning when there's no time or necessity to read "thoroughly." But remember, too, that research shows only a very weak correlation between mulling over every word several times and the levels of comprehension and retention achieved. It's quality, not quantity, that counts: a truth that applies to all executive life.

Any manager can spend longer and longer hours at work—and there will be times in every manager's life when the effort, in terms of concentration, emotional commitment, and long hours, will be of backbreaking intensity, but the spine won't crack. The human resource bank includes the ability to sustain superhuman performance for a spell, often a protracted one. That's one reason for leading a sane and reasonably planned life, with plenty of spare time, as normal routine: so that you can produce the abnormal effort when required.

There's a German saying: *"alle intelligenten Leute sind faul"*— all intelligent people are lazy. The intelligently lazy manager gets the maximum output from the minimum hours, and he exploits the time when he isn't "working" by using the intelligence which won him the time: in other words, he *thinks*. In this respect, as in all respects, taking good care of yourself makes it possible to take better care of others.

To summarize some of the important points I've mentioned in Step One:

1. Every one of the qualities needed for executive success can be acquired, developed, or improved.

2. Clarify your ambitions and your objectives before setting out to achieve them.

3. If you can't achieve your best performance where you are, buy yourself out: move to where you can.

4. Always assess a potential employer with as much care, and in the same way, as if you were buying the company.

5. Good leadership rests on 10 pillars: Trust, Teamwork, Atmosphere, Objectives, Clarity, Confidence, Back-up, Performance, Humanity, and Aggression.

6. Bad leadership stems from bad psychology, wrong attitudes of mind: clearing your mind and clarifying your motives will turn bad into good.

7. The single most important secret of Supermanagement is that there's no such thing: supermanagers combine many approaches, orthodox and unorthodox, to achieve their ends—and choose their methods for that reason alone.

8. The Supermanager manages himself as purposefully as his company, to get the physical and mental fitness he must have.

9. Above all, manage your time, always leaving (a) discretionary time after meeting regular commitments; (b) space to cope with unusual pressures; (c) room for study, personal development, learning new skills, and building personal relationships.

10. Don't waste other people's time: then you can ask them not to waste yours.

11. Management is thought expressed as action: take advantage of mind management to make yourself intelligently lazy.

Step Two: How to Take the Risks That Aren't Risky

1. THE WONDER COMPANY THAT TOLD ALL

An American electronics company came to market on the strength of a revolutionary new computer gadget, incorporating a revolutionary new technology. The rules of the Securities and Exchange Commission on full disclosure were followed scrupulously. The Wall Street punters were advised that none of the parts of Product Wonder were in production; that the losses (more than $2 million in fifteen months) would get worse before they got better; that the new technological gadgets hadn't been used in the prototypes—and hadn't been designed or tested, either.

There was just as bad to come. Prices and deliveries of the essential Wonder components might well not be satisfactory. Independent consultants (not surprisingly) doubted that the company could succeed. The management, which had only "limited experience with cost control and other commercial production and marketing techniques," proposed to live by leasing, of which it knew nothing whatsoever. There was no patent protection, and much better-heeled competition would probably come into the market. If the leasing were successful, the company would need to negotiate lease financing from the banks (it couldn't). Finally, the $11 million-odd to be raised by the share sale would all be swallowed up, and more funds would be needed, in large quantities, before any profit was made.

Obviously, nobody would buy a share in a company whose *friends* said all that about it, would they? Yes, they would. At $15 a share, it was a heavily oversubscribed sellout. Within three months the share price had doubled. Six months later, the price was four times the issue level—even though hardly any sales of Product Wonder had been delivered.

Better (or worse) still, the company had lost another $10 million. It thereupon had the gall to seek $25 million more, on exactly the same kind of totally terrifying prospectus as before. It obtained every cent.

It's dead, of course.

2. TOYOTA'S WINNING LOST CAUSE

No doubt about it, the investors who flocked to pour money into The Wonder Company That Told All showed rotten judgment. The risk wasn't moderate, and they didn't calculate it carefully at all. Yet no doubt they consoled themselves, even as their good money poured down the drain after the bad, that the gamble was worth the taking—after all, wonder companies have sometimes won through against all the odds. To illustrate that point, there couldn't be a more amazing story than that told by Seisi Kato in *My Years with Toyota* about the awful events that followed when he was dispatched to America to initiate sales of the Toyota Crown—the company's very first American export

Kato's boss had seen Volkswagen Beetles scuttling along the freeways and turnpikes and saw no reason why another maker of small cars couldn't muscle in, too. His counterpart on the production side agreed, after an American consul in Japan had urged him, "The Crown is great—why don't you try exporting it?" There were misgivings. Was the strategy premature? Was the Crown's technology up to American standards? But production and sales were unanimous, and the principle that "the key to business success is good timing" carried all before it.

Arriving in August 1957, Kato started seeing dealers, and gained from them the idea that four to five hundred cars could be sold each month—so a goal of selling 10,000 a year seemed easily attainable. Then Toyota (literally) ran into a bit of trouble: "When the Crown was tried out on U.S. freeways at 80 m.p.h., loud noises soon erupted and power dropped sharply. . . . Our engines, designed for the narrow-road, low-speed driving of Japan in those days, could not even begin to handle the performance and endurance demands placed upon them. As our dreams sank out of sight like a ship with a giant hole in its bottom, we wrote to Tokyo that it was advisable to simply throw in the towel."

To its eternal credit, Tokyo said, "No": just fifty or a hundred Crowns would do as a beachhead. Even when the technical troubles multiplied, and the cars had to be withdrawn completely from U.S. sale, Tokyo stuck to its guns. To defend its little beachhead, Toyota sold the four-wheel drive Land Cruiser instead. Were the Japanese guilty of a gamble just as imprudent as the investors in that Wonder Company That Told All? On the face of it, perhaps; but not on closer examination.

Any numerically based analysis of the U.S. project would have produced a very high score. So, of course, might a similar exercise for the Wonder Company. The difference was that on the evidence of its own past record, Toyota quite plainly had the resources required to succeed—the men, the management, the money. The only question was whether Toyota's humiliated engineers could overcome their technical problems, and that was a very fair bet.

Kato recalls that the failure "served as a burning stimulus to develop better products. In that sense, what was regarded as a rash and premature attempt to penetrate the U.S. passenger car market was in fact the 'glorious defeat' that served to stimulate and to develop products specifically for the export market." In hindsight, Tokyo's refusal to withdraw from the U.S. was inspired—for Toyota eventually surpassed the Volkswagen company, whose Beetles had initially sparked off its hopes. But one other fact needs to be weighed: the victory over Volkswagen took nineteen years.

Of course, Toyota had become a successful and probably very profitable exporter long before then. Victories against the odds, though, usually take far longer than triumphs in which every important factor is on the side of the victor—what else would you expect? When venturing into an unpromising market, or one which suddenly proves to promise nothing but pain, you need a quality which isn't logical at all: persistence, meaning the ability to stick with the task for years, if need be, until the rewards begin to flow.

There is one highly material element in the moral virtue of persistence—the ability to afford it. But make no mistake. The path of progress for those whose judgment is more brave than shrewd is about as stony as a road can be. Just listen to Kato:

> "The reality was that the first ten years of Toyota's export efforts to the United States had been nothing but a series of humiliations and frustrations, with little to sustain us but a burning ambition to realize this dream of dreams. Effort was piled upon effort, and our perseverance was pressed to the limits as, little by little, we inched open the doorway to success. Thrown into confusion by the Nixon shocks and weakened by the upward revaluation of the yen, still we had kept on trying, determined that we would take two steps forward for every step backward."

If all that is true of a company with such great intrinsic strengths as Toyota, it must apply with grand slam doubled and redoubled force to any lesser body. Persistence can turn a losing cause into a victory, provided that the essential resources are available. But it makes no sense to choose a losing cause deliberately. After all, people with winning causes have one great advantage—they win.

3. THE ASH THAT FAILED

There's no sadder sight, though, than a would-be winner in a losing, lost cause. The Supermanager reputation that Roy Ash acquired at Litton Industries propelled him into the Nixon Bureau of the Budget—although in truth Litton's performance had ceased to be superior, and became downright inferior, long before Ash left. Still, it's understandable that the board of Addressograph-Multigraph thought Ash a great catch, even for (maybe especially for) a company in deep trouble.

The candidate had some outstanding qualifications: long experience in a technology-based corporation with an early record of fabulous growth; great familiarity with Washington; articulate and impressive intellectually. Against that, his minus points can't have seemed too serious: as the financially oriented number two of Litton, Ash had never really been an operating manager of a major enterprise, still less of a business having to push through radical marketing and technological change in adverse circumstances: indeed, Litton had never found a way to recover from its own technological mistakes in Ash's day.

The result was a corporate disaster for AM and a personal one for Ash (which he survived in better shape because of his own great personal fortune). The trouble wasn't that Ash lacked ability. The AM board chose excellently—if it wanted somebody to run an operation where continuity was the keynote. But the essence of AM's problem was that, because of long past neglect, it needed—and urgently—the discontinuity that could have been provided only by a hungrier man than Ash, an entrepreneur annealed in the fire of tougher experience and versed in the science and marketing of the new technology.

The Coca-Cola board, also needing a new boss, could easily have opted for continuity (as the corporation had always done): instead, it set the cat among the pigeons in Atlanta, Georgia, by naming a chief executive officer precisely for the discontinuity he embodied. When Roberto C. Goizueta was placed in charge as chairman in 1981, he quickly demonstrated that he was different from the traditionalists, who had long dominated Coke, by a controversial buy of Columbia Pictures—the first major diversification of the giant outside soft drinks. But while the cash flow from hit movies has been useful, the prime reason for Goizueta's appointment over the heads of others can be put in one word: Pepsico.

In 1977 there seemed a good chance that Pepsi, the long-time number two, would wrest the U.S. market lead from the all-time champ. Goizueta's mission was thus perfectly clear. Beat Pepsi back where it belonged. In the best Japanese style, Coke went over to the attack, combining a militant policy on prices and promotion with a greatly enhanced new product program. Four new colas in under twelve months represented as sharp a break with Coke's tradition as the Goizueta appointment was in the first place.

Two quotes to *Business Week* from Coke executives sum up the strategic change that the newcomer has wrought. "We're a changed company," says one. "You can expect to see a lot of new concepts, new products and packages from us. This marketplace wants, needs, and responds to innovation." Says the other, "Goizueta's message to us is loud and clear. He says that for too long we treated Coke as a warehouse of equity and that we had better realize that what we are is a factory."

The other crucial changes at Coke followed from this basic change of stance, like the tightening and reshaping of the vital bottling companies (all franchisees) into a far more powerful force that can put greater marketing muscle behind the Coke innovations: like Diet Coke, which in 1983 shot 50 percent ahead of planned penetration to match Diet Pepsi's 1982 share. Once again Coke is the boss—all because it picked the right boss.

4. PICKING THE WINNING PERSONALITY

The one area of management where objective judgment and measurement are ultimately impossible is picking people—the right people for the job. Psychologists, of course, do have their batteries of tests; eccentric employers may take refuge in graphology or even horoscopes to reinforce their own subjective opinion. But it would be eccentric to the point of stupidity to hire somebody because you receive an excellent psychological report, when you're highly doubtful about the fellow for other reasons; and just as irrational (though people do it) to reject somebody who otherwise convinces you because the company shrink, or some Swiss handwriting expert, turns thumbs down.

Like a reference from a previous employer, recourse to technical experts is simply another of the factors you must weigh in the balance. But there's no cause for distress in this necessity of relying on personal judgment. The combination of past record and interview works quite efficiently. One Oxford college proved this by abandoning the traditional method of selection (interview plus written examination) in favor of interview alone, plus the report from the applicant's school. In consequence, the college shot right up from the bottom of the Oxford academic degree league to very near the top.

Success in exams was known not to be an especially good predictor of career achievement. It now appears that it isn't even especially good at predicting success in future exams. Thus much of the art of picking others must depend on the intepretation of the past track record and on the interview process itself. Neither is good enough on its own.

With résumés and *curricula vitae,* the first point is to be sure they are truthful—not doing so is a mistake the *Washington Post* presumably won't repeat, after being quite royally conned by a woman reporter who then proceeded to invent a phony but Pulitzer Prize-winning account of juvenile drug addiction. That's one clear use for the references (which should always be taken up): to check the facts of life. It's also wise to seek devil's advocates—people who will point out the black spots in what might otherwise seem a snow-white record.

That's because you need to counteract the possibility that, just as some students are good only at taking exams, you may be dealing with somebody whose main talent is being interviewed. Meet a clever man who talks well, oozes self-confidence, and has an apparent quick grasp of everything you say, and (especially if he's got physical presence to match) you're likely to be bowled over.

In cases where this happens, the appointment can prove totally pointless. You hire somebody like Lumpo, a spoof soap that *The New Yorker* invented in the Depression: guaranteed not to cleanse, lather, smell, or float, it just kept you company in the bath.

Or take the case of a conglomerate that needed a new boss for one of its problem subsidiary companies (indeed, nearly all of them were—and still are—problems). The consultants employed to conduct the search recommended the promotion of the existing number two, at a salary of $200,000. The management rejected the consultants' proposal, and turned instead to a foreign manager with international experience—for a salary of $700,000. They didn't demur when their choice demanded a ten-year contract—with the whole $7 million deposited with a Swiss bank in advance, in case the company was closed down before his ten years were up.

Since he had a natural, healthy aversion to paying tax, the new man also had his income paid (out of the bank account) into a private company owned largely by himself. He also demanded, and got, many and wonderful perquisites and expenses—including a $50 a week allowance for haircuts (he was bald). None of these demands, not even the haircuts, put off the eager management. The man was appointed, secure in the heartwarming knowledge that he would still get his money if his service with the company was terminated for any reason—for that, too, was a condition of his acceptance.

The appointment was not a success, and a few years later the international wizard departed—sadder, perhaps, for all anybody knows, but certainly richer. The company is now being run by an appointment from inside: the old number two, of course. The bald man with the costly haircut had an excellent track record, but the exorbitant and silly demands he made on conditions of employment should have put off any employer.

When interviewing, you should certainly watch not just for absurd demands, but for signs that are the mirror image of the behavior which psychologists Mackenzie Davey and P. McDonnell recommend in *How to Be Interviewed*. Such signs may tell more than the gift of gab and good looks.

1. Is he observant (does he look around your office to see

53

whether there are things in it which give indications of your interests and personality)?

2. Is he too familiar? (A bad sign: a conventionally polite manner is right.)

3. Does he listen (does he show positive interest in remarks, acknowledging them with nods and other signs that he is alert to what is being said but without saying "Yes" or "Right" after almost every statement)?

4. Does he show understanding of why you're asking the question (what you're trying to get at)?

5. Does he do more than just answer "Yes" or "No"?

6. Does he encourage you to do some of the talking? (Resist the temptation to do too much of it yourself.)

7. Is he irrelevant? (This kind of thing: "I was made manager in July 1975. No, it was August. No, it must have been July because August was the month that . . .")

8. Do be alert to signals. (Look out for signs of boredom or impatience—fiddling, doodling, leaning back in the chair, scratching, looking around the room, taking surreptitious glances at the watch. Watch your own signals, too, including the above.)

9. Does he ask about the job?

10. Does he boast—modestly? ("It was rewarding for us all when, after two years' hard work, we moved from a $3 million loss to a $4 million profit.")

11. Does he overstate his qualities? (Or is he honest enough to say "I would need to learn more about X"?)

12. Does he volunteer any failures? ("I then joined the ABC Corporation; that was one of the biggest mistakes I ever made.")

13. Does he admit ignorance? If he doesn't know the answer, does he say so?

14. Can he laugh (without overdoing it)?

15. Is he overdetailed?

16. Does he try to teach you to "suck eggs"? If he doesn't assume that you're knowledgeable, it's another bad sign.

These pointers alone will help in forming a judgment: and if the interviewee does go too far, he could be a Lumpo. But remember you're trying to *hire*—the purpose isn't *not* to hire. You should have made up your mind beforehand what qualities and abilities you want, and you're looking for proof that the person has them—in hope, but never in desperation. Once you hire or promote because there isn't anybody else, you're trusting not to judgment but to luck. You should also follow the rules that employment consultants Sanders and Sidney list:

1. Don't interview at the end of a tough day.
2. Be yourself.
3. Relax your candidate. He'll reveal more—the interview setting should calm him, too.
4. Treat the candidate as an equal.
5. Make an initial judgment from his resumé.
6. Concentrate closely on his behavior.
7. Focus initially on less personal subjects.
8. Don't interview behind a desk.
9. Conduct interviews in private.
10. Define the information you want.
11. Maintain enough interview control to cover all areas.
12. Stress value/attitude questions—not factual ones.
13. Make no judgments. Don't agree or disagree.
14. Word your questions to get new opinions. Avoid those with "yes/no" answers.
15. Use pauses . . . "ummm's" . . . to encourage elaboration.
16. Compliment candidate as appropriate.
17. Ask permission to take notes—but take them unobtrusively.
18. Don't cut off candidate answers . . . but interrupt when necessary to pursue a key point.
19. Don't give him the answers.
20. Show interest. Be a good listener.
21. Don't be afraid to show ignorance.
22. Don't anticipate your next question.
23. Use short questions.
24. Probe choice points.
25. Respond quickly and naturally.
26. Ask superlative-type questions—what is "best," "worst," etc.
27. Ask industry (not just company) questions.

28. Talk about problems.
29. Register sympathy with interviewee.
30. Base your interpretations on the obvious.
31. Confirm key observations several times during interview.
32. Some people say: look *first* for intellectual efficiency
    ... look *second* for emotional maturity/stability
    ... look *third* for human relations skill
    ... look *fourth* for insight into self and others
    ... *finally,* look for ability to organize/direct.
33. Look for what the candidate will bring to the job that you don't have today.
34. Look for what he has—not what he lacks.
35. Look for enthusiasm.
36. Does he ask questions about job satisfaction? He should.
37. Listen carefully to words he chooses. Outward appearances aren't everything.
38. Smile.
39. Keep him talking. The less you talk, the better.
40. Use humor when it fits.
41. Avoid loaded questions.
42. If you seek collaboration, ask another person to interview, too.
43. Don't use panel interviews.

If you do a lot of interviewing, it's a good idea to keep this advice on a handy piece of card and run your eye over it before the victim is shown in—just to remind yourself what to do, if you want an interview to succeed in sweetness and light.

But what if you want it to succeed in *Sturm und Drang*—the so-called stress interview? This is where the victim is put under pressure of different kinds; in a job interview the idea is to get an indication of how the man would stand up to pressure in an actual job. Thus the interviewer may ask "tough, even offensive, questions—sometimes touching on matters normally regarded as highly personal." He may criticize, appear to disbelieve, make accusations or insinuations about the fellow's honesty. But Davey and McDonnell (rightly) don't think this technique is socially acceptable, or necessarily valid. As they say, "The way people behave under artificially imposed stress in an interview may not indicate how they will cope with 'normal' pressure at work, however extreme it may become at times."

In other words, if you're running a civilized, humane, intelligent operation, you hire (and fire), promote (and demote) in a civilized, humane, intelligent way. In making the final judgment, however, reason alone can't come into play. Hunch is important: when it comes to hiring or promotion, if the hunch says "Yes," go to endless trouble to get the instinct confirmed by facts as far as you can. If the hunch says "No," the response is easier. Obey it.

5. THE TRISTAR THAT NEVER TOOK OFF

Be very careful, at all times, to isolate the facts and reasoning within a hunch. Gut feelings are never enough—in fact, they may be much too much. Only hark back to the late 1960s, when a civil project called the L-1101 was the pride and joy of Lockheed, the most proficient builder of military aircraft in the U.S. It was precisely to reduce its dependence on the military that Lockheed, despite a previous unmitigated commercial disaster, the Electra turboprop, pressed ahead with the three-engined L-1101, which became known as the Tristar. Orders proved few and far between, largely because the rival Douglas DC-10 scooped the pool. But still Lockheed bulled ahead, regardless.

Regardless of what? First, that the (inadequate) money borrowed for the project, at $400 million, came to *more* than the entire stockholders' equity. Second, that the engine supplier, Rolls-Royce, on whom the project totally depended, was financially about as safe as Mount St. Helen's before an eruption, a fact of which the Lockheed management seemed oblivious. But the Lockheed management apparently didn't know how precarious its own position was either, even though the problems were obvious. It wasn't a case of using spare military capacity; the Tristar needed a massive new office building merely to house the engineers, plus equally massive new production facilities to make the giant plane itself.

Clearly, these new investments needed a substantial order book to produce any payback, and Lockheed simply didn't have the orders. Small wonder that the company in the end effectively went bankrupt (following its engine supplier by a few years) and had to be rescued by President Nixon. Finally in 1981, Roy A. Anderson, the chairman of Lockheed, had to bite the bullet. If he didn't get any more orders, Anderson warned, he would completely stop making the plane (still losing money in large dollops). A few months later, he did precisely that. As the man said, "The company is sound and determined to stop the heavy cash drain." The question is, though, who started the drain—and why?

6. GO AND NO-GO AT HONEYWELL

How does one avoid Tristars? Or Ford Edsels? Or other, smaller calamities which are, nevertheless, still more disastrous for smaller operations? The margin between go and no-go is often narrow, though the arguments for, which are usually positive and aggressive, nearly always tend to outweigh those against, which are negative and defensive. Who knows? The billions that weren't made by the might-have-beens could be even more mind-boggling than the billions wasted in the has-beens, the Edsels and the Tristars.

Still, anybody involved in great disasters knows one truth: the venture didn't receive all the painstaking, logical, fact-based analysis of which the organization was capable; nor was any analysis supplemented by the most effective devil's advocate test-to-destruct criticism that could be mustered. In the end, the subjective element must be decisive. But in disaster cases, the subjective decision often precedes the analysis and prejudices it decisively. For instance, this is what an eyewitness told *Fortune* magazine about the fateful initial meeting at which a conglomerate boss, Harold S. Geneen, first heard about a tentative, grandiose scheme. The leader "went gaga. . . . I remember thinking, this project is all but approved."

That particular leader had a passion for growth, which in this case cost ITT $600 million before the inevitable end. Here beginneth the difficulty: passion is inseparable from great success in any field, including business; it mustn't be eliminated, but it must be controlled. Thus, few decisions involve more passion than whether or not to close an operation—a decision which had to be taken several times with the Tristar as with other benighted aviation projects, like the Anglo-French Concorde. Every corporate emotion will be mustered on the side of the menaced marvel, even if it loses millions by the hour.

The emotions can be defused by carrying out an analytical process which three experts—S. M. Dobson, J. C. Bailey, and J. E. T. Shorrock—used in their work for Honeywell's European operations:

Table 1

RATINGS FOR BUSINESS SEGMENT STRATEGY VALUE (BSSV)

	ESI RATING		ISI RATING
Market potential (size)		Gross margin	
0–100,000 units	0	less than 15%	0
1–300,000 units	1	15–25%	1
3–500,000 units	2	25–40%	2
5–700,000 units	3	40–50%	3
over 700,000 units	4	above 50%	4
Real growth		Material/sales	
negative growth	0	more than 80%	0
0–2.5%	1	80–60%	1
2.5–5%	2	60–40%	2
5–10%	3	40–30%	3
above 10%	4	less than 30%	4
Market share		Return on net assets	
less than 5%	0	less than 10%	0
5–10%	1	10–15%	1
10–20%	2	15–20%	2
20–40%	3	20–40%	3
more than 40%	4	more than 40%	4

The left-hand side of the table measures external factors, the right-hand one measures the internal considerations. These criteria were used in the example of Company X, which sells domestic gas boilers in Germany, France, and the Netherlands. In Germany the potential for the entire market is tops at 850,000 +, but real growth is expected to be only a low 1 percent, and the company's market share is 15 percent. In that knowledge, using its judgmental weightings (market size most important, followed by growth and share), the management can calculate an external strategy index.

Table 2

	WEIGHT	RANKING					SCORE (WEIGHT × RANKING)
		LOW 0	1	2	3	HIGH 4	

EXTERNAL STRATEGY INDEX

	WEIGHT	LOW 0	1	2	3	HIGH 4	SCORE (WEIGHT × RANKING)
Market potential (size)	10					4	40
Real growth	8		1				8
Market Share	7			2			14
	25			ESI			62

It can do exactly the same for the internal factors. The gas boiler operation has a gross margin of 30 percent, the material/sales ratio is 26 percent, while return on net assets is 21 percent. The management has judged that gross profit is the key requirement, followed by the material/sales ratio, with these internal strategy index results:

Table 3

INTERNAL STRATEGY INDEX

	WEIGHT	LOW 0	1	2	3	HIGH 4	SCORE (WEIGHT × RANKING)
Gross margin	10			2			20
Material/sales	8					4	32
Return on net assets	7				3		21
	25			ISI			73

Now you draw a graph with the ESI on one axis and the ISI on the other. The point where the two intersect will come either in the area of 100–80, or 80–60, or 60–40, or 0–40. In this particular company, the ideas of the Boston Consulting Group have been arranged and weighed to arrive at the following conclusions:

Table 4

BSSV	STRATEGY	DEFINITION OF STRATEGY
100–80	Invest	Refers to detailed tactical action plans to promote these products.
80–60	Continue	Refers to a continuation of current business practices and strategies.
60–40	Harvest	Follow strategies designed to reap high profits from high prices.
40–0	Divest	Follow plans which lead to ultimate withdrawal from the market segment.

Two objections spring promptly to mind. It's all very mechanistic; and, anyway, it all depends critically on judgment in matters like the weightings and the projections. It's also true that the Boston approach has lost a great deal of its recent popularity—partly because it is so mechanistic a way of approaching creative corporate strategy. But all the objections are beside the point. There's a world of difference between judging whether return on capital is more important than gross margin, on the one hand, and judging whether the company should or shouldn't enter a whole new market, on the other. The latter broad judgment must be better for drawing on the results of detailed assessments like the former—judgments where prejudice, stupidity, and distortion are far less likely to apply—and where misjudgments are unlikely to be crucial, in any case.

For instance, if an analysis such as the above yields a 0–40 score, it would be a foolhardy management that proceeded to invest heavily, either in a continuing venture or in a new one. Having a screening system also makes it much harder for the kind of thing to happen that was reported in *Management Today* by consultant Simon Majaro:

> In one recent acquisition, the hidden justification for the whole strategy was the chief executive's desire to find a suitable job for a close member of his family. Every conceivable justification was put forward as a reason for the acquisition choice, except the true one. Millions were spent to buy a company, and a few more millions were pumped into what proved to be a

61

very ailing enterprise. It was a high price to pay for an unemployment benefit, even for a dear relative.

An assessment system reduces everything to a common basis of fact, so that justifications that aren't factual have less chance of swaying the outcome. Of course, it's possible for a management with the bit really between its teeth to cook the sums in the system; maybe Lockheed would have had little trouble in getting a business segment strategy value of a full 100 for the Tristar. But it wouldn't have taken very long for the wildly optimistic figures to have been falsified by the horribly pessimistic events. The score would have sunk like a falling plane into the 0–40 sector. And the management would have been stimulated into making its final no-go judgment several years and several hundreds of millions earlier—maybe, just maybe.

7. THE BUSINESS THAT DIDN'T DIE

There's far more to making right decisions than producing sane assessments, though. Take another case from the corporation just mentioned, Honeywell. It was about to drop a business that made aircraft fuel gauges. This excellent Midwest manufacturing company, which grew originally on thermostats, was making the gauges in the same factory as special gyroscopes. These are far harder to manufacture than the gauges, and the high costs on the latter, which just wouldn't come down, seemed to spell their death warrant.

But the manager in charge asked for $20,000 and three months of extra time before the decision to withdraw from fuel gauges was implemented. The use to which he put the $20,000 was so successful that the business was breaking even in six months—and was reprieved by the company.

What did he want the money for?

8. HOW TO GROW 600 TIMES

A clue to the problem of the fuel-gauge business is that many a mickle makes a muckle. . . . The old Scottish saw about small savings, or small earnings, adding up to a great pile of wealth has all manner of applications to business management.

It also applies to business organization. Divide and conquer, another ancient maxim, conveys the same principle: divide a business into profitable, self-contained units, and develop the strengths of those units and their managements, and the whole operation is far better set up. That better setup in turn will generate many a muckle (if it doesn't it isn't a better setup).

The argument in favor of what one company (alas) calls "subsidiarization" is only one part of the dynamic theory of organization. That is, how an organization is set up will determine not only its levels of achievement but the behavior patterns of people in the organization, for good or ill. Errors in structure produce mistakes in practice. The faults can also be horribly difficult to eradicate, because vested interests will always gather protectively around their organizational bastions.

As an illustration of the impact of organization on management style, there's one corporation which is impeccably organized on "many a mickle" lines. From a tiny head office, the maestro makes no attempt to manage the autonomous subdivisions of his empire. He manages by budgetary control, reinforced by continuous invigilation of results and brought sharply home to the operating managers by sharp telephone calls.

The men at the other end of the line are supposedly free (as they should be) to run their own operations in their own style. But in fact they tend to imitate the maestro, working from their own desks in their own offices, largely because they never know when to expect a probing phone call and don't want to be found missing from the desk when the call comes.

This effectively rules out the quite different style of getting down on the factory floor, or out among the customers, and spending as little time in the office as possible—even though that might have suited certain managers and certain businesses much better.

It's not just the organization principle but how it's applied that determines how the outfit is actually run.

What is clear is that a clear-minded management—clear about the organization's aims and how it is organized—often carries away the most glittering prizes. For instance, a bunch of American corporations now belong to a conglomerate which, a few years back, nobody in the companies knew at all. The company, BTR, has enjoyed an expansion that seems to come more from fairyland than business actuality. In a decade this conglomerate of down-to-earth businesses has flown up from $100 million of sales to $4.4 billion.

What its chief executive, Owen Green, calls the "ethic" isn't religious:

1. Growth is the objective.
2. Profit is the measure.
3. Security is the result.

To this triple end the Supermanager executed a seven-point plan:

1. Corporate center reduced.
2. Authority vested in line management at the operational center.
3. Plant bargaining with unions.
4. Improving the annual profit plan system.
5. Determining the real nature of BTR's business.
6. A commitment to growth.
7. Reducing risk by broadening product range and moving into expanding markets abroad.

Note that the first three items (which were fundamental) are strictly organizational. Any management can, for instance, opt to centralize its labor relations (or any other function). But a local management that isn't responsible for something as critical to performance as wage costs and industrial harmony can hardly be held responsible for much else: neither can those who do conduct the bargaining at the center be held personally responsible for the financial outcome. It's a recipe for irresolute and irresponsible management.

Put things the other way around: where and when the manager knows that he and he alone carries the can, worms and all, for union bargaining, the responsibility is sharp and clear. His budgetary performance will reflect his management application and nobody else's—other than those who work with him inside the subsidiary operation. Moreover, the group as a whole escapes from the possibility of a general strike—with a bad piece of negotiation shutting down the whole company from Anchorage to Tampa.

Plainly, the soundest of organization structures won't work without the sound strategic thought that can come only from the center (as in Green's points 5–7); these days, too, the best results are unlikely to flow without an effective method (like the "improved profit plan") of stimulating executive response. Nor does organization by itself help to achieve the necessary continuous updating in the five areas of technology, production, marketing, cash management, and investment in capital equipment, which Green also highlights as integral to his corporation's upsurge.

There's nothing original in the last. Any manager knows that in these tough times survival, let alone success, depends on those five factors. The test of organization, the proof positive of the setup, lies in whether that setup impedes the updating and improving or whether these necessities are built into the responsibilities and powers of individuals down the line. Split the company into mickles that make sense and you may get a mighty muckle. Try and run the whole operation from the heavy top, and you may end up, like so many of the great and allegedly good companies in the West over the decade of the 1970s, with a mere mickle for your pains.

Which comes right back to Honeywell and its fuel-gauge business. The $20,000 was used to put up partitions physically separating the gauges from the other activities. Separated out, and left to sink or swim, the gauge men swam—as, in similar cases, any of us would.

9. THE BUSINESS THAT DIDN'T LAST

The evidence that organization profoundly affects results has become overwhelming. That's why, as the 1980s began, while attention concentrated on the megamergers, with bills in the billions, a funny thing was happening in American business. Companies were selling off divisions at the rate of $12 billion a year—and much of the stuff being sold consisted of companies that had previously been bought. This was literally de-merging: undoing past mergers by off-loading part of the merger—all because either the strategy of diversification or the performance of the merged company, or both, had proved a failure.

At City Investing the chairman talked of an "attic sale" of divisions. In summer 1981, at American Can, after over a decade's diversification into glass containers, forest products, printing, pharmaceuticals, publishing, aluminum recycling, and mail-order retailing, the management announced that a fifth of the company would be severed. Pharmaceutical company Squibb sold food revenues of $600 million plus. Beatrice Foods sold twenty subsidiaries in two years—including Dannon yogurt.

In another example, related by John Thackray in *Management Today,* Holiday Inns, which had ended up with a hodgepodge of thirty different businesses (aircraft sales, shipping, bus transportation, furniture manufacture, and so on), re-evaluated everything in the mid-1970s. Nearly all were junked. By sticking or returning to markets where it had managerial expertise, Holiday Inns also turned in record profits.

In many of these instances, diversification is the apparent villain of the piece. But the existence of highly successful diversified corporations shows that diversification in itself cannot be the explanation. The truth is that companies which manage diversity successfully are organized to do so. The organization principle is exactly the same whether the merger or acquisition is in the same business or a different one. The de-merging managements never mastered the principle, and haven't now. That's why they present their failures as errors of diversification or strategy, not as what they really are—mistakes in managing, generated and perpetuated by organizational goofs.

10. HOW TO ORGANIZE PROFITS

As organizations develop away from their single-cell starts and bifurcate into other activities, so one managerial requirement becomes paramount. The task, no matter what business you're in, is the same: to organize the place so that efforts are coordinated, but the results are as good, if not better, than the separate cells could have achieved on their own. While the task is the same, the approaches are as varied as the fauna in a pond—or the people and activities which get thrown together in a company. But choose the wrong approach, and the organization is damned beyond redemption, all the way from profits to productivity.

The conclusion that, where lagging productivity is the problem, organizational deficiency is usual, emerges loud and clear from the findings of consultant Arnold S. Judson, writing in the *Harvard Business Review.*

1. Management ineffectiveness is by far the single greatest cause of declining productivity.

2. Most companies' efforts to improve productivity are misdirected and uncoordinated.

3. Tax disincentives, the decline of the work ethic, problems with government regulations, obsolete plant and equipment, insufficient R&D, and poor labor relations—they all have little to do with faltering productivity.

The role of organization, on the other hand, comes across powerfully from Judson's survey of 236 top-level executives representing a cross section of 195 U.S. industrial companies. They weren't exactly a productive bunch: 52 percent of the companies studied reported annual productivity gains of less than 5 percent; another 19 percent reported gains of 5 percent to 10 percent; only 3 percent had gains exceeding 10 percent; and 25 percent didn't even know what their performance had been. Worse still, because roughly half the companies didn't correct their information for inflation, even the figures above didn't reveal the sorry truth—that 32 percent actually saw their productivity decline.

When it came to establishing causes for any success in improving productivity, the reasons given by executives were overwhelmingly (1) capital investment in plant, equipment, and process—72 percent; (2) top management commitment and involvement—61 percent; (3) good financial controls and information systems—45 percent. Nothing else got as much as 40 percent of the votes. But these conventional findings teach much less than the reasons for disappointment in attempts to boost the vital statistics.

(1) A piecemeal, unplanned approach to improving productivity—66 percent; (2) inadequate coordination among departments or functional areas (excessive functional or departmental autonomy)—42 percent; (3) insufficient investment in management and supervisory training and development—41 percent; (4) lukewarm commitment and involvement by top management—40 percent.

Leaving aside the last (for if top management is ever lukewarm, uncommitted, and not involved, forget it—indeed, forget everything), the productive problem is evidently organizational. You can't adopt Judson's prescription without altering the way in which the business is set up. He advocates a company-wide program, aimed not at eliminating symptoms (scrap, excessive rework, absenteeism, accidents, sloppy standards, etc.), but at removing causes—and doing so over the long term, with nothing lasting less than a year (three quarters of his unproductive sample ran their programs for only a year or less).

The expert goes on to advocate that productivity efforts be based on explicit plans that are consistent with and support overall business plans—which assumes that such plans exist. If the company isn't set up to form and implement business plans, it can't organize a proper drive on productivity. The multicell organism needs the governing principle that in vital matters will force it to operate as one.

The balance between autonomy and anarchy is a fine one. But failure to find that equilibrium explains why individual Ford or GM plants can boost their performance and quality to near-Japanese levels, while the customer who buys a Ford or a Pontiac may not note much difference, because other plants, ostensibly in the same company, have been (it's changing) allowed to lag far behind, so the high-quality engine gets fitted into a low-grade assembly job.

That's the description that fits the failed mergers: low-grade assembly jobs. The guys who masterminded (or misminded) the failed mergers had no organizational object at all: they were just adding businesses and markets they didn't know, and only integrating them (if that) by imposing common financial controls. The latter are essential, and cannot function in a ramshackle organization. But they don't constitute organization. To be worthy of the name, an organization must enable and encourage people to perform at their best, pursuing their individual aims but within a common philosophy.

If that sounds too vague and pious, consider the very precise advice which Arnold Judson gives to a boss on the productivity hunt.

1. Inform each head of an operating unit that he's to draw up a productivity strategy for his outfit—plus a forecast of the resources he'll need and the results he'll expect; a rationale that supports his choice of options; and a detailed set of action programs that will implement them.

2. After the operating managers submit their proposals, review each submission, seeking answers to several key questions:

(a) Does the proposal fit the relevant business plan?

(b) How feasible is it in light of the unit's strengths and weaknesses?

(c) How credible is it as a blueprint for implementation?

(d) What is the probability of success?

(e) How accurate is the assessment of risks?

(f) Have all central issues been identified?

In fact, the (a) to (f) routine applies to any business plan, that being the whole point. The Supermanager makes it clear to all his people what he expects; he leaves it to them (as he must) to tell him, with equal clarity, how they are going to deliver; he checks, continuously and critically, to ensure that planning is likely to produce performance—and then that performance is going according to plan.

Of course, it won't—much of the time. The good organization is flexible enough to absorb standard deviations. But what if the deviation is gross? If a business, bought or not, is bad, the right course is obvious. You fire the bad managers, starting from the top, and you promote anybody who seems halfway good into the vacated places. Allegedly, the success of Citroën after the Peugeot takeover followed the removal of the top tier of management and the promotion of the second tier, which had already drawn up a recovery-and-revival plan for the company.

But with a good business—again, bought in or not—extreme care must be taken not to disturb or undermine its existing strengths. The careful manager starts by defining objectively what those strengths truly are. He gives the local management full confidence and encourages them to come to the center for help and support that they cannot provide for themselves.

The problem of reconciling corporate and divisional interests, of balancing autonomy and anarchy, will remain in an organization of any size. Sometimes the center must say "No." But the well-tuned top management tries to head the subsidiary off at the pass, before commitment becomes too deep. If possible, it persuades the subsidiary management to take part in the negative decision. If the worst comes to the worst, it sugars the pill—holding out some other prospect, perhaps, or encouraging some other pet project where no conflict with corporate policy exists.

But the indispensable response—at all times, but especially at delicate moments like this—is to take special care of the once-independent management, and to encourage a management that has never been independent to feel that it is.

The central figure must at all times show more concern for their internal cohesion and success than for the group's. This has the disadvantage of making it more difficult for him to appear clever, or to work his will on the subsidiary operation. But what's good for the subordinate activity will more often than not be good for the whole. What's bad for the part, though . . .

11. THE MAN WITH THE FOURTEEN-HOUR DAY

What's bad for the boss, too, is bad for the organization. Here is how one Supermanager spent one day in his working (his all-working) life.

1. He started the day very early—got into the company car at 7:18 A.M. and plunged immediately into frenzied activity, riffling through papers, making notes, and dictating into a pocket recorder. To help him cope with the incessant output that resulted, he employed a battery of secretaries—one on the 7 A.M. to 1 P.M. shift, another from 12 to 7 P.M., with an assistant to help both of them with the huge load he generated.

2. He had a working breakfast starting at 8, with a large number of outsiders.

3. He followed that up with a conference at which he did all the talking, starting at 9:30, ending at 11, followed by individual interviews running until 1:45 P.M.

4. He ate a hasty lunch—two sandwiches only.

5. He went into the next outside meeting at 2:30, breaking for tea at 3:45.

6. He returned to his office, for the first time that day, for a series of meetings with outsiders.

7. When the last of his visitors had gone, he got down to the paper work. He was now also available, for the first time that day, to his colleagues.

8. He arrived home at 9 P.M., fourteen hours after starting the day.

9. After supper, he went to bed—and started off on another fourteen-hour run the next morning.

At the time of writing, the Supermanager concerned is still alive, well, and doing reasonably well. But is his *modus operandi* good for him—or for the company?

12. CLOCKWORK AND CORPORATIONS

True, at certain times in the history of nearly all enterprises, entrepreneurs, statesmen and states, everything, including a sensible personal and organizational life-style, has to be willingly sacrificed for some greater object. In the Second World War, as Lord Alan-

brooke's diaries painfully reveal, the mostly middle-aged men surrounding the elderly Winston Churchill had to maintain, day in,
day out, a punishing pace interrupted by alarmingly brief passages
of sleep, and alternating very late nights with very early rising in the
same small hours. How they functioned at all is amazing. How they
functioned so well is a miracle.

Still, nobody would bet on marvels and miracles if they could
organize events and themselves better. The pressure on Churchill's
aides wasn't entirely exerted by the war itself: a good part stemmed
from the irregular habits, including the penchant for the small
hours, long indulged in by their boss. That is the inevitable result
when the head of any operation adopts any form of eccentric working life-style. Willy-nilly, the others in his entourage have to alter
their lives and styles to fit.

That fourteen-hour man's frenetic activity, for instance, must
spur frenzy in others. His three secretaries won't just have work
created for them by the boss—they will create work for him. He will
generate still more work for himself by all that note scribbling and
dictating. It sounds quite impressive to hear an executive say,
"When you get back from lunch, you can find three or four memos
on pieces of yellow paper on your desk with instructions, suggestions, or questions." But the three or four memos (multiplied by
heaven knows how many executive recipients) mean a heavy flow of
replies for the boss to deal with—which sounds like a sure-fire
method of guaranteeing another fourteen-hour day.

That's only one reason why the memo is a dangerous organizational tool. Another is that it can serve as a poor substitute for more
effective methods of keeping in real touch with what is happening.
Worse still, because of the stream of paper, the memo machine may
be deceived into believing that he's in control when he isn't.

A proper setup limits the scope for Management by Memo by
(a) giving operating autonomy to people with clearly defined responsibility; (b) keeping close tabs on them and their performance
by very frequent controls (mostly financial) and frequent (and regular) face-to-face meetings; (c) freeing the man at the top to think,
plan, invigilate, goad, and so on; (d) leaving spare time and capacity
for emergencies when the fourteen-hour hurly-burly becomes
(briefly) unavoidable.

More usually, close examination of a fourteen-hour stint will reveal (a) superfluous activity that didn't need to be done at all—by anybody; (b) activity that could have been delegated without either difficulty or disadvantage; (c) activity that uselessly generates activity in others—like that spate of memos mentioned above; (d) almost, by definition, no time whatsoever in which to think and reflect.

Very probably, the magnetism of the memo, though, is that it does at first blush seem more economical of time—especially if the comparison is with the meeting. Almost any organizational gathering tends to take much longer than planned or expected, and to accomplish less. Just as memos breed memos, so too, meetings breed meetings. In organizations where politics is important (as in the great game of politics itself), meetings become inescapable, and the results can be seen in the stress inflicted on the poor fellows who are expected to combine the endless internal and external politicking (i.e., meetings) with arduous executive jobs.

The key word is *executive*. Organizations should be set up so that those with executive responsibility can execute. That means using fundamentally nonexecutive appointments (as the Japanese use their chairman and president) for the nonexecutive, political, or policy roles. Moreover, the executive responsibility must be real. The reason why the command structure works badly in American corporations with large central staffs is that the people proposing executive action have no responsibility for carrying it out. Churchill knew better. For all the merry dance he led his military staff at home, he never deviated from the military principle that the general in the field is in command—operating within the higher strategy laid down higher up.

Even if the same principle is followed properly inside a peacetime (if not peaceful) organization, you'll still find work addicts who will slave away for fourteen hours—and create other slaves in their wake. But at least ensure that the fourteen hours are actually devoted to the executive affairs of the organization. Don't let the manager's mental and physical powers be tested to the limit in optional exercises of his time and tension. There always is a limit.

13. THE MAN WHO WENT AHEAD

A keen entrepreneur, returning to the fray after setbacks that might have killed the spirit of a lesser man, wanted to tackle a project that, he knew, some friends in a larger firm had rejected. He talked to them, and they explained fully and frankly why their thumbs had turned down.

The market, they pointed out, was dominated by a single, long-established competitor. This tough nut was especially hard to crack because of its low, low prices. Even though doubling its prices might not have affected its turnover at all, the market champion, with the arena virtually to itself, stuck to quotations that would inevitably make life hellishly hard for any challenger.

While the top dog could make indecently good money, despite its prices, because of its optimum volume, any would-be assailant would bleed to death during the long years needed to get on anything like level terms in turnover. Since number one held so heavy a lid over profits in this market, the big company considering a challenge decided that this wasn't its cup of hemlock.

Despite the arguments against, the small entrepreneur went ahead. He didn't succeed.

14. WHAT MADE SONY WIN

In theory, a big competitor, as in boxing, will always beat a little one—and the bigger they come, the harder it should be to make them fall. They, after all, have more resources of every kind almost by definition. They can afford both the positive strategies and effective tactics which make the most of their markets and also the counterattacks or preemptive moves which protect those markets against invaders.

One of those negative strategies is price. So long as Goliath commands a price structure that allows no room beneath, he can't be attacked by any David using price as a weapon—not unless the challenger can afford to lose money indefinitely. The price leader in a case like this is vulnerable only if David can go over the top—getting a higher price for a product selling in lower volumes.

This is the classic method of launching an expensive innovation: charging the highest possible price, on a new wonder drug, say, and bringing it down as volume rises and competition arrives, hoping to end up with a Goliath command over prices in the market as a whole. But the strategy can't work unless the product truly is a marvel, a better offering whose advantages will attract enough customers even at a higher price.

There is a related alternative, in which the new entrant, coming in at a higher price, persuades the market leader, by its example, to follow suit. But this demands a sleeping giant. There can be only two reasons why the powerful firm isn't already using its power to extract the last penny that the traffic will bear: either it simply doesn't *know,* or it simply doesn't believe, that higher prices actually can be charged—or it is deliberately using those low prices as a weapon to deter and repel competition.

Only in the first case can the higher-priced, smaller competitor hope to reverse the usual price game of following the leader. In the second case, the object of the giant's self-denying exercise (for it is forgoing profit) is very specifically to squelch any midget, which is what it will usually proceed to do. The strategy, though, is one whose advantages and disadvantages are finely balanced.

On one side of the scales is the real, quantifiable loss made year in, year out by the policy of underpricing: that cumulative, heavy, and purely voluntary cost must be set against unquantifiable rewards of repelling an as yet nonexistent adversary. In fact, business decisions taken solely to spike an enemy's guns are very often disasters—certainly if the decision involves any long-term commitment, and possibly even if the response is short-term.

The giant has actually made a classic error. Its managers think (if they are thinking at all) that their low-price policy is the cause of their market domination. It isn't: the *product* is the key—and as long as they concentrate all their resources on strengthening the product, they can afford some competition (it's the competition that will usually be unable to afford it). Anyway, new entrants nearly always make a monopoly market larger.

In a few cases, but only a few, the giant doesn't even have to trouble its head about this problem: for example, where the price of challenging Goliath—the cost of entry—is made prohibitive by technology or economics. For instance, he who challenges Hughes Tool in its immensely profitable business of oil-drilling bits is a braver man than I am, Gunga Din—and will very probably end up a poorer one, too.

In those circumstances, market hold cannot be broken except by a violent change in technology. But otherwise monopoly markets are always vulnerable, not to price competition, but to erosion around the edges. The Japanese are especially adept at this technique, but have often needed the unwitting cooperation of their American victims for it to succeed. Thus Xerox let in the Japanese by refusing to recognize (despite urgent warnings from its European outposts) that customers wanted small desk-top copiers. The U.S. television manufacturers similarly let in Sony because they foolishly thought the customers wouldn't want color portables. These companies, and many others, frittered away a priceless advantage of being big—that you can actually afford to take all forms of competition seriously.

By the time the victims had counterattacked, the Japanese were already firmly established. Even in U.S. and European industries (like television and copying) where the Japanese were not the leaders, they quickly became in some respects the side to beat—and the Western Goliaths (those that will survive, that is) are having to compete, not on price, but by taking leaves out of the Japanese book. That means:

1. If you have an overall edge over the competition, exploit it for all it's worth—and go yourself for the highest levels of productivity and competitive power.

2. Never rule out the possibility of effective flanking competition, but, if it appears, counter at the earliest possible time—on product strategy and tactics, not on crushing price warfare.

3. Where your advantage doesn't apply across the board, concentrate on the markets where you *are* strong.

4. Don't compete where you can't—get out and, unless circumstances change profoundly, stay out.

None of the four points adds up to traditional monopoly policy, in which the giant uses all its economic power, from control over distributors to saturation advertising, to kill off competition. On the contrary, it's a policy of competition—and that, in fact, is the key to Japanese success. A company like Sony will even own half of another one, like Aiwa, which does its utmost to plaster its parent. Merely consider the awesome, thriving number of car, camera, and hi-fi makers in Japan, and compare these serried ranks with the shrinkage of competitive numbers in the West.

The Sony style gives multiple sources of innovation, multiple points of attack on the market, multiple places for executives to make their marks—and their markets. It's lack of Western internal competitiveness, as much as lack of external competitive activity, that has lost markets to the Japanese marauders. But for Davids, the success of the latter is a happy omen. In today's increasingly segmented markets it takes a marvelous mammoth to defend all his products successfully at all points. And, since marvels are rare, Davids can multiply—provided they follow precisely the same four-point policy that the wise Goliaths and the wily Japanese are forcing home.

15. THE GUY WHO CAME IN FROM THE COLD

You don't have to be big to think bigger. A maker of marquees and tents got nearly all his profits in the usual way, hiring out the canvas for weddings, horse shows, agricultural shows, and so on. This raised an acute problem. Sales, profits, and capital turnover alike were limited by seasonal demand: all but 5 percent of the hirings came between April and September. Using a device called the "marketing workshop," the firm tried to answer a famous marketing question first posed in a famous *Harvard Business Review* article by a professor named Theodore Levitt: "What Business Are We In?"

Very obviously, as Ted could have told them, they weren't in society weddings or shows. The firm actually provided speedily erected weatherproof covers enabling the user to carry on with whatever activity he had in mind, come rain, come shine. This true definition of the true business led the marquee man to look to (1) using marquees after factory fires to get the plant back into production fast; (2) using his beloved tents when factory extensions ran into building delays and winter was drawing nigh so that, with a marquee above, builders could complete their work whatever the weather; (3) enabling building contractors to use their labor, bid for contracts, and work on sites all through the year.

Four workshop sessions after this dazzling perception of reality, the company had a new business plan. Thereafter, its hirings and profits rose dramatically—until it was getting 35 percent of its sales in the once dead and dreary months of October to March.

A small food manufacturer, selling branded products to the retail trade by van, used the same workshop technique to solve his problem: marked increases in the cost of van operations. With raw material prices up, fuel costs rising, and capital stuck in buffer stocks at depots, the firm couldn't escape by increasing prices—the pressures of competition and the buying power of the major supermarket chains were too great.

The workshops reviewed the financial ratios used to measure the performance of the departments that incurred costs. The review led to examining the buying patterns and delivery and service requirements of customers instead of looking at the problem from the old angle of fixed depot locations. The improvements subsequently introduced cut the van fleet by 40 percent, eliminated one depot, and produced an overall saving in operational costs of over $225,000 a year. A new strategy for major accounts was also developed, including changes in delivery methods and tighter control of buffer stocks. The estimated reduction of about $375,000 in working capital alone must have paid for the workshop time and time again.

16. WORKSHOPS OF SWOT

Many a business underperforms because it is underestimated by its own managers. Just as these individuals are often blind to their own faults, and even to their real virtues, so they may not see the realities of the business: not just its failings (though myopia here is common, and often fatal), but its strengths. There are all kinds of reasons for this blurred vision, including the pressure of day-to-day events and the weight of habit. But all the reasons in the end can be boiled down to one proposition: managers don't make the best of their business because they never give the matter any serious thought.

If that sounds unlikely, three questions provide the acid test.

1. What are the current goals of the business?
2. What are its Strengths and Weaknesses?
3. What are its Opportunities and Threats?

Unless the answers to the triad come trippingly off the tongue, the manager isn't really managing in anything more than the present, and probably isn't even doing that to the best advantage. As for the future, it is a closed book as long as questions 2 and 3 are unanswered. The capital letters in those questions are there because together they form a SWOT analysis. Do that properly, and you can answer a vital fourth question:

4. How should you change long-term company objectives and strategies as the environment and your own management intentions change?

The questions, as recommended by marketing expert John Lidstone, set the scene for the marketing workshops which he likes to stage for the entire board of a client company. Why the lot? Because

too many boards, instead of considering the future, frequently get bogged down in bread-and-butter matters or sidetracked by current crises. Added to this there is the inevitable conflict that arises from the composition of most boards of directors, however creatively they have been planned and balanced, between the three main functional heads of marketing, production, and finance.

79

In sober truth, most boards are planned and balanced about as creatively as a pyramid of circus elephants. But Lidstone's strictures don't apply only to boards. Most managers come under the marketing, or production, or finance heading; or, as line managers, preside, wittingly or not, over a perpetual conflict between three functions which are supposed, in jest, to be mutually supportive. With different, though interdependent objectives, the three types of manager often speak with different, forked tongues.

As Lidstone points out, finance men can become too preoccupied with the financial events of the past and with the cost implications of every decision, rather than the opportunities for profit around which the decisions should revolve. With the accountants stuck in history, the production people seldom remove their noses from the grindstone of the present. What they get stuck into is the marrying of men, materials, machinery, and time to produce the necessary from the plant (since they so often fail to achieve that, you can understand their preoccupation—and their preoccupied air).

The marketing man is the one everybody expects to have his eyes on the future, on identifying, anticipating, and satisfying the customer needs of tomorrow (at a profit, preferably). But is he? In practice marketers can be as myopic as anybody, concentrating on the here and now with every bit as much fervor as a production honcho. The workshop idea is aimed at the marketer's weaknesses as much as anybody else's.

The same needs, the same principles, apply even if the three functions are all rolled together into one boss: he still needs to talk and work through—with his colleagues—the direction of the company, in both senses of the word; where the company is going, who is going to take it there, and how.

In the system run by Lidstone's firm, Marketing Improvements, a couple of consultants attend the workshop, one acting as chairman. The outsiders make sure that the information and evidence needed to answer some searching questions are available. First, you need to master some general issues:

1. Is there a detailed up-to-date analysis of what business(es) you are in?

2. Are there clear profit and profitability objectives, broken down into goals for each chunk of the business?

3. Have growth rates been defined, and is there an optimum rate and/or size beyond which you don't want to expand?

4. Are the objectives practical, specific, expressed in numbers where possible, timed, competitively advantageous and limited enough to ensure commitment?

With those answered satisfactorily, the detailed marketing discussions follow:

1. Have the categories of strategy, such as market penetration, market development, and diversification, each been investigated in turn—and thoroughly?

2. Have you evaluated the selected strategies to ensure their relevance to the marketplace, to the corporate objectives and resources (you know these, of course), the marketing activity, and the competitive situation?

3. Have your strategies been checked and brought together into a combined approach which in turn could lead to redefining or extending the firm's objectives?

4. Do you have an effective way to consider and decide your marketing direction?

At every stage, conclusions must be drawn so that specific decisions can be taken. You may not know the answers. If not, start some research to provide them. You may need to construct theories, which must then also be tested by research. And you don't just end your one or two days together (which is all that a workshop should last) with large drinks all around—the closing is in some respects the most important moment.

That's when the chairman makes it clear to everybody what decisions have been reached, what conclusions have to be validated, what further information is still needed. Everything is summarized in writing, and the workshop members are given specific responsibilities, again in writing, for follow-up and action. One workshop won't be enough. Nor will the company's own premises be ideal for the conclave—hold it somewhere else.

Remember, above all, that this is no social get-together. That acronym SWOT hangs over all: Strengths, Weaknesses, Opportunities, Threats. It is axiomatic that the organization, like the individual manager, can never make the optimum use of all its strengths or do enough to eliminate all its weaknesses. That can constitute a threat as ominous as the Bermuda Triangle. But it also provides an ocean of opportunity.

17.   THE WELL-DRILLED BLACK & DECKER

The threat can be overcome by quite simple approaches—the simpler, indeed, the better. The formidable U.S. management and marketing machine Black & Decker has had a penchant for British executives ever since its U.K. operation was set into ferocious growth by an Englishman named Robert Appleby. B & D regards all management activities as integrated—but it has a problem, of sorts: so high a dominance of its main U.K. market (power drills and accessories for the home handyman, with 95 percent) and such penetration (over half of British homes have the drills) that new products and new markets are indispensable to sustain its growth.

The new products all bear a strategic family relationship to the power tools. For instance, the domestic tools suggested powered equipment for the garden, leading to lawn mowers, hedge trimmers, chain saws, and so on. Domestic tools suggested industrial ones. Here, the company ran into troubles early on. So what did Black & Decker do?

1. It cut its product range (eliminating the non-successes).

2. It designed new products which it could sell right across Europe, generating higher volumes and lower costs.

3. It worked to cut down the motor variants even further, applying a basic principle of maximizing the millions of motors made in one plant by rationalizing designs.

In its base market, do-it-yourself, Black & Decker concentrated on adding to the range, with new products for new jobs. It plans the manufacturing side so that output can be switched rapidly from, say, saws to lawn mowers and back again in response to market needs. It monitors these very carefully: for instance, it studies returned warranty cards to identify actual retail trends as early as possible. Then it adjusts accordingly, not only production schedules, but advertising and selling pressure.

Nothing in these deeds is especially complicated, but none of it can be accomplished easily, either. Doing the simple things superbly brought up the U.K. business of Black & Decker, based in a recessionary economy, from $90 million of sales and $9.5 million of profit to $765 million and $21 million in a mere four years.

18. GE'S SIMPLE STRATEGIES

The difference between the smallest, simplest marketing operation in the world and the largest and most sophisticated thus turns out to lie in practice rather than in subtlety of theory, even though the theoretical gurus, like Professor Philip Kotler of Northwestern University, do tend to concentrate their preaching (and their consultancy practices) on the giants. At first sight, their approach may seem hideously intimidating. Just look at Exhibit A.

That's how General Electric in the U.S. evaluates a business that it already owns or is thinking of entering. Before blanching, though, look at the factors listed in the two boxes for industry attractiveness and business strength. If you don't know where your business stands on these fourteen factors, you should—and in most cases the information is already in the businessman's head. The matrix makes him quantify his knowledge and set it down—as in Exhibit B—where the question is the status of his precious product in the marketplace.

The advantage of being forced to put into words, to make explicit, what has been left unshaped, is to bring the mind hard up against reality. For instance, a low-quality, medium-priced product (the so-called shoddy goods strategy) is no good in the long term,

EXHIBIT A

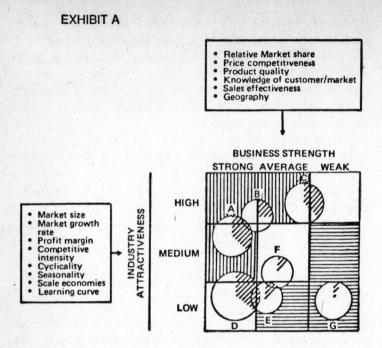

and not much use in the short run, either. As for the hit-and-run strategy—you can't build a business on a fleet turn of foot.

Turn to a truly great marketing company like Procter & Gamble and there's no such nonsense. In markets ranging from soap to food, disposable diapers to toothpaste, P & G looks first to "better than average quality" and second to "improved quality over time." Turn to nonconsumer goods, and Caterpillar, a hugely successful industrial marketer, until clobbered as the 1980s recession began, puts first "premium product quality."

The deep significance of quality is important in and of itself. In the context of markets, though, the virtue of quality is that it positions you in the three highly defensible (and highly aggressive) strategies at the top of the matrix: earning a premium price; gaining deeper penetration of the market; plastering the opposition with "superbargains."

In fact, the P & Gs and the Caterpillars aim to use their quality

EXHIBIT B

PRICE

		HIGH	MEDIUM	LOW
	HIGH	PREMIUM STRATEGY	PENETRATION STRATEGY	SUPERBARGAIN STRATEGY
PRODUCT QUALITY	MEDIUM	OVERPRICING STRATEGY	AVERAGE QUALITY STRATEGY	BARGAIN STRATEGY
	LOW	HIT-AND-RUN STRATEGY	SHODDY-GOODS STRATEGY	CHEAP-GOODS STRATEGY

advantage to finance the backups that consolidate their positions in the marketplace. The former, for instance, will plow its high cash flow (from high margins) into things like product innovation, brand extension, heavy advertising, and effective sales promotion. Caterpillar, in its very different business, plumps for strategies like "superior service and parts management" and offering a full line of products.

The overall object of all such strategies is to obtain the greatest possible market share times the greatest possible unit price. Now, "greatest possible" isn't by any means precise. One manager's possible is another man's poison. In any event, "market share" is by no means as straightforward a concept as it might seem. The reason isn't simply because companies commonly exaggerate their market shares (not just for the hell of it, but to make themselves feel better in the long, dark hours of the night).

A more scientific difficulty is that "market share" has several dimensions. Kotler likes companies to look at four different measures.

1. *Overall market share.* This means the company's sales expressed as a percentage of total industry sales.

2. *Served market share.* This means company's sales expressed as a percentage of the total sales to its served market.

3. *Relative market share* (to top three competitors). This means the company's sales as a percentage of the combined sales of the three largest competitors.

4. *Relative market share* (to leading competitor). This means the company's sales as a percentage of the leading competitor's sales.

All of these have their utility. But the one you want to watch for the sake of marketing strategy is number three—"relative market share" to the three largest competitors. An American outfit called the Boston Consulting Group made amazing headway in its own highly competitive market by the use of another matrix in which number three provides the bottom line. Here it is in Exhibit C.

EXHIBIT C

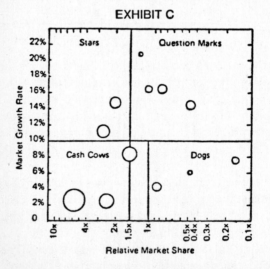

The box is easily read. If the market is growing by 22 percent annually, and you've got ten times the combined sales of those three largest rivals, the business is not merely a star—it's a supernova. At the other extreme, if its sales are a tenth of the enemy trio's (with the boot on the other foot) and the market isn't growing at all—go, and wait not upon the order of your going.

The Boston formula is simplicity itself: invest heavily in a star; close or sell a dog; keep a cash cow going on care and maintenance while you milk as much cash as possible; if it's a question mark, find out if you can turn it into a star.

Now the word "simplicity" is dangerously near to "simplistic," and the fact that highly sophisticated planners have used the Boston formula or variations thereon doesn't mean that a matrix is a substitute for management or marketing. But marketing strategy should always aim toward the top left-hand corner of the matrix boxes given here. As noted earlier, the theory isn't subtle: get the best price for the largest market share, and you must win. The difference that takes the P & Gs and the Caterpillars to that point isn't subtle, either. They simply (as simply as possible) *make* it happen.

To summarize some of the important points I've mentioned in Step Two:

1. Don't persist in a losing cause unless you truly know you can turn it into a winning one.

2. Always look for obviously winning causes.

3. Pick people not just for what they are, but for what you want them to do.

4. Never ignore a gut feeling: but never believe that it's enough on its own.

5. Always measure alternative decisions before choosing between them—and always remember that there are alternatives.

6. Separate a business into its effective parts so that they can sink or swim—but make them swim.

7. Establish a balance between autonomy and authority that gives *them* immediate powers and *you* ultimate control.

8. Organize yourself so that the organization isn't organized around you.

9. If you have an overall edge over the competition, exploit it for all it's worth—and go yourself for the highest levels of productivity and competitive power.

10. Never rule out the possibility of effective flanking competition; but, if it appears, counter at the earliest possible time—on product, strategy, and tactics, not on crushing price warfare.

11. Where your advantage doesn't apply across the board, concentrate on the markets where you *are* strong.

12. Don't compete where you can't—get out and, unless circumstances change profoundly, stay out.

13. Check at all times that you know the current goals of the business, its strengths and weaknesses, its opportunities and threats.

14. Wherever you can, aim to get the best price for the largest market share.

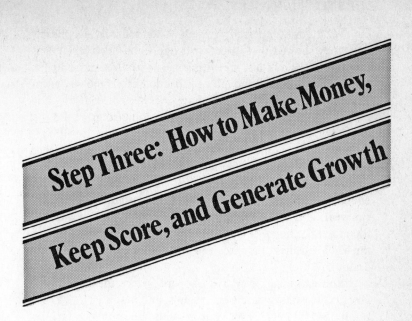

Step Three: How to Make Money, Keep Score, and Generate Growth

1. THE FIGURES THAT DIDN'T ADD UP

A successful businessman had a disconcerting experience with one of his very best businesses. In his own words, this is what happened.

> I thought 1980 was a great year for one of my firms. I wasn't running it directly—I have, as you know, many other interests—but the man I put in has always seemed extremely competent, and the figure I've always looked at first, the turnover, was rising like a rocket.
>
> But this, I've discovered, is the point where it's all too easy to make a mistake. I'd just had to change the accountancy staff, and the new lot took a long time to settle in. The figures—the detailed figures, that is—got later and later. So what? Knew the turnover, didn't I?

Well, you've guessed the rest. When I finally got the figures, they showed that direct costs had risen much faster than turnover. That still left me with a substantial rise in contribution—but not nearly enough of a rise to absorb the whopping jump in overheads. Murphy's Law operated, of course (whatever can go wrong, will); with business going so great, I'd just opened a new factory—in a good location, but it still cost money; and I'd launched an export drive, and that, too, racked up a great amount of expenses.

The net result was no net, not one red cent. We lost an enormous amount of money in the closing months of the financial year, and we've gone on losing since. In fact, if I hadn't found out the horrible truth when I did, just before Christmas, the whole business, factories and all, might have gone down the drain.

You can imagine what's happened since then. I've hired new accountants, put in new systems, and made a New Year's resolution: I'll never, *never* put up with late or inadequate figures. I want a forecast of monthly profits a week after the month ends, and I'll have final figures at the end of the month, or else. If they aren't the same as the estimates, more or less, it won't just be the accountants who get fired.

2. FIGURES THAT DO

Any organization, high or low, large or small, commercial or charitable, bureaucratic or entrepreneurial, is guided by a management information system. The only difference is that some are good and others downright dangers. But they all purport to speak in the same language—money—and they are all expressed in some kind of financial report. From some nobody can deduce anything at all—there are management accounts, believe it or not, from which it is impossible to discover even the gross sales. From others, the whole progress of the business can be read clearly at a glance, and that has as much to do with presentation as content.

Table 5

A TYPICAL MANAGEMENT INFORMATION SYSTEM

A.B.C. LTD CASH CONTROL
CONTROL

($000)   RESULTS TO: May 31, 1983

LINE NOS.	(Figures show cumulative position for current year)	31.5.83		XYZ DIVISION QUARTER 30.6.83		QUARTER 30.9.83		QUARTER 31.12.83		QUARTER 31.3.84	
		Actual	Budget	Forecast	Budget	Forecast	Budget	Forecast	Budget	Forecast	Budget
1	Profit before Tax	817	560	979	712	1408	1100	1650	1299	572	
2	Depreciation	228	233	276	281	462	510	654	703	155	
3	Movement in working capital	(888)	(917)	(967)	(609)	(956)	(575)	(12)	171	(992)	
4	Capital Expenditure	1110	1313	1610	1566	2247	2247	2589	2589	550	
5	Cash Flow from operations	(953)	(1438)	(1323)	(1184)	(1333)	(1212)	(297)	(417)	(815)	
6	Net loan movement	327	114	389	107	389	61	389	52		
7	Movements of Reserves	258	578	258	578	258	578	259	578	209	
8	Net cash flow	(1538)	(2130)	(1971)	(1868)	(1981)	(1850)	(945)	(1046)	(1024)	
9	Surplus versus budget	592		(113)		(131)		101			

To prove the point, look at Table 5, which represents the typical kind of report that the typical management information system produces. The items it contains are by no means the only ones a particular company might demand in its reports. Every business has its own individual vital statistics, whose identity can readily be discovered by asking two questions: If I could press a magic button and get any information I wanted at once and at nil cost, what would it be? But, what would it actually cost, and are the benefits worth that expenditure?

They aren't the easiest questions to answer honestly. But whatever answer you come up with, one general observation applies: the information can be presented far more intelligibly than in Table 5. That comes from a lecture delivered by A. S. C. Ehrenberg. His observations on it ran as follows:

". . . the data are difficult to take in. This is partly because of the archaic layout. Years ago the readings used to be entered by hand with pens, and so today each figure is still entered in a separate box. This stops the eye from moving from one figure to another. In many companies such control sheets are still on foolscap—often the only forms that are. And the form has usually been Xeroxed so often that it is almost indecipherable. But even when the reproduction is more adequate, as here, the data remain difficult to grasp."

How do you improve on the so-called experts who prepare such reports for great companies? The basic principles—on paper or video screen—are simplicity itself.

1. It's easier to compare figures when the eye is made to run down, rather than across, the page, so you put the figures you want to compare in columns, not rows.

2. It also helps if figures to be compared are expressed in the same form, i.e., as monthly averages rather than cumulative totals for periods of different length, so that's how control figures should be summarized.

With these two principles in mind, a company can arrive at something like Tables 6 and 7 (see page 93). They contain exactly the same information as in 6, but presented in a far more accessible

Table 6

(MONTHLY RATES IN $'000)	PROFIT BEFORE TAX		DEPRECIA- TION		MOVEMENT IN WORKING CAPITAL		CAPITAL EXPENDI- TURE	
Year to date	F	B	F	B	F	B	F	B
31. 5.83	163*	112	46*	47	−180*	−180	220*	260
30. 6.83	163	119	46	47	−160	−100	270	260
30. 9.83	156	122	51	57	−110	− 60	250	250
31.12.83	138	108	55	59	− 1	14	220	220
31. 3.84	191		52		−330		180	

* Actual

Table 7

YEAR TO DATE $('000)	PROFIT BEFORE TAX		DEPRECIA- TION		MOVEMENT IN WORKING CAPITAL		CAPITAL EXPENDI- TURE	
	F	B	F	B	F	B	F	B
31. 5.83	817	560	228	233	(888)	(917)	1110	1313
30. 6.83	979	712	276	281	(967)	(609)	1610	1566
30. 9.83	1408	1100	462	510	(956)	(575)	2247	2247
31.12.83	1650	1299	654	703	(12)	171	2589	2589
31. 3.84	572	—	155	—	(992)	—	550	—

way: Table 6 has the figures converted into monthly averages, Table 7 gives them straight. Note, however, that the figures are rounded as well, and Ehrenberg in fact recommends rounding even further, to two digits, even for the biggest number. He points out that only a tiny loss of accuracy (3 percent or so) is involved. But it's purely a matter of habit. As a company president, quoted from the *Harvard Business Review* by Ehrenberg, frankly observed, "the first few times my controller sent me a report with the figures rounded to the nearest 1,000 dollars, I felt very uneasy. The report seemed lacking and incomplete. Now that I have grown used to the shorter figures, I find I mentally round all figures I look at down to two or three digits."

Ehrenberg says that "rounded figures seem naked because it is easy to see what they say (that 35 percent is about twice 18 percent), but it is not necessarily obvious what we ought to do about it, what conclusions to draw or actions to take. In contrast, figures like 17.81

percent and 35.24 percent are less disturbing, because, while we clearly do not know what they mean, they are at least very precise."

That passage comes direct to the heart of the matter: "what conclusions to draw or actions to take." There are other technical tricks that help in presentation (like the use of single spacing rather than double; the avoidance of complex graphs; reducing typed tables by about 15–20 percent for optical comfort). All these useful tips spring from knowledge of how the human brain actually works. But the only purpose is to provide a better trigger for firing its response mechanism.

The figures, as Ehrenberg stresses, should always be accompanied by brief written summaries that emphasize the main patterns and exceptions. But don't react as some of the world's largest companies tend to do if the main pattern is a terrible shortfall in sales and profits. Typically, those dozy giants merely record (and no doubt deplore) the dreadful events—and do absolutely nothing about them until the next annual budget season: then, *mirabile dictu*, all manner of fat is cut out of the corporate hide, and the beneficent results are hailed with hosannas on all sides.

The whole point of modern management accounting (as in Table 3), with its comparison of actuals, budgets, and forecasts of actuals, updated every month, and revised as necessary every quarter, is to react to change and to avoid nasty surprises—to shut stable doors before horses gallop off into the blue. Used in that way, a management information system is not merely worth its weight in gold—it can create gold by alerting managers not only to their problems, but also to their opportunities. Used properly, management accounts are not just history but history, and money, in the making.

3. THE DISAPPEARING PROFITS

Never forget that the numbers in those accounts are just that: numbers. In a world which takes it for granted that profits are the be-all and end-all of business, most incentive and sharing schemes are tied to that number—despite all the evidence that profits are a movable feast. Take the case of a girl who had her own imprint with a large New York publishing house. Although the books under her imprint sold well, there were no profits at all—not one penny. Finally, she worked out what profits should have been made, confronted the president (also a woman), and demanded her money or her life. The president reluctantly handed over the money. She then added these immortal words: "Let this be a lesson to you, honey. There ain't no profits in American business!"

Such individual calamities only serve to rub in the truth exemplified by one successful and amazingly swift turnaround. The turnaround artist in the case simply dismantled a centralized bureaucracy, making the bosses for each company totally responsible for all aspects of the business and rewarding them accordingly—but not just on a straight profit link. The philosophy is get on, or get out; failure is tolerated for no longer than one year. But the definition of failure, and that of the success that earns a fat bonus, includes profits as a ratio of capital employed.

Why? Because the biggest risk in this particular business is an excessive pileup of inventory. Reaching a high figure for return on capital forces the bosses to keep their expensive stocks as low as they possibly can. The key performance and target measures for managers, and the company itself, must cover many dimensions as well as profit—just to ensure that the profits that ain't become the profits that are.

4. RATIOS OF SUCCESS

Actually, no single statistic in business tells you anything about the calibre of its performance—not sales, not profits, not even the growth of either. To acquire real meaning, every statistic not only has to measure accurately what it purports to measure, but it must also be related to some relevant statistic that measures something else. Thus profit as a percentage of sales is one of the most significant tell-tales around—and if this percentage, or ratio, is growing, that, too, has far more meaning than growth in either of its constituents alone.

By the same token, only in reverse, the right ratio can give a most accurate picture of a business going wrong—before it does. Which ratio? Thanks to the expert work of D. A. J. Marais, who investigated a bunch of failures and nonfailures, you can see, using the evidence of their history, what the best ratios are for separating the sheep from the goats.

The work isolates one particular financial ratio, easy to work out, which is basic to evaluating the performance and prospects of any company. It's cash flow to current liabilities. Why should the proportion of cash flow to current liabilities matter so much? Because it measures the firm's profitability and its ability to meet its short-term commitments.

For example, bank debt is a major part of the current liabilities figure. According to the Marais study, "The failed group tends to have a much greater proportion" of bank debt relative to the size of the company. In fact, bank debt averaged 22 percent of gross total assets for failed firms—only 8 percent for the survivors. Set the simple cash-flow statistics (which measure the money coming in from current operations against the money flowing out to finance them) in relation to the claims on the cash resources, and you see how vulnerable or otherwise the business actually is.

On this score, the survivor firms had $40 of cash flow for every $100 of current liabilities. As for the failures, three years before they joined the ranks of the Great Unloved, they had only $20 of cash flow for each $100 of liabilities. A year before failure, the ratio was zero—that is, they had no cash flow at all. The moral is that the *trend* in a ratio may tell more than the figures obtained at any one stopping point—for the failures, the trend was a straight downward line heading toward extinction.

Many other ratios can be used to test performance and staying power alike, such as

1. Cash flow as a percentage of total debt (30 percent for the survivors; 20 percent and falling steeply for the flops).
2. Current assets divided by current liabilities (1.6 was the an-

swer for those who made it; 1.5 and falling fast for those who didn't).

3. Quick assets (cash, etc.) as a percentage of current liabilities (over 80 percent for the survivors; well below 80 percent for the failures).

Funnily enough, after dropping to 60 percent, reflecting a further year of miscreant behavior, the last-mentioned ratio perked up slightly a year before final disaster. So, whatever the trend, a quick-to-current figure of 60–70 percent is a sign that something, somewhere may be grievously wrong—whether the business is large or small. It was simple calculation of such ratios that convinced a couple of professors that the great Rolls-Royce aero-engine firm was being sucked into its own jets—although, of course, the day of reckoning was delayed by the sheer size (and reputation) of the firm. As Marais notes, "The very size of a company may often act as a buffer against external turbulence."

For all that, and for all the large firm's financial advantages (like lower cost of capital and its greater availability), the "size equals security" syndrome shouldn't be given too much weight. The expert also points out that "size in no way guarantees survival in an increasingly competitive environment."

He can say that again. Anyway, there's survival and survival. Being kept alive by a creditor who won't foreclose because you owe him too much money (the key to Chrysler's original survival) isn't the object of anybody's exercise. The right idea is to be at no man's mercy, but to have the freedom of liquidity—plus the confirmation of knowing that your company has passed the acid test of performance, proving that it can pay its way in the here and now.

The Marais Ratio, cash flow to current liabilities, shows a discrepancy between the failed and nonfailed (remember, the latter recorded a figure *twice* as good as the former did three years before their failure) which is much sharper than that recorded by other leading indicators of corporate insolvency—so much sharper that it's one nobody can afford to ignore, along with that critically important trend. Note that the survivors maintained a very steady performance on this truly vital statistic. Year in, year out, cash flow stayed at around that safe 40 percent of current liabilities. Just as the steeply falling line points straight to failure, the steady state indicates precisely that—a steady state, the stable platform on which solid growth and ultimate survival can be built.

5. PAYOFF IN YEAR ELEVEN

That stable platform is growth in the real worth of the business—a crucial point which many otherwise smart managers fail to grasp. Thus, once upon a time, an aggressive and sharp-minded company got wind of a competitor's pending new product. So marvelous was the wonder, so certain to reap ripe profits, that the very entrepreneurial operation concerned decided to beat its rival to the punch. However, the rival refused to be outboxed, accelerated its launch with might and main—and left the other company temporarily high and dry.

But only temporarily. It licked its wounded pride, watched to see whether the market did burgeon as expected, and finally, pleased with what it saw, launched its own me-too product after all. The product was late by definition, later than the management had originally planned and several months after the opposition. It was thus clearly number two in a market which, for all its strength, couldn't support two competitors. And the product was thus certain to make losses.

The entrepreneur in charge, however, rationalized his position as follows: he was prepared to lose $100,000 a year for ten years, as long as he was making a profit of, say, $100,000 at the end of that period, in Year Eleven. Then, he would only have paid $1 million, he reasoned, to create a property worth at least that amount.

He was taking the same view, in a slightly different form, as often surfaces when a project misses the targets on which the initial capital investment was based. The temptation for managers (especially those who backed the awful thing in the first place) is to hang on, because of all the money already poured down the same drain.

Their fate is usually the same as that of the ten-year investor just mentioned. The company eventually closed the project because of the horrendous losses it had been making—in Year Eleven, of course.

6. LIVING BEYOND INFLATION

A hidden risk of letting losses run and run, even if the business finally turns that usually retreating corner, is that the early losses may be worth very much more than the later profits—even if the latter look bigger—because of inflation. Inflation on the horrible scale of that experienced from the 1970s onward has caused two problems for anybody measuring his activities in money. First, you needed far more money just to stay where you were—let alone to expand your game. Second, the whole basis of accountancy was thrown into disarray. It was in a tricky enough condition before double-digit inflation butchered the books: but what is the poor (or rich) businessman to make of accountancy now?

The answer begins with the knowledge that one thing hasn't changed. In Victorian times, when prices were as likely to fall as to rise, the mill and mine owners just counted all the lovely loot piling up in their treasure chests—and they were right. To this day, you haven't truly made a profit unless you have piled up real, bankable money, or goods which can be swiftly converted into money, that comes to more wealth than you began with.

This is a principle which management accounting, the cement that holds all sound companies together, has long observed. The "contribution" which is basic to management accounts measures the surplus or (heaven forfend) deficit after all the direct costs of operations have been charged against the direct revenues. The measure is always in current money, and automatically adjusts to changes in the purchasing power of the money. But this simplicity evaporates when financial accounts are prepared.

For instance, suppose that the firm holds $100,000 of stocks which have appreciated by 20 percent at a time of 20 percent inflation, but which will have to be replaced at a cost of $140,000 when used. Has the company made $20,000 profit (as conventional accountancy would argue), or no profit at all, or a loss of $20,000?

In fact, there's no final answer to the conundrum, which hasn't stopped all manner of clever men from trying to square this particular circle. The only hard fact to grasp is that the best accounting convention is the one which leaves you paying least tax: the $20,000 loss in the case just given. Conventional accounting has left firms paying tax on profits they have never made.

On the Commerce Department's traditional figures, the domestic earnings of nonfinancial U.S. corporations totted up to $97.4 billion in 1978—a whopping figure that was in turn an enormous 16 percent up on 1977, and 2.6 times the 1965 level. But, if you adjust for inflation, by taking away phony profits on stock and jacking up depreciation to take account of higher replacement costs of plant and equipment, the $97.4 billion becomes $59.6 billion; and in constant money that's way *down* on 1972—by about a third, in fact. So which figure do you believe: up 2.6 times, down a third, or somewhere in between?

Plainly it's the same conundrum, on a grand national scale, as the stock profit question. A sensible way of living with the problem has been provided by Professor Eugene Fama, writing in *Fortune* magazine. As he notes, the problem cuts both ways. Suppose you had borrowed $1,000 at 17 percent to invest in inventory which, after a year of 17 percent inflation, cost $1,170 to replace. You were down $340 before tax, weren't you?

Not if you remember that you will only be repaying $830 after 17 percent inflation has done its bit: meaning a $170 tax-free profit. So the true cost is simply the interest cost, which will be reduced by around half through tax relief. As Fama points out, though, interest rates at a time of inflation will tend to rise above the rate of inflation: only the difference really represents an interest charge; the rest is repayment of capital. So forget about the paper profit—you never made it and never will. You repaid the $1,000 with $1,170 of steadily depreciating money, and you got away (which won't happen often) with a nil interest cost and tax relief on the whole caboodle.

That will plainly help to produce a respectable yield on the total capital. But, in inflationary times, what's respectable? To take advantage of Fama's researches, this is what you do:

1. Define the capital for your business as its *total* capital—the money you, and any other shareholders, have to put into it, *and* all the debt.

2. Calculate depreciation on what you reckon it would cost to replace the equipment concerned, and on your realistic assessment of how long the stuff will last.

3. Value the consumption of inventory on the LIFO basis (last in, first out), meaning you value the stock consumed on the latest price you've paid.

4. Include in your calculation of the return on capital
   (a) all interest payments;
   (b) tax payable;
   (c) dividends paid.

5. Compare the resulting figure with the current rate of inflation and yields available on fixed interest investments—and think very, very carefully if you aren't beating them all. You can see the logic behind this if you take a mythical company which has the (highly mythical) good fortune to be paying only 10 percent interest on a debt which represents 30 percent of the total capital: i.e., the "stockholder's equity" (or capital minus debt) is 70—and on this equity figure the firm earns a respectable 20 percent return before tax at 50 percent. The total cash flow from operations as a percentage of the total capital of 100 is thus 7 percent (after-tax profit) + 10 percent (depreciation) + 3 percent (interest) + 7 percent (taxes): a grand total of 27 percent.

But wait—the depreciation isn't just a figure, but a genuine expense of the business. Deduct that, and the return comes down to 17 percent—which, in a year of 17 percent inflation, is no return at all. The logic ultimately has nothing to do with inflation *per se,* but a great deal to do with business reality, which is a matter of finding the right sums to do and doing them.

Take the case of "the Payoff in Year Eleven." The maestro

made several mistakes, but the main one, in this context, was to confuse capital with income. The same money that he was losing, at $100,000 a year, could have been used to purchase capital—borrowing it and paying interest. But that wasn't what he was doing: he was just losing money; he was thus reducing, not enhancing, the worth of the business, all in the remote hope that, one day, it would turn the corner. A business which isn't replacing the nominal capital destroyed by inflation is on a similar downward slope—and it will never be earning a real payoff, in Year Eleven or any other year.

But there's one further lesson, one which the German electrical giant AEG didn't learn—to its ultimate terrible damage. All AEG's business decisions were subjected to inflation accounting. Not so with its highly successful rival Siemens. As Peter Drucker writes in *The Changing World of the Executive,* "What Siemens did was quite simple. Its day-to-day operation, including money management, was run in accordance with the reality of inflation. Everything to do with the making of tomorrow was run as if inflation did not exist."

As Drucker explains it, "To inflation-proof the business, the activities that make tomorrow—scientific and technical research, product and process innovation and development; maintenance of plant and equipment; market development; customer service; and the development and training of professional, managerial, and skilled people—are run as if the interest rate were 3 percent, that is with disregard for the inflation charge." This point is that neglecting these activities, simply because they don't make financial sense when you discount the inflation rate, is to neglect the whole future of the business. Do that for long enough and, like AEG, you end up with financial figures so awful that there's no point in correcting them for inflation—or anything else.

7. THE MAN WHO TOOK CHRYSLER BACK

When the case gets terminal, you don't need to worry about inflation, or the distinction between capital and income. Money is what you desperately want, in any shape or form, if you're faced with a Chrysler-type crisis. Ever since the Eisenhower era, the Chrysler Corporation has staggered from crunch to crisis, each one worse than the last. Even when the U.S. auto industry did relatively well, Chrysler's performance was hamstrung by its feeble number three share of the home market, weak foreign operations, and management errors as it sought vainly to match the might of General Motors across the board.

Inevitably, cash ran shorter and shorter, making an awful situation still more desperate. By all odds, Chrysler should be as dead as the Model T. Rescued from imminent bankruptcy in 1979 by Congress, the company lost an all-time record of $3.5 billion in the three years including 1981. Yet the next year Chrysler actually made a profit—and its chairman, Lee Iacocca, had become, according to a businessman poll, easily the most respected business executive in the U.S.

A major part of Iacocca's achievement rests on the escape from bankruptcy, which meant twisting arms in Washington and the banks, and still left Chrysler owing a perilously high $2 billion in long-term debt. On August 12, 1983, though, Iacocca triumphantly repaid the last $800 million of the federally guaranteed loans borrowed three years before. What gave Chrysler its chance of climbing that debt mountain successfully was the following set of dramatic and drastic changes:

1. The work force was cut from 157,000 employees to 74,700.
2. Thanks to concessions wrung from the United Auto Workers, the remaining workers were costing only $1.5 billion in wages and salaries—a reduction of 28 percent in three years.
3. Businesses that Chrysler didn't need were sold off—including that unsuccessful overseas side.
4. The fifty-two plants Iacocca inherited were cut by a third to thirty-six.
5. To reduce inventory, the practice of building cars for stock was stopped: smaller, quicker trucking of parts replaced large rail shipments (annual saving $45 million); parts in use came down from 70,000 to 40,000 (annual saving, some $300 million).

As a result of these five crucial measures, and other changes, a company that had a mere million bucks between it and closure in November 1981 had $900 million in cash at the start of 1983. More important, and astonishingly, the company can now make money by building 1.2 million vehicles—about half the number needed in 1980, a year when the auto-maker made its biggest ever loss of $1.7 billion.

Whether or not Chrysler makes it, to win a long-term and successful future, depends on products (on which Iacocca planned to spend $8 billion over five years) and their marketing—always corporate weaknesses in the past. But without the basic changes made by Iacocca, there could have been no future, no products, and no markets. Chrysler can now go forward because its boss went back in two senses—getting smaller to get bigger, and returning to the eternal basics that form the simple foundation of all successful management.

8. COSTS THAT ARE CONSTANT

It's much easier to state the basic formula of business than to apply it. If X is your revenue (that is prices multiplied by volume), then the trick is to keep Y (costs) as far as possible below X. The wider the gap between the two, the more money must pour into the ever-open coffers.

Businesses commonly underestimate the extent to which they can reduce Y. One boss discovered that, having in adversity "ripped the guts out of the business ... we were really feeling quite smart"—until, that is, a calamity fell on his division's head yet again, and the company had to re-examine its entrails. Under this new pressure, it found four more ways of reducing Y.

1. The work force was cut by 130.
2. Steps were taken to raise productivity: for instance, changes in the shift system cut absenteeism from double figures to 2 percent or so.

3. The traditional weekend shutdown went.

4. In consequence, production of commodities rose by 10–15 percent in volume, and that of packaged products by 30 percent.

Because the boss feared a volume decline, he also galvanized the sales side into selling harder. In fact, total sales fell all the same—by no less than $1 million. But entirely because of the reduction in cost, X − Y equaled a jump in profits of no less than 37 percent.

Those figures should be wholly convincing. But never underestimate the perversity of man, or the complexity of his affairs. Most businessmen have at least a hazy notion of the true quantity of X—that is, they know how much money is coming in. But many businessmen (perhaps most) don't have accurate figures on costs, and continually spend more than they need—often much more. It's very easily done.

One excellent method is to use more fixed assets than are actually required. Machines and buildings cost money, which means that their use equals money. The man who uses more machines than he needs, buys them when he can lease, and hangs on to machines he will never run again is conspiring at his own downfall.

Consider rather the Lesson of the Leaseback. Many an entrepreneur has turned rapacity into riches by this simple strategem. You find a sitting duck—a company sitting on beautiful, delectable properties, say—buy the company; sell its property to a financial institution; pocket the cash; lease back the real estate—and carry on trading.

These days, finding such asset-rich companies to buy is less easy than it was. But any corporate real estate is what you might call ripe for plucking in this way. The company frees capital. It's true that the price of its liberation is a rent—and rent has to be paid. Surely, the leaseback has *increased* the costs, not reduced them?

The cost was there all the time. At any point, the owner could have ceased trading, rented the freehold himself, and pocketed the market rent. If the market rent is greater than your business itself is earning, either you, or the business, or both, are hopeless. Far better to quit, and become a landlord. In fact, many big-time managements now charge their subsidiaries a market rent for the premises—even if they are freehold. The hidden costs, as well as the obvious ones, must be covered to arrive at a true, good, and honest profit.

The leaseback points to one cost pitfall: the money already sunk in the ground and what's on it. But there's also the money that flows—in, out, around, and about. The simple $X - Y$ formula applies here, too. If the actual, bankable cash flowing in exceeds the real, exchangeable cash flowing out, you're solvent. If Y is greater than X, for reasons other than soundly financed expansion, sooner or later the great day will no longer dawn.

That's why many businesses die from "overtrading" or being "undercapitalized"—accountants' jargon for two sides of the same coin. It means that the company simply doesn't have enough ready money available to pay the immediate bills before the cash owed comes flooding in. Unwary entrepreneurs think they can solve this difficulty by delaying payment on their own bills into the dim and distant future, while demanding cash on the nail for their own offerings. It works for a while: the creditors' column on the balance sheet gets bigger and bigger, while the debtors' column doesn't budge—until one day the financial genius wakes up to find that he owes far more money than he can possibly repay, and that the creditors are all knocking, if not thundering, on his door.

It may seem paradoxical that these disasters can happen when the business is actually booming away. But the paradox is the same as that to which accountants Touche Ross draw attention when advising a business how to manage financially in what they delicately call "a changing economic climate"—in other words, the Anxious Eighties. "During recession," they warn, "cash shortage is usually caused by lack of profitability; recovery can prove to be an even greater cash trap, as the need for additional working capital is immediate and the profits follow."

It's another aspect of the same problem that concerned two American experts, Bradley T. Gale and Ben Branch, writing in the *Harvard Business Review*. The authors point out that having a negative cash flow isn't some dreadful sin, like "beating your wife."

A low rate of cash flow year after year does not carry the same stigma as recurrent low return on investment. Even negative cash flow is not necessarily a serious problem. As long as a business has established the strategic position required to earn an attractive return, it generates cash when the market ultimately slows down. But, while rapid growth continues, the company may still require additional resources.

That's because the costs of production and sales (and of expanding both) have to be financed before being recouped via the revenue from sales. The faster sales rise, the more working capital required—hence the drain on cash. There's a fascinating chart, drawn from Strategic Planning Institute studies, which shows a positive cash flow with a *negative* ROI (return on investment) of nearly 20 percent—as long as the sales are also declining by something over 10 percent per annum.

But even a business enjoying a 30 percent sales growth and an ROI well above 20 percent will still have a negative cash flow. In fact, a fast-expanding business like that will have to earn over 40 percent pre-tax before it breaks even on cash flow.

The other way around, generating cash can result from policies that sound (and are) absolutely terrible. "Managers can generate cash by harvesting the business's present market position, reducing marketing expenditures, and withholding introduction of new products." That, too, must ultimately sound the death knell.

What's the answer? The authors call for something called "aggressive asset management." In other words, a businessman is passionately interested (or should be) in how fast he turns over his capital. Inadequate utilization of plant is a bugbear exceeded in threat only by excessive stocks. The assets in a business are a cost that never disappears—until or unless they are sold. The fewer the assets used in relation to turnover, and the higher the sales revenue in relation to direct costs, the more profitable the business will be— profitable enough to support even the weight of high-speed expansion, with its insistent demands for money. Get the cost/revenue basics wrong, and cash will quickly crucify you. Get them right and the cash will (almost) look after itself.

9. THE BITE-BACK OF SMIRNOFF

In watching Y (costs), never forget the price in X. Heublein, the proud producer of Smirnoff vodka, faced a determined attack from Wolfschmidt in the 1960s. Like most such attacks, the onslaught hinged on price: a dollar less a bottle. An attacked market leader is apparently in a no-win bind: if it cuts price to match, it loses profit massively across its much bigger volume; if it doesn't budge, it loses volume to the price cutter—and down come the profits.

Heublein escaped from the bind by a brilliant strategy cited by Philip Kotler and Ravi Singh as a classic business example of military counteroffensive. The distiller *raised* the price of Smirnoff by one dollar—making it two dollars more than Wolfschmidt, and thus clearly a "better" vodka. Then Heublein launched two new brands: one at the same price as Wolfschmidt, the other at one dollar less. With the tables turned on the attacker, Smirnoff continued to dominate its markets—rapidly growing ones at that: in 1982 it sold 7.33 million cases. And Wolfschmidt? Just 1.26 million—a mere sixth.

10. THE PRICE OF UNDERPRICING

A business can be destroyed by charging too much money. But that is a far less common disease than charging too little—and very often the underpricing stems from simple misunderstanding of the dynamics of the market. Price by itself means nothing. It's the relationship between price and volume that is dynamic, and that determines whether or not a price should be cut—or raised.

It's also the relationship with a competitor's price that determines what a price really means. For example, say that a competitor puts up his prices. What do you do? Play follow-my-leader? Or stay where you are? In fact, if you take the latter course, you are not standing pat. You're *cutting* your own price. *Relative* price is what counts, and by not following suit, you must really be dropping your own price.

Mostly, managements confronted with this fact will rub their hands over the competitive advantage that their rival has handed over on a silver platter. That's falling into a trap, psychological as much as technical, which centers around the concept of "critical volume gain." This psychological trap is a powerful inhibition, which helps to persuade managements, especially on the sales side, to shun price rises as if they were poisoned fish. But consider the sums presented by a Deloitte, Haskins & Sell consultant, David Connell.

The "critical volume gain" or CVG, Connell points out, is the amount by which sales must rise to compensate for the loss of profit that results from refusing a me-too price rise. If the product is selling at $90, and the competitor goes to $100, the result may seem to be a foregone conclusion. But just look at Table 8.

As the figures show in stark black and white, even with a 25 percent rise in volume, the company is still $10,000 worse off in this particular case. It would need to raise sales by *half* simply to match the financial consequences of raising the price to $100. The improvement in market share might seem worthwhile at a first careless glance. But think: can you really wrest 25 percent more sales, let alone 50 percent, from a 10 percent price advantage?

The answer to that question is a matter of judgment, and pricing decisions must always rest to some degree on subjective thought. But the thinking must be tested by objective numbers. Critical volume gain is the mirror image of critical volume loss (CVL)—which

Table 8

		AFTER COMPETITOR'S PRICE INCREASE	
	BEFORE COMPETITOR'S PRICE INCREASE	INCREASE OWN PRICE	MAINTAIN OWN PRICE AT CURRENT LEVEL
Price	$90	$100	$90
Volume (units)	2,000	2,000	2,500
Variable cost	$70	$70	$70
Contribution per unit	$20	$30	$20
Contribution (percent)	22.2%	30.0%	22.2%
Total contribution	$40,000	$60,000	$50,000

WHEN FOLLOWING MY LEADER MAKES SENSE

applies when it's your company that wants to lead prices upward. How much can you afford to lose in sales? At what point will the drop in volume cost you more than the rise in price can deliver to the cashbox?

In Connell's example, the company is selling at $100 a unit, with variable costs of $75, and thus making a contribution of 25 percent. Its management (over the dead bodies of its salespeople) wants to raise prices by 15 percent. The outraged salesmen protest that volume will fall, but their boss calmly asks them to put numbers on their outrage. How much? Anything from 15 percent to 30 percent, they angrily retort.

The boss can now do a simple sum. He multiplies the price (100) by the percentage increase in price (15) to get 1,500. This he divides by the percentage contribution (25) plus the percentage price rise (15), which adds up to 40. Divide 1,500 by 40 and the answer is a critical volume loss of 37.5 percent. That is, the company's sales would have to fall by 37.5 percent, or worse than the aggrieved salesmen's worst estimate, before the benefits from the price increase would drop to break-even point.

You can work to the same conclusion the hard way, but Connell's equations are a short cut. You need to know only X (decrease or increase in price percent) and C (percentage contribution). 100 times X divided by $X + C$ = CVL, or critical volume loss. With the mirror held the other way, when you want to cut prices, 100 times X divided by $C - X$ = CVG or critical volume gain.

Real life never works out as neatly as casebook examples or algebraic sums. But the principles behind the equation are immutable. That same real life is full of cases in which companies have at long last reluctantly raised prices in fear and trembling—only to find that sales have powered through the increase, which in turn has contributed, in full, to the bottom line. Nothing else can achieve the same results, except a saving in costs—and that is seldom so painless.

These facts do not rule out the opposite approach, the one which the first Henry Ford used to such devastating effect. This is where you bring prices down rapidly, achieving a volume gain well above the critical point, and piling up huge increases in profits as the fixed costs are spread over greater volume, and as the variable costs come down with greater output per man.

But old Henry had the consequences of his policies worked out on a blackboard, which is lesson one. The second lesson is that the Ford finesse is more difficult to play in modern conditions. As actually happened in microcircuits, the point is reached all too soon where tumbling prices in competitive markets fail to yield critical volume gains, and where the economies of scale are canceled out by the rate of price decline. And that's the point where price strategy comes into play—where a higher price for greater perceived value is the critical equation.

11. THE FAT OVERHEADS

If price is the most important number on the revenue side, the leading figure on costs has to be overhead: the fixed costs that have to be paid whatever the level of sales. A turnaround specialist seized on this point when sent by an American medical products giant into a newly merged operation. Ostensibly, the difficulty lay in a number of strategic problems that he swiftly and clinically analyzed. Some products were fairly mature, but subject to sharp competition and price pressure. A couple more were good concepts, but thought expensive by the users. There was one unique product, but it was growing slowly, and powerful competition was on the way.

Finally, the boss had what was described as "a dream product that turned into a nightmare." Wrong for that particular national market, the product had already run through several million dollars, and the losses were still heavy. What, apart from all this, concerned the new man, though, was the high and unnecessary level of overhead spending, on everything from office cleaning to sales support. How could he get his young managers to cut down on their overheads?

As he pointed out, this meant asking them to reduce their own domains, cut back on the financial resources available to them, fire perfectly good and willing people, and so on. Not surprisingly, they were reluctant to respond. What to do?

When this same question was put to managers in the Bank of America and an engineering conglomerate, their answers tended to center around various schemes for encouraging managers to identify their own interests with the reduction of overheads and thus the increase of total performance—one even suggested giving them shares in the company.

As one of the bankers spotted, all these schemes (like the above turnaround man's hesitation) had a fatal defect: *they gave the managers an option.* The correct answer was brilliantly summarized in a *New Yorker* cartoon. The boss is pointing dramatically at the open office door and summing up the whole issue, for an unfortunate subordinate's sake, in just seven well-chosen words: "Get out there, Denby, and cut fat!"

12. UNFIXING THE COSTS

A peculiar and not terribly endearing trait of the manager is to put off the evil day until the evil day: that is, he doesn't get around to making elementary improvements in the business until ruin, or the threat of ruin, is staring it in the face. Come recession, and nothing in the business will be sacrosanct, even though much of the waste being eliminated, and many of the faults being cured, could and should have been dealt with long before.

Any consultant worth his fee can find large savings in the direct costs—labor and materials—although these are areas to which management does pay some kind of attention. But when it comes to fixed costs, the indirects or overhead costs which the direct operations have to support, "relatively little systematic management effort has been devoted to them." The authors of that statement, management consultants Urwick Orr, know whereof they speak. Even under the spur of recession managers tend to react unthinkingly and unsystematically: for instance, by imposing 10 percent cuts across the board, instead of first answering a management catechism like this:

1. Does your company overcentralize decision-making?
2. Does it hold too many meetings?
3. Is it concerned more with prestige than with profits?

4. Does it rely too heavily on complex statistical reports, with vague decision-making responsibilities?
5. Does it train potential managers to move into new responsibilities?
6. Does procedure loom larger than commercial judgment?
7. Does it duplicate common data?
8. Does it encourage communications among departments?
9. Does the technical excellence of any service exceed what it is required to do?

Don't imagine that these questions have nothing to do with fixed costs. One international drug company carried out what looks like a simple corporate reshuffling. It created a single division profit center, cut out one tier of top management, and centralized the selling operation. The potential economy was $1.2 million a year. In the same industry, a European firm decentralized to autonomous (and profitable) units, eliminated product groups that weren't making money and concentrated on those that were, and simultaneously cut central overheads. Its reward was $900,000 a year.

One of the great arguments for small (preferably tiny) head offices and autonomous, decentralized subsidiaries is precisely that they should allow the company to operate with much lower overheads. Harold S. Geneen, when boss of the ITT conglomerate, boasted to a congressional committee about the 1,000 management experts at head office. When you think that every ten head office managers probably represent a total overhead cost of a cool million dollars, you can understand why one U.S. company, hunting acquisitions in Europe, won't look at anything that returns less than 30 percent on sales—otherwise any purchase would be turned into a loss-maker by the mountainous corporate overheads.

Once you've got the management right, the next issue is that of the systems and procedures being used. Here's Urwick Orr's guide to the most common areas of waste:

1. Reporting systems based on extensive computer print-outs, from which line management gets so divorced that it can't take remedial action when needed.
2. Complex costing systems that aren't appropriate.

3. Complex routines that take over the shop floor supervisor's job.

4. Using computers to unreal effect—so that people have to use manual systems in parallel.

5. Overcomplicating sales estimating and order processing.

6. Ignoring the need for adequate standardization of product design.

7. Recording data unnecessarily.

Here, too, the sins can be much greater than reading through the list might suggest. One vehicle components company simply— very simply—modified its distribution procedures, and pocketed (or, rather, didn't unpocket) $750,000 yearly as a result. Even that vast saving pales beside the $3 million of economies obtained by an insurance company solely by improvements on its clerical side. Admittedly, clerical work is a far bigger proportionate expense for an insurance company than for most other businesses. Yet all the insurers did for their couple of million was to install clerical work measurement, to use organization and methods techniques to program the work, and to win better machine utilization.

Even in a business without the hunger for paper of the insurers, the clerical savings can be enormous. A battery-maker cut clerical costs by $300,000 by reviewing staff levels, introducing a staff efficiency scheme, and vetting recruitment of new staff. Clerical effectiveness is an area that can't be ignored; a lot of money hangs on the answers to these questions from the consultants:

1. Is the work relevant to commercial results?
2. Does office layout encourage efficiency?
3. Is mechanization effective?
4. Does work flow follow an efficient plan?
5. Is clerical work properly managed and measured?
6. What's the relationship of staff turnover to efficiency?
7. Is there an effective incentive scheme?

Suppose you've been through all these checklists and believe your management to be perfect (it isn't, but still). Can you apply some general check via a ratio of overhead costs to the rest of the business? The rule of thumb will vary enormously from trade to trade and company to company. Overheads can go as high as 40 percent of product costs, which is certainly too high. You must have a rule of thumb: say, keeping overheads to 25 percent of turnover—and the lower the better. For there's one other percentage not to be forgotten. According to Urwick Orr, a systematic attack on fixed costs may well reduce them, not by that standard 10 percent across the board, but by 20–25 percent—and not by reducing the company's efficiency, either, but by raising it to new heights.

13. THE MAN WHO MADE TOO MUCH

After overheads (or maybe before them) the cost item that attracts most management attention is usually labor (often wrongly—materials may offer much more scope for savings). Now, the less you pay labor, the less it costs. But is that obvious truth the right principle? Is there any regular, reliable guiding light?

Such a light did, apparently, shine in the mind of the multinational managers who bought the nice, fat subsidiary of another, smaller company. Naturally, the local general manager went with the deal. He relished the thought of the new independence he would gain, the expansion he would be encouraged to promote, not to mention the personal rewards that would be heaped on him if all went well. He was already quite handsomely rewarded—a salary of $45,000; a car worth $16,000; and a commission on profits.

After only a few weeks, he began to feel that the salary was inadequate recompense for the extra loads thrust upon him by his new masters, whose corporate size seemed to breed meetings, memos, reports, and procedures like rabbits. Coping with all this bureaucracy (totally unknown in his former parent company) made it extremely difficult to find the time for managing—and the new subsidiary, which the new owners had planned to use as a springboard for expansion, had promptly run into terribly tough trading.

Anyway, the general manager put in for a higher salary. The head office response was to entrust the matter to a certain firm of management consultants. The general manager hadn't realized that all executive salaries in his new, huge bureaucratic parent were fixed on this consultancy firm's system: all jobs were assessed, weighed, given points, and paid accordingly. He thus had to spend half a day being interviewed by a nice man from the consultants, who went away saying that a report would follow in due course.

When the document did arrive, the general manager didn't know whether to laugh, cry, or resign. After analyzing the job and talking about the median for the industry, the consultant recommended that the $45,000 salary should be revised—downward, to $34,500. The $16,000 car, moreover, should be replaced with one worth $10,500. And the commission on profits should be abolished as "wholly inappropriate." The best thing about the report was the consultant's closing observation: "We anticipate that there may be some difficulty in implementing these recommendations. . . "

14. HOW TO HANDLE HOWARD

In one Jules Feiffer cartoon strip, his ubiquitous put-upon character, known only as Howard, approaches a grimly lantern-jawed boss for a raise. The boss reacts warmly: in their organization, they like a man who knows his own value. But a man who comes in demanding more pay, that's a discontented one; and, in their organization, they don't want discontented employees—"Think it over, fella." That's the problem of salaries in a nutshell: in the end, the salary rests on a bargain, and whoever is in the stronger position, or succeeds in appearing stronger, runs off with the better end of the deal—or else (as the general manager mentioned above did), just runs off.

Looked at from Howard's point of view, the question is relatively simple. The employee, rightly or wrongly, makes his judgment about his market or his internal worth, on real evidence or just on supposition, and then attempts to get his employer's agreement. If the latter refuses, Howard either slinks away with his tail between his legs or finds another employer (preferably before actually quitting Lantern Jaws) who will pay more. But the employer is in a much trickier position—because Howard's pay is his cost, multiplied by all the Howards he employs.

There are various scientific or pseudoscientific methods for working out how much Howard is worth. In any organization of significant size, whether these methods are used or not, the system of pay tends to degenerate into a civil service structure, in which status, and status alone, determines pay. In theory, achievement should determine status, but in practice seniority is the major determinant, rather than contribution to the success, however measured, of the outfit.

Any sensible company would obviously seek to link pay to performance; to make Howard's visit less necessary; and, above all, to achieve the far better performance that would make Howard's extra pay seem a mere mite.

Two McKinsey consultants, John Dembitz and John Woodthorpe, set down in *Management Today* the rules for paying managers for performance.

1. Distinguish between long-term and short-term reward schemes: the top managers should take part in both, because it's their business to look after the future while maximizing the present. But don't link the pay of people to long-term results over which they have no influence.
2. Pitch the rewards high enough: between 10 and 20 percent on an annualized basis, or 60–120 percent of annual salary at the end of six years.
3. If the company isn't a high-flier, treat the bonus as a "carve-out," i.e., you hold back half of a 20 percent pay rise conditional on the low-fliers hitting a realistic but challenging performance target.
4. If the company is flying high, make the incentives "compensation-plus." Give the boys their 20 percent rise, but pay the bonus if they go on upward.
5. Link payments on a sliding scale to achievement—with a minimum level below which they get not a nickel.

6. If it's motivation you're after (it should be), go for cash payments rather than shares.

7. Tie short-term schemes to annual performance, but long-term ones to overlapping periods of three to six years—with the overlap designed to allow for any changes in strategy that will affect performance.

In fact, the experts advise leaving room for discretion, so that if an incentive scheme comes up with a dotty result (say, profits have been hit by a change to new technology), you don't penalize people for a profit setback that's no fault of theirs. By the same token, you don't want to pay money because the purchase of another business has raised earnings without anybody lifting a finger.

As these two obvious traps show, truly fair incentive schemes that benefit all parties equally aren't easy to design and operate. It helps if you follow some other principles: (a) have clear rules and stick to them; (b) KISS—keep it simple, stupid; (c) make it clear who runs the scheme; (d) don't let it penalize managers who move inside the company.

But there's one principle that dominates all the rest. *Don't let the scheme deteriorate into a giveaway.* In the U.S. many bonus payments (some of unconscionable size) are not genuinely tied to performance and have about as much incentive effect as a three-martini lunch. The final absurdity is the seven-figure transfer fee, in which the man pockets his loot before he's done a hand's turn for the company. The true object should be to pay good people very good money for very good performance—but only *after* they've proved their goodness in practice.

That doesn't solve the problem of base pay, although it should ease it. The base should reflect market rates and also bear relation to responsibilities inside the firm—but not slavishly. As noted earlier, there are several scientific and pseudoscientific methods of handling Howard. They can have unfortunate effects—witness not only the man who made too much, but also the following case of the star subsidiary.

This ace performer was the pride of its conglomerate owner, which called in consultants to grade all its managerial staff according to a points system. Of course, you can't really grade people downward—you can only grade them up. The net result was a huge increase in the salary bill—and the star subsidiary, weighed down with those additional overheads, fell from the heavens. It has since been closed.

That's no way to handle Howard or anything else. Pay for good performance, but only for that, and the means of payment will look after itself—and Howard.

15. THE MEN WHO PAID $3 MILLION FOR NOTHING

Pay for good performance is easy to say, very hard to implement. Consider the case, reported in *The Chief Executive* magazine, of the man who headed up a $300 million division of a large chemical company, with a base salary of $100,000 in 1979. This genius would get a year-end bonus of $40,000 as well, but only if he hit his pre-tax profit goal of $20 million and held investment constant. But if he could push profits to $26 million, his bonus would soar right up to $100,000—doubling that base salary.

Could he? Well, his division had a "strategic plan" calling for price reduction and heavy advertising on several product lines in 1979; the idea was to gain market share over the next two to three years. Of course, the above-mentioned 1979 profit goal of $20 million took into account the planned expenditures and the effect on revenue of the price cuts. But the boss could beat the target substantially and pocket $60,000 more in bonuses very easily—if he held back just a bit on the expenditures and price reductions.

He did just that. Profits duly reached $26 million in 1979, and his bonus check was a nice fat $100,000. So far, so good—for him. But not for the business: Jude T. Rich and Ennius E. Bergsma, both McKinsey consultants in New York, report that "Unfortunately, a competitor hit the market with a better product six months before his company. As a result the manager's division suffered a serious setback in the market position."

And the horrors multiplied. There was a long-term incentive plan, too—designed to pay out a total of $3 million in cash to fifteen senior executives (including our boy) as long as corporate earnings per share grew at an annual rate of 12 percent over the four years from 1976 to 1979. Helped, in part, by that big, fat year in 1979, the company hit its 12 percent target. With cumulative earnings of $300 million, the $3 million—it was a mere 1 percent of earnings, after all—was paid out by the board in 1979 with nary a qualm.

But stock prices remained unchanged over the same period, and so did the dividend payout. So what did shareholders get for their $3 million? The answer is a great big nothing. But don't jump to the conclusion that this only shows (a) how useless incentive pay schemes are and (b) how bogus they can be. The idea of tying pay to performance is great. The defect in the horror story is the *measure of performance.*

Pay for short-term results at the expense of the long-term and even the medium-term interests of the business, and that's what you'll get—only short-term benefits. On the other hand, if somebody takes a business that's worth $500,000, say, and without requiring any more capital develops it in a couple of years to the point where it's worth $1 million or so, the increase in economic value is $500,000—and the laborer is unquestionably worthy of his hire and his bonus.

But how do you build worth? And how do you know that you've built it? The two authors explain, very obviously when you think about it, that a company financed entirely by borrowed capital is adding wealth if its cash inflow from profitable operations exceeds its cash outflow from servicing the debt. If you borrow money at 14 percent and invest it at 18 percent, all's well. But if you borrow money at 18 percent and invest it at 14 percent, you're subtracting wealth just as surely as if you had burned the dollar bills.

Of course, no outfit exists on all-borrowed money, apart from divisions of groups, that is. But equity also costs money. The 18 percent capital cost and 14 percent return figures given above are those for the company in the horror story: although its after-tax return on equity had stuck at 14 percent while all the shenanigans were going on, the cost of equity capital had risen during the period from 12 percent to 18 percent. As the authors say, "No wonder the stock went nowhere. The market had read between the lines of corporate earnings statements and penalized the stock accordingly. Executives cashed in, shareholders lost out." That's nonsense: the only sense is, no increased value, no bonus—period.

16. MAKING THEM ADD TO YOUR VALUE

If the economic value is enhanced, that should settle one controversy that goes right to the heart of any organization—and which will never die. The issue is whether to pay people a straight, unadulterated wage or a salary, or whether, in some way or other, to link their reward to performance—either theirs, or the organization's, or both. Evidently, payment by or for results is much more complicated than a straight wage, which is one reason, good or bad, why performance pay hasn't swept all before it.

But there's another reason: the apparently unbreakable rule that all such payment systems degrade over time, so that, even if you started by getting the performance you were prepared to pay for, you end up with getting less—which is bad for the digestion, if nothing else. In the worst, the most degraded schemes, firms pay far more than they need for precisely the same performance they would probably have gotten anyway—as in that chemical division, with its executives overpaid by $3 million.

Applied across a whole labor force, such nonsense can be disastrous. But there must, in logic, be an answer to the puzzle of pay—and it may be offered by a measure which is as basic to assessing corporate performance as economic value and sounds similar: added value. This is one of the rare financial measures that isn't primarily intelligible to accountants. It rests on two figures that are about as simple in concept as business measurements can be: the sales value of all the goods produced, and the cost of all the materials and services directly used in making said goods. Just as the executives create economic value by earning more than the true cost of the capital they use, so the work force does the same with the bought-in cost of materials and supplies.

The difference between sales value and cost is the added value. It follows, as the night does the day, that this added value is the only source (not counting borrowed money) from which all the claims on the company can be met—which consultant A. R. Swannack neatly categorizes in three chunks:

1. Earnings
2. Overhead
3. Profit

That's how Swannack presents the figure when operating a value-added scheme, explaining them as in the following example: "Overheads include salaries, rent and rates, advertising, depreciation, etc. Profit includes taxation, dividends, provision for expansion, etc. The earnings pool is *your share* of the added value. The bigger the added value, the bigger your earnings pool."

A model scheme divides the basic earning pool between (1) basic wages and (2) productivity bonus. Basic wages in turn come from (a) the hourly rates, (b) overtime premiums, if any, and (c) long-service payments. Productivity bonus is what's left in the earnings pool after basic wages have been paid, calculated monthly, and shared out on an agreed formula. As for the hourly rates, jobs are carefully assessed and graded, and each grade carries its agreed rate. The aim is to have all jobs fairly rewarded—from the pool.

You could run a payment scheme on these lines and still end up in trouble for many reasons—not least the possibility that the earnings pool will be too big. As a rule of thumb, if labor costs come to more than two thirds of added value, they shouldn't. Otherwise there simply won't be enough to finance the future and reward the investors or lenders (because the lenders and investors will sooner or later need reward and repayment, it's no use regarding debt or new equity as a substitute for adding enough value). If a company doesn't add any value, or doesn't add enough, it will, sooner or later, have only one way to go—down and out.

But value-added schemes per se don't guarantee adding value. As Swannack warns:

1. All payment schemes need constant monitoring and revision to ensure that they are doing what you want—and added-value schemes are certainly no exception.

2. A lot depends on the employer's willingness to disclose the necessary information. Without the latter, the scheme won't work.

3. To make the best of the idea, you need (a) very good supervision and (b) a style of management that allows employees to contribute to ways of adding value.

4. The whole scheme could be torpedoed if your ratios are liable to vary significantly through causes outside anybody's control. You don't want to reward people for windfall profits—or penalize them for accidental losses.

Of those four points, the third calls to mind a long-standing paradox: that, to make an incentive scheme work, you need very good shop floor management, but if you've got very good shop floor management, you don't need an incentive scheme. The gibe neglects the reinforcement factor that performance pay schemes can bring even to the best performers—in management or lower down.

The reinforcing agents can be seen in the list of claims which proponents make for added-value plans:

1. It's noninflationary; the control exacted by added value means that wage drift can be arrested.

2. Employees get interested in all factors that affect added value, such as excessive scrap, insufficient material yield, high service costs, etc.

3. Pay related to added value emphasizes the benefits of better methods, machine improvements, correct quality, and generally the desire to improve.

4. An AV scheme creates a real and effective sense of participation in company affairs.

5. Communications are improved, and people feel they have some influence on company affairs of the organization.

6. It can help to secure redeployment of labor and introduction of new methods and machinery.

7. It helps to remove restrictive practices.

8. It isn't costly to administer.

THE SUPERMANAGERS

9. Unit costs are reduced by material savings as well as by improved labor productivity.

If all that sounds too good to be true, it isn't—for the principles are simplicity itself.

1. Money motivates everybody;

2. Limit the money, by tax or anything else, and you limit the motivation;

3. The more the money, the more the motivation;

4. Establish sufficient motivation, and the extra output, or greater added value, call it what you will, pays for itself;

5. The simpler a reward scheme is, the better it works, the easier it is to run, and the more satisfied managers will be with the results. As one of them noted about his people, "When they have completed one job, they look around and get moving on another. Previously they would have clocked up excess time. I'm getting more production, they're getting more money, the IRS is getting more tax, and the customer a lower price." Who could ask for anything more?

Of course, it means hard, careful work to ensure that a scheme is acceptable to and understood by the employees and operates effectively all the time, with proper control of the inevitable problem areas. A pay system—no matter what—that's unacceptable, not understood, ineffectively run, and full of uncontrolled problems will definitely damage the company. But a management that can achieve that constellation of failure is probably well along the road to ruin without any help from added-value schemes.

17. THE AMERICANS WHO MADE MORE

The right system can even ensure that managers 3,000 miles away do the best they can—working for a foreign company that owns 100 percent of the business. Making sure was a problem that assumed bigger and bigger proportions for Hanson Trust as its U.S. interests grew larger and larger within the group total. Hanson didn't even have a U.S. office for its first couple of years, but then built up its own management team in New Jersey, headed by a man who had been chief executive of Hanson's first (and vitally important) fishing-company buy.

That man ran the companies, with businesses ranging from Ball Park frankfurters and shoe shops to lace-making and hand tools, largely by budgetary control. Approval or disapproval at budget time (when, says Hanson's Gordon White, "there's always a big fight") very much depends on "how much capital they want"—all budgets are geared insistently to return on capital employed, and the desired returns are duly made. In 1980 Hanson received $44.5 million of pre-tax income on the near billion of sales in the four older U.S. divisions.

But the key wasn't only the big budget fight, or the insistence on high returns. If the American managers make their figures, they receive big bonus payments. The result of this "incentivization" is that "some earn more than the chairman"—and good luck to them.

18. MAGIC INGREDIENT X

Hanson had hearkened to the Holy Trinity of personnel policy—to "attract, retain, and motivate" the hottest, best, most effective executives in Christendom, or anywhere else. A logical response is to use fast promotion to kill all three birds with one stone, but logic doesn't accord with the facts in one study of salesmen which showed that the turnover of salesmen is *higher* in fast-promoting companies. So what does retain people? For salesmen, at least, the answer is simple: money.

Higher-paying firms lost half as many employees as lower-paying companies. There's no question but that the obvious is true: pay is the lynchpin of the relationship of people to the organization, and it's most unlikely that what's true for salesmen is false for their bosses.

Even in those outfits (like charities or arts organizations) where pay is miserable, the lack of reward has to be balanced by very heavy extra weights (prestige, perks, prerogatives, etc.) if the operation is to manage and be managed at all. In any organization that can afford it, pay should be at the highest level consistent with performance and continuing incentive.

How that balance is struck has no objective answer. But it's a prime mistake to pay (or expect) a basic salary that is vastly in excess of the going rates in an industry or locality. The policy of the acknowledged masters in these matters, such as IBM, is to pitch salaries just above the average—enough to make a real difference, but not so much as to constitute sheer extravagance. That sounds sane and reasonable enough, but it doesn't allow for Ingredient X.

Going from Year One to Year Eighteen, a sample of U.S. companies blessed with the possession of Ingredient X showed the following performances in (a) market price per share, (b) earnings per share, (c) balance sheet net worth per share, and (d) index of sales revenue: (a) + 682 percent, (b) + 311 percent, (c) + 376 percent, and (d) + 258 percent.

Compare this with a sample of companies, alike in most respects except for the absence of the magic ingredient:

(a) + 298 percent, (b) + 119 percent, (c) + 157 percent, and (d) + 166 percent.

Ingredient X appears to work wonders—and it is merely some kind of scheme for extending share ownership to the employees. True, all such conclusions are subject to a strong word of caution. If a company riding high makes shares available to its employees, who can ever prove that the high performance and the share scheme have any connection?

Put it another way, though. Would you accept the following deal? Your employer asks you to give up 2.5 percent of your pay until the end of the financial year; if profit hits 7.5 percent of turnover, you will get four times the amount held back; if profits don't make the target, you lose your 2.5 percent. The arithmetic shows that the deal is highly attractive to both parties. The employee is gambling 2.5 percent of his salary for a chance of a 10 percent rise;

the employer, for a small increase in wage costs, gets a massive rise in profits, plus a healthy boost to cash flow.

The idea, which comes from Eastern Airlines under the management of former astronaut Frank Borman, presumably played some part in its ability to survive the industry's 1980 recession without layoffs (things got worse for Eastern later on). If that's indeed so, the explanation can lie only in the identification, via the profit motive, of the interests of the private individual with those of the corporate management.

But you don't have to prove that this has actually happened. If the results are excellent and the company has a profit-sharing scheme, or some similar deal, it's a fair conclusion that the two have some connection—even if the link is only the existence of a management that is good enough, in general, to recognize, in particular, that the laborer is worthy of more than his hire.

Take a case like Dana Corporation. Until the 1980 recession hit its auto parts business between the eyes, Dana won a 10 percent rise in output per man-hour year in, year out. Ingredient X wasn't a share ownership scheme but the Scanlon Plan, which shares the benefits of higher productivity between employees and company on a three-to-one basis—and employees means everybody, from janitor to plant manager.

Any productivity scheme works better the more inclusive it is, and the more rapid and evident its results. At Dana the share-out isn't a year-end bonus, but a monthly check—and always a separate one. The bench marks, or targets, are devised so that a bonus of around 10 percent is paid, with the identical percentage applied to everybody.

Only a sentimental fool would suggest that results like Dana's flow only from profit sharing or share ownership or the excellent welfare systems usually found in firms that have either or both (they are not mutually exclusive). Every management zone has a profound bearing on the possibilities of a Scanlon scheme like Dana's: or those of value-added payments; or those of Ingredient X ways of extending ownership to employees; and on what level of productivity even the best-motivated workers can achieve.

The phrase "best-motivated," subjective as it is, has its objective roots, though. The productive efficiency of the business, which can be measured objectively, must have an impact on motivation. Obviously, having the best machinery, allowing neither idle plant nor idle hands, getting high output per busy man-hour and paying highly for it—all these are key motivational forces, but above all, the last. It may be fun for social scientists (and moralists) to sniff at the motivational might of money. Take no notice.

To summarize some of the important points I've mentioned in Step Three:

1. Never, never put up with late or inadequate figures.

2. Use your management accounts to help react to change, avoid nasty surprises, and alert you to problems—and opportunites.

3. Pick the key figures which, when combined, will tell the real health of your business.

4. Aim to replace the capital value eroded by inflation—and then some.

5. Keep Y (costs) as far as possible below X (revenue, or prices multiplied by volume).

6. Manage assets aggressively, with the fewest possible assets used to generate the most in sales revenue.

7. Watch *relative* prices (relative to the competition)—and don't cut them unless you will win a commensurate gain.

8. Cut out the overhead fat continuously and rigorously.

9. Don't economize, though, on wages and salaries—pay high for high performance.

10. On the shopfloor, relate that high pay to higher added value.

11. Remember that money is the most powerful motivational force of all—and use it accordingly, right throughout the business.

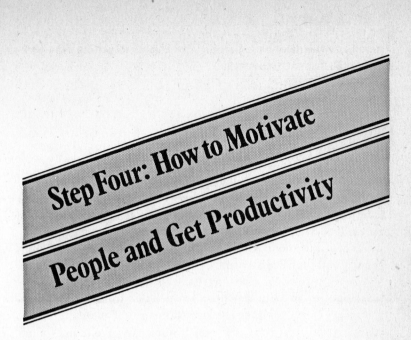

Step Four: How to Motivate People and Get Productivity

1. THE MAN WHO ASKED WHY

The treatment of people doesn't revolve only around tender loving care and kindness, as one Supermanager, now retired, used to demonstrate. He was famous for asking, whenever a key manager or other employee left, and a new hiring was proposed, "Why? Do we need to replace him?" The first answer was always "Yes." But the boss was never satisfied with that. Very often he proved that by reorganizing the department, or redeploying people and responsibilities, the job could be evaporated.

His reasoning was that, the more indispensable the manager and his job seem to be, the less likely it is that anybody will ever query what he does, or ask whether that work is still as appropriate as when he was appointed; the efficient man with his ineffable reputation may actually have become an obstacle to getting the operation into a more effective state.

2. TOO MANY COOKS SPOIL THE PROFIT

There's no virtue in employing more people than you actually need—not even for the excess employees themselves. Sooner or later, the ax will fall, perhaps on the whole company. And, while they will be overpaid for the work they are doing, or not doing, they will probably be underpaid in relation to what they could earn from genuine full-time employment.

A truly splendid employer has the minimum staff paid the maximum reward. But staff numbers are like forms in a bureaucracy: they breed, until the company becomes a *Watership Down* of countless and sometimes uncounted rabbits. What the right numbers are, let alone achieving them, poses considerable difficulty. One guide, though, is comparison with other operations, like a study that a man named Paul Finlay carried out for his multinational employer.

So detailed a comparison would normally be impossible, which makes its crystal-clear results impossible to ignore. Finlay's investigation was designed to find out why a British plant had 1,191 employees, while a comparable German unit managed perfectly well with 463 fewer. Output was much the same. What was the explanation?

Forget the obvious one, that the Germans worked harder. Man for man, the direct workers put in the same effort. Before even considering end-result productivity, would-be number cutters should begin at the beginning with:

1. *The Setup.* Are you using the most efficient layout of the most productive machinery? Or, in an office or service industry, are you using the most efficient system to carry out only essential work in the most productive way?

The answer will seldom be a resounding "Yes," if you are honest; and it may be "No," partly for reasons beyond your control. For instance, the U.K. management in Finlay's case had a three-story plant built long before the single-story one in Germany. That alone involved greater numbers, as did the lower degree of mechanization in the U.K. Altogether, setup factors explained *half* the U.K. over-manning, or 219 people. Even these are not factors to be ignored—no matter how good the excuses.

But there are no excuses when it comes to . . .

2. *The Establishment.* This word, which came to stand for the whole inner knot of people who run Britain, presumably derived from the very center of that knot—the Civil Service. In Whitehall, the word means the people somebody has decided to employ to fill a given function. Establishments are hard to reduce and often even harder to justify.

In Finlay's case, the British numbers were swollen by causes he dubbed "versatility" and "cultural and social." A fifth of the total discrepancy in numbers arose, for example, because the British boilermen, working around the clock, did not, like their German counterparts, double up by doing night-time security checks. The German electricians could be trained as mechanics, or vice versa, and asked to work in either capacity. Without versatility and doubling up, waste of labor is unavoidable.

"Social and cultural" can mean anything from the staff (usually uncounted) required to administer perks and fringe benefits, to the tea ladies who could have been replaced by dispensing machines, to full-time cleaners whose work could have been contracted out, to ultimate nonsenses, wrong in themselves, such as having several canteens or dining rooms instead of one for everybody, from driver to chairman. Finlay's British company had four restaurants for its 1,191 employees, including two for different grades of management.

Management itself, in fact, is one of the most lavish spendthrifts of labor. The waste comes overwhelmingly through disregard of . . .

3. *Thinking Straight.* Another fifteen of the 463 people needlessly employed in Finlay's U.K. plant came under this heading; they arose from failure to ask or answer the basic question of the Man Who Asked Why: can we justify employing anybody at all to man this activity?

For instance, the British plant checked material for losses at five separate points. The Germans knew that nobody would want to steal the stuff, anyway, so they checked only on receipt and at the monthly stocktaking. By comparing the figure with the volume of finished product, they knew as much about wastage as the British—but at much less cost.

Pursuing their irrational fetish about security, the British had thirteen more people than the Germans to check that employees weren't running off with the product. Employees were even checked (nobody knew why) when leaving the working area for the canteen. The Germans (thinking straight, and implementing straight thought beautifully) operated a random search at the main exit only. Everybody had to press a button on leaving, and whether or not they were searched depended on whether a red or green light came on.

Duplicating head office functions is a thoughtless habit to which subsidiaries are prone—and this U.K. one was no exception. That explained part of its superfluity of managers—thirty-five, against just two (the factory manager and the general manager) in Germany. True, some of the British managers did jobs the supervisors handled in Germany, but there were twice as many British supervisors, as well.

One further explanation is that the British had a whole gaggle of specialist departments, such as work study. Not only did this one require four people, but four people naturally require a manager—and so the rabbit breeding continues. It can be stopped at any stage—but is far better contained (like rabbit breeding) before it starts. Get the setup right; keep the establishment small; think straight; and you save yourself and everybody a great deal of profitless pain.

3. THE ROLLS-ROYCERS WHO DIDN'T KNOW

"How many?" isn't the only key to productivity, by any means. How?—how people are handled—is just as vital. When Rolls-Royce audited communications among the 50,000 people in its aero-engine plants, it discovered, among other horrors, machinists working on a component for years, without ever knowing what the thing was for; barely anybody ever looking at company bulletin boards; few people, even managers, who could tell you how much one of their cherished engines sold for; and, often, people who couldn't name the chairman, managing director, or even the local general manager.

Some communication methods did work, though: like mass meetings of groups of three hundred managers—with the general manager in charge; smaller groups of 40 percent—with executive directors talking to them; open days for all the families; single-subject exhibitions right down on the shop or office floor; and using the loudspeakers to broadcast messages and information—which nobody regarded as a Big Brother device. The reasons why those methods worked (and others didn't) appear clearly from another approach, which seemed to be the best seller of them all.

Michael Stanton, writing in *Management Today,* calls this the "accountable team concept." What the manager in charge of one particular product center did was to meet with a different section of his work force every Wednesday afternoon. At the meeting were the shop superintendent (who also chaired it), his foremen, the production engineer, the production control manager, and the plant engineer, the shop stewards, and three or four workers elected from the section.

The workers were different at each successive meeting, so over the year every man had a chance to sit around the table with his boss. The discussions covered things like quality, customer complaints, engine performance reports, marketing performance, and complaints or suggestions from the shop floor. Tight agendas and accurate minutes gave the essential continuity.

Why did this way work so well? (1) The boss was personally visible and accountable to his work force. (2) Everyone was treated as part of a team in which everyone was interdependent—something which, at first, some supervisors and managers found hard to accept; now, says Stanton, they wouldn't have it any other way. (3) The manager firmly but unobtrusively policed subsequent action and made sure that there *was* action.

In other words, successful communication involves everybody

in the company, from top to bottom, and it goes right down to the bottom. If Mohammed goes to the mountain, miracles will follow— why, people in the company may even find out who Mohammed is.

4. FROM HIGHEST TO HUMBLEST

You'll find the top-to-bottom (or, better, bottom-to-top) principle in Supermanagement after Supermanagement. Nobody can prove that any particular system of man (and woman) management is best. You can demonstrate, by anecdotal evidence and on commonsense grounds, that companies which spend a great deal of time and trouble on work-force relations—almost irrespective of what they do in the time—get much better results than those which don't. But take a company where this concentration on industrial relations is a paramount consideration, like Black & Decker; some parts of its prevailing philosophy appear to have no direct relationship with such highly desirable consequences as, say, flexible working, which lets you take maximum advantage of the savings possible in production methods.

For instance, Black & Decker operates from the moral conviction that all staff, from the highest to the humblest, should be treated as far as possible alike. In consequence:

1. In each plant, there is one staff restaurant; everyone lunches there.

2. Conditions of employment are roughly the same, and there's only one life insurance scheme.

3. Everyone gets the same percentage raise, paid on the same day.

4. A set scale of notice ranges from six weeks after two years to thirteen weeks after five years (employees need to give only one week's notice).

5. General managers have their offices either literally in the middle of the factories or very near the production lines, and personnel officers are available to deal with trouble on the spot and as it happens.

6. An elected works committee meets at least once a month. The general manager chairs it; he tells his people about the company's sales results (profit, for the whole U.K. company, is disclosed once a year), and discusses any problems or issues that are raised.

7. The really important commitment, though, is to avoid redundancy at most, if not quite all, cost. Maintaining employment levels comes very high on the list of priorities—which gives extra urgency to finding new marketing opportunities, and to making managers go out and sell their output.

These seven principles are in ascending order of utility to management purposes: that is to say, with each step it becomes that much easier to demonstrate the payoff in terms of production, productivity, or profit. For a start, nothing poisons the attitude of workers more than insecurity—the fear of redundancy that excellent companies (IBM is a notable example) strive to remove from their workers' minds, with obvious consequences for the stability of the company and its performance.

Next, the personnel officer on the floor plainly provides an immediate and effective channel of communication. In fact, Black & Decker installed three channels to ensure that employees not only understood what the management was up to, but trusted managers to do their best for all concerned. Channel one is the personnel officer; channel two, the plant-level joint committee; channel three, the complaints procedure—under carefully laid-down rules, any employee with a grievance can go all the way up to the chief executive officer. (Good communication can't be achieved through monochannel systems.)

Again, IBM operates a similar procedure. Again, IBM has a similar emphasis on communication. The remarkable similarity in the kind of personnel policies adopted by experts in these arts and crafts carries its own lessons. Organizations that do their best for their people (in the nonaltruistic expectation that this makes it more likely that their people will do their best for them) don't use communication as an end in itself. It provides a bond that ties all the organizational residents together.

Even the seemingly unproductive aspects of personnel policy are deeply significant. The provision of only one staff restaurant, where everybody lunches, from the boss to the bottom boy or girl on the ladder, is no news in the U.S. or Germany. It's a big deal in Britain. That in itself provides one explanation for poor industrial relations in the U.K.—because separate dining facilities for the management (and even for several different groups or castes) convey a very powerful message.

You can interpret that message most easily by listening to the defenders of separate eating.

One, they say it's bad for confidentiality if the workers can sit near the managers. Interpretation: the managers have secrets from the rest of the staff, and lots of secrets, at that.

Two, they say the workers don't like it themselves, and there should be perks and privileges for people who rise above the rest. Interpretation: the company is divided between a proletariat (if not a *lumpenproletariat*) and other castes who are socially superior, and must be seen as such.

Three, they say the workers do dirty jobs and mustn't take their filthy clothes (and/or hands) into the same premises as those who wear suits. Interpretation: the company is too idle and/or mean either to clean up working conditions or to provide decent changing facilities and overalls for use before the midday meal.

If an organization is run by a management that withholds information from its employees, is pervaded by snobbery, is indifferent to elementary welfare, and considers the nonmanagement employees—or even just the blue-collar ones—as a lower breed, it may just possibly still succeed. But it won't, in all probability, succeed for long, especially these days. The modern worker isn't inclined to be humble. The modern manager, though, needs a modicum of humility—if, that is, it is humble to treat others with as much consideration as yourself.

5. THE 22,000 OLIVETTI KEYS

Consideration takes many forms, just as you sometimes have to be cruel to be kind. The hottest (and one of the richest) of Italy's businessmen is Carlo de Benedetti. In a country whose business heroes have often been exposed as supervillains (Calvi, Sindona, etc.) the man who saved Olivetti and its work force stands out as a rare example of the triumphant turnaround against the turbulent backdrop of Italian business and politics.

The savior came to Olivetti from a career that had already made him rich and controversial. Hired by the Agnelli family to run Fiat (another long-troubled giant), in a few months de Benedetti fell afoul of the internal politics in the Turin colossus. After a short spell enriching himself in another line of private business, he was tempted by what Olivetti offered—though many would have been more appalled by its prospects than thrilled by the chance "to show the world that seemingly intractable problems can be solved by resort to capitalist principles and methods."

What de Benedetti solved was the problem of a company with a vast turnover, and no profits, and with debts that came to $850 million; the loss for 1978 was about $100 million. Olivetti looked doomed, especially since servicing the mountain of debt was costing a thundering 13 percent of turnover. The equity capital, in contrast to that mountain, was a ludicrously small $60 million.

De Benedetti corrected the financial imbalance by a variety of means, including the injection of $12 million of his own wealth. But Olivetti, in heading for bankruptcy, had built up one asset to show for all the borrowing: an array of new products. The new man felt sure that he could use these sophisticated office machines to turn the company around—with one proviso: that he could take an ax to some staggeringly high production costs, or, to put it another way, horrifyingly low output per employee.

He calculated that in 1977 his new company's output per man-year ran at about $25,000, "compared with anywhere from $40,000 to $55,000 for some of our strongest competitors, and I'm not even talking about IBM. What do you have to do in such circumstances? Quite simply, increase revenues and reduce costs. So I set about doing both."

One of his first steps was to increase prices "against all the advice of my marketing people; but I was convinced that Olivetti had been selling too low compared with the competition." Another was to reduce the labor force worldwide in the first year by some 6,000. "Don't get the idea this gave me any pleasure; I don't like being the chief executioner. But I really had no option. The decision I took had been deliberately postponed for years by the previous management, which had failed to face up to the implications of the widespread switchover from mechanically to electronically operated equipment in the product range. This involves a ratio of one-to-ten; in other words, it takes only one tenth of the time to assemble an electronic machine, compared with a mechanical one."

Without the cuts, de Benedetti could never have exploited the big switch to electronic typewriters, which four years from the new man's arrival totaled 20 percent of its turnover, giving the Italians a claimed half of the European market and 30 percent worldwide. Even without cracking the crucial American market with the success he wants, de Benedetti has doubled Olivetti's sales to $2.2 billion, pushed it firmly into the black with profits of $65 million, and switched the sales from 60 percent in business machines on his arrival to two thirds business systems now, all based on the electronic typewriter.

In the process, de Benedetti's own investment in the company has quadrupled in value. The only thing that has gone down (apart from the debt) is the payroll. Those 6,000 original job cuts have swollen since to more like 22,000. But those were the 22,000 keys to a trebling of the productivity that had compared so badly with the competition in Olivetti's darkest hour. Overmanning doesn't defend jobs, it destroys them—as all those at Olivetti would have been destroyed.

6. TREATING BOEING'S PEOPLE PRODUCTIVELY

"Optimists who work at Boeing bring lunch. A pessimist leaves his car running." That was the bitter gibe in Seattle, when the aerospace firm, by far the biggest employer in the city, was making gigantic layoffs. But in early 1981, a prosperous Boeing still employed 108,000; in the ghastly year of 1969 numbers employed had been truncated by 46,000 souls. Two questions stand out. Why did Boeing have to sever so many people? And what would have happened if the severances hadn't been made?

The second question is the easier one to answer. Boeing would have gone bankrupt, or would have been rescued from that condition (like its competitor, Lockheed) by the federal government. In 1969 it lost $14 million on sales of $2.8 billion. A decade later it made $875 million—and you can understand the difference by comparing two figures: in 1969, Boeing used 25,000 workers to produce seven 747 jumbos a month; a decade later it needed just 11,000.

The overmanning arose, as fundamentally as it always does, from managerial failure. It was only one of the symptoms of the same disease: putting the 747 into production before the engineering was good and ready. As various inevitable snags hit the project, they were tackled on the factory floor—which meant hiring extra people, or "buying your way out of a problem," in one executive's words. In this ghastly situation, a new chief executive took some ghastly decisions, as recounted to Elizabeth Bailey in *Management Today.*

1. Boeing would cut employment even more drastically than it needed—so it could build back from below floor level.

2. The cuts would affect management as much as staff—"We cut a slice off the pyramid. We got rid of as many vice-presidents as we did riveters."

3. To identify areas of inefficiency, those who made the planes would be separated from those who supplied services.

4. Elimination of parts shortages would be achieved by computer cataloguing of all 100,000 parts used in the 747—and every employee who used them.

5. Management systems were reorganized until the company felt that proper control was again being exercised.

Observe that there's not a word in this program about employee motivation, productivity schemes, work-force participation—or anything that comes within the normal compass of a personnel department. That omission emphasizes an inescapable truth: that security of employment rests on efficiency of output and organization—one measure of which, of course, is whether you need 25,000 or 11,000 people to make your jumbos.

It's also true that the possible efficiencies are always greater than expected. Boeing didn't actually have to build back employment: "As we pared and pared we found that we didn't really need any more people." Another truth is that fat builds up on the corporate body in the most unlikely places: "We found that there were maybe ten people who spent full days working on organizational charts. Every time someone was promoted, a new chart would be worked up. We decided to do without the charts for a while."

For those ten people, and maybe for those who had to tell them the bad news, that decision was terribly painful. Being able to take and execute painful decisions is part of good management. But it's better management by far never to reach the Boeing Bind, which means that the highest criteria of efficient use of manpower must be built into the systems. Otherwise people will end up paying a heavy price for failures that are not their fault.

For instance, at one point in the crisis half-finished planes were taken off the production line and left outside while a missing part was awaited. There were something like 1,600 parts shortages a day, according to a Boeing executive, each one slowing down production and productivity; now, he says, there are about twelve.

That smacks of exaggeration, but it doesn't exaggerate the lesson that high productivity in modern business isn't the product of high physical effort, or even mainly of high morale. It's the consequence of integrated management that knows what it's doing and what it wants—and uses its will, know-how, and investment to achieve the most in output with the least in manpower.

Management and morale meet at this point. Men whose work is stopped by missing parts aren't going to be in love with the management. Nor will overmanning and other forms of waste (which the workers will spot long before management does) make people think any more highly of the bosses. On the contrary, the elimination of incompetence with the employees' help has been the most positive contribution achieved by "Participation, Communication, Sharing, and Enrichment"—to quote the PCSE recipe of one consultant, Adam Thompson.

He defines participation in precisely the correct sense: "treating people productively." The productive results in his experience include, among things like converting an annual loss of $1.5 million into profits of more than that, and in another case cost savings of over $750,000 a year, one example that is right out of Boeing's book: "a budget based on hiring over fifty extra employees, achieved with no extra hands."

All this, remember, was achieved with the active *participation* of the workers, with full *communication* of what was afoot, and with their *sharing* in the proceeds (as well as the decision). But, of course, they always do share in the financial results, even if there's no formal means of doing so. For if the Boeing Bind isn't untied, you can't guarantee *enrichment* for anybody involved.

7. THE SALESMEN WHO SLID AWAY

As noted, it isn't only numbers that count in Supermanagement—it's also relations with those numbers. But if the relationship is conducted solely with and via the union, look out. Many Supermanagements dodge the unions altogether—like IBM. When IBM faced a challenge from one white-collar union that was seeking to enroll its work force, the management took the threat very seriously. In fact, companies that (like IBM) pay premium wages and give liberal benefits can still end up with the poorest morale and worst labor problems (unlike IBM), but not if they apply the same thoroughness as IBM does to their worker relations. The IBM management, leaving no stone unturned, no matter how often the turning, communicated so effectively on the unionization issue that the work force overwhelmingly rejected the union. It cried foul play—but the company stayed un-unionized. . . .

At another company, less thorough in these matters than IBM, the sales director believed that he knew his salesmen. But he got around only rarely. When he did, his sole preoccupation was with sales performance. He never encouraged discussion about the salesmen's jobs or their concerns. He didn't know, because he didn't inquire into the matter, that they were deeply disillusioned with their lot; nor that they were actively, but quietly, joining a union—at their own invitation. The sales force of that company is now fully unionized, and the management doesn't like it one little bit.

8. VISIBILITY IS VIRTUE

The trouble with a permissive, participative, cooperative approach to management is that by implication it devalues its opposites: clear, firm direction and leadership. The trouble with that runs to the heart of relationships with employees. If you ask them what they want, they'll tell you: clear, firm direction and leadership. These are the findings of many surveys of employee attitudes, including those carried out by a consultant named Graham Cole. He also found that, whatever the employees do need, they don't get it.

For a start, answer Question One: *Are you visible to your co-workers?* Time spent touring the factories and offices, attending sales meetings or factory committees is never time wasted. Employees vote overwhelmingly in favor of knowing their bosses. Yet in large companies, and even in some much smaller ones, many staff wouldn't know their directors if they saw them. As one man working in the stores put it, "I wouldn't recognize our director if he walked through the plant. We are told that they are professionals, but how can we believe that?" There's only one answer: they can't.

Question Two: *Are you in touch with the realities of your job?* It's all too easy to spend too much time in your own office; typically half that time is spent with immediate subordinates, about 10 percent with peers or superiors. After allowing for paper work, that leaves all too little time for talking with people further down, keeping them informed, "walking the job," or visibly displaying, not only yourself, but your leadership. A common complaint of the workers interviewed by Cole was that their bosses sometimes didn't know the answers to this essential checklist.

(a) How well (or poorly) are company policies being implemented?

    (b)   What problems are currently concerning employees?
    (c)   What do they think of management?
    (d)   Is the state of employee morale good or bad?

If you don't know the answers, or, having found them, don't follow up by seeking explanations and, where necessary, improvements, you can expect trouble—including union trouble. As one supervisor explained, "The main reason why we are in the union is to get our jobs done. We use the union not so much to get pay comparability, but to get daily decisions and actions out of the management."

Question Three: *Do you encourage unity of purpose between employees and the company?* There's a simple enough method of encouragement: holding meetings, and enough of them, to discuss with employees the company's objectives and performance, departmental issues, future changes likely to affect employees, etc. And there's an equally simple way to ensure that these meetings are effective: allow employees' own opinions to be heard. People being what they are, most will stay silent, but they must feel from the experience and evidence of others that their voice matters.

Question Four: *Are you fair and accurate when judging individual performance—and especially when selecting people for promotion?* This issue matters greatly at all levels in the company. Attitude surveys show a widespread feeling in many companies that the wrong people get promoted—and often for the wrong reason. Incompetent managers or supervisors can undermine employee morale and create organizational chaos like an army of industrial saboteurs. Appointing them must also undermine the respect of the underlings for the idiot who made the appointment.

Question Five: *Do you make sure that employees know what they want to know about the matters that concern them personally?* Come to that, do you know what those matters are? According to Cole, the list includes their work, departmental issues, industrial relations news, results of pay negotiations (don't leave the last two to the union, whatever else you do), the company's future plans, changes in work methods, promotion prospects, reasons for management decisions (they almost certainly won't challenge the latter—they merely want to know why). At all points, employees are more interested in the future (on which you should concentrate) than in the past (which is why last year's financial figures don't sing in their ears).

These five are basic questions. But others are also of great importance. Do you ensure that you have open channels of communication down to the lowest level of your responsibility—and up from all levels to yourself? Do you keep what Cole calls "a zone of management silence" about certain vital but controversial issues? If they include matters like progress of negotiations, reasons for work stoppages, manpower cuts, plant closures, automation and future prospects, you're asking not only for trouble, but for the union to take over the communication role from management.

Do you foster rigid class distinctions? Anybody who has separate dining rooms, separate parking lots, separate entrances, separate lifts, and separate toilets, whatever their conveniences (you might say), is conveying a message to employees that he almost certainly won't want them to hear—and that they won't like. The convenience may not be worth the real cost.

Finally, do you recognize that your work values are different from theirs? Cole found that the qualities the managers surveyed tend to value most are cooperation, loyalty, hard work, reliability, punctuality, efficiency, and output. For their part, employees value job security, good wages and benefits, fair treatment, interesting jobs, personal recognition, and opportunities for promotion. Mistakes founded on this difference in values can mean that anything advocated by the boss is automatically mistrusted or unacceptable to the work force and the union (if any). They won't believe a word he says. And that's doubly pathetic—because believe him is what they desperately want to do.

9. THE MAN WHO SIMPLY DID IT

A new general manager was installed at the largest plant of a manufacturing company that, back in the 1960s, had taken eighteen months to negotiate with the unions a totally inevitable revision of the rate paid to the production workers, who were all on incentive pay. The problem arose from a fundamental change in technology, involving the introduction of new machines with far higher rates of output, which owed nothing to the efforts of the operator.

A few years later, when the painfully negotiated rates had become hopelessly uneconomic for the company, it suffered a damaging strike when it sought to reform them. Then severe recession struck the industry—and the new boss was taking over a plant that was losing money hand over fist. He decided that the nonsensical incentive system had to be changed completely.

This time, there were no eighteen months of negotiation. He just did it—in a fully unionized plant. The unions, faced with a like-it-or-lump-it choice, were forced to accept the *fait accompli*. And the successive cuts in manpower that were needed to move the plant toward profitability subsequently went through smoothly. The unions had gotten the message that the new man meant business.

10. WHEN TO TAKE A STRIKE

Meaning business may mean labor trouble—bad trouble, bad for everybody. Nobody ever "wins" a strike. If the men settle on the management's original terms, the company has still suffered the costs of the dispute—and something within management's power must be wrong for a strike to have started in the first place. If the management settles for more than its last offer before the walkout, the men rarely recover the loss of earnings during the stoppage until so long after their return that it hardly seems worth all the bother.

Add to these basic facts of life the risk that your side might lose, and a strike is clearly not likely to be a sensible option for either party. In fact, nearly all managements, nearly all the time, are extremely reluctant to face a strike—and most workers are equally reluctant to stage one, especially over nonpay issues. Men will walk out for more money, seldom for anything else, and, if they do, seldom for very long.

It follows that a prolonged strike over a nonpay disagreement points either to massive management ineptitude or to managerial use of a pretext to force a showdown. The motive might be to weaken the union or to reassert managerial authority (which may be one and the same thing). But the engineered or provoked strike is an expensive and heavy sledgehammer which should only be used to crack something vastly bigger than a nut; and its use, anyway, is an admission of gross failure somewhere back down the line.

Remember that, on an issue of principle rather than money, recovery of the wages lost by a strike, dubious even when pay is at stake, is impossible. It's true that many nonpay issues have pay embedded somewhere within them. But little ingenuity is required, even in an atmosphere of something less than peace on earth and good will to all men, to overcome opposition and, without a strike, accomplish, say, changes in operating methods that will improve efficiency. But you must be prepared, if convinced that changes are fair and proper, to introduce them—even at the risk of a strike.

Plainly, a well-managed company never gets near that point. Efficient, productive working is something from which everybody benefits and which should be the normal condition. Even in less happy circumstances, a reasonable management should be able to get reasonable changes by reasonable negotiation. But the management isn't managing if it is prepared to compromise on anything but those areas which truly are negotiable—or if it enters negotiation without a time limit by which the changes will be instituted, come what may.

Canada's International Thomson Organization gave a classic $45 million example of what not to do during its agonizing dispute with the staff of The Times. It did indeed name a deadline for agreement on reforms that were vitally needed to stem huge losses. But when, after protracted negotiations, no agreement came, the Thomson managers "suspended" their papers. All that meant was a far greater loss during the year when the presses didn't roll, followed by resumption of printing without any substantive gains for the management proposals. If the management had simply pressed ahead, with or without agreement, the printers would very likely have gone on strike—but that would have forced the unions to make the running. Merely look at the strength of this position: a struck management sets a deadline for a return to work on its conditions, or else it will close the company for keeps. The men and the union have far more to lose by staying out than by returning, and return they usually will.

The precondition, though, is that they must sincerely *believe* that the management is prepared to close the company—and they must care, truly care, if it does. In the Fleet Street jungle, many print workers are not directly employed full-time by the paper that pays them, a fact which makes it singularly difficult to get tough. If you can't be tough, though, acting tough is a great mistake. Where toughness is tenable, it should be displayed unemotionally, reasonably, but with total firmness. Let one chink develop in the wall of resolution, and the game is up. Of course, your object is not to close the company. But there is a transcendent aim, which is to preserve the company as a genuinely going concern—and an efficient one.

Here's how the great Soichiro Honda did it—or used to. "A bolt that had been tightened by a young worker made a few more turns when Honda did it himself. 'You damned fool. This is how you're supposed to tighten bolts,' shouted Honda, as he hit his employee over the head with a wrench." Just try that at Ford in Dearborn.

In other words, don't take all you read about Japan's participative team management too seriously. But that perhaps dates back to an earlier time, before Honda learned worker wisdom, aided by his partner, Takeo Fujisawa. For instance, what would most Western managers say in reply to this question from the head union negotiator? "What do you think of the pay offer you're making to us?" I know what they *wouldn't* say, and that's what Fujisawa actually did say on one occasion, according to author Tetsuo Sakiya: "The offer is so low, I think it's ridiculous."

The boss went on to admit that "It is our [management's] fault that the situation has become such that we had to make such a low offer"; predicted that sales would pick up in March; proposed a new pay negotiation at that time; and received thunderous applause. All the same (another Western theory exploded), the company ran into serious labor difficulties. Honda himself stayed clear (wisely, no doubt, in view of his penchant for hitting workers with wrenches); yet it was he who stumbled on the management style which eventually got the company out of its mess.

Honda got angry with "workers who played baseball on the

plant grounds," saying to himself, "In collective bargaining, they complain about having to work too hard. But when it comes to playing baseball, they do it until they become completely exhausted, even though baseball does not bring a single yen to them. What kind of men are they?"

But then he thought, "I must recognize that man achieves the highest degree of efficiency when he plays. If someone says he works out of loyalty to the company, he is a damned liar. Everyone must work for himself. Even I work because I like working. I must create a workshop where everybody will enjoy working." Which is what Honda proceeded to do.

That's what happens when the best comes to the best. But if the worst comes to the worst, and a strike begins, the situation changes by virtue of that alone. One highly successful chief executive won't tolerate any subordinate who settles a strike on materially better terms. That's because he insists on establishing the principle that strikes *never* win concessions from his management. If major concessions are the only way in which a manager can get the strikers back, this chief executive fires the personnel manager or his boss, or both—because they should, of course, have agreed to the demands *before* the strike.

In that period a game of two-sided cat and mouse is inevitable as both sides attempt to test how far they can push the other. But nobody on the management side can ever afford to forget that one vital principle is always at stake in any negotiation: management's own freedom, right, and duty to manage effectively.

11. THE MILL WITH THE THREE-DAY WEEK

The prime reason for that is clear—without effective management, you won't get effective anything. All the cases of improved productivity anybody knows stem from management effectiveness. For example, at Crompton, a textile firm with a plant in Leesburg, Alabama, the mill hands were put on a three-day, twelve-hour-a-day week—and also got a full week off once every eight. If employees actually worked the thirty-six hours (i.e., no absenteeism), what's more, they got paid for forty. Result: the last few hours of the three-day week became the most productive, and labor turnover dropped to only a tenth of the industry average.

Other cases of productivity boosts in U.S. companies, culled from *Fortune* magazine, include the following: at Burger King, the fast-food chain that is running McDonald's a good race, TV terminals were put into the kitchen. The chefs could thus read their incoming orders from the screen, as taken from the cash registers out front. Result: the cooks made fewer mistakes and wasted less food.

New technology can help people other than burger kings to still more amazing effect. The new electric furnaces at Corning Glass are three times as productive as the gas- or oil-fired varieties—and the higher the price for energy, the more financially attractive a saving that becomes. In fact, Corning reckoned it was "avoiding" $24 million in fuel costs a year, mostly because of the new furnaces.

These three examples of higher productivity show where it always really comes from: not from the sweat of the brow, but from the Supermanaging brain behind the brow.

12. PAYOFFS FROM PERSONNEL

By the same token, low productivity generally stems from low-brow management. Not so long ago, a large multinational company wanted to make one of its executives production manager of its most important plant. He agreed—on one condition: that he should have nothing whatsoever to do with industrial relations. They still gave him the job, which makes them equally brainless—and guilty. Any company that leaves personnel work to a personnel department, and doesn't make it a central part of operating management's responsibility, deserves what it will probably get: troubles, if not with personnel, at least with their performance.

The "at least" is misleading, because performance is everything. The proper objects of employment policies are many and varied. But unless those policies add up to a convincing corporate result, they may be worth nothing at all—because the company itself may crumble, in whole or in part. Look at it another way: why would you want people to accept changes in working methods eagerly? Not, for sure, to please some professor in the social sciences, but because the new methods will benefit everybody, including the workers.

The equation in soft minds of high profits with grinding down the poor working man may be ineradicable. But the manager doesn't have to take note of such external nonsense. His time is far better spent in eradicating the internal nonsenses which abound in most operations. Physical inefficiency, for instance, impedes productivity and worsens labor relations, so the work of even a brilliant personnel department could be negated by sloppy work layouts or inefficient use of equipment.

The point where these idiocies will be most apparent, and where their solution will be most obvious, is where they occur. That's the rationale for the various and increasingly popular schemes for involving work people in work problems. Whether or not this kind of involvement represents anything you could call "worker participation" is irrelevant.

Three basic questions lie behind the actions in the mill with the three-day week—and all the myriad of similar steps that truly progressive managements have taken. The questions are:

1. Can my work organization be changed in any way that will boost output or improve quality?
2. Can the manufacturing or other technology be changed in any way that will cut costs, and/or raise quality and/or output?
3. And last, but by no means least; what, if anything, am I doing to motivate people to be more productive, anyway?

Only the last is directly related to the traditional concerns of the personnel people—and the best answer that anybody can provide for the third question is largely useless if the two questions above are languishing in abeyance. Excellent man management isn't a substitution for Efficient Physical Management; on the contrary, EPM is the precondition of managing personnel well.

That being said, there is a great deal that modern ideas of personnel management can contribute—across an enormous range of organizational life. Most of the highly publicized ideas have to do with getting voluntary cooperation—mostly over matters which, by simultaneously boosting EPM, kill two if not three birds with one stone. Other ideas utilize payment systems to the same productive effect. The governing concept is that willing hands make light work—or do more of it. But cooperation doesn't *exclude* discipline: it supplies disciplined behavior without coercion—or fear.

In any organization, fear and its running mate, insecurity, are easily aroused. One chief executive, deciding to cope manfully with the recession, put in a major program designed to strengthen the sales effort. At the last moment, as a complete afterthought, he added to the snappy catch title of the program the initials OMJ—standing for Orders Mean Jobs.

An innocent and obvious enough thought, you might say. But it had cataclysmic results. The sales staff, operating in a sedate industry where firing was almost unknown, assumed that the jobs referred to by OMJ were *their* jobs: i.e., no orders, no jobs. The boss, who meant only that the more orders they got, the more work there would be for the factory, succeeded overnight in generating a totally counterproductive atmosphere of fear.

The disadvantage of fear is that it substitutes negative emotions for positive ones. Very often, if you analyze a fear-ridden and -driven workforce, you find inadequate management at the top.

In the end, though, discipline and cooperation do rest alike on the fear-inducing principle that the undisciplined and uncooperative (or just plain unproductive) will have to be "let go," i.e., fired. While it is true, as Saul Gellerman once wrote, that "most cases of inefficiency and poor work are the result of a weak organization or bad ways of doing things . . ."—note the "most"—in some cases, the person is at fault. What do you do when an employee down the line gets out of line?

As with any management problem, you should approach this

one fast, fairly, informally, factually, and hopefully. The hope is that the firing may be unnecessary after all. But if after all your fair, friendly, and patient efforts, any or some of the following conditions still exist, go ahead.

1. The employee is a troublemaker and continually looks for ways to disrupt the outfit and to lower the morale or alter negatively the attitudes of others.
2. Nobody can get along with him or her. Many quarrels and misunderstandings result from their actions or inaction.
3. The person doesn't do his job because he refuses to apply himself. He is not interested in learning.
4. The employee makes your company look bad to the public, suppliers, or clients.

The principles come from W. H. Weiss in *The Art and Skill of Managing People*. A fifth one should be added: when you know, in your heart of hearts, that sooner or later you're going to have to ask whoever it is to leave—do it now.

13. THE SHIPYARD THAT WAS NEVER LATE

There's a sixth principle of employment policy, too. Expect perfect performance from everybody, including yourself. Supermanagers always do, as a shipping-line executive found. His economics depend critically on having the right ships at the right price at the right time. The economics always meant having his ferries built in West Germany—no matter who else was asked to tender bids. After one such decision, the two sides settled down to the usual arduous detail, a clause-by-clause process that takes many hours of hard negotiation—but not one particular clause, not this time.

When they came to the matter of delivery, the German relaxed and said, "Put in what you like." Taken aback, the shipping boss asked what he meant. "What I said," replied the German. "Put in what you like." The customer, still amazed, pointed out that he could stipulate, say, a million bucks a day as a penalty for late delivery. "Put in a million," said the German calmly. "We have been in this business for 150 years, and we have never delivered a ship late yet."

The saga wasn't quite over. Some time later the two men met socially, and the customer asked the shipbuilder if he could give him a rough idea of when the new ship would be handed over. "No," replied the German. "I can tell you *precisely*." He then named the time and the day; and that appointed hour was exactly when the line got delivery of its new bauble; not as some special favor, the result of some extraordinary exertion, but as a matter of established practice and reliable routine.

14. FORGETTING ABOUT WHOOSH!

Any operation that prides itself on an achievement like being on time with a delivery has got it wrong. That kind of performance is supposed to be a norm, not a special event. If the operation isn't set up, stimulated, and managed so that the norm is indeed normal, then it needs urgent attention—no matter how successful it appears to be at the time.

In fact, even flagrantly failing outfits are indifferent to this most visible sign of why they are failing. As what became the *Queen Elizabeth II* was moving slowly (very slowly) to completion, somebody asked anxiously about the obvious signs that it was running hideously late. The inquirer was told that he had ignored "The Whoosh Factor. . . . When we've only got a little time left I call everybody together, and they all pull their fingers out, and everything goes, 'Whoosh!' "

That is not, to take a different kind of on-time performance, how they order things at Cathay Pacific Airlines. This operator has an "on-time committee" that meets each week to consider the airline's performance on arrivals and departures and to investigate the reason for failures. The point of selecting this particular area is not only that delays annoy passengers (which they do), but that investigation of the failures gives a swift and sure insight into the airline's operating efficiency. Acts of God like bad weather are obviously outside Cathay's control. But if it's an engineering or administrative problem, then the management knows there's a fault and knows, too, that it must be eradicated.

Some managers try to achieve the same effect by going through a random sample of customer complaints. It's an excellent idea, which should certainly be tried, if only from time to time. But as an efficiency control system, the method has the defect that the complaints may be unjustified. It's a *subjective* check on efficiency, as against the on-time performance check, which is *objective*. The choice of measure must vary from business to business. But in many engineering firms, and in similar kinds of manufacture, on-time performance is exactly the right approach.

The weakness may first appear, not in the actual performance, but in the answers to two questions.

1. Is there a regular report on the status of deliveries?
2. Is there a formal mechanism for investigating the causes of failure to meet target dates?

If the answer to either question is "No," the correct response is obvious, although further inquiry is needed before the answer can truthfully be changed to "Yes." A major on-time problem almost certainly results from defects in the systems for scheduling and order intake. This is a different problem from simply taking far longer over manufacture than you need. The problem in these cases, millions of them, is that, however long it takes, the process isn't finishing when somebody said it should and would.

Maybe they shouldn't have said it in the first place. Study complaints about not meeting delivery dates and you may well find that the fault doesn't really lie with the plant; its production times may not differ that greatly from those of the competition. Often, it's the salesmen who have made promises that the plant could never conceivably keep. This establishes the first question in a seven-item catechism.

1. Are sales people taking orders on unrealistic delivery dates?
2. Does the production side have any realistic idea of how long orders do currently take to pass through the system?

3. Is there an effective method of communicating the up-to-date delivery position from production to sales?
4. Are the realistic delivery times satisfactory from the viewpoint of current and potential customers?
5. If not, where are the bottlenecks, and how can they be removed?
6. Is the delivery performance erratic, in any event? If so, why?
7. Who in the company knows about on-time figures? If it isn't everybody—well, it should be.

Any of these questions can be translated into terms of any other objective measure of performance—like the time it takes a subscription department to answer a query; the physical output of a typing pool; the date of completion of monthly accounts; the percentage of successful distribution of a product; the number of times a company is caught out of stock; and so on.

Very often, the information is initially hard to come by—for a reason that arises from a Cathay Pacific observation: the remark that airlines in general are extremely shy about revealing their on-time figures to anybody, inside or outside the company—no doubt because the statistics are generally poor. That's the worst possible reason for secrecy, and also the worst possible approach to improving efficiency.

The best approach is to publish the information, not just as a whip, but as a spur. The purpose of making on-time performance a standard operating objective is to achieve the systems and the system management that are required. Collecting the facts and analyzing them are essential to establish the defects. Establishing what the defects are is essential if the faults are to be cured—and if the objective is to be converted, as it should be, into a target.

People love targets, and adore meeting or beating them—even if there's no extra monetary reward for doing so. The Japanese build such targets into their way of business life. For example, you see signs posted in factories with such poetic and inspiring messages as:

"Fight to Wipe Out 0.1 mm. Error"
"Fight to Cut 0.1 Second Inaccuracy to Zero"
"Everybody's Wisdom and Effort to Zero Accidents"

"Campaign for Top Technology in the World"
"Meet Delivery Schedules Without Fail"

Follow suit, and you build in something that will benefit everybody concerned—a *permanent* Whoosh! factor.

15. THE NUT WHO CHOSE MANUFACTURING

In manufacturing, without built-in Whoosh! you won't get very far; with it, you can get very far indeed. A twenty-nine-year-old Harvard Master of Business Administration named Peter Smith found this out when he voluntarily quit his existing job to go into factory management. To other MBAs, Smith must have seemed like some kind of nut. MBAs mostly go into head office jobs such as studying mergers and acquisitions, the kind of job Smith left when he went off to manufacture vacuum cleaners for his employer, General Signal. Manufacturing is not only the least likely route to the top—it's also the hottest place at the bottom.

Smith discovered just how hot: "We worked at a run all day." He found that human relationships were fundamental, and he proved to himself, too, that the impact of manufacturing on profits is decisive. To quote what Smith told *Fortune* magazine, "If the scrap rate is 5 percent of material costs, and you can get it down to 2 percent, you can make a 30 percent improvement in profit without adding a dollar on sales. Nobody else in the company can do that."

Easy said may be easily done. Smith spoke to a worker (actually speaking to people being the first and most important step in human relations) who suggested using a switch in the cleaners instead of making clumsy electrical connections. The switch cost twice as much, but with union cooperation Smith got the productivity he needed to offset the cost—and the rejection rate fell from 20 percent to under 1 percent.

His work wasn't all done by kindness. When a female worker hit a supervisor in Smith's early days at the plant, he sacked her at once in the interests of shop-floor discipline. Without discipline, he couldn't have worked such wonders as reducing the costs of assembly from $1.56 to 88 cents per unit over three years, while saving his company a total of $12 million. Which worked wonders for Smith's career, too—maybe he wasn't such a nut, after all.

16. HOW TO BE COUNTERPRODUCTIVE

Note that technical improvements were basic to the big advance at General Signal, and also how much room there was for improvement. There nearly always is. Just before the Second World War, reports production expert John L. Burbridge, a factory management decided to find out just how productive its plant really was. It came up with the following grisly results:

1. If it took ten hours to machine a particular batch of parts, it would take 1,000 hours—100 times as long—for the batch to pass right through the factory.

2. For every $2 million of products the factory actually managed to make and sell, an average of $1 million was tied up in stocks and work-in-progress, in roughly equal proportions; the stocks, again, divided roughly equally—half raw materials, half finished products.

3. Less than half of the completion dates given for each quantity of parts were actually met in full; even fewer of the goods ordered for delivery to the factory actually arrived in the quantities required and by the specified dates.

Some four decades later, the same tests of efficiency were repeated in various batch-production engineering plants. The results were just as awful—as would only be expected by anybody who has been following the relatively poor trend of manufacturing productivity in the West. But before any tongues are clucked, would-be cluckers had better check their own efficiencies, using commonsense

157

measures like the above. If the measures don't reveal substantial inefficiency, they almost certainly haven't been properly applied.

Burbridge argued that five common practices found widely in industry, and by no means just in the backward reaches of America and Europe, militate against efficiency. He identifies as villains of the counterproductive piece:

1. Line production, in which different machines or work stations are laid out in a line, along which the materials flow continuously.

2. Process organization, in which, line production being impossible, the materials visit many different departments and sections in turn, before all the processes required to make parts are complete.

3. Functional organization of managers and office workers, so that, in the paper work as in the manufacture, several departments or sections are involved in managing and processing the work.

4. The pursuit of economies of scale, in the belief that, the bigger an organization becomes, the more efficient it will be.

5. The habit of ordering the different parts needed to make the same product in different sizes of batch, some twice a year, some four times, some ten times, etc.

Burbridge amplifies the last point with the following account:

> Perhaps the best illustration of an alternative and much more efficient approach to this problem is the wartime production of Spitfire aircraft. At the beginning of the war there were very few factories for building aircraft, and access to materials, particularly aluminum, was very limited. Nevertheless, a major increase in output of finished aircraft was achieved by restricting the production of components each month to the exact quantity needed for the assembly and maintenance of Spitfire aircraft during the following month.

Look closely at his five points, and two facts leap out: first, the five are fundamentally organizational—you don't have to be an expert production engineer to see their logic; second, the main obstacle to doing things differently is that what Burbridge proposes *is* different. Managers are much happier managing as they have always done—and that is probably the principal reason for low efficiency and for missing the countless opportunities for improvement which exist in all operations, manufacturing or not.

The psychological upheaval of what Burbridge recommends is enormous—for instance, the switch from line production to small assembly groups which manufacture, not just a piece, but the whole product. According to Burbridge, when Philips of Eindhoven went over to making black-and-white TVs in small groups (with no foremen) it gained a 12 percent advance in output per worker and a 60 percent reduction in rejects found by the quality control inspectors.

In factories that aren't suitable for line production (which means at least four fifths of them), a change to product organization can work wonders: that is, each department completes either entirely or almost wholly the parts on which it works. As the expert points out, "Under these conditions departmental managers can be held fully responsible for the output, quality, and costs of components, and any decisions concerning this output can be delegated fairly and efficiently to them."

Much the same argument can be applied in favor of "group technology" or "cellular production"—names for ways of dividing large departments into mini-factories, each of which (again) has full responsibility for the components which it manufactures *in toto*. Add to the mix the Spitfire ordering methods, and you can hope for greater flexibility and a huge improvement in the efficiencies (or inefficiencies) that thorough and honest investigation should have turned up.

Note the indispensable point that, while the above argument was expressed in terms of inefficient factories, the principles apply just as strongly to inefficient anythings. The principles are:

1. No operation can be called efficient unless you have objective, obvious measures by which to judge its efficiency—and apply them rigorously.

2. Organization can have as profound an effect on efficiency as anything else—and the optimum efficiencies won't be obtained un-

less the organization principle is challenged and, if it fails to meet the challenge, changed.

3. The way things have always been done is unlikely to be the best way in which they should be done now—and is guilty of promoting inefficiency unless proved innocent.

4. Divided responsibility is a source of inefficiency, where concentrated responsibility has the reverse effect.

5. By and large, people are happier operating in small groups with defined and complete tasks.

The last lesson goes back much further than Spitfire production in the Second World War: all the way back, in fact, to the old medieval craft organization, in which a *Meister* led his own group of workmen, and the group itself was the focal point of output. The principle ties up with small-is-beautiful organization, with quality circles, with man management techniques, and so on. It's no more a panacea than these other reflections of the spirit of the times. But counterproductivity isn't a cure, either—it's a disease, and a social one at that.

17. THE STOCK THAT WASN'T SOLD

The key to Supermanagement, then, is responsibility—or, much more precisely, the exercise of responsibility. That's what separates the men from the boys, and the businessmen from the clerks. A genuine eighteen-carat businessman made the point when called in to advise on a specific problem in another company. The little local difficulty was heavy overstocking of a commodity on which the businessman was an expert: wine.

It was easy for him to work out exactly how heavy the overstocking was. The bureaucratic business concerned had the amount of stock held on computer, and also the weekly sales—on two different computers, of course, which had never been put in touch with each other. He got them talking, and the computers duly informed him that there was enough Chablis, for instance, to last for half a dozen years or more at present rates of consumption.

To a real businessman, the solution was obvious: get the stock down to appropriate, sensible levels by the swiftest, most economic route. There were bound to be some losses, because some of the stock had been bought far too expensively. But the carrying cost of the excess inventory was in seven figures, and a committee formed to consider the proposals gave its blessing—except that, at the last moment, it agreed to set up a subcommittee to examine the matter in more detail.

The subcommittee then voted down the stock-clearing proposals. The matter then went to the full board, which supported the original committee decision, but set up its own subcommittee to look into the matter more fully. By then eight months had been consumed, while the stock was still eating its financial head off.

The businessman, used to exercising dictatorial powers of decision, was amazed. But when he suggested that part of the stock be cleared quite painlessly by dropping its price, the bureaucrat-minded man concerned dug in his heels. Even though the realized dollar profit was the same as on his best-selling line, he wasn't going to sell anything at less than the margins in his budget—and nobody else in the firm was prepared to be any more businesslike.

18. WHEN MANAGEMENT ISN'T BUSINESS

The difference between business and management is as subtle, but as crucial, as the distinction between fine art and mere illustration. It may not always be obvious where the difference lies. But you sense it as sharply as the contrast between black and white. You use good management for one purpose and one purpose only: to get good results, which, in a commerical organization, must mean good business results. If you don't get the latter, then you haven't, to all intents and purposes, got good management.

The bridge between the two is willpower. For instance, it's

standard management routine to install budgetary and control procedures. Any competent finance director knows how it's done; textbooks exist to explain the techniques, and where there's a textbook, there's management. But you can readily, even in the 1980s, find companies that don't complete their budgets for the next fiscal year, as you might expect, in the final quarter of the preceding year. No: they finish them in June—not six months in advance, but six months *after* the year in question has begun.

Equally, subsidiaries of quite large and apparently sophisticated companies, when faced with the bad results that such budgetary control systems are supposed to throw up, deal with the difficulty by not sending along the bad news to the center—which does nothing about the ominous silence. That isn't how they manage in any company whose management is a well-chosen means to a desirable end.

The devices available include estimated accounts within a few days of the month's end, and final management accounts before the end of the next month; flash reports on variances; cash flow forecasts, including forecasts of cash balances; and so on. But the devices are used as a key to (a) knowledge of exactly how the business is doing, as early as possible, and the earlier the better; (b) spotlighting variances from planned performance, up or down, so that any necessary action can be taken; (c) exerting basic performance discipline on the reporting manager.

This doesn't mean that the budget is a rigid constraint, a holy tabernacle. That's what a *non*manager thinks—that the figures in a budget are sacrosanct and deviation from them a mortal sin, to be punished accordingly. A budget is a forecast of revenues combined with a plan for generating those revenues by incurring costs. The forecast will probably be wrong; the plan, too, may have to change—and the managerial sin may lie, not in varying from budget, but in failing to make necessary changes.

Prevention in management is far better than cure. A system which throws up information too late for anybody to do anything about the situation revealed is a nonmanagement system. If you want to find out why famous names like Jaguar and Raleigh lost so much ground in their crucial U.S. markets, ask whether they were guilty of the following sins: (a) not updating their product lines; (b) not supplying products when the things were, despite their misapplied efforts, ordered; (c) not visiting their dealers, who, of course, defected in droves; (d) not receiving any information that would have told the head office what was going on—and, as it happened, going wrong.

Failures like these often have nothing to do with the products: it's a failure of that essential driving will, starting from the center, that's at fault. You can restate the essential difference between management and business another way: it's the difference between bureaucracy and nonbureaucracy. For instance, this is a bureaucratic definition of management (which occurred under the weirdly inapt title "Job Performance"): "Each manager performs two roles—as a functional specialist, such as a production manager, an accountant, or an engineer. In this role it is the technical competence of the manager that is important." In the second incarnation the manager "contributes to the overall performance of the team. A role in which important and personal relationships count for more than technical expertise."

This isn't business, or even management. It's administration. There's not the merest hint that a manager is supposed to achieve anything as an individual. If he just performs his function and fits into his team, that's good enough—and his company can go on losing something like $1.5 million a day. In fact the document being quoted was aimed at an organization that *was* losing just that amount. It goes on to define a manager as someone "concerned with setting objectives, deciding priorities, devising and implementing plans and assessing the results achieved."

That makes him sound exactly like a civil servant. You can just see a manager assessing the results achieved, noting that the objectives have been missed by miles—and doing nothing about it. Going through the motions is the death of real business management. But the motions can be used to achieve real forward dynamic—as in the case of an electronics group, whose new financial executive found that "We had budgets frontways, sideways, and upside down"; the only trouble was, managers were able to pass the budgetary buck. The new man ensured that "once they were hooked on the budget, they weren't able to wriggle thereafter. There was no excuse mechanism." By charging subsidiaries interest on the productive assets they used, charging rent for the land and buildings, and crediting managers with interest on the cash they remitted to the head office, the financial Supermanager aimed to stop them from "behaving like squirrels with bloody nuts," hoarding "their assets, their stock, and their people." The result? Pre-tax profits shot up by 83 percent in two years, and return on capital soared to 31.1 percent. *That's* the difference between business and management.

To summarize some of the important points I've mentioned in Step Four:

1. Never employ anybody without asking whether they are really needed—and never employ them if they're not.

2. Be personally visible, accountable, and highly communicative to a workforce with which you're on equal terms.

3. Make sure the work people participate in getting productivity—and in its benefits.

4. Be fair, be firm, say what you mean, mean what you say—and make sure it's understood.

5. If it comes to trouble, never compromise on management's freedom, right, and duty to manage effectively.

6. But never forget that efficient organization of machines and methods is the precondition of managing people efficiently.

7. With that in mind, always set stiff criteria for effective performance—and see that they are met.

8. Reorganize work to make individuals and individual teams responsible for quality and performance.

9. If you give a manager excuses, he'll take them: don't give him any.

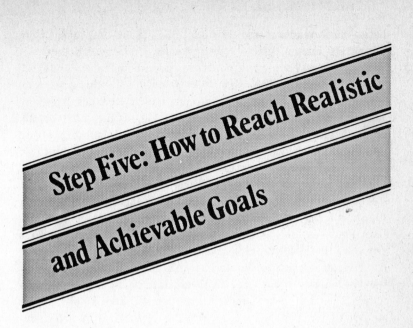

Step Five: How to Reach Realistic and Achievable Goals

1. THE SECRET OF JAPAN

When it comes to goals, few—very few—companies in the West would have dared to set objectives as high as those that the Japanese have proved to be realistic—by achieving them. How has it been done? Not by Eastern magic, nor by following what Western mythology holds to be the Japanese secret formula—rather by managing in the best Western tradition.

One of the best management writers around, Kenichi Ohmae, has used his vantage point in McKinsey & Co.'s Tokyo office to demolish myth after myth about Japan's success. Forget about the idea that Japanese firms adhere rigidly to predetermined long-range strategies. The essence of their remorseless advance lies in paying scrupulous attention to performance on a monthly or even a weekly basis—performance measured not against a three- or five-year plan, but against budget, against <u>return on sales,</u> against competitors.

In that last list the key words are underlined: "return on sales." Ohmae, writing in *The Wall Street Journal,* calls this a fixation, especially among diverse, multi-product outfits. He notes that many Japanese companies are quite content so long as they see *"Zo-shu, Zo-eki"* (increased sales and operating margins). In other words, they insist on adding value and take little or no notice of return on capital—a measure of profit, true, but a much more abstract one, used by "a tiny minority" of big firms.

Using the harder return on sales figure, Japanese businesses in the short term will rob profitable Peter to pump money into long-term Paul—as long as the corporation overall is still okay. Thus Omron Tateishi Electronics, says Ohmae, spent the profits from its component business to develop Japan's first cash dispenser terminals for automated banking. "We wanted to be the leader in cybernation," according to Omron's president, Takao Tateishi. "We wouldn't have spent $28 million on bank terminals if we had calculated the return and decided on that basis."

You can see how the process works from a Toshiba executive's description: "Our measure is not ROI by product or by business unit, but the ROS of an entire division. How an operating head supports a losing business with more profitable ones is entirely up to him, as long as his total ROS today and in the immediate future looks good. His performance is measured monthly. We use an equation that gives a 60 percent weighting to a compound measure made up of return on assets, return on sales, and monthly results relative to budget and relative to the same month in the previous year. Other factors—specifically, consistency with medium- to long-term strategies—get only a 40 percent weighting."

This doesn't happen in a cozy environment. The success of the Japanese when competing with the West rests on ferocious competition at home. Japan, Inc., is a bunch of fiercely warring tribes, who almost never merge or take each other over—for that would mean subjugating one company's "spirits" to another's. Just count the number of Japanese car, hi-fi, TV, and camera firms—all of them far more numerous than in the West, and mostly far more successful in world competition.

That's how it was once upon a time in the West—or as it is now in the mini- and microcomputer market. But if you want to survive in so hotly competitive an environment, you've got to innovate continuously. That's how the four Kashio brothers behind Casio broke into a calculator market comprising nearly fifty fivals; the Kashios introduced new models in swift succession with the idea of shortening the model's life cycle, and lowering prices at the same time.

Prices duly fell like stones, until the volume increments, explains Ohmae, no longer paid for the share growth. "In fact, Casio itself was almost a serious casualty of the price war it had started. What rescued it was the advent of new technology (C-MOS, liquid crystal display, and voice and music chips) which enabled Casio to add value through innovative features and introduce new-generation products."

It was the Kashios who masterminded and powered this drive, though. As Ohmae points out, the most dynamic Japanese corporations are amazingly alike in one way to which Western mythology gives little credence—the influence of a single man, or occasionally of a small group. This may fly in the face of myth, but not of management sense—as long known in the West. The McKinsey man gives several examples, among them zipper giant YKK, Toyota, and Sony.

Sony was founded and run from 1946 to 1971 by one man, Masaru Ibuka, and its U.S. operations were again developed by one man, its current chairman and CEO, Akio Morita—who made the famous decision to go ahead with the Walkman cassette player in the teeth of opposition from his top management colleagues. The prosperity of Yamaha (the leader in music and sporting goods) was the work of a tycoon named Genichi Kawakami. In 1977, after remaining in charge for more than twenty-five years, Kawakami stepped down with the words, "While my steps are still firm, I'll say good-bye to all of you." Three years later, he removed his successor, and resumed his former position in Yamaha; like all major Japanese companies, it has a corps of talented managers, yet the critical decisions are made by one man.

There's no surprise that the rule that strong firms need strong central leadership applies in Japan—as can be seen from the turnarounds that have been required by some of the greatest names in

Japanese business history: Toshiba and Nissan, Canon and the Teijin textile giant. In all four cases strong men took strong hold of the business; what was really "top-down" management was converted into something that looked to Western eyes like "bottom-up" through a mechanism of apparent consensus. As one such executive put it to Ohmae, "I'm led to make decisions; I don't really make them on my own." (Or, "All my decisions are made on behalf of the chief executive.")

As Ohmae goes on demolishing or undermining myth after myth (quality circles, robotics, Japan, Inc.) there emerge from his account half a dozen real lessons—much more important than the mythical ones.

1. Maximize current overall returns on sales.
2. Use short-term profits to finance long-term strengthening of the business.
3. Build decision-taking around strong central leadership.
4. Make getting the best out of people, and doing the best for them, a central preoccupation.
5. Get all production, etc. processes to maximum efficiency.
6. Make beating the competition a constant objective.

In other words, the Supermanager of Japan is very good at the one thing that matters above all, East or West—his business.

2. WHY OMMIT SPELLS SUCCESS

What applies to big Japanese business, including those six principles, applies to smaller operations anywhere. Take a once-small printing company, which saw the light initially only because the founder wanted to publish a little magazine devoted to birds and rabbits. While the publication never took off, the printing work accepted on the side did expand until, after the war, the outfit was in a fair way of business—but not of profit. Even though the printing industry was inundated with far more orders than it could handle, the boss was charging much too low, uneconomic prices.

A group of young eager beavers in the company went to him

and, with some difficulty, convinced him that this was no way to run a business. They then pushed through price rises that transformed the profits. But to transform long-term prospects, more was needed. The younger men decided to build up strength in printing catalogs—a relatively obvious choice, since two of the largest catalog companies in the country were headquartered nearby.

By the 1970s the business was a moderately successful public company, the technology was changing fast, and photogravure—a process in which the firm had no experience at all—was the technology of the future for the huge catalog jobs. Within a decade every single machine in the plant had been changed; the work force had been retrained for the new technology; and sales had risen by 1980 to $22.5 million, a 552 percent rise from 1970, as the company built on its special expertise in catalogs and magazines.

Profits, moreover, had multiplied by 570 percent to $3 million, before interest and tax, which represented 13 percent of turnover. That early decision by the young dissidents—that they didn't want to be in the printing business but in the business of printing—had taken them into the very top echelons of an industry which offers some trenchant insights into the nature of Supermanagement, and its opposite—the secrets of success and of failure.

Of course, in the house of business success there are many mansions, many recipes. But it's always been tempting to believe that there must be some highest common factors, or lowest common denominators, that bind the successful companies together. Only find those common features, and you should have the elixir of success. Alas, elixirs are as hard to find in business as in love. But a study of 350 firms in that industry of printing threw up some fascinating clues.

One clue is that only a small proportion could be ranked as successful. The vast majority of people run their businesses ineffectively. They do so partly because they are headed in the wrong direction in the first place. The point is crucial. The three obvious objectives on which a manager might seize for his company are continuity, or profit, or growth. In fact, only 8 percent of the successful companies named continuity as their business objective—compared to 53 percent of the weaker brethren.

That majority vote, you might think, still left a fair number who saw profit or growth as their aim. Not so—only 14 percent went for growth and a mere 4 percent for profit. The residue (and residue is the *mot juste*) simply had unclear objectives or none at all. The strong 30 firms were in no doubt. Growth attracted 46 percent of them, and an equal number opted for profit.

The purist might argue that all firms were in the wrong, since continuity, growth, and profit are all essential. But the pursuit of growth implies profit, because that is required to finance the expansion; and the pursuit of profit implies growth, since the funds generated will have to be plowed back into the business, and thus into its expansion, if the profits are to be maintained and increased.

If you've got profits and growth, there can't be much doubt about the continuity of the firm. But without either, the pursuit of continuity will be quite literally a dead end. Even when they think they have objectives, companies of the weaker sort can fall over their own feet in a way that makes failure equally inevitable. Consider this quote: "Our objective is to improve quality and increase our market share and profits. Investment in machinery will be reduced. Expenditure on operator training and selling costs will be reduced."

The words come from real life, but the speaker is living in a fantasy world, where the destructive consequences of his actions are concealed behind mists of misunderstanding. Such businessmen shy away from reality in many ways. The man above, for instance, probably didn't have any sales targets: 95 percent of the weaker brethren didn't. In contrast, 87 percent of the Supermanagers not only set sales targets but (far more important) acted on them.

Success, by no means incidentally, was not based on subjective notions. The stars were in the top quarter of the companies surveyed on three hard and fast counts: (1) the ratio of profit to capital employed; (2) the ratio of profit to sales; (3) the value added to wages. They also had five common features that make up the acronym OMMIT.

1. They defined their business Objectives and operated to meet them.

2. They identified Market opportunities and coordinated their commercial efforts to achieve planned business results.

3. They had a clear understanding of Money and its use as a company resource.

4. They had good Information systems in support of good decision-making procedures.

5. They had organized the management to operate as a Team, developing and training executives to meet the changing needs of the business.

That may sound slightly like preaching virtue as the pathway to goodness. But you omit any of the OMMIT five at deadly peril; and they in fact refer to matters far more explicit than being virtuous. Take the matter of market opportunities: the colossal difference between the weaker and stronger firms in this study was that the stronger ones tended to specialize in certain types of customer and certain products. They didn't see themselves as defined by their technology or by their processes.

It's the difference between saying "We're in printing," on the one hand, and "We supply labels to wine companies" on the other: between "We supply a range of materials to various industries," or "We sell a single product [tickets, say] to a large number of users." The idea is to identify a particular area, or segment, which you can make your own. The wrong idea is to stick in your thumb like little Jack Horner without having any very clear idea of what plums you hope to pull out.

Once again, the statistical discrepancy is amazing. While 86 percent of the Supermanagements specialized in one or more market areas, and 77 percent in one or more product areas, not one of the weaker companies had identified a market in which to specialize. Nor were things much better when it came to finding a specialized product area—only a fifth of these feeble fellows had done so.

Don't think, either, that the differences gained from following the winning policies are insignificant. Some of the strong firms made 100 percent on their capital employed—the average for the top quartile (in which they all fell) being over 37 percent. The average for profit as a proportion of sales was more than 12 percent. And that same top group had an added value of over $2.95 per $1.00 of wages. That compared with less than $2.00 for the bottom quartile, which almost certainly means that they weren't making any real profit at all.

The OMMIT policies, then, don't tell you precisely what to do. They are, however, a highly effective guide to what you should avoid, and a framework within which the detailed decisions that will create business success can be taken. Within the fivefold framework, anything can be achieved. Without it, even continuity, the name of the game for the misguided weak brethren, becomes unlikely.

3. THE SECONDHAND ARMS SALESMAN

With OMMIT, though, a management can proceed to super status from the most unlikely starts. Two U.S. companies have leading positions in a special area of defense electronics. One, Optic Electronic Corporation of Dallas, Texas, makes mostly optical fire-control equipment; the other, Ni-Tec of Chicago, is one of two prime producers of image intensification tubes, the crucial components in night vision equipment. They have one other thing in common. In the late 1970s they passed into the hands of a British purchaser, United Scientific Holdings. Its bill for the pair was $7.5 million down, with maybe another $5 million to follow; yet the buyer had *sales* of only a little more than $1 million when it became a public company as recently as 1968.

Even more bizarre, USH began life selling war surplus goods, like binoculars and compasses, in London's Tottenham Court Road. It got into defense business proper as a sideline—buying up replacement parts to sell to foreign armed forces. A young university graduate, Peter Levine, was told to catalog the military stuff, and under him the sideline swelled into the mainstream business. Shortly after going public, Levine made two tiny buys, moving into production of vehicle cupolas, incorporating periscopes and gunsights, and military optics—including, eventually, laser range finders.

The former secondhand company could therefore bring to its Dallas business valuable firsthand laser know-how, while drawing on the American firm's greater technological skill in passive night vision and thermal imaging equipment (which is what enables a soldier or fire control officer to hit his target in an almost total blackout). Along the route to this unlikely success, in the decade up to the end of September 1980, USH multiplied its turnover by 1,020 percent and its pre-tax profits by1,400 percent; earned 16.3 percent on turnover and a stunning 45.1 percent on capital employed. It was thus handsomely positioned, not only to make its U.S. buys, but to raise and pay $40 million for Alvis, the maker of the British army's brand-new tanks—all from a small secondhand start.

4. THE STATISTICS OF VICTORY

That kind of success can't be denied. But can you measure Super-management more precisely? Stockbrokers Vickers da Costa have come up with a clutch of criteria which they use for the understandable purpose, given their business, of selecting winning shares, one of them being the aforementioned United Scientific. For a management, stock market performance is not, as it happens, a satisfactory measure of success. The market is captious, fickle, and undependable; and, when it falls in love with a company, the results can be disastrous. The buying pushes up the share price to an unsustainable multiple of earnings—and that makes disappointment absolutely inevitable, no matter how brilliantly the company performs.

That's why IBM, the outstanding company of any description in the whole postwar era, could reward its shareholders with only a miserable 1.5 percent total return (in inflated dollars, at that) over a whole decade in the 1970s. So forget the share price, even though that is one true measure of the "wealth" of the business. The object of the Supermanager is to enhance the real *worth* (not wealth) of the business year in, year out. That is an objective which the private company can pursue just as fervently as one whose shares are quoted on a stock market, which is where they may excite the attentions of a broker like Vickers da Costa.

But this broker, being very choosy, won't look at candidates for business success unless they have a value (in its terms, obviously, the market value of the shares) of at least $11 million. Second, there has to be a rising pattern of pre-tax profits. The assessors recognize that every business (like every economy) has its off years. But a successful business is allowed to have only one off year; the profit fall in that off year mustn't be more than 15 percent; and the business must make up the decline in full in the following two years.

The third criterion needs more explanation. "Retained cash flow" (RCF) has to run at an average of no less than 15 percent of "equity funds" (EF) over the years of study. RCF, to spell it out, is the balance retained in the business—profit *after* tax, plus depreciation, and deferred tax (if any), less minority interests and the dividends paid out to shareholders. EF equals shareholders' funds, plus any deferred tax reserve, minus "good will" (unless, that is, any other business where good will arose has been bought in the past half-dozen years).

These three criteria, which supply the raw material for an English service called Testing for Success, carry crucial lessons for businesses and organizations that will never go anywhere near the stock market. First, size. To know that it has succeeded, a business must be run with some notion of what scale equates with success. It may be a great deal less than, say, $10 million, but in every activity there is a point at which an operation is significant and one at which it is not. It isn't a question of size for size's sake, as the other criteria make copiously clear. The point is rather that, below that critical point, the long-term viability of an organization (and hence its ultimate success) can't be guaranteed.

The size criterion, though, must be coupled with the very difficult one of regularly raising profits—difficult, not only because of the environment of the firm, but because of factors, including technical accounting and tax considerations, but more especially fluctuations in economies and markets, which may make year-to-year comparisons invalid. The essential, though, is that, under Anglo-Saxon accountancy conventions a business that increases profits by 15 percent in the year to December 31 is worth 15 percent more (before the tax man gets his claws on the proceeds) than it was on January 1. Forget the accountancy and concentrate on the facts: how much has the underlying worth of the business actually risen year by year? A rise of 15 percent is by no means an excessive target or an excessively demanding standard for a successful manager.

The trend in declared profits could, of course, be adversely affected by a sudden bulge in investment. But the accounting treatment of investment is of infinitely less importance than the existence and quality of that investment. The reason for looking at retained cash flow with such passionate regard is that this RCF figure measures the ability of the company to maintain its expansion—without which its share price will rapidly cease to be an object of wonder.

True, a company may well be able to finance its growth by raising or borrowing funds—as United Scientific did before making the Big Buy into Alvis tanks. But new money has itself to be financed, and the weight of that new cash will pull the company down unless it continues the progressive rise in earnings and the high ratio for retained cash flow, which won it the financing ability in the first place.

The stockbroker's three tests are thus valuable for underpinning a share price. But they are far more valuable for underpinning a business—and they form a troika. Each of the three horses depends on the others, and they have to pull together. Thus the secondhand arms salesmen used their rising profits to achieve first a bridgehead, then a "critical mass"—a viable size—in their chosen line, and as the business grew, so its debts shrank to a smaller and smaller proportion of its worth.

"Critical mass" feeds earnings growth, which generates the investment resources—and with those, completing the benevolent circle, critical mass and progressive earnings growth can be maintained. At the end of the day, expansion can be financed only from the earning power of the business, meaning its ability to generate cash—from old and new investment alike. And that is the true business of management.

5. LORDS OF THE MARKETPLACE

There's more to it than that, though—more to it, too, than can be found in the Peters-Waterman book, *In Search of Excellence* (already referred to). Not that the authors can be wrong in picking up examples from the excellent companies they studied. How can you err by copying, say, the DEC trick, which, instead of allowing 250 engineers and marketeers to work on a new product in isolation for fifteen months (the usual approach), is to form bands of only five to twenty-five people and test ideas out on a customer, often with cheap prototypes? That takes only a few weeks.

The authors quote, again wisely, IBM marketing vice president Francis G. (Buck) Rogers, who says, "It's a shame that, in so many companies, whenever you get good service, it's an exception." At the really excellent companies, in contrast, "Everyone gets into the act." At such companies they know that the best product ideas can come from customers—if you listen, intently and regularly. Nor will you get innovation without the kind of approach shown at 3M—a company that has been called "so intent on innovation that its essential atmosphere seems not like that of a large corporation, but rather a loose network of laboratories and cubbyholes populated by feverish inventors and dauntless entrepreneurs who let their imaginations fly in all directions."

That may sound a mite fulsome. But when Texas Instruments chairman Mark Shepherd talks of every worker being "seen as a source of ideas, not just acting as a pair of hands," he's plainly realistic. That's how to make a company's outstanding productivity record better still. Another way is certainly to have bosses who "are legendary for walking the plant floors." At McDonald's, chairman Ray Kroc rightly and regularly visits stores and assesses them on the factors the company holds dear, QSC & V (Quality, Service, Cleanliness, and Value). The single-minded Kroc would also doubtless echo the former Johnson & Johnson chairman who once said, "Never acquire a business you don't know how to run." Not to mention the past chief executive at Procter & Gamble who noted, "This company has never left its base. We seek to be anything but a conglomerate."

The Peters-Waterman book also stresses at several points the importance of simplicity, lean central staff, and what the pair call "simultaneous loose-tight properties." On the looseness side, "At Digital the chaos is so rampant that, one executive noted, Damn few people know who they work for.' " As for the tightness, "Digital's fetish for reliability is more rigidly adhered to than any outsider could imagine."

Yet do these points really add up to more than anecdotes? Are they what really makes the star companies so starry? The authors select as particular examples the following list of fourteen: Bechtel, Boeing, Caterpillar Tractor, Dana, Delta Airlines, Digital Equipment, Emerson Electric, Fluor, Hewlett-Packard, IBM, Johnson & Johnson, McDonald's, Procter & Gamble, and 3M.

Take a look at *Fortune* to see how these companies fared in the years up to and including 1981. The magazine measures performance on four criteria: (a) total return to investors, 1971–81; (b) growth in earnings per share over the same decade; (c) net return on shareholders' equity in 1981; and (d) net return on sales in 1981. Here's how, ranked out of five hundred companies, ten of the "exemplars" did on those four counts:

Table 9

COMPANY	POSITION			
	A	B	C	D
Boeing	24	46	122	228
Caterpillar Tractor	211	158	206	131
Dana	162	222	317	276
Digital Equipment	133	30	281	31
Emerson Electric	321	205	77	80
Hewlett-Packard	130	47	168	64
IBM	369	249	109	27
Johnson & Johnson	354	176	102	66
Procter & Gamble	347	295	199	194
3M	381	245	85	38

It's not a magnificent showing. Out of twenty numbers for the long-term ratings, these ten luminaries chalked up only four single-figure ratings—that is, came into the top fifth of the largest U.S. companies. The average rating was strictly middle of the road.

Turn to the single year of 1981, and the performance is better—particularly on return on sales. But again, eight single-figure ratings out of twenty hardly add up to a very wonderful performance: especially not when there are seven ratings of 190 or worse. In other words, "excellence" adds up to mediocrity on the longer-term performance figures and only better-than average on the short haul—although you would logically expect it to be the other way around.

So while the qualities Peters and Waterman specify are all very good, any one company might well achieve better results, much better ones, by a quite different approach—one that suits it, its people, and the market in which it's operating. Nor is it clear that the best figures on the long-term rating, which happen to be Boeing's, establish it as a better-managed company than, say, IBM or 3M—which Boeing far outshines. For that matter, was 3M really a better managed company in 1981 than Procter & Gamble?

The answer is that there's a ninth quality, one which isn't measured by the *Fortune* criteria, or the Peters-Waterman analysis; and number nine is the highest common factor of the highest Supermanagements. Look at those ten names, and it emerges unmistakably. All the other attributes and anecdotes revolve around one thing: maintaining the corporation as the King of the Market. The markets of the companies vary tremendously: their number one status in those markets does not. From that insistent determination on being number one much else flows: and that is why these companies will be around when higher-ranking performers in the 1970s and 1980s will not, with one proviso: that the Supermanagements never forget that insistence on performance, and readiness to change if you don't get it, are the only way in which you stay King.

6. STRATEGY FOR SURVIVAL

In other words, the figures in the accounts, from however many angles you examine them, don't give the full measure of Supermanagement. Being the King, and staying there, depends, not on the current score, but on the innate strength. William K. Hall, writing in the *Harvard Business Review,* made some highly pertinent observations on the matter. He looked at sixty-four companies in depth to determine those with the best hopes of surviving in a hostile environment—the equivalent, as a measure of business management, of the medieval trials by fire and water. From his study, Hull concluded that:

First, the best business survivors are the firms which can deliver their products at the lowest cost and/or which have something called "the highest differentiated position"—which, being translated, means having the product which the customers perceive most clearly as being different to and in important respects (important to them, that is) rather better than the competition. That is, these companies are Kings.

The essential two tricks of difference and superiority can be achieved either on a *full* product line (like IBM's, say) or just in a specific, viable segment of a market (BMW in high-performance sedans, for instance). But companies which attain the loftiest status, however they do it, win the highest growth rates, the greatest returns, and the best prospects of a payoff when plowing back capital. They're the Supermanagements all around.

The next best position, according to Hall, is no surprise: to be second-best at either low-cost delivery or differentiation. But the second-best do second-best on growth returns—and they can be pulverized by competition either from number one or from outside. In the car industry, Hall rightly quotes the agonies of Ford in the U.S. as GM and the Japanese stepped up the pressure from both sides. An English critic would say much the same of British Leyland in Britain, caught between Ford U.K. and the importers, in another embrace reminiscent of the Iron Maiden of Nuremburg.

Third, with bleak and unhappy prospects, are those businesses which run neither first nor second in the cost and differentiation stakes. Unless firms in this position can find a radically revised slot in the market, or diversify radically, they will fall into the fourth category. There, they will find a fate which isn't worse than death—it *is* death.

This fourth category is the marginal or failing position. To quote Hall, "Competitors who end up last in mature, hostile environments ultimately must fail or be subsidized, either through government ownership or aid, or through cash infusions from a diversified parent. Despite efforts to use such subsidies to resegment and refocus their operations, the survey data shows no successful efforts in such turnaround attempts among the sixty-four competitors in eight basic industries." As Hall says, his data raise a fundamental question as to "whether there is any real possibility of strategic turnaround."

Well, there is. But it can be done only by severe surgery—as one group of managers found when confronted with a severe choice: make the company work, or see their own careers take a nasty downward curve. The strategic priority, if they wanted to save themselves and the company, was clear: close the company's largest plant, a money-munching mammoth. This was no easy task when the managers asked to run down the works would lose their own jobs in the process. Since the closure was utterly crucial, unlimited hours and care were poured into the preparation and the planning—and the closure was effected without losing any production anywhere else in the group, which ended up with half its former capacity, but making three times as much money.

Sans the money muncher, it was in a position to implement the second leg of its strategy: to acquire another leg for the group. The managers were still too poor to buy any public company, so they lowered their sights to divisions of public companies. By various routes they ended up with an important business in specialty chemicals; another in disposal of chemical wastes; pre-tax profits up nearly nine times from the figures of half a dozen years before, on turnover which hadn't quite trebled. The return on capital, a wholly illusory figure in the years when that capital was truly being destroyed, had doubled—and was a very real return indeed: so real that the purchase price, when the relieved and enriched managers sold out, was no less than $100 million.

Here, radical strategy and radical surgery had produced a radically different business. What is true of the business giants with millions or billions of sales applies just as sharply to the lower end of the economic scale. Everybody in business, and in every segment of a business, has to answer one basic, unspoken question: Why should people trade with me, rather than anybody else? Unless there is a convincing, unique reason, and unless that vital difference is kept alive and well, the management has not succeeded and will not succeed. As Hall says, you can get by, and for a long time, as second-best. But who ever thought second-best synonymous with Super-management?

There's a slippery slope that can be traced through Hall's classifications. At first, the firm is King of the jungle—lowest in costs, highest in customer esteem. Then it allows some disregarded competitor to establish a lower-cost, different product which is more favorably regarded in the market. Before long, two or three more rivals have established themselves in slots above the original number one. From that point on, unless heroic efforts are made, the one-time leaders fall into "the marginal or failing position" from which ultimate collapse is inevitable.

Businessmen who preside over this kind of Rake's Progress (and there are countless examples) have not only achieved failure themselves, but wished it on innocent bystanders. The managerial rake has a similar personal decline and fall: from accepting his own second-best, and then third-best, performance to the stage where he's actually unaware how bad he is. Like some of Hall's sick subsidized managements, he may even convince himself that, simply by being there, he is both good and successful. His successors will know otherwise. Supermanagement has to be measured like a Victorian fortune: not only by what you make in your lifetime (for which read career) but also by what you leave behind.

7. THE TWO LITERS OF TOYOTA

That continuity from one generation of Supermanagers to the next is an outstanding characteristic of the best firms in Japan. Yet it took the great Japanese company Toyota Motor a huge stretch of time, from 1935 to 1962, to make its first million passenger cars. The next nine million took only a decade. In the following five years, to July 1977, the cumulative production doubled—another ten million cars. By January 1980, a scant thirty months later, a further ten million had taken Toyota, the world's third-largest manufacturer, to the thirty million mark.

In this barely credible expansion (probably the greatest single achievement in postwar manufacturing industry), Toyota was led by its sales side—set up as a completely different company, at the insistence of the banks, after the whole company nearly collapsed financially in 1950. A crucial decision by the sales company came in the middle of that decade. Already successful with a light truck, Toyota had launched the first all-Japanese car, the Crown, and was about to introduce the Corona. It decided to set up a second, separate retail sales network. As Seisi Kato recalls in *My Years With Toyota,* the idea "immediately met sharp opposition from our established dealers, and all of us ... had an extremely difficult period putting our plan into effect."

The Toyota sales chiefs persevered, "believing it had to be done if Toyota was to grow to its full potential." The president of the company, Shotaro Kamiya, had a famous admonition at the time: "A one-liter container can hold only one liter of water." He meant that a company "had to expand its sales capacity first, if it truly expected to achieve more than the volume of sales being made at the time."

Once its domestic sales were in full and growing order, Toyota turned its two-liter technique to exports. By 1975 the five millionth export had been shipped. Less than five years later, the cumulative total had doubled. Nobody could say that Toyota had failed to grow to its full potential: least of all its one-liter competitors.

8. GO BIG, YOUNG MAN

Sooner or later, in every businessman's life, there comes a moment when growth in his single product or market no longer seems enough. If he's under pressure, it may actually not be enough. Diversify or die, says the writing on the wall. Unfortunately, diversify and die is a much more common result. Going into a new market with a new product—or, like Toyota, into a new country with an existing product—can be about as safe as putting out fires in ammunition dumps.

Only a very innocent manager ignores this truth. The less innocent adopt a sound, sensible, sane policy to limit the risk. They start small and, if the venture shows signs of success, they reinforce their bridgehead with more money, more management, more of everything. It's a sound, sensible, sane policy, as noted: but it's absolutely wrong—if you believe the researches of a professor from Virginia named Ralph Biggadike.

He looked at 68 ventures in the first two years of operation and 47 in the third and fourth years. Why the drop from 68 to 47? Because several of the ventures never saw Year Three. Biggadike, writing in the *Harvard Business Review,* ranked his ventures' performance on four criteria: (1) return on investment (2) cash flow as a proportion of investment (3) pre-tax profit as a proportion of sales and (4) gross margin as a proportion of sales. The results (see table) were shattering. The median return was minus 40 percent in Years One and Two, and minus 14 percent in Years Three and Four. In fact, by the end of the whole period, less than two-fifths of the ventures had made any kind of profit.

Collectively, though, they showed a startling rate of growth—a median figure of 45 percent per annum. Before anybody calls for three hearty cheers, note that the median market share after two years of this hectic growth was only 7 percent; a couple of years on, the share was still no more than 10 percent. In other words, to quote

Table 10

FINANCIAL PERFORMANCE IN THE FIRST FOUR YEARS OF OPERATION

PERFORMANCE RATIO	MEDIAN VALUE	
	YEARS 1 AND 2	YEARS 3 AND 4
Return on investment*	−40%	−14%
Cash flow—investment†	−80	−29
Pre-tax profit—sales	−39	−10
Gross margin—sales‡	+15	+28
Number of businesses	68	47

* The ratio of net pre-tax income to average investment. Income is calculated after deduction of corporate expenses but prior to interest charges. Investment is calculated as working capital plus fixed capital (valued at net book value).
† Cash generated by after-tax earnings minus cash absorbed by increased working capital and increased net investment in plant and equipment.
‡ Sales revenues minus purchases, manufacturing, and depreciation as a ratio to sales revenues.

the HBR article, they had nearly all followed this siren call: "Far better to enter small, learn as you go, and expand with experience."

What goes wrong? The fact that losses are incurred from or at the start is no surprise; that's inevitable. But it doesn't follow that, once the corner has been turned, the sun will continue to shine on the just. According to the research, seven of the businesses that did manage to break into the money in the second year were out of it, back in the red, by Year Four. In other words, "early profitability in a venture does not necessarily guarantee continued profitability."

The seven that slid back, what's worse, were among a mere dozen ventures that made any profits in that initial two-year period. After that, for the sample as a whole (as the table shows) things did improve—but for only one reason. The sales volume rose. The comforting theory is that, after the inevitably expensive launch period, costs will become less heavy. But they didn't for Biggadike's sample companies. Their costs went on rising, often at a fast clip—sometimes even faster than sales.

Having absorbed and believed those facts, you may still brace your shoulders manfully and be prepared to carry on for the payoff *beyond* the four-year period. The shoulders had better be stiffly braced—it took a further four years before the typical venture entered the promised, profitable land. Even then, the returns were paltry—seemingly only 7 percent.

To quote Biggadike, "A sample time projection suggests that ten to twelve years elapse *before* the return on investment in ventures equals that of businesses that have matured." Nor can you count on the cash in exceeding the cash flowing out until a dozen years have passed.

If you don't believe the data, you're in good company. When Biggadike showed these results to managers, they queried them strongly—until they found, on checking the data against their own corporate facts, that the figures more or less tallied. Given the small market shares, already quoted, achieved over the first four years, it can't even be argued, remember, that the long profitless grind is a worthwhile investment in market position.

The immediate reaction to all this calamity might seem to be, no new ventures. Biggadike puts it another way: "Any corporate venture that promises losses for a period longer than the job horizon of most managers seems unlikely to survive"; in which case, after looking at all the above facts, it would be better not to attempt the ventures at all, in which case commercial development would come to a standstill—which is absurd.

How do you accentuate the negative and turn it into a positive? One positive clue lies in a highly negative rule laid down by one of the Biggadike companies: "Kill new businesses if they are not profitable at the end of Year Three." That would have killed almost all the ventures studied—and a good thing, too. Losses are there to be cut, not extended into infinity.

With that understood, you do as follows. (1) Go (like Toyota) for the biggest possible market share. (2) Launch any new ventures few and far between. (3) Only back the business as long as its market share is rising. (4) Don't back it, even if the business is profitable, if the profit is gained from a loss of market share. (6) If it's a choice between a new venture and developing an existing business, pick the latter every time.

Of the six, the first is most important—go big, young man!

9. THE MAN WITH TWO ACCENTS

The best, or the easiest, way of starting big in a business is to buy into it—especially in a foreign country. Back in 1973, frustrated when the government of the day killed off a big buy in England, two British businessmen, Gordon White and James Hanson, decided to invade the U.S.—"the last bastion of capitalism," in White's words. He thought that "the values [what he could buy for Hanson Trust's money] were streets ahead of values available in the U.K." Eight years later, after only five purchases, Hanson had the twenty-fifth biggest foreign-owned business in the U.S., worth perhaps $400 million.

To land those five buys, though, White (1) spent a preliminary six solid months researching the American scene, "steeping myself in American business methods and rules"; (2) built up files on nearly 1,000 companies that he studied closely, but which were nearly all abandoned; (3) went after three times as many companies as he actually netted; (4) did it all with an initial investment of just $3,000.

December 1973 saw White's first catch: appropriately, a fishing company. The old-established J. Howard Smith (now Seacoast), second-largest in the U.S. fish-oil and fish-meal trade, cost the buyer $32 million. On the day of takeover, there was $20 million in the Smith company coffers—more than enough to cover the first $14 million installment of the purchase price. In its first year under Hanson ownership, the company made $13 million before tax, while substantial quick profits also came from selling the rich real estate which the previous owners had built up over the years.

When, later on, White bought some U.S. textile interests from German owners, he paid far below book value for the assets, and then sold off one of the purchased companies. In 1980, profits of the textile interests exceeded the net purchase price. The adroit U.S. buys played a dominant part in raising Hanson Trust's earnings per share 362 percent between 1973 and 1982, while building up per share assets by 274 percent—and still climbing.

White made one false step when he bought control of a U.S. conglomerate because he thought (wrongly) that a ready-made American management team came with it. That taught him to be "doubly careful" in constructing deals ("I agonize over every one") in the tooth-and-claw atmosphere of U.S. business—an environment he exploited with some zest, passing as an American if it helped: "I can switch my accent to confuse the issue." What the company hunter won't do, ever, is give up the chase too readily: "You win in this life by bloody brute persistence."

10. HOW TO BUY A BUSINESS

There are two kinds of business growth, organic and, presumably, inorganic—the kind at which White became an expert. While the first adjective means growth generated inside the company, by selling and investing more, there's no single descriptive word for growth by purchase—buying all or part of another business. Yet acquisitions have played a role, for good or ill, in the growth of virtually all companies, large and small. Like a house, a business isn't necessarily for staying in. It's an asset for buying and selling, for any one of a myriad of reasons.

A good reason, though, doesn't equal a good purchase. Like a house purchaser, the business buyer should seek to pay less than the business is worth to him—with worth measured by some totally objective yardstick. For instance, the U.S. giants have been bandying billions about in the battles for oil companies, like Marathon and Conoco, because of the widely held belief (which had better be right) that the oil which the targets have in the ground is worth much more than the billions being bandied.

Whether or not the sums are right, the principle certainly is. The buyer must ask, "What am I really buying? What is that truly worth?" Sometimes, as in the oil example, both questions seem easy to answer. More often than not, though, the buyer is only acquiring profits, or the hope of them—and hope automatically throws objectivity out of the window, opening it wide to subjective speculation. Even if the reason is to enter a new business area, the proof of the pudding can only be in the eating.

The great art dealer Lord Duveen used to clinch amazingly expensive sales of masterpieces to American millionaires with the immortal line "If you're buying the priceless, you're getting it cheap." As a general rule, if you're buying the future, it's going to cost you. On the whole, no business can prove that it's worth buying unless the sellers can produce a run of yearly accounts that show a continuous buildup in its internal value—in the profitability and growth of the assets.

The canny buyer will never, never neglect his homework. In the process he will put a key ratio like profit to sales (it should go without saying that turnover is no criterion unless a profit is made) under the microscope. How fast have both sales and profit gone up? And has the profit to turnover ratio been increasing, showing that the company is containing its costs and keeping up its prices? How patchy is the record? Can the dips be explained away for good reasons (*not* plausible excuses), or is bad management to blame? The other vital ratio, return on investment, is subjected to exactly the same scrutiny.

Suppose the buyer is satisfied that the profits are as stated in the accounts (a supposition that must never be taken for granted), how should the company be valued? At any time there will be a going rate, linked to the price of money established via the stock market, for a given type of business in a given set of circumstances. The temptation, if the buy has any potential (and why else should you want the thing?) is to price the company on its future, rather than the past and the present. *Don't.* At Hanson, White looks only at past, existing figures (hoping to find evidence of an upward corporate run like Hanson's own) and at the "downside risk"—that is, what the worst possible outcome of the purchase might be. He won't proceed if the risk isn't acceptable (it wasn't, in what otherwise looked like the bargain of the century—the Avis car rental business—and White let somebody else drink the poisoned chalice).

If satisfied on this point, White looks at the net outcome of the deal: what will Hanson end up by paying, after selling off any bits and pieces it doesn't want and taking hold of the buy's liquid assets—its cash and so forth? If the deal has been really well constructed, the buyer can get his money back in a year or so—and there aren't many investments in this world of which that can be said.

Get it wrong, and the money will never come back home, which is the point at which purchasers less astute than Hanson will start jabbering on about the other, intangible benefits they have received from the buy. Pay too much for a company, though, and the balance sheet will suffer for years to come. From that follows a simple but hard-to-keep rule: when you've made up your mind on a price range, stick to it—unless new and compelling reasons establish that the assets are worth more than originally thought. British companies scouting for American acquisitions bought several pups (actually, whole kennels full of the things) because they didn't understand the cheerful habit of American entrepreneurs in such circumstances—which is to ask for much, much more than they expect to receive.

As with selling a house, the hopeful entrepreneur may get

lucky—there's a sucker born every minute, if not in your neck of the woods, then somewhere else. White lost one purchase when the seller dropped dead at the last minute; it would have cost Hanson $163 million. A few years later, the company went to another buyer for $800 million. But in the buying game it doesn't pay either to mourn the fish that got away or to set the heart too passionately on the object of desire. More fish will escape than ever get landed (as White's one-in-four experience shows). But being frustrated is part of all pursuits, financial, sexual, or whatever. Insist on your passion being requited at all costs, and that is probably what you'll get—all costs.

11. THE FOUR MILLIONAIRES OF CALIFORNIA

Four young West Coast millionaires made their piles in four apparently very different ways:

◊ One, a hang-glider ace himself, had gone into making and selling the gliders.

◊ Another had become the largest packager of herbal teas in the entire U.S.

◊ The third was the inventor of the Dolby method for suppressing unwanted noise on sound reproduction systems.

◊ The fourth had begun by repairing tennis and other athletic shoes, and now made them as well.

In fact, the four had one highest common factor of critical importance. They had each identified a new trend in leisure or other life-style activities and had concentrated on serving these trendy new markets with their needs.

In this, they followed the same growth path as Mohan Murjani, an Indian citizen based in Hong Kong, where in the mid-1970s the family made clothing, bicycles, toys, and electronic gadgets. Dropping in on Bloomingdale's on a visit to New York, Murjani discussed with an associate how to get the firm's goods out of the bins and into the windows. How about clothes with the name of a famous designer—Yves St. Laurent, say?

When the latter showed no interest, Murjani had other celebrities researched. Eureka! The answer was heiress Gloria Vanderbilt. With the rich and famous celebrity showing off the stretch denim trousers (and her own middle-aged slimness) on TV, the product bearing her name took off. Within four years, sales had topped the ten million mark, and the Murjani fortune was also measured in the millions. And that's how one nowhere company rode to fame and fortune on the designer-jeans boom.

12.   THREE A'S OF EXPANSION

Tomorrow's millionaires will probably find their magic markets in the same way. Usually the growth path leads from some activity in which the future titan is already interested or established. Thus, the Hong Kong clothing manufacturer sees that jeans are big and lasting sellers—and cleverly finds his own way onto the bandwagon. Sometimes (though rarely), it happens the other way around: by deliberate, random choice among all the infinite possibilities the worlds of taste, technology, and turnover have to offer.

There's no shortage of forecasts for searchers after loot. For instance, according to one Cleveland-based business information and market research firm, Predicasts, home video cameras, solar collectors, waterbeds, and rug fresheners rank high among products which will "achieve spectacular growth over the next several years." Home video cameras markets were expected to grow by 65 percent a year in sales in 1982; solar collectors in use will "increase by an average of 30 percent per year over the next dozen years"; sales of waterbeds would be 35 percent higher in a year than they were right now; and rug freshener sales would double.

There's no surprise in the overall Predicasts finding that computer and other electronics-related industries still offer the greatest opportunities, especially in such areas as desktop computer systems (34 percent p.a.), communicating word processors (41 percent p.a.), automated office equipment (41 percent p.a. for personal business terminals), electronic games (24 percent p.a., including video), telephone management systems . . . and so on.

Most of these, of course, aren't products you can start making in the twinkling of an eye; nor are such other favored products as carbonless paper, thermoplastic rubbers, synthetic engine oils, enhanced oil recovery chemicals, industrial robots, high-speed facsimile equipment, or industrial excimer lasers (whatever they are). But note the common theme: technology.

In today's markets, research and development are more important than ever. In some cases you can't even get in without high technological know-how. In others you'll never keep abreast of the competition unless you can inject technological sophistication.

This is one investment in the future not even a retailer can afford to miss—spending money to ensure that he stays in the right markets with the right offerings. That doesn't only mean spending money on forecasts, because the essence of forecasts is to be wrong, in part, and to miss some trends while spotting others. Many a product now blushing unseen will beat those named above to the punch. No—you spend money to ensure (a) that, even if you spot them late, you note all significant and interesting trends as soon as possible; and (b) that you can exploit to the full any opportunities that they offer.

That really encapsulates the whole process of growth. Opportunities and Exploitation are the twin names of the game: deciding on a site for your business mansion, and then building, extending, and developing the estate until it has reached the limits of its potential. Only a minority, by definition, have the imagination to spot the creative opportunity that makes millionaires. But the majority can at least nurture one indispensable trait—enough imagination to stop the automatic "No."

It's a notorious fact that some of the world's richest commercial seams were hawked around unsuccessfully (like xerography) before anybody saw the light. But the number of wrong initiatives rejected inside companies is literally numberless. Sure, most ideas deserve their fate. But any company built on the concept that anything new "will never work" will never be built very high. The eternal vigilance that is the only safeguard demands taking all opportunities and threats seriously.

The search for growth has two parts: internal and external. Internally, the existing business should throw up ideas for new or extension businesses that build on the company's strengths and develop new ones (the surest way to grow backward is to forget that the base business must continue to receive every bit as much attention as in the past). Externally, you watch developments in your own or associated markets, plus developments or trends in the whole environment, as economies and life-styles evolve.

Like the Predicasts numbers quoted earlier, forecasts of such trends can be quite precise and more or less obvious. Thus nobody would be surprised to hear that the following will see strong or fast growth in the years ahead: wine and spirits (particularly wine), electronic equipment (both at home and at work), leisure activities (hobbies, collecting, reading, music-making, health and beauty, gifts, foreign holidays, eating out), plus telephones and office equipment.

Mostly such predictions extrapolate what has happened in the past, as do the following:

Using the home as a leisure center, reduction of housework, home health checks, lighting and color, security systems, hobby education, do-it-yourself, more sport, using a "more savory palate," a more varied diet, foreign travel, a second holiday away, increased craft work, shorter working hours (but more shift work), more moonlighting, six weeks' holiday, better working conditions, the robot factory, worker education and retraining, moving away from cities, improved public transport, etc., etc.

Every single one of these areas is currently generating business growth for somebody, somewhere. But those who've seized the chance, like the four millionaires of California, have found their own angles—ones that are perfectly logical in hindsight, but which occurred only to them. For instance, would you have been convinced that there was enough growth and money in hang-gliding, or herbal teas, or noise suppression on cassette players, or repairing athletic shoes? Easy enough to spot the booms in sport, health foods, or audio, but harder by far to find the angle.

In the consumer markets of the future, built on desire rather than need, the angle will be all-important; in the industrial markets of the future, built on the urgencies of competition, lowering costs and improving performance will be the areas of growth. Those who reap the biggest harvest will be personally involved up to their ears, and they won't be diverted from their main path.

The tale is told elsewhere in this book of the Dirty Dozen firms who did everything wrong, while only the Wise Little Pig manager did everything right in pursuit of his ambition to have the biggest and best tool-making shop around. So what happened in the worst recession in postwar history?

Despite their aging equipment, poor marketing, and low efficiency, the Dirty Dozen, when it came to the crunch, worked harder, scurried around—and stayed in business. The Wise Little Pig made a bad mistake: he strayed from his chosen path to take on component work for aero engines, which demanded heavy investment, but, because of technical problems, generated only a few thousand bucks of turnover in nine months. The owner sold out to a new majority shareholder (a man in his seventies) at a time when the turnover, which had never exceeded $1.5 million, was sharply down. You need the three A's—not just Angle, but Application and Acumen as well—to stay on the royal road of expansion.

13. THE COMPONENTS THAT WERE TOO LARGE

You also need the Big C—customers. In a deeply troubled industry nobody was making any profits—indeed, nearly everybody was losing money in buckets. As usual in those circumstances, the afflicted managers were being urged to market their way out of their troubles. One of them, though, retorted that it was impossible to market in his business—and he had a sad case history to prove the impossibility.

His predecessor as boss had spent some years, and hundreds of thousands of dollars, on perfecting a piece of technology. As a result the firm could produce components far larger than anybody else could manufacture. The only trouble was that nobody seemed to want components of this enormous size. The company did think of one use itself, and put the resulting, unique product on the market. In a whole year, it had sold precisely none of the offending articles.

The new boss went on to explain that he had even hired a marketing expert to come up with ideas for uses for the new technology. "He's been working away for twelve months," said the afflicted manager, "and he still hasn't come up with a single idea. So you see how difficult marketing is in this industry!"

14. WHEN MARKETING IS BUNK

Marketing is as difficult, or as easy, as you make it. A leading figure in the marketing game was touring industry to diagnose its health. In one sick region, he found, praise be, a successful businessman, whose company was actually thriving—but who strongly expressed his belief that marketing (as Henry Ford said about history) is bunk. "I'll tell you what I do," he said. "I find out what the customers want, I give it to them, and I follow up with excellent after-sales service—and that's why I'm successful. So don't give me any of that bull about marketing."

The real nonsense in marketing is to preach it, but to practice something completely different: like not finding out what the customer wants, which is standard malpractice (as in the case of the overlarge and unsalable components). Finding out is easy enough in principle: you ask. Some managers are put off because this simple principle is called "market research," for which some tricky professional expertise is required. It would be no more logical to shun computers because their components carry esoteric names and employ technologies far beyond the normal managerial comprehension.

Expert research can find out, not only *what* customers are buying, *how* and *why*, but what *price* they are prepared to pay. Using a technique called the "buy response," in which customers are asked whether they would or wouldn't buy at various prices, provides a piece of information vital for both marketing and profit—the price above which people's readiness to buy is likely to fall off.

An expert in pricing research, Peter Kraushar, tells how one managing director "kept on increasing the price of a well-known product which didn't have much direct competition. The sales effect was small, but everyone else was terrified that such a policy might eventually kill the product. Research showed that the product was still price-insensitive and so could stand still more price increases—within reason. The managing director continued his policy, and sales volume of the product concerned has remained steady since, despite the forebodings."

Another much less happy example is that of a new drink which (like the overlarge components) had taken years to develop. Research had been done among consumers, and they liked its taste. The company's managers had the sense to worry about price, and research showed that, however much consumers liked the product, they wouldn't pay the price that the company needed. It didn't, alas, have the sense to heed the research. The product was launched twice, "and each time," writes Kraushar, "it had to be withdrawn ... just as the research predicted, because of the price."

Note that the company did realize (uselessly) that knowing the consumer tastes isn't enough. While it is theoretically possible to know too much about a product, new or old, or about its market, in practice a great deal of valuable information is not obtained—and sometimes not even sought. And as in the drink case, still worse, information is often ignored because it's unpalatable. The news you like least is the *last* news you should ignore.

It's no use, for instance, trying to establish a valued difference in the marketplace if customers don't actually think your offer is anything special. Another writer, Alan Melkman, regards a policy of *"Differentiate or die"* as having "inescapable logic" in the current phase of business. His other five marketing musts are *dominate the market and keep it; relentless pursuit of the basic strategy; carry out ruthless analysis to increase marketing productivity; take tactical initiatives; systematically adopt new marketing aids and techniques.* All six musts hinge on the accurate compiling and analysis of market information.

As Melkman notes, a "competitor comparison survey" can show you what matters to customers, when thinking about buying a particular product or service. Once you know "how each of the main competitors rates in the customer's eyes against each of the criteria ... only a small step is needed for a company to identify the elements of its product service package on which it must concentrate."

Any aspect of the marketing mix can provide the vital advantage. Where a Neiman Marcus concentrates on high quality combined with superb retail service, a McDonald's depends for its burger bonanzas on the consumer appeal of what was originally a new, unique, and economic way of eating out. Where Beecham's has based its marketing success on very strong branding (the key, for instance, to U.S. breakthroughs with two toothpastes, first Macleans, then Aquafresh), Laker Airways (in the brief heyday before disaster) broke through on the Atlantic route with aggressive pricing. And Melkman is certainly right in attributing much of Ford's success in Europe to its tight control over distribution channels.

Whatever the strategy, the success of its application depends on the information at hand and how it is used. Look at the buying process in depth and you can identify what the best level, type, and frequency of contact are—from the customers' point of view, naturally. The discovery can pay handsome marketing dividends. For example, one office supplies business stopped operating a very expensive field sales force and replaced it with carefully trained, well-motivated, and tightly controlled people selling by telephone. Result? Much lower selling costs, a zero loss in sales in the short term, and a fatter turnover in the longer term.

It all comes back to the same three points. (1) You find out what the customers want; (2) you give it to them; and (3) you follow up with excellent after-sales service—just like the man who thought that marketing is bunk. There's only one thing he forgot (because, no doubt, he took it for granted)—you do it all at a profit.

15. THE CATERPILLAR'S COST

The higher the price, other things being equal, the higher that profit will be. Marketing guru Philip Kotler uses Caterpillar, the great manufacturer of earthmovers, as his example of exploiting how customers view the product—by using that "perceived value" to set a better price on the product. Caterpillar aims to outsell the competition even though a competitor's similar machine might be priced, say, at $20,000 instead of Caterpillar's $24,000. When a prospective customer asks a Caterpillar dealer why he should pay $4,000 more for the latter's love object, the dealer answers:

$20,000	is the tractor's price if it were equivalent to the competitor's tractor
$3,000	is the price premium for superior durability
$2,000	is the price premium for superior reliability
$2,000	is the price premium for superior service
$1,000	is the price premium for the longer parts warranty
$28,000	is the price to cover the value package
− $4,000	discount
$24,000	final price

The stunned customer is supposed to learn that, although he is being asked to cough up $4,000 more for the Caterpillar tractor, he is actually getting a $4,000 discount. So he ends up choosing the Caterpillar tractor, convinced that the lifetime operating costs of the Caterpillar deal will be smaller—and never mind the four thousand initial bucks.

16. VALUES OF PERCEPTION

In sophisticated companies of Caterpillar's ilk, decisions on vital matters like price aren't left to haphazard emotion. The decisions are taken in the context of full knowlege about the customer, including:

1. *Penetration:* the number of customers who buy from your company expressed as a percentage of all customers.

2. *Loyalty:* the purchases from the company by its customers expressed as a percentage of their total purchases from all suppliers of the same products.

3. *Selectivity:* the size of the average customer purchase from the company expressed as a percentage of the size of the average customer purchase from an average company.

The wise company also wants to know about the "price selectivity" of the market—meaning the average price charged by the company expressed as a percentage of the average price charged by all companies. The effort required to find all that information isn't merely worthwhile, it's indispensable. The customers and their perceptions, whether the supplier agrees with them or not, make the market—and influence others. Accordingly, if you're doing badly, the customers *must* perceive you in an unfavorable light, and there *must* be a reason for that.

The right place to discover that reason (as you must) is with the customer, and that answer may well not lie at the opposite end, that of the technology. Rolls-Royce cars, for instance, have commanded a premium price for decades without, in the more recent ones, commanding a reputation for pioneering automotive technology. In computers, some of the giant companies that took on the thankless task of competing with IBM fell right into the technological trap. They poured investment into trying to steal a technological jump on the master, and some even succeeded. But it did them no good at all in the marketplace.

IBM continued to be perceived as *the* computer company—the automatic first thought when it came to business systems. Being perceived better is also the key to being dearer and more profitable, that is, being able to command better prices in the market. Using a typical business profile, you can show that, if a 5 percent rise in volume with no price increase bumps up profits by $30,000 on a $70,-000 base, a 5 percent increase overall in price *by better segmentation* plus a 5 percent increase in volume by better selling will more than double profit to $155,000.

The better segmentation and better selling are closely linked. It's the special expertise and reputation in a closely targeted, differentiated product line that gives power (as in the Caterpillar case) to the salesman's elbow, and force to his price quotations. The more differentiated the product, the less likely it is to suffer from direct price competition. But what if it does? What do you do?

Only in the last resort (which means *in extremis*) do you sacrifice the image—the idea of difference and value—which you have so painstakingly achieved. You *don't* cut prices automatically (especially since, to use the same example, a 5 percent price cut with no rise in volume will kill stone-dead $50,000 of your $70,000 profits). You react along the lines recommended by André Gabor in *Pricing: Principles and Practices.* When a competitor's price is cut you put the following questions to yourself:

1. Ask: Is it likely to be a permanent drop? If *no,* you hold your price at its present level and keep on watching the competitive prices.

2. If *yes,* ask: Is the drop likely to have a significant effect on my sales? If *no,* proceed as in (1) above.

3. If *yes,* ask: Would a permanent reduction of *my* price damage *my* image? If the answer is *no,* drop the price to the competitor's level or to your limit, whichever is higher.

4. If *yes,* ask: How much has the price dropped?
   (a) If it's 1–5 percent, run temporary price deals.
   (b) From 5.1–8 percent, introduce self-liquidating promotions (like offering some bargain, say a kitchen gadget, for six package tops and 25 cents: the cash payment plus the profit attributed to the extra sales should cover the whole cost).
   (c) If the price has dropped by 8.1–10 percent, design a limited advertising campaign.
   (d) And if it's over 10 percent, ask: Is the product important enough in terms of profit to support a major revamp of packaging, advertising, etc.?

5. If the answer to 4(d) is *yes,* you design a new treatment accordingly. If *no,* consider "milking" the product, stopping all adver-

tising and other promotion, and letting the thing linger on, perhaps at a reduced price.

The above five points refer to fast-moving consumer goods, but the principles apply generally. It may, for instance, be worth revamping the product, not just its promotion, to restore the vital difference that will protect its prices and profitability. If the goodie arrives at the milking stage, though, the game is over. The product is a commodity, all difference and passion spent, and sooner or later Gabor's final advice will come into play: "you must always check up with one last question; has my reaction been effective? If *not*, consider other alternatives, including dropping the product altogether." *Vive la difference,* indeed—because, in the final analysis, *la difference, c'est la vie.*

To summarize some of the important points I've mentioned in Step Five:

1. Remember those six lessons from Japan: (a) maximize current overall returns on sales; (b) use short-term profits to finance long-term strengthening of the business; (c) build decision-making around strong central leadership; (d) make getting the best out of people, and doing the best for them, a central preoccupation, (e) get all production, etc. processes to maximum efficiency; (f) make beating the competition a constant objective.

2. Practice the OMMIT principles: define business Objectives, identify Market opportunities, understand and use Money, maintain good Information systems, and operate as a Team.

3. Use a high retained cash flow to fuel the growth of the business to critical mass—meaning a viable size in its chosen market.

4. Aim for the lowest cost of supply and the highest differentiation from other suppliers.

5. Make sure you have all you need for growth before going for it. Then go for the biggest possible market share—and back new ventures only if share is rising.

6. Buy other businesses only cheaply—and only after exercising

the utmost care, ensuring that, even if the worst comes to the worst with the buy, you can stand the strain.

7. If entering a new market, find the new angle that will provide your venture with the critical advantage.

8. Find out what the customers want, give it to them, and follow up with excellent after-sales service—all at a profit.

9. Aim for the best perception in the market, so that you win the best price.

Step Six: How to Control Your Own Destiny

1. THE TURNAROUNDS THAT TURNED

The belief that you can control your own destiny is never more valuable than when fate seems to have turned against you and the organization. Time and again, in corporate turnarounds, the Supermanager demonstrates that the insoluble can be solved, the incurable cured, and the irremediable remedied. Such men have proved that fate can be countermanded in the U.S. and Britain, Germany, and France—and in Japan.

Canon, for an outstanding example, looked down and out when Ryusaburo Kaku took charge of a lagging camera firm that was still licking its wounds from the price war in calculators. Kaku re-established Canon's leadership in photography with a flood of innovations, becoming the first of the top-of-the-market single-lens-reflex makers to launch snap cameras, and also broke very successfully into plain paper copiers. The key, according to McKinsey man Kenichi Ohmae, is Kaku's often-used word "first-class," i.e., he demands (and gets) superb performance.

Another Japanese turnaround case is Toshiba, whose performance looked anything but first-class in comparison to Hitachi until 1976. Then Takeo Iwata took over. He (1) disposed of businesses that were going nowhere, (2) pulled money-losers around into profit, and (3) stressed profit as a major theme throughout the corporation. Within four years, operating profitability at 9.4 percent was clearly ahead of Hitachi's 8.1 percent.

But one man or one firm's competitive success is another firm's headache—and maybe its disaster. Thus, Japanese competition, from none other than Hitachi, Toshiba, etc., has struck with such great force in consumer electronics that few Western makers have been left to face the onslaught in hi-fi and radio—and even television has seen massive inroads from the East. One small firm in audio, family-controlled and modest in size, duly slumped into a $4 million loss as what its boss called "a bloodbath" of a market drenched the accounts in red.

The family had kept the business alive by concentrating especially on hi-fi "music centers," complete with turntable, cassette deck, radio, and speakers. The music-center market fell away as Japanese imports flooded in and prices collapsed; the firm was left stranded with huge stocks and no hope—not in audio equipment, anyway. As one executive put it, "We were caught in this trap. We had to get out of it with something new." His chairman expressed it another way: "What do you do to get out of recession? You either sink or plug the gap."

What they found as a plug sounded bizarre: they went into television, a market the company had quit years before. In the teeth of Japanese market domination, the company got out its first black-and-white portable, from design to launch, in a few months, and then developed its first color set in only ten months. Unlike Toshiba, it didn't have four years to spare. Both products gave an instant boost to the company's fortunes and pulled it into the black. But if the TV decision succeeds long-term, it won't be because of the wisdom of that decision alone. It will be because of the basic strengths on which the self-helpers could call in their hour of desperate need.

The strengths included ultraquick response to market changes, low overheads, obsession with production, high flexibility, and (above all) true grit. As the self-helper-in-chief once growled, "We're not going to crawl under a stone and die." Those who crawl, whether they're as big as Canon or as small as the family with true grit, aren't killed—they kill themselves.

2. THOSE WHO HELP THEMSELVES

Whoever, back in the mists of time, observed that God helps those who help themselves should have patented the observation. It must have been repeated a million times—which doesn't make it any less true. For a manager, the unkindest act of God must be a recession. Nothing within his individual power could have averted the evil hour, and nothing can prevent economic downturns like those of the Sick Seventies or Anxious Eighties from striking every business in the land with the commercial equivalent of the bubonic plague.

The unfairness and horror of it all must be compounded if you've been zipping along for years at a seemingly unstoppable pace. But the worst possible response is to wring the managerial hands. Far better to set them, and the mind which activates them, to work. For an incisive example of self-help in these circumstances, consider the case of a young Supermanager, still in his early thirties when this saga began, who had known nothing but growth in his career. His turnover had in three successive years chalked up the following remarkable progression: $9.75 million, $17.5 million, and $27 million. Then came recession, the worst to afflict the West since the Great Slump.

The Supermanager's first mental response was to look long, hard, and realistically at the economic environment. Of the adverbs in the previous sentence, "realistically" is the key word. Self-deception is the sin no manager can afford even in good times; in bad ones, the vice can be lethal. Look how and where he could, this wallpaper boss could see no lightening of the gloom in the economy at large or in his particular sector of consumer goods. He also identified factors in the international economy which, in his view, made his gloomy conclusions logical.

Now, it's not necessary for every manager to turn himself into an economic forecaster—there are too many of those around as it is. But an informed and impartial idea of the context in which you have to operate must be the starting point for any intelligent plans. Indeed, that's how the superplanners in megacompanies start, with an economic overview. The conclusions for this particular business became obvious:

1. Accept that lower growth will arise this year.
2. Accept that there will be few growth markets.

At that point it might sound as if he was throwing in the towel. Even though the success of the past had been won against the background of a decline in overall sales in the market, the impact of the firm on its competitors meant that it had less and less opportunity to expand its share at their expense; to put it another way, the larger your share of any market, the less your scope for enlarging that share.

If realism produces this kind of prognosis, there's only one possible response: retrench, and fast. "Reassess cash-intensive plans" is how the Supermanager put it. The economy drive that a firm customarily calls for in times of stress should be primarily aimed, not at protecting profits, but at preserving liquidity—or cash. The company was building inventory to support the launch of its new product line with an announced policy of 100 percent stock availability and a rapid replenishment service for the retailers. To cut the borrowings that financed the stock, the Supermanager cut production—halving stock levels within three months, and doing so even though he knew that actual retail sales were running well above the previous year.

Retrenchment alone is not enough. The other side of the self-help coin is income: cut your costs while raising income, and recession can be surmounted. The business was facing a tough time in overseas markets because of the strength of the currency. It didn't withdraw—*it sold harder.* Three additional area managers were hired to promote the overseas selling effort as part of this new, more aggressive stance. The logic is self-evident. The export markets, despite the difficulty, offered more scope than the domestic ones, primarily because the existing presence abroad was relatively minute.

Nor was that the only positive response. The CEO recognized that "high growth will come only from diversification or market extension." Widening and developing the product range is the only answer if you're seeking real expansion in static markets, which for this company meant taking a sideways step into the equally depressed textile market, where the company could hope to repeat its favorite trick of expanding market share rapidly from a small, indeed tiny, base. But at any time (and remember that recession compounds all risks) the diversifier must never take his eyes off the main business; even the general rule, that the king-sized leader in the market is in the strongest position to survive, won't remain valid without continual care and feeding.

After three years, the company could realistically claim to have won the lead in terms of product, quality, service, and creativity, having reinforced the lot by heavy investment and constant reorganization over its short life. If you can bring your business out of recession with the best designs and most modern machinery—fitter, stronger, and healthier than the competition—then recession will have been deeply profitable.

Not that it's ever fun. As the man said, "Recession is a bitter pill to swallow and provides a meager diet for growth." But never mix gloom with doom. As he went on to abjure everybody (and, above all, himself) in tones which strike exactly the right note of defiance, "if recession is a meager diet, we won't just survive on it, we aim to thrive on it."

3. TEN TERRIBLE SINS

But what do you do, in or out of recession, in the following nonthriving situation? You're sent in to correct the Ten Terrible Sins of a self-supporting independent division of a company with 750 employees. This is what's wrong:

1. A particularly difficult, long-running industrial relations mess.

2. Not enough output to meet customer delivery requirements.

3. Not enough profit to give an acceptable return on capital employed.

4. No suitable general manager.

Your first step is to identify the underlying problems (the overlying ones being bad enough), which in the case in question turn out to be, in short, that. . . .

5. Nobody at senior management level relates customer orders and priorities to shop-floor capacity.

6. Control has been lost over stock and materials; hence the classic combination of excessive and obsolete stocks of components, finished products, and work in progress, together with shortages and incomplete orders that can't be delivered.

7. Design standards and tolerances don't match the production facilities.

8. Shop-floor operators refuse to complete any returns on quantities produced or times taken, so you have no accurate data available either on historical or standard costs.

9. There are some two thousand products—many of which are called for in various combinations to be fitted to any of the one hundred core products.

10. Lack of product control through R&D and marketing means that obsolete products are still being produced as special orders.

As if that wasn't enough? Oh—not surprisingly, management morale is at a low ebb, employees are completely demoralized, and militant union guys have filled the power vacuum—they have shop-floor control, and middle management doesn't. The top management, naturally and stupidly enough, has blamed all the problems on bad industrial relations.

So what do you do? (Running away isn't allowed.)

4. WHAT THE DOCTOR DID

In any mess of the dimensions just recorded, you haven't the time to sit there—you must do something, and very fast. The Case of the Ten Terrible Sins was reported by James G. Keir, who describes how an expert in curing rampant corporate diseases—a company doctor—went about his healing work. Since speed is of the essence, the management medico always starts with the elementary and the obvious. At the particular sickbed that meant:

1. Checking stock and work-in-progress.
2. Determining customer priorities and relating them to available stocks.
3. Putting an embargo on all production and purchases, except stuff required within the next month.
4. Making a task force set about correcting all parts and materials lists *for the products/components in greatest demand.*
5. Holding frequent meetings, formal and informal, with middle and senior managers and employee representatives—not only telling them what's being done, but getting their ideas and full involvement.

Keir adds that it is most important to ensure that the normal working disciplines are gradually reintroduced, however much opposition you encounter.

These five steps must be followed up by rapid, ruthless reform of the setup. Seven of the top management people who blamed labor relations for their own shortcomings went; that still left five to hold the fort. The lunatic product range was also rationalized. Marketing, R & D, and production had their heads knocked together. All employees would receive their reward, not in heaven, but in hard cash, as production and productivity increased and costs were brought under control.

As for the side effects of this drastic treatment, while some senior managers went, others were demoted. Two token half-day strikes culminated in a four-week stoppage when the men were told that additional wages had to be earned before they would be paid. After that, the majority, silent or otherwise, accepted that management intended to manage (though with more consultation than ever before)—to manage, that is, after deciding and stating clearly what they were going to do, and then doing it. From sales of $9 million in 1977, output rose to $22.5 million in 1980, at which point the potential for further expansion, but without further capital investment, was $30 million.

Company doctors can work such miracle cures, not because they are miracle men, but because the diseases of very sick companies, unlike those of very sick people, follow similar courses—even though the causes of infection are as different in kind as botulism and sleeping sickness.

For another Keir instance, take a private company with 150 people working in three different operations: electrical control systems, heating and ventilation design and fabrication, and subcontract machining and fitting. The owner who had built up these businesses had an autocratic approach and found it difficult to confide in and delegate to his senior managers. When the owner had two serious illnesses, his subordinates couldn't cope, and the company suffered heavy losses.

The five faults diagnosed by the doctor all have their counterparts in the Ten Terrible Sins:

1. Low caliber of management.
2. Fragmented control.
3. Decision-making, even about trivia, was heavily centralized.
4. Aging machine tools and other equipment.

5. All of which meant low productivity, late deliveries, lost customers, and a whopping bank overdraft.

Once again, the company doctor followed the first principle: apply the elementary, straightforward management disciplines fast. He analyzed the outstanding orders; introduced rudimentary procedures for shop-loading and control; raised productivity by planning the sequence in which work was carried out; installed an incentive scheme; got the bank overdraft extended (by showing off the new, improved facts and figures)—and after all that, he was able to complete the cure by more elaborate efforts.

He strengthened the sales side, contacted current and lost customers, developed a product that was exclusive to the company, trained management in relevant techniques, and improved the setup—all with delegation of decision-making to lower levels of management. The company returned to profits, and stopped losing its skilled operators.

The obvious lesson to draw from these cases is that company doctors can be good medicine if you have a business that has been allowed to deteriorate into disease. But prevention is vastly superior to cure. Every manager should be his own company doctor, mastering the basic, well-known principles of management, and insisting, via the well-known ways, that they be applied. As Keir says, too many managers, when faced with problems that are new to them, try to reinvent the wheel. Often, they design it square.

Constantly putting out fires and attending to details take managers' eyes off the necessity to think through and decide on the company objectives. In this formless, frantic state, they also lose sight of the fact that operators and middle management may know some of the answers. But nobody asks these people the questions, so the answers go begging, when improved consultation and communication could easily tap the latent knowledge.

In both the cases described by Keir, the company doctor was required to inject, not just the specific skills, but the will to make the company work. Even where the will exists in abundance, you may still need the medicine man—because value-added incentive schemes, or shop-loading and inventory control, or employee communication, may not be the strong points of anybody on hand. It's an observed fact (or at least an article of faith) among consultants that the more expert and professional a manager is, the readier he will be to seek outside advice and assistance. What's more, the better the management, the more successful that help will usually be.

5. THE CONSULTANT'S CASEBOOK

The kind of management that doesn't call for help when needed is either (a) dumb or (b) conceited—usually because it thinks it's done pretty well already. Maybe it can look back, like one electrical equipment firm, at a rise in productivity of over 17 percent in three years after some fairly heavy treatment. The management had mechanized some labor-intensive operations, it introduced computer systems into engineering-related functions, it reduced overall material costs, and it upgraded its quality assurance program.

Good enough, you might think. But you'd be wrong. Consultants found that the management had allowed several mistakes to be made.

1.   It didn't recognize that its two separate product lines, one selling on quality, one on cost, had quite separate needs.

2.   Its engineers paid scant attention to manufacturing costs, materials, and equipment utilization, or the products of competitors.

3.   It couldn't get the worker contribution it wanted because employees feared they would lose their jobs if they improved productivity.

4.   It didn't involve staff functions in the effort to get productivity on the line.

Take another case—that of a large consumer durables maker who had a traditional assembly-line approach to production, based on the usual low-skill, highly specialized, repetitive jobs. This worked fine, except for one thing. The workers didn't like their jobs and stayed in them, on average, less than six months. When a high rate of turnover is combined with low morale and chronic absenteeism, a big boost in the number (and expense) of production defects is bound to follow. An extensive repair effort, which needed quality engineers, materials handlers, and schedulers, salvaged most of these defects; but at any one time almost a third of the units were being recycled and reworked.

It was another case where the corporate management could see the trees, but needed consultants to help it see the wood. The examples come from the casebook of consultant Arnold S. Judson, of the Judson-Gray outfit in Boston. They show precisely where the outside eye can look beyond the trees, which is one of the crucial approaches to raising productivity, just as keeping your efforts too narrow—concentrating on cost savings in one or another part of a company (usually in manufacturing) rather than throughout the company as a whole—is the death of productivity programs.

The consultant described in the *Harvard Business Review* what happened after the two managements above had seen the light and the overall view. The electrical equipment firm (1) treated the two product lines separately; (2) involved production managers at the earliest states of the engineering work; (3) got marketing and manufacturing to work together to develop export opportunities. This last change, in turn, paved the way for a joint strategy to control sales growth and capitalize on economies of scale with longer production runs—and it stabilized employment. With the job fears removed, the workers really played ball. Overall, the new organization-wide approach, with careful follow-up, yielded productivity gains almost double those achieved in the past.

As for the consumer durables business, it abandoned its attempts to raise productivity by orthodox methods. Instead, it set up a management/employee council with an agenda of some two hundred conditions or practices that needed to be changed. That was the basis for alternative manufacturing plans—and the plan that the council ended up by accepting involved small, autonomous, and partly self-managed work groups.

The council established a pilot operation to test and evaluate these new work-design options. Two of them proved especially successful. When put in place after some two years of effort, they achieved overall productivity gains of from 40 percent to 50 percent.

Note how the improvement was won: half from more efficient assembly, and half from lower overheads. A third of the gross savings, not so incidentally, went back to the workers. Ineffective management had become Supermanagement—by inside effort with outside help.

6. PHYSICIANS, HEAL THE OTHERS

You wouldn't believe that outsiders could help if you believed this about consultants: "They waste time, cost money, demoralize and distract your best people and don't solve problems. They are the people who borrow your watch to tell you what time it is and then walk off with it." That's Robert Townsend's celebrated gibe against the management consultant in *Up the Organization*. Perhaps it shouldn't be taken too seriously. But the following *cri de coeur* from a company boss does support the charge.

On the record, he told a reporter, "Both their impartiality and expertise were very useful." Off the record, the same man had this to say: "We paid them $50,000 and wasted a further $100,000 in lost management time. They prepared a report, and then, when asked to refine it, applied a totally different judgmental basis. It was an expensive, protracted, and very frustrating exercise."

In another case, though, an international construction company, about as lackluster as any builder could be, with a miserable 5 percent return on capital employed, called in the McKinsey consultants. The changes which followed included:

1. Bringing forward a younger generation of management.
2. Changing the company from a functional structure—with building and civil engineering as separate entities—into a geographical one.
3. Setting more demanding targets.
4. Cutting back overstaffed departments.
5. Centralizing in some cases—bringing control over types

and prices of domestic contracts back to the center, but decentralizing far down the line in other, international cases.

The changes took effect just in time for the group to seize some sweet opportunities in the oil-rich Middle East, Australia, and the U.S. As the rich chances were taken, revenue rose in nine years by some 350 percent. But that was nothing compared to the surge in profits: up 31.5 times before tax, and 27.5 times after. As an executive remarked, "It probably didn't matter much exactly how management was restructured—the important thing was that the reorganization (and the consultants) administered a salutary jolt."

Any earnest explorer after consultancy truth can find plenty of similar sob—and success—stories. What do they all prove? All management consultants are not good, and neither is all the work done, even by the better ones. In that, consultancy is no different from any other human endeavor. It must run the gamut of performance from mediocre or worse to excellent—and the responsibility doesn't lie entirely with the consultant.

As another boss said, "You've got to be prepared to spend time with consultants—to brief them properly, and to make sure that the chemistry is right between them and your staff. And you've got to keep control—monitor the operation regularly to keep tabs on the progress." In other words, employing a consultant encapsulates the management process itself—briefing, human relations, control, and monitoring.

Spelling this out, author Rosemary Brown notes that anybody using a consultant for any purpose will have different aspirations from anybody else, but the golden rules of the collective wisdom on the subject are nevertheless general—and sound.

1. Decide what you want.

2. Tell the consultant what you want precisely and completely—and make sure he understands.

3. Take time and trouble to tell your own people what the consultants are up to and why. It will help in winning their keen co-operation.

4. Insist on regular meetings with the consultants to monitor progress.

5. Make sure that the consultants are fully involved in implementing their recommendations.

6. Don't be afraid to call an immediate and early halt if (a) you don't like the work being done or (b) you don't think you can live with their recommendations.

Because of the infinite variety of purposes to which consultants can be applied, the rules are made to be honored in the breach—as long as you know exactly why you're breaking them. For instance, if the consultant is being used for a specific expert purpose, it makes absolutely no sense to argue against his expertise—unless he's no good, in which case you shouldn't have hired him in the first place.

The error is often seen in advertising (ad agencies being the highest paid form of consultant by far). Because this is an area in which any fool can express an opinion, any fool does. If he is a powerful fool, the interference can ruin an expensive campaign. Advertising men do know more about advertising than their clients—as you would only expect. But, because agents like to eat, they will by and large go along with their clients' mad mistakes. Most consultants, if the choice lies between losing the job or losing a debate with the client over what should be done, will take the latter course.

In that knowledge, the wise customer checks and double-checks to make sure that the consultants aren't merely saying what they think he wants to hear, which would negate the whole point of hiring or hearing them. You want consultants to say what you don't truly want to hear, but always know to be true—that some part of the operation is a shambles. If, to take one example from real life, you're losing $550,000 a year on building fire engines, you desperately want the consultants to point to your defects of production and product control—and fix them. Within nine months of the management fire brigade going into that operation, it was breaking even, thanks to the fixing.

Needing help, or calling for it, are nothing to be ashamed of or surprised about. Another writer, Hugh O'Neill, tells of a management consultancy that discovered this truth the hard way, by its own experience. In the course of a complete audit of the consultancy's operations (it wanted to protect its income in the recession), one of its own computer consultants found that, over the years, as the payroll and accounts had been computerized, systems had evolved or been produced singly; that computerization had not led to any reduction in staff; that, furthermore, the staff used the machine for everything from desk-top calculations to handling complex simulation models on capital appraisal assignments. With this can of worms revealed, the analyst was assigned to the problem full-time for seven weeks. Major savings resulted.

The audit concept is one which can open many a can of worms. Here are some blunt questions that go to the heart of the faults found by auditing consultants in many companies.

1. Has the management thought out what needs to be done if targets are to be achieved? *Are* there any targets?

2. Does it have any real idea of the problems with which employees down the line are struggling?

3. Does it know how much the problems that are being "lived with" are costing?

4. Does it relate production and other problems to business results, and is it prepared to make the necessary investment in solving problems?

5. Is it more concerned with fire fighting than with fire prevention?

6. Has it learned to live with high costs and low productivity by waiting for problems to occur and then buying its way out?

7. Is it always taken by surprise when a new difficulty or unexpected (though quite predictable) problem occurs?

These are such uncomfortable questions that many managers are incapable of answering them honestly. But there's an eighth question. Would the management prefer to continue operating inefficiently rather than admit to shortcomings and get them corrected—by outsiders if necessary? If the answer is "No," the company certainly won't make good use of consultants. But it won't do much else right, either.

7. THE MAN WITH FOUR QUESTIONS

Knowledge is control of your fate; ignorance is helplessness. But the best knowledge is the simplest. Thus, one of the most successful practitioners of management science in the U.S., named Oliver Wright, is the high priest of a discipline known as "Material Requirements Planning"—a technique designed for the very important task of keeping stocks (and thus the cash tied up therein) as low as possible without hampering the smooth operations of the factory. Naturally, MRP is usually applied with the aid of a computer. Yet Wright, according to *Fortune* magazine, has reduced MRP to just four questions:

1. What you gonna make?
2. What's it take to make it?
3. What you got?
4. What you gotta get?

Answer those four questions accurately, based on an annual sales forecast, and revising stockholdings as you go along, in line with actual sales, and you could save so much money that you end up rich—maybe even richer than Oliver Wright.

8. RANDOM WALK AND PERPETUAL PRESSURE

Those four not-so-deceptively simple questions on inventory go right to the heart of one area that can hold the key to the collapse or continuance of the entire organization. If stocks are too low, the company can't produce or supply in the necessary quantities. If they are too high, financing costs will eat voraciously into the profits, and sooner or later cutbacks in production, exacerbating the financial damage, will become inevitable.

But stock control alone won't reduce stocks to the minimal level. Poor production methods mean, among other horrible things, excessive stocks. For instance, successful adoption of group technology (with fairly autonomous groups of workers completing all or most of the production operations) can cut work in progress by 60 percent and stock levels by 40 percent.

This doesn't mean that anybody can afford to neglect improved methods of controlling stock. The cost even of sophisticated stock control—$100,000 or more for small companies, over $1 million for the bigger ones—is as nothing compared to the savings which the computer can produce by doing its sums. A study by some Minnesota academics showed that the average increase in the number of times stock was turned over went up by *half* when sophisticated methods were introduced.

Observe, though, that getting the full benefits from efficient stock control will involve the most efficient system of production; and *that* will involve . . . and so on. The process goes on *ad infinitum*—one part of a business relates crucially to another, which relates crucially to yet another.

For instance, having too much paper work is in itself a bore and a nuisance and a waste of time and money. But that's not the worst of it. Take the case of a company that required seventeen pieces of paper, entries in four different ledgers, and up to thirty-five steps to purchase its supplies. The result was a two-and-a-half-month backlog in processing orders, while the staff involved were far too busy to do their proper job—buying cost-effectively. They just placed the orders. Eliminating the excess paper work in a case like this often means simultaneously cleaning up an inefficient system (the cause of the paper explosion); and, if the project involves all the people affected (as it should), a blow will be struck for better morale as well, for everybody hates paper work.

The levels of efficiency vary embarrassingly between firms and between countries. Inside one multinational, the American "accounts payable" system processes about 20,000 invoices per man-year; the German can manage 12,000; the British only 5,000—just because of the difference between effective and ineffective systems design. In all these areas, the difference lies in knowledge—in knowing where a business is subperforming and knowing (or finding out) how to correct the faults.

One way of checking your knowledge is to check—via a checklist. Any point-by-point run-through of any activity will probably yield gold. It's perfectly possible to write your own checklist—indeed, that is an excellent basic method of forcing the mind to concentrate on some part of the business that has been taken for granted, but really needs to be taken to the cleaners.

The trouble is that you can't do everything. In theory, in a business where authority has been properly delegated, everybody will be going through the same criticize-and-correct routine in their own areas of responsibility. But human nature demands that human beings be checked just as thoroughly as lists, and there are two ways of doing it: the Random Walk and the Perpetual Pressure. The first means what it says—bobbing up anywhere or everywhere at random, visibly or not, asking questions and, above all, demanding action. The second means fixing on one aspect vital to you and pressing away all the time until you get not sub- but super-performance.

Thomas J. Peters gave *The Executive* an example of the first technique reinforced by the second. At United Airlines, Ed Carlson practiced what his people called "management by walking about." On his return from these peregrinations, he applied "deadly efficient, personally managed follow-up routines that brought action within days after he returned from the field with lengthy 'to do' lists."

How do you exercise Perpetual Pressure—and where? On the where, almost anywhere will produce savings, from the procedure for paying salesmen their expenses to (a very obvious case) energy consumption. The case is obvious because, when the oil crunch came, companies were galvanized into taking action that had been available all along—for instance, one car plant obtained energy cost reductions of $400,000 a year for only $36,000 of current expenditure and a capital cost of just $400,000. Until the crunch, large savings had just gone begging.

As for the how, you run project teams. It doesn't matter at all what you call them, or matter much how you compose them, whether it's quality circles, or some other shop-floor grouping, or even "action learning"—the approach by which managers learn through tackling real-life problems. When one company used this learning approach for a couple of dozen supervisors, for example, not only did their performance as supervisors improve, but absenteeism in the plant fell from 9 percent to 7.1 percent and annual labor turnover from 10 percent to 7 percent.

Looking at it another way, the company suffered from over 40 percent more turnover than it needed—before the team approach took hold. Any task force, indeed any concerted approach to any aspect of a business, will usually yield similar payoffs. Such Supermanagement can mean making systems better, or bypassing them altogether; interfering or leaving well alone; technical improvement or commonsense change. The only thing that is constant is the determination to go on asking and answering hard questions, key area by key area, until there are none left to ask—which will be never.

9. THE SURE-THING DISASTER

By the same token, the best way to invite the hardest blows of fate is to be misinformed. A company that felt in a strongly expansionist mood decided to launch a new product in its most strongly expanding market. The sheer strength of the market seemed to reduce the risk to vanishing point—the company's market leader was reporting an upsurge in orders of about three quarters compared to a year before—and this came on top of an excellent performance in the year that was just coming to an end.

Greatly encouraged, the management proceeded with its new product launch. When the sales turned out to be negligible in the new year, another look was taken at the market. It showed that, if all competitors were taken together, sales in this sector weren't booming at all—they had flattened right out. That meant not an inch of room for the new product, which was losing money in alarming amounts.

Greatly chastened, the managers realized that they had looked at the wrong data—their own figures, not those for the market as a whole. The product was withdrawn and relaunched in another form, where the losses were much smaller, and in a sector where the prospects of penetration were real—only this time, the decisions were based on the real facts.

10. INFORMATION'S GOLDEN NUGGETS

No talent in management is worth more than the ability to master facts—not just any facts, but the ones that provide the correct answers. Mastery thus involves knowing what facts you want; where to dig for them; how to dig; how to process the mined ore; and how to use the precious nuggets of information that are finally in your hand. The process can be laborious—which is why it is so often botched.

For instance, take this case from *The Sabine File*, A. C. Neilsen's system for providing people with essential information. You are selling spirits, but the brand share has been declining since the introduction of new variants. Should the variants be withdrawn? You look at licensed liquor stores that handle various combinations of the original brand and the variants, and you find sales volume and share in each of these subgroups over a twenty-month period. The evidence is that your overall position has been maintained in outlets handling the full range, but has fallen in outlets handling only the original brand. What do you do?

The initial temptation, to cut your losses and kill the new variants, can't be justified by the above data. So you keep the variants; more than that, while re-establishing the identity of the original brand, you *reinforce* the commitment to the new beauties. But note how detailed the data had to be before the company had enough ammunition to avoid a dumb decision and make a bright move.

The brightness and rightness, of course, must be corroborated by further information, more hard homework, and total realism. Here's another case where the conclusions are simpler: selling household products, you are testing a new brand in a fast-growing

221

market. Working through agents, distribution is so far confined to a limited number of very large outlets. You need more information about the brand's performance in these stores before deciding whether more support is justified. Comparing the brand handlers with nonhandlers—for both the current period and before brand introduction—gives you sales shares, prices, and distribution broken down by your brand, competitors, and the total. You find that, although your brand has the smallest share across the whole of its test area, this is due mainly to its low distribution. In shops handling the brand it is actually the leader. What do you do? Plainly, you go for an all-out effort to boost the distribution of the new brand.

Those two real-life cases are taken from marketing, but any problem provides the same necessity—you've got to establish things like:

1. Definition of the problem.
2 Description of the problem in four dimensions: Identity, Location, Timing, and Magnitude.
3. Extraction of key information in the four dimensions to generate possible causes.
4. Testing for most probable cause.
5. Verification of the true cause.

The five vital points are taken from *The New Rational Manager*, by Charles H. Kepner and Benjamin B. Tregoe, inventors of what has become a famous fact-finding method of problem solving. It formalizes the nugget-mining process described above in the first paragraph. For instance, a piece of plant is playing up. The pair would set down (using the Identity, Location, Timing, and Magnitude routine in [2] above) all the facts in painstaking order. What unit is malfunctioning? What's going wrong? Where exactly? When was it first spotted? When has it been noted since? At what point in operations? What's the extent of the problem? How many units are affected? How much of any one unit?

Note that the information obtained doesn't supply the *answer* to the problem of the leaking oil—it simply gives you the data without which you might make a hopelessly wrong decision.

For instance, in a personnel problem described by Kepner and Tregoe, a manager obviously wanted to sack a clerk who was making costly errors and seemed to be poorly motivated. Going through exactly the same routine as above established these points: neither fault had appeared in his previous job, nor when he was working temporarily in another department. Thus the recommended routines pointed to what should perhaps have been obvious all along:

Bob, accounts payable, is making too many errors; Jim, expense accounts, and Betty, accounts receivable, are not making errors.

Bob is making errors now; was not for over a year when he worked in marketing.

Bob does make errors on comptometer work, accounts payable; does not make any errors at all on other work, as when he filled in for Jim on expense accounts.

Conclusion? The young man was bored out of his tiny mind operating a comptometer all day, and sacking him would merely have lost the company a potentially good employee.

Now some facts look so starkly clear (as in the above case) that it may not seem worthwhile going through a whole rigmarole to arrive at the equally clear solution. But remember the Sure-thing Disaster: the new product would *not* have been launched if the "obvious" fact (the strength of the market) had been tested for validity.

With those new variants of booze, too, brand share had fallen since their introduction. What would have been more obvious (and wrong) than to have linked the variants and the fall as cause and effect? Similarly, the new household product wouldn't have gotten the support it deserved without the backing of necessary information. And the inefficient clerk might have been dismissed. A fact is only as good as its proof—and an incomplete or inaccurate factual picture is a time bomb that could, and probably will, explode. A true, full view, though, can set off explosive success.

11. THE EASY MONEY

Incomplete learning is another time bomb. But what does learning mean to the Supermanager? A professor whose son worked for an enormously successful conglomerate once asked him a question. How on earth could the group buy a company that hadn't made money for years, and was losing heavily at the moment of purchase, and then, in what seemed no more than a trice, get the thing earning a 20 percent return on capital?

The son explained the recipe: take charge of the cash; analyze the business; identify the useless managers and remove them; identify the good ones and promote them; with the help of the latter (and preferably on their own instigation) make the basic changes in market strategy and production arrangements that may be necessary. Then simply insist on getting performance, which you monitor by means of excellent financial controls.

The professor shook his head wonderingly: "You make it sound very easy to make a lot of money," he said.

12. THE LESSONS OF LEARNING

It's understandable that an academic, used to the difficulty of his own academic discipline, and accustomed to the still greater difficulty of putting it over to students, should believe that so weighty a matter as management must have more to it than the simple principles of effective organization. So it does. But just as the principles of learning can be mastered quite simply, much more easily than the subject being learned, so managing can be grasped quite effectively by people who know very little about management as taught in academic courses.

This doesn't mean that the academic knowledge is useless. It means that managing is ultimately about action, about ideas turned into deeds, not ideas alone. Useful management knowledge is always specific to cases—very little is like a knowledge of botany or

Spanish grammar, valid in the abstract. But the lore is none the worse for that. Even people who do manage with effective, even brilliant success, without being able to explain on paper what they're doing, can have their performance improved by a little learning. In managing, a lot of learning can sometimes be a dangerous thing. But conversely, a little learning can go a very long way.

Any list of courses for managers will show the limitless range of subjects that can be taught and which somebody in any organization should understand thoroughly. Examples include, say, the prevention and detection of fraud—an absolute necessity when the computer and the skills needed to run it have opened the door to sophisticated and enormous crookery that the nonelectronic manager could never hope even to suspect. Then there are subjects which constitute the banal bread and butter of business life, but for that reason are the scene of much incompetence and waste—like export documentation, duller than ditchwater, but no less important for that.

Another crucial area is the improvement of everyday performance by employees in areas where constant tuition and updating have been proved to pay dividends. Selling is the most obvious sector, especially in markets where the excitement and hugger-mugger of the consumer goods world are missing, as in most industrial products. Basic nonmanagement skills which are essential to managing shouldn't be neglected either. You really can teach grown-up men and women to think better or write far more logical, comprehensible, and effective reports; you can show them vital things like distinguishing between facts and opinions.

Several subjects can always be slung together to form some sort of comprehensive management course. But the more students are asked to absorb, in variety as well as quantity, the less likely their education is to stick. Concentration is the watchword, in every sense. However, a major subject almost certainly can't be covered in less than two days. Trying to cram too much into one day will be self-defeating (and the same applies to in-company get-togethers, when the participants are given, say, ten minutes each to rattle through the affairs of their divisions; that kind of operation is purely social and inspirational, you hope).

The minimum of two days is by no means a maximum, of course. But if the instruction is going to run for more than a couple of days, don't expect one instructor to carry the load alone—two voices are always better than one, anyway. With just a pair, the most they can manage effectively is four days, and that in turn will depend on careful planning and orchestration of the time.

This comes naturally to the best course designers. In all cases where courses pass the only test—the approval and direct perceived benefit of the participants—you'll find that the lecturers have gone through a closely designed and well-packaged routine, probably one that they repeat again and again. Training courses are not glorified after-dinner speeches; they are no place for ad-libbing. The planning can and should include breaks and passages of pure entertainment, which are essential if the concentration is to be maintained when it counts. But the preliminary organization always preconditions the final results.

Efficient administration is part of the teaching. Petty aggravations, like projectors at ankle level, and failures of equipment, like inoperative mikes, will ruin the best of lecturers' attempts to hold an audience. The planning should also avoid confusing concentration with brain-bashing. Many course organizers delight in making the participants work their tails off, burn the midnight oil, go through the mill—and all the other cant phrases for unnecessary abuse of people's willingness to be maltreated. It's far better to give people plenty of time to absorb the teaching with clear heads and reasonably bright eyes. The combination of macho-ism and masochism is more appropriate to one of the Californian cults than to serious, precisely aimed management development.

But what about *general* development? All the subjects referred to above are closely defined. The more general a course ("modern management" or "management in the 1980s," or whatever), the less likely it is that people will actually learn something useful. It's customary to conceal this fact beneath another cant phrase—"widening their horizons." If that truly is the objective, the assembled executives would be better off receiving instruction in general cultural subjects. Indeed, one U.S. company does claim great success for a policy of refreshing and broadening its managers by immersing them in art and literature for a few days.

Be that as it may, the lesson is valid. The object of any education for managers is to provide something which they can take away from the course and use in their lives. (What they take away should include, incidentally, complete and excellent documentation on whatever the course was about.) The take-away food for thought and work can consist of specific lore which will help both the manager and the company at once (like being able to avert a computer fraud), or it may lead to improvement of the manager's abilities in some wider but valuable way (from better report writing to an appreciation of Picasso). Either way, it must be possible to write down what specific objectives the training will achieve. Only then will anybody know—or care—if the lessons, as they must be, have been well and truly learned.

13. THE THEME-OF-THE-MONTH MAN

The most valuable teaching, though, always takes place on the job. And the most beneficial tuition of all stems from the values which the men at the top impose on the corporation. But the job, like all teaching, must be done properly by good teachers. Thus, in one large U.S. corporation, one boss insisted that his major preoccupation was stimulating the flow of new products. Analysis of how he actually spent his time over a three-month period showed, however, that no more than 7 percent of his effort went into the new product area.

In another similar-sized company, the boss said he was obsessed by quality. Yet no matter how hard he tried to raise the level of quality, he was unsuccessful. When his subordinates were questioned by a consultant, they explained why: "Of course, he's for quality, but he's for everything else, too. We have a theme of the month here."

In stark contrast, at Procter & Gamble product quality is achieved on the "do-one-thing-well" principle, according to Thomas J. Peters, writing in *Business Week*. And over at Hewlett-Packard "every operational review focuses on new products, with a minimum amount of time devoted to financial results of projections." That's because David Packard, part founder of the company, believed that "proper implementation of new-product plans automatically produces the right numbers." Packard also made it a point to start new employees in the new product process because that was the theme, not of the month, but of the company—all its life.

14. DO IT, FIX IT, TRY IT

Lessons are not learned for their own sake in Supermanagement. They are learned to be applied. And nobody applies them better than the companies that are both biggest and best. One of the great mid-century myths is that bigness is ugly—that large corporations are by definition inefficient, incapable of innovation, cumbersome, overcautious, unprofitable, and generally helpless.

Not so. In fact, the record of certain great businesses with sales in the billions compares favorably with the finest small firm there ever was (which, of course, if it were that marvelous, would sooner or later become big). For decades companies like 3M, Procter & Gamble, Digital Equipment, H-P, and IBM have, in and out of most seasons, shown brilliant business form, and their secrets are—well, simplicity itself.

Here they are, as divined by Peters as a McKinsey consultant. The features he found in common among thirty-seven well-managed companies in an article have become famous as the basis of his book *In Search of Excellence,* written with Robert Waterman, Jr.

1. A bias toward action
2. Simple form and lean staff
3. Continued contact with customers
4. Productivity improvement via people
5. Operational autonomy to encourage entrepreneurship
6. Stress on one key business value
7. Emphasis on doing what they know best
8. Simultaneous loose-tight controls.

Of those eight virtues, the first is in the right place. The credo of success is exactly six words long: DO IT, FIX IT, TRY IT.

How this credo is obeyed in practice has a strong smack of Churchill's famous wartime habit of marking his memos with the immortal words "Action this day." For instance, senior executives at IBM were given assignments whose sole function was to process customer complaints—within twenty-four hours, at that.

Many problems, of course, can't be solved in a day, and disaster will follow if anybody thinks they can and acts accordingly. But if something needs FIX-IT action, the well-managed company will react like Digital Equipment. A DEC executive told Peters, "When we've got a big problem here, we grab ten senior guys and stick them in a room for a week. They come up with an answer [note the next three crucial words] *and implement it.*"

Separate the responsibility for deciding policy from that for its execution, and you open up a huge gulf into which large parts of the company may inadvertently fall. The tendency in large, ill-run companies is for senior managers to become divorced from the action. Not so at DEC. Its task force members (all of whom are volunteers) tend to be busy senior managers who are anxious to get the problem solved and to return to their main jobs. Whether for that reason or not, DEC task forces seldom stay in business for more than ninety days; nor do they at Hewlett-Packard, 3M, or Texas Instruments.

At TI, managers are given action goals as precise as the objectives for any task force: dates by which a new plant must be operating, for example, or by when a certain percentage of a sales force must have called on customers in a new market. In the wonderfully true words of a TI executive, "The bottom line for any senior manager is the maxim that more than two objectives is no objective."

The essence of such a system, though, shouldn't be compulsion. Again at TI, shop-floor teams set their own targets for production—and apparently set goals that require them to stretch and are at the same time reasonable and attainable. By much the same token, managers are expected to act on their judgment and not *against* it. This isn't the preaching of permissive management, but the lesson of hard TI experience—"In every instance of a new product failure, we had forced someone into championing it involuntarily."

How do you balance the need for freedom with the equally urgent necessity for control? Not, if those thirty-seven companies are anything to go by (as they are), through constructing an elaborate system of controls. The thriving thirty-seven tend to concentrate on very tight control of very few variables—for instance, at 3M, just return on sales and number of employees. At Dana, a new president threw out all the policy manuals (which tend to breed like minks in big groups) and substituted a one-page philosophy statement plus a control system that made divisions report costs and revenues on a daily basis. There's no point in having controls that tell you more than you want, but those which do convey the essential information must be tightly applied.

Exactly the same principles of brevity, simplicity, and relevance apply to business plans. At 3M, new product ideas must be proposed in less than five pages. At Procter & Gamble, one-page memos are the rule, but woe betide any manager whose single page contains a fallacious figure. In keeping things simple and direct these companies help themselves by splitting up the operation into small, entrepreneurial units; keeping activities to small manageable groups; and placing a tight lid on staff numbers—fewer than a hundred people, says Peters, run Dana, with its $2.4 billion of sales.

Peters was also impressed by the way in which the successful top managements incessantly banged home whatever was most important to the company, "whether it's customer service, productivity improvement, new product development, product quality, or, in a food business, quality, cleanliness and value." The outstanding companies have one theme and stick to it.

Underlying that pattern, however, is the action emphasis of DO IT, TRY IT, FIX IT, and the knowledge that the only ultimate test of action is its results. If they include, as at 3M, a 17.8 percent return on sales after tax and a 24.4 percent return on the money invested in the business, then it's a beautiful business—big or small.

15. THE PLANNING THAT WASN'T

The Supercompanies, though, are in a minority in at least one respect. When consultant Michael G. Allen decided to investigate the strategic planning strengths of 145 leading U.S. companies, he found not strength but weakness. He tested four dimensions of planning:

1. The provision of corporate strategic direction;
2. The development of strategies for business units;
3. Central review and integration of plans;
4. Linkage with operating systems.

Dimension by dimension, using the companies' own assessments, he found that on the corporate strategy question only financial objectives and goals, quality of earnings, and development of key resources were rated as "strong." Everything else was on a rising scale of weakness, with development of new businesses and markets weakest of all. The overall score was −7.

Much the same story was true of planning individual businesses. "Financial resource strategy" was strongest. Creative strategies to improve position, resource strategies, and innovation in venture management were "extremely weak": overall score, −13.

Moving on to central corporate review of plans, nothing was thought adequate except "review of plans for analytical consistency," which isn't worth too much. The overall assessment, not surprisingly, was low: −23.

But the worst was to come on action to implement plans. As Allen reports

In the 145-company survey, linkage of plans to operations showed adequacy only in top management involvement in strategic planning (+26), and middle management involvement (+ 8).' ... "Very weak" were the calibre of planning resources and staff (−17), linkage of strategic priorities with budgets (−21), degree of implementation and impact of strategy (−28), and toughness of operating plans to execute strategy (−30). Rated as "extremely weak" were the board of directors' in-

231

volvement in strategic planning (−40), organization for effective strategy implementation (−41), management selection linked to strategic task (−46), and coupling of strategic performance with pay and promotion (−52). The overall assessment was a miserable −34.

The initial failures of some great American businesses in the face of Japanese and European competition aren't surprising, given those facts. What's surprising is that the failure hasn't been greater—to the point of no return, where they couldn't fight back. Those that lived to fight another day did so because of a precious resource: the innate fundamental strengths of U.S. business.

16. WHY BANK OF AMERICA BOOMED

The truth is that generations of managers come and go, in companies big and small; they strive and strain, but in the end the results are often determined less by their labors than by the direction that some Supermanagers, or bunch of them, imposed on the company, maybe, long ago. In April 1981, John Thackray took a look back at the eight U.S. companies that he had studied for *Management Today* in its first year, 1966. Fifteen years later all except one, Fairchild Camera and Instrument (swallowed by takeover, despite its high technology positioning), were still extant—but after the most extraordinary vicissitudes.

Half had one striking fact in common: as Thackray wrote, "At RCA, ITT, Singer and Grace, most of the top managerial attention has gone into fashioning portfolio strategies to achieve the optimal diversified mix of divisions—buying into new businesses, shedding existing investments that didn't meet management's pleasure." Part of the rationale for this ever-popular game of abandoning or downgrading the base was the search for greater consistency of financial performance. It wasn't found. Over the four years from 1975 to 1979, for example, return on investment at RCA fluctuated between 9.5 percent and 18.4 percent; at ITT the range over a decade was 6.8

percent to 13.9 percent; at W. R. Grace the lowest for the decade was 5.5 percent and the best 14.5 percent; at Singer the oscillations of the bottom line were even wilder.

In the futile quest for stable, perpetual growth, terrible errors were made. Singer moved into defense products, hosiery- and clothing-knitting machines, carpet-tufting machinery, electronic laboratory and test equipment—and a major effort in business machines. A mail-order business and home entertainment products were also taken on board. The write-offs came to $411 million—that was when a new boss started to try turning the company around. That man fondly believed that the original base in sewing machines was in good order. The horrible truth? As a Singer executive said, "We neglected our product development. We neglected manufacturing facilities. We neglected our retail stores. It's a classic case that will be studied for a long time to come."

What lessons can be learned from such a classic? Singer's sorry decline is only one: there's also the almost unbelievable halving of profits at the mighty ITT in 1979, as one dopey project pulverized a single division; and the disastrous, $490 million failure of RCA, once the king of color television, in computers; and the extraordinary moiling and toiling at Grace, where two hundred companies were bought and fifty divisions sold—until one of those plays, in energy, at last launched the company on a winning streak.

The lessons can be seen more clearly by looking at a success story: Bank of America, with an average rate of return on investment of 16.4 percent since 1974, and a net income growth of 18.7 percent. The record was not only far better than that of any of the industrial firms Thackray studied; it outstripped any of the other major money-center banks, which were by no means immune to the lust for whoring after strange corporate flesh.

When, as president of the bank, the Supermanager Tom Clausen set his face against this go-go philosophy, "it took guts," according to a senior colleague, "because there was a lot of that go-go mentality around here." In Clausen's own words, "People around here used to be very concerned about size and volume. Ask any officer, 'How's business?' and you'd immediately hear how many loans he'd made. I tried to leave my stamp by making everyone aware of profit."

What Bank of America did is not only easier than go-go diversification—it makes more sense. Every one of the conglomerate disappointments possesses several excellent businesses; this must be true, or else they would have disappeared from sight long since under the burden of their own gross and grossly visible mistakes. Clearly, the managements either failed to capitalize fully on the excellence of the good (as Clausen capitalized by banging his drums of profit and safe, sustainable growth) or else the failures obliterated the effects of excellence by buying (or growing) rotten apples.

In fact, they were probably guilty of both sins: the Singer Syndrome. It's easier to prove the bad buys than the bad stewardship of the good businesses—that's because today's managements are now throwing out (and thus identifying) the bad apples bought by their predecessors; and in some cases they have brought all buying to a near-halt (as at ITT, RCA, Singer, and Grace). Of course, when it's a *predecessor's* mistakes, casting them into outer darkness is easier; but another fact is that there are an awful lot of predecessors around.

At ITT, when Harold Geneen was forced to retire because of age, he shortly thereafter led a boardroom movement that toppled his successor. At RCA, the door has been revolving at top speed ever since Robert W. Sarnoff paid the price for his computer fiasco. The latest casualty (at the time of writing) was Edgar H. Griffiths, but another boss was slung out between Sarnoff and Griffiths, while the latter hired a president for the company in 1980 only to sack him six months later. The hectic political infighting which must accompany such gyrations would also explain why, allegedly, Griffiths concentrated on the short-term at the expense of the long—the official excuse for his ouster. "Long-range planning at RCA," according to a quote from *Business Week,* meant "What are we going to do after lunch?"

The lessons of the Illustrious Laggards for the Supermanagement of all companies stick out several miles.

1. Stick to that basic theme—or allow the separate entities of the company to stick to their basic themes.

2. Concentrate short-term activity on improving basic efficiencies.

3. Couple short-term emphasis on efficiency with plans for medium- and long-term defense and improvement of market positions.

4. Use acquisition sparingly, either to strengthen the above tactics and strategies, or to add *immediately* to the returns on assets.

5. Make stability, in management and in business development, a prime aim.

6. Last, but not least, never succumb to the notion that you're a genius—even if (which is unlikely) you are.

The Illustrious Laggards were run by people with a high, a very high, opinion of themselves; so, no doubt, were the 145 companies whose planners told Mike Allen such appalling truths. Conceit is the worst possible basis for corporate strategic direction. And misdirection is the best possible basis for failure to control the destiny of the corporation—and all who sail in her. It's easily avoided.

To summarize some of the important points I've mentioned in Step Six:

1. In times of general business retreat, look for specific opportinities to advance.

2. If you need outside help, get it.

3. When you've got it, manage it purposefully and critically, like any other resource.

4. Combine the Random Walk about the business with Perpetual Pressure, asking the right questions and getting answers—at once.

5. Never make decisions on less than the best information you can find.

6. Train your people in the skills that they need—and you want.

7. If something has to be done, DO IT: if something has to be remedied, FIX IT: if something might work, TRY IT.

8. But don't try to do too much—stick to one or two basic themes at a time.

9. Planning is vital—but it must be planning for action. Couple short-term emphasis on efficiency with plans for the iron defense and golden improvement of your market position in the medium and long term.

Step Seven: How to Learn From Managerial Mistakes

1. THE DEAD-WRONG DECISIONS

Everybody makes mistakes. The only unpardonable error is to refuse to recognize a mistake when you've made one. So never argue, even (or maybe especially) to yourself that some rotten decision was okay, merely misunderstood, or misrepresented, or badly implemented by somebody else. Almost certainly, you were mistaken, and you can derive more benefit from the painful analysis of the mistake than from the pitiful pretense that it was never made—or from analyzing the best decision you ever took.

Witness the confession of a successful executive about a market failure that preyed on his mind for years:

> What galls me is that almost every decision I made on this venture was wrong. Now, of course, they weren't my decisions

alone—others were involved. I can't in all honesty say I would have done any differently if I had been entirely on my own. Who knows? Yet perhaps that's where the trouble began— there were always too many cooks.

Another problem was that the cooks weren't all in the same kitchen, geographically speaking, and that most of them had many other weighty matters on their minds. In fact, of the inner group of five, four were chiefs and only one was an Indian; and he was the only one bringing concentrated, undistracted attention to bear on the subject.

That might have been all right. He was the general manager of the new thing, after all. But he was the wrong man. Faced with no obvious candidates inside, we had opted for a man who was available and had worked for us before—even though we all knew that he almost certainly didn't have the qualities needed for the job. Not his fault, mind you. He just didn't have it.

So why didn't I make a stand against it? First, because of that most dangerous procedure in making appointments, settling for any port in a storm—it took us off the hook. At least we had a boss, even if he was the wrong one. But I can spot another failing on my part. If I'd fought against the appointment, that's what I would have had to do—fight.

It was another reflection of the too many chiefs, not enough Indians problem. With all those powerful figures around, the temptation was always to go for the easily obtained consensus. But because we'd made a weak appointment, we couldn't leave the guy alone to get on with it, and I took personal responsibility for making sure the venture got properly off the ground.

The only catch was that matter of geography I mentioned. My office is in Manhattan, and the new venture had been established in New Jersey with one of our biggest subsidiaries, partly because it was sharing some management services and personnel. In hindsight, I see that I should have moved nearby. As it was, whenever we had to meet on the project (which was all too frequently) I had to get in a car—and, of course, there was always some pressing appointment somewhere else that curtailed my appearances.

That partly explains why I tended to be too uncritical of the new company when it started operation. Again, we all were. But I think now that a far more basic reason underlay our failure to judge the new project harshly enough. We were trying to do too many things at once, so the venture was a muddle, and our judgment was muddled in consequence.

Why the muddle? Well, we were replacing an old product range. But two of the old products, some of us thought, had strong market appeal, which we didn't want to throw away completely. So we incorporated some of the features in the new product, which was also heavily influenced by our desire to outmatch the competitor who had been setting the pace.

Now, it makes every kind of sense to analyze the strengths and weaknesses of a competitor in the marketplace, so that you outscore his product on the strong points and don't repeat the weaknesses. But I've always strongly believed that, once you've done that, you forget about the competitive product completely. You concentrate on producing, within the criteria you've established, the best and most different damn product you can.

But we were a bit mesmerized by the competition, and so our new range was a mishmash of me-too and old-hat features, rather than an integrated concept aimed fairly and squarely at the market. We couldn't have produced that, of course, because we hadn't defined the market clearly. We were trying to reach two groups of buyers, to kill two birds with one stone, when in truth the groups had little in common.

All the attendant problems you'd expect arrived—bad morale among the staff, constant minor inefficiencies, administrative foul-ups. The day-to-day problems, equally unsurprisingly, tended to take our eyes off the market—and even off the budgets. When the feedback from the market wasn't good, we discounted it. When the costs ran far ahead of estimate, we dismissed it as worthwhile growing pains.

When the need for a new chief became inescapable, we even repeated our first mistake—the any-port-in-a-storm syndrome, grabbing at the first man who came along. Fortunately, by now the inner group was coming to its senses. In short order, we revamped the product, throwing out all relics of the old range; got the costs under control by some fairly radical measures; appointed a third CEO from outside with the qualities we needed; and started off again. This time, thanks be, we made it.

Here's what the repentant sinner learned:

1. Never put a man in a key job just because he's there; whatever the difficulty or delay, get the right man.

2. Never go along with decisions simply because that's the line of least resistance.

3. Always take time out to consider a project by yourself—before your ideas get shaped by the impact, perhaps forceful, of other people's views.

4. Don't let the control of projects fall into the hands of committees—especially top-heavy ones.

5. Always ensure that you've got the full-time attention of the key people and/or the key site.

6. Whether in design or market objective, aim to kill one fat bird with one big stone, and that's all.

7. Control costs on new ventures every bit as rigorously as those on established projects.

8. Take all bad news and adverse criticism very seriously—if necessary, go and talk to the critics yourself, rather than dismissing the words of those who relay the criticism to you.

9. Last but not least, if you're luxuriating in the success of a business and not being critical about it, why not? There's bound to be something wrong. Are you sure you're not turning a blind eye—knowing that, if you were to open your eyes, you would actually have to get out of your easy chair and *do* something?

10. If you think that the real trouble is that you're losing your grip—tighten it.

2. VITAL LESSON SIX

You can see the necessary process of making mistakes and learning from them at work in the life, not of a failed company, but of a Supermanagement—that of Texas Instruments. As its president said in 1982, a company of TI's status has to focus "on the right products, for the right growth markets, at the right time." So how come TI didn't do just that? For failure to do so is the diagnosis which the CEO offered to explain why his profits *halved* in 1981.

What's more, TI's long-standing reputation among the world's Supermanaged companies rested on developing superproducts and on doing both at the right time—i.e., before anybody else. Those became the very things that weren't being done at TI; and the reasons carry a profound moral for management.

According to *Fortune* magazine, the trouble at TI began with the two men at the top—who are "very autocratic, very powerful, very intent on controlling things," according to one veteran. Reams of memos, computer rankings of the performance of every operating manager, management meetings that were "sometimes punctuated by table-pounding, table-kicking, and flying objects"—all these were signs of top-down management in a company which prides itself on the bottom-up variety, in which people far down the line are supposedly encouraged to come up with innovations.

TI had forgotten Lesson One. *Practice what you preach.* If you don't there's a real danger that performance will get out of kilter, too.

It also ignored Lesson Two. *Treat different markets differently.* TI grew at astonishing pace in semiconductors, where the trick was to keep on widening markets by bringing down the price as fast and as far as possible, beating competitors to a pulp in the process. The management tried the same trick in digital watches—and the decision was wrong.

The two top men "kept pushing to slash the price to $9.95. That meant having a plastic case and band. We kept telling them consumers didn't want that, but they wouldn't listen." TI is now out of watches completely. That wasn't only because of the silly underpricing, but also because it used the wrong technology. You had to press a button to tell the time (via a light-emitting diode) instead of just being able to look (via an LCD, or liquid crystal display).

The reason for this wasn't technical incapacity—it was bad organization. The watch business was run via a so-called product customer center, or PCC; each PCC had a single boss with total responsibility for marketing, but none for manufacture. The manufacturing guys wouldn't agree to supply the LCDs which the marketing guys wanted—and that was the end of that, and of TI's watches.

It had ignored Lesson Three. *Ensure that responsibility is matched with resources.* TI responded by merging masses of little PCCs into much bigger ones to reflect this lesson, one it learned the hard way—for instance, in the market for programmable calculators. This was "once TI's exclusive preserve; but Hewlett-Packard grabbed more than half the business, mainly because for over two years TI's calculator group couldn't get updated circuits."

Another famous set of initials in TI's management myth is the "tactical action program," or TAP. As well as their operating responsibilities, managers (even very junior ones) were put in charge of these TAPs, two hundred of them in all, which were supposed to bring elements of the group's overall strategy to fruition. It sounds messy—and it was. Operating problems naturally took precedence, especially as earnings fell short, and, as the TAPs languished, so did the company's strategies.

This rubbed in Lesson Four. *Don't give people divided responsibility*—one clear task at a time is quite enough. Don't get the idea, though, that organization is the only thing that counts. As the *Fortune* writer observes, the overriding problem was that TI made many poor strategic decisions—going into magnetic-bubble memory chips, for instance, because they were expected to be cheaper, and having to back out expensively (for a $50 million loss) when it found that they weren't.

But there's a link between the two types of error, of managing and technical development. The company had outgrown the scope of its Supermanagement—especially one that was wedded to the secrets of past success. When that became clear at TI, in March 1982, it shook up the semiconductor group (as one example), "reassigning over a dozen vice presidents and operating managers." According to *Fortune,* former TI people ascribe such shifts to a "canary theory" of motivation through anxiety: "when you've got ten tons of canaries—or executives—in a five-ton truck, you beat on the roof now and then to make sure at least half of them are up and flying."

That ignores Lesson Five. *If the canaries won't sing, you won't make 'em sing by bashing on the roof.* Nor will that be the reason for any wonders that TI, as it manages to rise from its recent predicaments, performs in the future. That future success will result from realization that the past can become the enemy of the present, that even Supermanagement deteriorates over time, like a noble white Burgundy past its peak, that it must prove its ultimate quality by its readiness to recognize its own human failings—and to rectify them, with all means in its power and at all costs. That's Lesson Six. One lesson that TI is most unlikely to ignore.

3. THE WATER IN THE CEMENT

Some of the worst mistakes in management are in the realm of public relations, and many are gratuitous. Thus Morris Rotman, chairman of the Chicago-based public relations firm Harshe, Rotman & Druck, had reason to be "cautiously apprehensive" about somebody's brainwave for promoting Rival dog food's new meatball dinner. Rival's president liked to show visitors how wholesome the product was by eating it in his office. The agency suggested inviting journalists to a lunch at which the company president and a pedigree dog would share a table. So it came to pass. But the animal, either not hungry or frightened by the flashbulbs, showed total indifference to the meatballs. Finally, the desperate president reached into the dog's bowl and ate the stuff himself, to the cheers of the assembled scribes. The client took one look at the publicity that resulted—and fired the agency.

The above story is one of several public relations horrors recounted in *Dun's Review.* For another, in celebration of American Home Products' development of an improved Black Flag insecticide containing Baygon (said to be especially lethal to cockroaches), the PR people set up a press conference on a cold New York day. To demonstrate the product's superior killing power, the plan was to spray one dish of cockroaches with Black Flag and another with competitive Brand X and "watch the bugs sprayed with the Baygon product drop dead faster." Unfortunately, the product works by being absorbed through pattering insect feet, but cockroaches become lethargic in cold weather and don't patter—they just lie there. "After thirty minutes of spraying the hell out of the damn things, the bugs were in better shape than I was," says the PR man—or rather, the *former* PR man.

Another PR firm organized a press conference to mark the completion of a huge middle-income housing project in Manhattan, guaranteed to generate good publicity for its building-company client. When a reporter asked how it was possible to build so costly a project and still offer tenants such moderate rents, the beaming builder rose to the occasion and replied, "Easy—we just throw a little more water in the cement."

4. HOW PERSUADERS PERSUADE

Before deciding, on that evidence, that PR consultants are worth less, far less than their fees, ask how you would deal with a couple of problems that any manager would loathe to have on his plate—or his mind:

1. You sell soft drinks in nonreturnable bottles, and an aggrieved environmentalist lobby has dumped thousands of the horrible things on your doorstep in protest.
2. You sell motorcycles, but the entire market has collapsed, because people regard the machines (rightly, alas) as noisy, dirty, and dangerous.

The two problems have one thing in common (apart from being deadly serious). They both hinge around public opinion. Therefore, neither can be solved without changing, or influencing, that opinion. That process is the lifeblood of a management technique, public relations, which often isn't seen as a technique at all—because it's entrusted to consultants or in-house people who are seldom involved in the higher management of the business.

But PR power is not to be despised. Take the two cases above: the glass campaign featured "Bottle Banks"—bins into which the public could throw its bottles. By January 1980, they were operating in fifty cities and had collected thirty-five million bottles and jars for recycling.

The key to the motorbike campaign was to ignore press criticism and concentrate on "promoting the positive aspects" of bikes, starting with the relatively innocent two-wheelers, like mopeds. In 1979 nearly four million leaflets were distributed door-to-door inviting the householder to try a moped; in the same year over 100,000 column centimeters of "positive coverage," i.e., pro-bike stories, appeared, with at least an hour of national television and over five hours of national and local radio.

Be warned: it's a basic rule of PR that only the deluded businessman measures its effectiveness by column centimeters. But the pro-bike coverage easily swamped the anti-bike centimeters—and that's what counted; so did the results. Motorcycle sales rose steadily to three times the level at the start of the campaign.

The important words in that last paragraph are "so did the results." The impact of any PR campaign, like any expenditure on advertising, can always be measured—preferably in objective terms like bike registrations, but also, often by necessity, via more subjective assessments, such as attitude surveys. As noted, column centimeters or air time are fairly meaningless in themselves. But measures such as those do have a virtue: they rub in the inescapable fact that the media, love them or hate them, are the door to the hearts and minds of the great public out there.

For example, here's how Lever Brothers, relaunching a dishwashing product as Sunlight Lemon Liquid, bombarded its press target—and target's the word. In a concentrated three-week period, the shells fell successively on the leading trade magazine (which printed an exclusive feature), all other key grocery trade publications, every business and marketing editor in the land, women's page and shopping-page editors, and syndication groups. Two major editorial competitions had been negotiated, and the ammunition included three releases on specially designed Sunlight paper, contained in a bright lemon-colored press folder, with titles like "Lemon Power Rules, says Lever Brothers"; "The Power of a Lemon"; and "How to Tackle Washing-up." Also included were an attractive pack shot, a lemon verbena plant, and a product sample.

Of course, the media can be used for many purposes other than printing stories directly about the object of the PR man's passion. What Sheridan called "the puff indirect" in *The School for Scandal* can be even more effective. Thus, stories about "Bottle Banks" for nonreturnable bottles are more effective than industry articles saying what wonderful things said bottles are for decorating the landscape. The idea, the gimmick, is the foundation of most successful PR, whether or not the media are the main target.

For instance, Lever Brothers threw in a "Sunlight Cub Month sponsored washing-up service scheme" involving 60,000 Cub Scouts. This and other follow-ups could never have done the trick on their own. But they reinforced the press blitzkrieg and the advertising bombardment, to help achieve a 74 percent increase in market share for the lemony goo. Note the importance of the combination punch. PR is not out on its own, nor can it work effectively that way. It works only as an expression of the total company, especially in its public impact, from which it follows that PR can only be as good as its client.

Sooner or later, a promise that is belied by the product will blow up in the face of the guilty party. Provided that the promise is good and true, the more cynical aspects of any PR operation don't matter: for instance, the necessity to pour alcohol down the eager throats of the media in the hope of attracting their attention (and their column centimeters). The press party, though, is a legitimate management technique, whose special rules are general:

1. Don't waste your time or other people's on things that are of no interest to *them*. Good PR *makes* things interesting. (Never give a press party unless the subject is really interesting—not to you, but to

an easily bored journalist and, far more important, to the easily bored public beyond him or her.)

2. Envisage the result you are hoping to achieve and test that desired result against the realities of the situation. (Always ask this question: would I, if I was news editor/city editor, or whatever, of the paper concerned, give this any space?)

3. Whatever you do, ensure that the highest professionalism is applied to all its aspects (meaning that you must pay for excellent entertainment and presentation).

4. Make sure that your message is seen and heard and understood by all those to whom you are communicating (if you've got them there, speak to them).

5. At the media level, PR is greatly influenced by personal contacts—make them and keep them. (Meet media people whenever you can—and talk.)

6. Reinforce the PR message by every means in your power (even if it's only a ball-point pen or a lemon verbena plant). Successful public relations isn't just a matter of the power of the idea—it's the combined effect of the idea and its application, and you exploit that effect, not just for the short run, but for the long.

5. THE TEN CORPORATE STRENGTHS

You need to know and master the long-term lessons especially to help you through short-term disasters. The long-time Supermanagement of Dana had to report 1980 profits clobbered by recession in the auto industry, its chief market (for parts).

After that grisly year, when profits fell by 60 percent, it staged a 17 percent recovery. The management could cope with trouble using the following ten strengths—developed, please note, when *out* of trouble:

1. It had *decentralized,* pushing responsibility down to the level closest to the action. Dana has only one central management organi-

zation—the "policy committee." Divisional managers report to it, and plant managers to them, and so on down the line.

2. It had made *strategy* a key element in running the business, basing the strategy on separate, properly defined markets. (Dana has eight markets, and each strategist works with the divisional manager to find new niches and submarkets.)

3. It had formed management *groups* with no operational roles, to bring like people together to share information. For instance, the Catawba Group includes strategists and other advisers with line responsibilities. The Kiawah Group consists of Dana general managers, its entrepreneurs, and major staff department heads. The Ottawa Group is made up of key managers who meet annually to keep abreast of goals, objectives, and strategies.

4. It kept up the *pressure* for both performance and plans. Over seven days all Dana divisional managers meet the policy committee one by one to discuss their plans for one year ahead or more—and the week, significantly, is called "Hell Week."

5. It doesn't ignore any means of *communication* with everybody who needs it. Dana publishes scores of different newsletters; uses closed-circuit TV, telephone hot lines, etc.; and holds internal plant meetings conducted by plant managers and supervisors.

6. Especially important, its senior executives are *visible;* face-to-face visits of the top people at which they both inform and listen are vital.

7. It makes sure that its people are properly *trained.* The company runs Dana University, which provides over 2,000 man-weeks of free training a year in subjects like supervision, cost control, asset management, material control—and helps people to get masters' degrees in engineering and business.

8. It cuts out *layers* of management whenever it can. Dana's Hastings, Nebraska, plant, for instance, operates without direct line supervisors. At many facilities the line between manager and worker has become thin. Supervisory duties are often shared by several people, all of whom work and supervise in turn. At other plants, supervisors and office people spend some of their time actually producing the product.

9. It encourages people to *talk back*—that's the title used on

posters in Dana plants (Here's your chance to TALK BACK TO THE BOSS, Got a question or comment?—WRITE ME!) The posters have letter forms attached that are addressed to the chairman.

10. It keeps key *ratios* in mind—and aims to improve performance on those ratios. Thus Dana got its costs down from 83.4 percent of total sales to 82 percent in 1981—and every 1 percent of its sales is no less than $27 million.

But that isn't the end of the story. In 1982 Dana suffered another huge setback—this time of 56 percent in earnings per share. Let this be a lesson—especially to Dana. However good a company seems, however strong and various its strengths, bad times will always show the cracks that good times and fine words conceal.

6. USING <u>DIPI</u> IN THE DIPS

There's a difference, though. Some disasters in business are entirely the fault of the victim, although human nature generally prevents the victim from pointing the finger entirely at himself. But it's equally true that disaster can strike unbidden: for instance, when a whole economy—or the whole U.S. motor industry—collapses, many managers (like Dana's) will be caught in the crash, and there isn't too much they can do about it. Initially, that is. As noted earlier, when recession does strike, there's plenty that can be done.

Indeed, doing it—or not doing it—separates the winners, the survivors, from the losers—those who die unsung. The range of possible reactions is enormous, encompassing nearly two dozen choices, if you believe Abraham Shana, writing in the *Journal of Marketing*. His recipe for coping with hard times concentrates on the overriding objective of increasing demand—demand being what, in a recession, almost everybody lacks. The possibilities range from Product (narrow your product line, an excellent idea) to some more dubious advice on Price (lower prices whenever possible, etc.), better notions on Promotion (motivate sales force to sell more), some aggressive words on Place (increase distribution outlets), and intelligent ones on Consumers (treat consumers selectively to maximize sales).

But all Shana's preceding items, in my view, are easily outweighed by the last few: Diversify, Increase Productivity, Innovate—or DIPI for short. But they don't, of course, apply only to companies caught in general recession. The author himself recognizes this, for DIPI is also his concluding prescription for companies whose problem isn't lack of demand in a recession, but shortage of supply or inflation. It's hard to think of a single situation when, if not DIPI, IPI wouldn't apply—the point being that diversification will not always be an appropriate strategy, but increasing productivity and innovation never cease to be vital requirements.

Author Lionel Wardle points out that there are very few possible explanations if a company can't sell its products at a reasonable profit. Either:

1. There is no effective market for the product, or
2. The product is not being sold in the right way or in the right market, or
3. The product is not competitive in terms of price, quality, or service, or
4. There is "unfair" competition, possibly because of subsidies or tariffs, or
5. The company has internal weaknesses—thus, costs are too high, productivity is too low, quality control or delivery are poor, etc.

If you're really unlucky, the company will face all or some of these in apparently deadly combination. But once a management has determined which of the Fateful Five it faces, the door has been opened to solving the problem—unless you know which enemy you oppose, making the right choice of response is impossible. You end up like the Japanese fleet at the Battle of Midway. Starting off with two objectives, and uncertain what opposition they faced, the excellent Japanese admirals tried to cover themselves for all possibilities—and ended up by being caught flat-footed. They lost humiliatingly to their single-minded American opponents, despite an apparently overwhelming 4-to-1 advantage.

Wardle lists ten steps which, in or out of recession, will help a company to prepare its response to the identified enemy from a position of flexible strength:

1. Organize a systematic "reverse engineering" program on the company's products and those of its competitors. Take the things to pieces and apply value analysis to every component. Find out how they can be made better and cheaper—and don't be satisfied until your cost profile is at least as good as that of your best competitors.

2. Get comparative data from other departments, firms, and competitors and use it to identify where you need improvements. Establish performance criteria and standards. Involve the work force in planning any action that's required to meet the new standards.

3. Carry out a deliberate and systematic audit of the available business opportunities. Rank and evaluate them against clearly defined criteria.

4. Involve management and work force as far as possible in making plans to market and sell—and acting on the plans. (This is too important a task, says Wardle, to be left solely to the marketing experts.)

5. Use the information from steps 1-4 to establish a strategic plan, setting out the company's aims and specifying what must be done to hit those targets.

6. Identify and implement the changes required if the strategy is to succeed—and use, where appropriate, any techniques for developing the organization and its people which you know to be effective.

7. Make the company's management information, administration, and control systems more effective.

8. Look at possible alternative production systems for potential improvements in productivity, quality control, stock levels, delivery performance, etc.

9. Critically examine how well the company's purchasing and supply sides perform. Establish objective measures of purchasing

performance. See if you can work more closely with suppliers—providing them with technical assistance, training suppliers' staff, etc.

10. Set out the objectives which the company wants its reward system to achieve and determine how far what you've got meets those requirements. If the existing system doesn't meet those needs, then the alternatives available need to be investigated systematically.

Now, everything in this program can't possibly be done at once. Nothing in the program will stop a recession from developing, either; but nothing in it will ever be a waste of time. Quite the contrary. If a firm can survive and prosper in a slump, just imagine what it can achieve in a purple patch. DIPI in the Dips is worth even more in the Ups.

7. THE THIRD LEG THAT COLLAPSED

The worst mistake, because it's the most pervasive, is not to see yourself as you really are. The chairman of a one-time growth star wasn't far from retirement, a moment which he wanted to bring forward. He had a company president who had apparently saved the firm from extinction during a fairly recent cash crisis. That fact proved all-important in the new situation.

Up to that money crunch, crises of any kind had been foreign to the firm's experience. It had developed a growth product that had proceeded to grow without let or hindrance until the point had been reached where the business was so big that it was highly vulnerable. When the boom for the single product ended, the company began to suffer the torments of the commercially damned.

The point that worried the chairman was future strategy. The company had recently bought a complementary machinery business, which gave it a "second leg." The president wanted to find a "third leg"—and the chairman didn't know if this was sensible. He didn't have a clear alternative, but he did have reservations.

When asked if he was prepared to accept the departure of the president, though, the chairman said "No." That being so, he had no real option but to accept whatever the man decided upon. The alternative was to dismiss him and supersede his advice—in other words, to take over both strategy and tactics.

The chairman had no taste for such high-flown deeds and rapidly vacated the scene. A few years later the inevitable happened. The first leg—the original business—became so weak that it couldn't support any external load. The second leg, while profitable, proved to be too insubstantial to generate much wealth. That left the newly acquired third leg, which in the event, had too little to offer in terms of wealth or anything else. The effort to develop it, moreover, led to a huge overload of debt.

In 1976 the net capital employed of this company was $23.5 million, plus intangibles of $3.6 million. (NB: intangibles in a balance sheet are often a bad sign; the prudent company usually gets rid of them as soon as possible.) Against this, the company had $14 million of bank loans, and over a million in other debts.

Within a year, the chickens implied by this vast leverage had come home to roost. The overdraft was up by $600,000 (the bankers either had nerves of steel or the brains of the aforesaid chickens), although the company's reserves had been more than wiped out. The entire net capital employed of $15 million was accounted for by the overdraft and loans—and the company, first, second, third leg and all, was done for. All because, ultimately, the original chairman had made the fatal error of not seeing things—including his own position—as they really were.

8. HOLD THAT TIGER!

The third leg, and the company that went with it, didn't collapse because of intractable problems that sooner or later would have wreaked devastation. The problem of a growth product that turns into a commodity is difficult, exceedingly so. But it's one that has been solved many times. What went wrong in this case was *people*. The chairman's behavior was conditioned by his own irrelevant wish for early retirement, and so he took a weak attitude toward his president—about whose personal abilities he was plain wrong.

There's nothing special about the overwhelming importance of the human element in this disaster. It is the common factor found in every organizational tragedy; only rarely does an act of God, like a calamitous fire, explain collapse; usually, it is an act of man—misguided man. The misdirection comes especially easily to men who have been successful. Success is the product of talent applied to suitable circumstances. If the circumstances change, it's the talent that may no longer suit.

For instance, no TV mogul was ever more successful than Fred Silverman at ABC. His brilliant programming took the network from a poor third to the lead over CBS and NBC. Although Silverman built this leapfrogging act largely on situation comedy after situation comedy, nothing enhanced his reputation more than the screening of *Roots*. Silverman, by running the Alex Haley slavery-to-freedom saga in huge prime-time slabs on consecutive nights, broke all the rules of conventional TV programming and won record ratings for the ABC network.

The *Roots* triumph was only part of the achievements that made Silverman a legend in the business. He translated that legend into hard cash when he moved over to rival NBC for a salary of $1 million a year. There, alas, his touch was almost as unsuccessful as it had been golden at ABC.

In fact, according to a study published in 1981, the golden Silverman wasn't planning a revolutionary media coup with *Roots*. Quite the reverse. Thinking that *Roots,* in which a pile of ABC money had been sunk, would get low ratings, Silverman thought it best to take his medicine—and get the horrors over and done with in one week's fell swoop. The rest is history—and so is Silverman's career at NBC. He failed to repeat his success and is no longer with the network.

It wasn't that Silverman's skills had changed, but circumstances had—partly as a result of his own triumph's impact on the other networks while at ABC. Put another way, his luck, or rather his ability to ride his luck, had run out. Much the same thing can happen to companies; the same talents fail to work in a different situation, or (which comes to the same end) the famous talents don't work because, unbeknown to anybody, they are not being applied.

Take the case of a fashion industry boss who had learned his business the hard way. After a terrible struggle in his commercial youth, he had first built up his shops by selling high fashion on the cheap; when this had succeeded, he dedicated himself to "taking the risk out of fashion." That's a hard trick, given that fashion is inherently unstable, and nowhere more than in women's wear. But the techniques of tight computerized stock control seemed to work over the years, so that, for a brief season, the company even figured as a stock market darling.

The sudden collapse of the business, to the point where it had to be rescued from financial failure by a takeover, came as a shock to everybody—including the boss. What went wrong?

The weaknesses turned out to be the exact reverse of the previous strengths. The designs were not, as they usually had been, to the taste of the better-off younger women. Against a background of poor sales across the whole trade, the stocks had got out of hand—despite all the computer aids. The problem was compounded because the factories the company owned, whose tied production had guaranteed supplies but not final sales, suffered disproportionately as the effects of the overstocking worked backward from the stores.

The keystone of the whole edifice, just as the boss had always said, was design; and that in turn was founded on his personal identification with the design side. But as the business had expanded, and especially as international growth had begun to attract him, the fashion king was no longer able to keep so closely in touch. The design control began to slip away from him, and no computer born of man could save the day.

What can stop such evil days from appearing at all? Since the fault is human, the cure must be found in human terms. The rules are obvious enough from the many cases of failure.

1. Always put the organization above the person—especially yourself.

2. Never believe that anybody is indispensable—especially yourself.
3. Always listen first for the bad news—especially about yourself.
4. Always be highly critical of performance—especially your own.
5. Never take your eye off the main objective—especially one you have set yourself.

The defect of these five rules sticks out several leagues. If The Man is all-powerful, nobody will be able to point out the error of his ways, except himself—and he won't. In the dress shop case just described, and in most disastrous upsets, that is precisely the trouble—there is nobody around to hold that tiger and change his ways. One or two all-powerful people get beyond criticism and beyond control—and their decline and fall proceeds to the sound of a chorus of impotent yes-men. The dead giveaway is if people surrounding a manager are no good. Then neither is he, and neither, in all probability, will be his fate. The genuine Supermanager surrounds himself with the best people he can find—and listens to them.

9. THE CHILD THAT WASN'T OKAY

Good people can be made better, or turned into bad, by the way in which they are managed. The following tale is told by business expert Hugh O'Neill:

"The satellite factory of a major manufacturing parent was set up to produce a different but related product range. From the outset it had problems, not the least being that its very existence had been based upon a misguided assessment of market potential. The parent began to look down on the satellite 'child,' whose management soon adopted a 'We're not Okay' attitude. Every problem became a major disaster. And inside the satellite threats were made—solve this reject problem, or heads will roll."

One problem was making a particular product to exacting

standards of shape and appearance. In the three years of the product's life there were very few successful product runs. Most runs provided considerable quantities of misshapen product, and at times the level was so bad that the whole run was aborted. There had been several inquiries, at some of which specialists from the parent were present. No improvements were made.

Under the pressure from the parent, the child at last learned from its own mistakes. A team of operatives, supervisors, technicians, and engineers, together with a problem-solving expert, was called together. "The group took just one day to analyze the problem and propose a solution. Subsequently there have been several successful production runs and no recurrence of the reject problem."

10. HOW TO REJECT REJECTS

The worst mistake in quality control is to produce a product so awful that you can't sell it to anybody, or even try to—a reject. It's no small or occasional problem, either. To give some examples (again taken from Hugh O'Neill), one foodstuffs manufacturer had stocks worth $500,000 at retail which couldn't be sold because they didn't match the required quality standard—in appearance only. In a major engineering company, too, people had gotten used to a 73 percent-plus rejection rate on components that cost $450 apiece before they were chucked in the waste bin.

The giveaway words are "gotten used to." Not just managers, but everybody in a manufacturing company, comes to accept a certain level of rejects as normal, as inevitable. *Whenever malfunctions are accepted as facts of life, waste is occurring on a significant and unnecessary scale.* This general truth is as valid in service companies as among manufacturers. The only difference is that the waste can be more easily quantified in a factory—that is, if anyone is bothering to count.

Normally nobody bothers. But the waste must include:

(1) the raw materials consumed in rejected products (less any trifles received for the scrap);

(2) the wages and other costs consumed in taking the products as far as they got;

(3) the rework done on components that were almost, but not quite, good enough. Even where the operation is efficient enough to spot that the reject problem exists, the initial result may be more cost, not less, because time and money will be spent on trying to solve the horrible problem.

"Horrible" is the right word. According to O'Neill, the cost can run at 3 percent of gross sales value (an animal-feed firm) or 4.5 percent (an engineering company). In a precision engineering business, rejects ran at no less than 17 percent of total raw material costs. But another general truth rears its head at this point: *however great the cost of a malfunction appears to be, it is always much greater.* The only way to find the truth, the whole truth, and nothing but the truth also happens to be the only way to a cure, because, as in any management problem, full analysis either points the way directly to a solution or provides the basic information from which a solution can be generated.

Take the workings of another O'Neill case, a major international company. Direct costs attributable to rejects and waste came to 9.5 percent of manufacturing costs, including production costs, raw materials, and direct labor, but subtracting any waste recovery. Of this figure, 3 percent was attributed to "unavoidable" rejects arising during the learning curve on plant start-up or during product change (though the people thought that changes in method might reduce this by a further 1 percent); even at 3 percent, there's 6.5 percent that is "avoidable." In money terms the "avoidable" amounted to nearly $13 million per annum. With all indirect labor and overheads added, the 9.5 percent was bumped up to about 15 percent of manufacturing costs.

Rejects in the field will add a further 1.25 percent, calculated on materials costs only; adding labor and overheads, the figure rises to 2 percent. Much of this damage is done in distribution, with only a small part directly attributed to customer complaints. The breakdown shows .05 percent for complaints about the product itself and .75 percent caused by mislabeling or putting the wrong product in a package. Without counting a penny for consequential loss, loss of potential revenue, etc., the total figure for this plant (one recognized as being efficient) must exceed 17 percent of manufacturing costs. This equates to an annual sum in excess of $34.5 million, a whopping sum in relation to sales, let alone profit.

What do you do about such calamities? First, you ask where rejects are identified—whether the answer is the quality control department or some machine, that's where the inquiry must start. The questions to be asked will be many and detailed. How many rejects (per hour and per year)? What are the different types of rejects? As in any such inquiry, the probe has to go deep—behind what people say, to the actual truth.

Sometimes a simple answer will pop up, as in the case of shift supervisors who just didn't believe that management wanted the machines stopped for proper repair rather than go on churning out a substandard product. Sometimes the answer will be more difficult to achieve—solving the $500,000 feed reject problem mentioned earlier took thirty-two man-days of concentrated effort. It may be that total rejects elimination will itself be rejected as too expensive—but there are virtually no rejects problems that can't be solved, and solved, what's more, within the company.

O'Neill draws a moral which is of wider significance even than reject control: working on problems together is a remarkable way to achieve, well, working together. He calls this "the snowball effect." Once total reject control has been adopted, a number of things happen: (1) the solving of one problem often leads to the elimination of another; (2) people start to think of finding solutions rather than of how to live with problems; (3) there is an increase in formal and informal "suggestions"; (4) productivity increases follow—there is bound to be a rise directly related to the rejects eliminated, but there is usually a multiplier beyond this, which some ascribe to the improvement in morale; (5) morale certainly does improve—as epitomized in the change from an attitude of "we can't, it won't work," to that of "well, let's give it a try"; (6) interdepartmental and interpersonal conflict is reduced as quality becomes a more generally accepted and shared goal; (7) and, of course, costs come down.

To return to the case of the Child That Wasn't Okay, dramatic changes happened once the child had handled this major difficulty.

Not only did its management acquire confidence in its own ability, but the parent began to develop confidence in the management. No longer was the child a pariah; no longer was it denied investment; no longer was it refused a fair hearing; and no longer was it turning out an unacceptable level of rejects.

11. THE CATERPILLAR THAT GOT ITS PLUS

Service companies are in a similar fix. A firm distributing Caterpillar Tractor machinery, instead of advertising to its customers one year, spent the money on a promotion campaign aimed at its own staff. The firm had found defects in the company's service to customers. The faults weren't surprising, since most employees didn't seem to know (a) that their jobs had any bearing on customer service, or (b) that service levels had any impact on the company's fortunes.

So the advertising money was spent on selling to *the staff* a program called "Cat Plus"—designed to emphasize, among other things, service and quality. Employees even got invitations to briefings sent to their homes, as if they were ladies and gentlemen of the press. As the marketing chief put it, "We've gradually come around to likening ourselves to running a restaurant or hotel." The "Cat Plus" program thus covered everything—the distribution company even had its offices and workshops smartened up in the process.

Research among the staff after the program showed that 65 percent of them felt that "help and assistance" to customers had improved after the program (most of those who didn't so feel thought it was already very good). What mistake did the sensible 65 percent make in feeling so satisfied with that result?

12. SAMPLES OF SUCCESS

The mistake made by the Cat distributor was fundamental. The *internal* verdict on a company's quality isn't worth a plugged nickel if the *external* verdict, that of the customers who generate its livelihood, is adverse. The same goes for a bureaucracy. The wonderful opinion its inhabitants have of their own performance may speak volumes for their high morale, but has nothing to do with the purposes and achievements of the organization. A satisfied customer is the only real touchstone, and it is the only ultimate safeguard—as long as the customer is being satisfied at economic cost.

In other words, an unbreakable cord connects the happy user at one end and the efficient producer or purveyor at the other. Just as profit stems from efficiency, so does quality; and from economic quality, in turn, come market strength and market penetration. The tale has been told many times, but needs retelling again and again—how Japanese producers, in motorcycles, consumer electronics, cameras, cars, etc., have carved out dominant or leading shares of world markets by taking American techniques and developing their use to a higher pitch than any industry in the West has managed to achieve.

As with any management technique, the key to modern quality control doesn't lie in complex scientific brilliance, but in simple willpower. The method known as "statistical quality control" (SQC), true, is beyond the easy understanding of the average manager, though the statistically minded find it easy enough. But you don't have to be a mathematical genius to grasp the fact that only a minority of firms have been using SQC to control quality throughout their manufacturing operations.

Americans are significantly more likely to use SQC than Europeans, but U.S.-owned firms are mostly recent converts to the approach. Not so in Japan. According to Keith Lockyer and John Oakland,

> In Japan, statistical methods are commonly known not only by quality control engineers, but by all company personnel. They can all make practical use of SQC methods. . . . One

means of public recognition of a company's QC activities is the Deming Prize for Application, given on the basis of "the degree of dissemination, state of application of SQC, and future promise." This award is the most distinguished QC prize in Japan, and many companies make it a prime goal in their efforts to promote quality.

Another measurement of recognition is the Japanese Industrial Standards (JIS) certification mark, which gives a national guarantee of quality to Japanese products that bear it. "To be eligible for JIS approval, a company must practice SQC—and the JIS mark can be given only after this condition is satisfied."

In theory, skeptics could once have explained the Western reluctance to use these techniques (actually fifty years old) by the old excuse of claiming that they didn't work. But the recent rush of American companies to import this American lore back from Japan gives the lie to any such comforting notion. The explanation for neglect lies in two highly dangerous characteristics of managers—reluctance to change established ways, and reluctance to apply scientific or logical method to management. For instance, the established way of controlling quality is inspection. Large armies of inspectors are employed; their existence is itself a barrier to any change of technique, even though inspection is known (look only at the car industry) to be an ineffective and expensive method.

In fact, even 100 percent inspection yields worse results than the far cheaper SQC approach, in which samples are analyzed statistically. Research shows that inspecting every single item can still let through up to 15 percent of defective items; SQC, on the other hand, not only does away with inspection costs, but can reduce scrap by 2 percent and the costs of rework by 15 percent. The fundamental principle can be checked very simply by the unbelieving. The number of words in this book containing the letter "e" can be counted laboriously one by one, or easily from a few samples. The sampling result will be more accurate.

Now, since the technique can be demonstrated independently, and since its results in companies can be shown unequivocally, why don't people rush to pick up what Lockyer and Oakland describe as "nuggets of gold lying on the beach"? Part of the answer lies in a simple organizational boob. Even in some parts of the chemical industry, where quality control is crucial, only a third of the production managements are *directly* responsible for quality, according to one survey. As Philip Crosby, the author of *Quality Is Free*, has constantly stressed, one easy way to get poor quality is to make it the responsibility of a separate quality department—i.e., somebody else's business.

Quality is everybody's business, because it runs right through every business—right down to the bottom line. To quote from *Management Today*, "The crucial fact is that it is much less costly to prevent bad manufacture than to rework, scrap, or service it, a waste which can and does cost 15 percent of turnover." The charts of the statistical wizards will show quickly when a process is going wrong—and the warnings in one case (a paint company) saved $375,000 in a year. For instance (this instance), if you've got a worn friction valve slowly and continually vibrating open, letting too much paint into the cans, it's costing you money—and the sooner you know, the quicker you can get the wretched thing repaired.

More important than the detailed faults, though they can be hideously expensive, is the general principle. In any business, and not just in the vital control of quality, improvement can always be achieved if the will to improve exists. If the will, and the knowledge that improvement is possible, aren't there, neither the quality nor the business is under proper control. Get that control, and the rewards are endless.

13. THE QUALITY PROPHET'S LATE HONOR

If ever a prophet took a long, too long, time to be honored in his own country it's W. Edwards Deming—pioneer of the statistical quality control methods just mentioned which have been cardinally important to Japanese production successes, and the man who gave his name to the famous Japanese prize. Yet the master didn't start working for the Pontiac division of General Motors, as one example, until he was almost eighty years old—and the results were predictably quick and rich.

Item: at Engine Plant Eighteen, four different vendors supplied connecting rod bolts whose defective threads were causing perpetual bother. Putting in Deming's system showed at once that all the defective bolts came from only one of the supplying quartet. The defective vendor was dropped.

Item: in the 1981 model year, thirty-eight engines had to be removed from the chassis, or "pulled," at a cost of $38,000 or more, because a camshaft gear, which had to be bored to a tolerance of a few thousandths of an inch, didn't fit. Measuring the bores on three successive gears once an hour, *à la* Deming, proved enough to keep the boring accurate. Only half a dozen engines had to be taken out in 1982. In 1983 months went by without a single incident.

Item: the total "pull rate" for the 2.5 liter engine on which No. Eighteen works is down to below one in a thousand—it used to be over three and a half times as high.

Item: the percentage of engines passed by inspectors on the units' first arrival at the end of the line is up from 60 percent to 96 percent—or well-nigh perfect.

Reporting on this, *Fortune* magazine points out that Dr. Deming advocates much more than statistical control alone. He also stresses worker participation and training—something which this plant's hourly paid people had received hardly at all. After a full-time month of instruction, they now understand statistical controls and possess both a calculator and a magnifying glass. The last unsophisticated tool costs little but can save a fortune—it's used to examine tools with greater care.

Sounds childishly simple, doesn't it? Very often, that's what major improvements are—child's play. Making automobiles is a highly complex, difficult process. But it's not at all difficult to see that some traditional approaches are wrong and stupid. For instance, in another example quoted by *Fortune's* Jeremy Main, Ford broke with tradition in 1980. Although its Louisville plant hadn't officially been given the mission to build the new Ranger truck, the drawings, parts, models, and mock-ups were sent to Louisville for display alongside the assembly lines—and workers were invited to participate with comments and ideas.

The normal practice often sees the plant stuck with awkward, wrong, and counterproductive procedures that look fine in the drawing office, or more likely are just overlooked, but which don't work on the line. The Louisville workers, given the chance to get it right, came up with 749 proposals by early 1983, of which 542 had been adopted. In the December corporate audit, reports Main, the Louisville outfit had only 198 "concerns" (mistakes in Ford lingo) per one hundred cars, the lowest the auto-maker has found anywhere in the U.S.

None of this would surprise the high priest of quality control. Deming has always stressed that quality is a means to other ends. That Pontiac engine plant emphatically makes his point. As quality has improved, so has productivity—last year it rose by no less than 27 percent.

14. QUALITIES OF CIRCLES

Nothing about quality applies to quality alone, including the key questions that must be asked. They are: What are we doing that could be done differently—and better? What are we doing that needn't be done at all? What definitions that we use can be changed—and should be?

Take quality itself. The instant response in most managerial minds is to think of reported defects, scrap rates, more inspectors, customer complaints and returns, and so on. But in the wider, truer sense, quality stands for the overall service and satisfaction offered to the user. It isn't an *aspect* of the product or whatever—it *is* the product.

That's why the vital process of value analysis, coupled with value engineering, has such high—well, value. Like quality control, VA activities must be undertaken by skilled technicians, but their underlying principles are universal. First, value analysis is conducted by a *team*—many cooks make the broth. Second, the team literally pulls the product to pieces—nothing is sacred. Third, the classic criterion of management is applied—the price-performance ratio, or how can we obtain better performance at lower cost? Fourth, the exercise is not academic—it is expected to result in implemented change.

In nearly all cases, successful VA efforts to reduce the product's manufacturing costs, by cutting down the number of components or substituting less expensive materials and methods, result in benefits for the user as well. You can see the process over the life of very long-running items, like car engines, which may power half a dozen different models over their lifetimes. With each successive modification, the engine delivers more power for less noise and often achieves more economy. That's because the original specifications and performance set a bench mark, the minimum standard on which the engineers will inevitably seek to improve.

There are cases where the product and service are too good, in the sense that they cost too much to supply or are too expensive for the market. "Goodness" is not an absolute—you don't make throwaways to last. However, it's rare to find a firm whose quality is genuinely excessive. One cynical Supermanager had a division which reckoned it had cured the previous fault of supplying "a Rolls-Royce product at a Ford price." According to the boss, it hadn't been doing anything of the sort—it had been making a Ford at Rolls-Royce costs. Self-deception comes in the door when the value analysis principle goes out of the window, as at Rolls-Royce itself before the aero engine and auto company went bust in 1971.

Among the various and horrible problems which brought that great business to its knees was sheer excessive cost. Thus the making of aero engines was troubled by a gruesome 24 percent tally of defective welds on turbine blades, and machining problems on the same, leading to a scrap rate of 4 percent. Business problems, of course, needn't be technical to waste wealth; in another company, time was being lost through conflicting job instructions, at a total cost of $250,000 a year. In yet another firm, people had to search around looking for precision tools—and that cost $100,000.

Both the last two problems were identified and solved by the same business technique that undid the damage at Rolls-Royce. The latter's 24 percent of defective welds was corrected, after investigation, by amending the weld parameters and increasing the "slope-out" (the time taken for the electron welding beam to decay) from eight seconds to twelve. The defect rate came down to 1.8 percent—saving $90,000 in nine months. The machining problems on the blades were corrected by clearing up the work space and reorganizing the layout of the equipment. The scrap rate duly came down to an eighth of its previous level—annual saving, $40,000.

The magic technique that was applied to these diverse cases, and can apply to an infinite number of other ones, is the quality circle. It costs money itself, but it's worth it—the return on the investment is commonly five or eight times. And at Rolls-Royce that meant no mere bauble—a total saving of $750,000 in only thirty months.

The principle goes to the heart of the extraordinary Japanese economic achievement. The Japanese know that quality isn't something stuck on to a product after it's made, but something built into the original design, and into the ensuing modifications, and into the whole production process. It's the achievement of a permanent advantage in perceived value and reliability.

However much quality is built into design and methods, though, its achievement is ultimately a matter of men. Hence the Japanese development of "quality circles" in those first months after wartime defeat when Japan began building its peacetime victory. There were no instructors other than the foremen, so the latter began training the workers, naturally in groups.

Then the great discovery was made—that solutions to problems arise very simply from the interactions of the *group* (remember the same point about value analysis *teams*). In the words used at Honda, "we want people to display their ability." Once again, the object is not simply to cut the reject rate. That will be the wonderfully valuable by-product of something far more wonderful—getting the best out of people because they want to give it.

The key principle is well known in the West, anyway—that workers, as Ford found at Louisville, are an excellent source of ideas for improving their work. Why the source isn't tapped for its flow of pure mountain-spring water, managements themselves scarcely know. Part of the trouble lies in the psychology of the workplace, in which command and everything else flow from top-down, and nothing moves from bottom-up. The lack of a mechanism for reversing that flow is one of the major barriers, which is where the quality circle comes in.

Here are quality control expert David Hutchins's rules:

1. Involve *everybody*, from top to bottom, and especially not forgetting the middle.
2. Pick the place to start with great care, and start small.
3. Appoint the supervisor who will run the circle with equal care.
4. Give him, as the first job, the training of the circle in this way of solving problems, and hark to Hutchins's words on this:

> Remember that in all probability, the members of a quality circle will not have been to school for many years . . . and it was probably not a happy experience. The supervisor and the trainers must be able to talk the same language, and explain without the use of statistical analysis and technical terms and concepts. The people most likely to prove best at this form of training will themselves have spent a considerable part of their working lives on the shop floor.

5. After training, have the circle pick the problem. They must choose it, not you; it has to be *their* problem.
6. The circle (seven or eight members) then sets about the problem—and the solution. You should make sure that the people concerned get a cut out of the savings; remember, those are potentially five to eight times the financial cost of implementing.

The cost in time shouldn't be enormous, either; one hour once every two weeks is usually enough to do the trick—and it's some trick. You should be able to get the following benefits, apart from the crucial money savings: better morale on the shop floor, less frustration, more effective supervision, the breakdown of shop-floor indifference to quality, and a much more critical standard of quality, when self-applied, than you can get from inspection.

It's also necessary to keep the Pareto principle in mind (Pareto was the eighteenth-century Italian economist who discovered that 80 percent of the profits come from 20 percent of the product line). What that means is that you don't want the group to devote its time and energies to the 80 percent of the operation that generates only 20 percent of the costs or the quality problems. It's the vital fifth that gives you 80 percent of your troubles, and that is obviously where attention should be concentrated. Exactly the same Pareto principle applies to value analysis teams; indeed, quality circles can be regarded as VA of work itself, and, like VA, the QC inevitably goes into internal methods of manufacture en route to the external objective. That can be stated with beautiful simplicity—better quality in the hands of the user, or, even more simply, turning mistakes into Supermanagement.

15. THE DYING COMPANY THAT DIDN'T

Resurrection can be achieved even in cases where the mistakes not only outnumber the correct procedures—but swamp them entirely. This is what one set of investigators found in a case where the company wasn't so much sick as moribund. The list of its ailments was so long and grave that it's hard to think of anything else that could go wrong (or of anything that was going right).

1. Poor profitability
2. Low morale throughout, with expectations of closure at any time
3. Badly run-down buildings and plant
4. High levels of waste and customer returns
5. Excessively high costs of production and ancillary operations
6. No selling activity

7. Four to five years behind competitors with new products
8. Poor housekeeping
9. Substandard office facilities and canteen.

If a list like that doesn't frighten you off altogether, at least, once you know what's wrong, you can use the atrocities as the basis for a plan of counteraction. That was what happened, with the consultants' help. Before long the dying company had sprung back to life, was making reasonable profits, and was able to plan a progressive future. How was the kiss of life administered?

16. HOW TEAMWORK WORKS

In crises, managers commonly do the sensible, sane, necessary things they could have done before—thus averting the crisis altogether. If people working in a company don't know what's happening or why, they will work less effectively and think more suspiciously—a heavy price to pay for the dubious comforts of secrecy. In the case just described, the chief executive officer began his cure by telling the truth and telling it to everybody. He called a general meeting of employees, explained the company's critical situation, and outlined the action planned.

Don't speed over this point. A crucial part of the battle for men's minds is to back words with deeds. One reason for Jimmy Carter's lack of success as President (for instance, take MEOW—his "Moral Equivalent of War" speech on the energy crisis) was failure to support his rhetoric with effective action. The boss in this case was no Carter; he followed these steps, and at once:

1. Bulk purchase and storage of high-consumption materials;
2. Tight controls on use of oil and electricity;
3. Tight controls on waste and new materials usage;
4. Increased machine speeds;
5. No recruitment, not even to replace leavers or retirements.

All boring, humdrum, and necessary measures. But negative programs (to reduce costs, eliminate waste, etc.) must always go hand in hand with positive moves. Where cutting costs is coupled with souping up sales, the results must obviously be vastly enhanced. So the CEO also went for increased turnover by:

1. Increasing prices where possible;
2. Selling a wider range of products to existing customers;
3. Seeking new customers for existing products;
4. Concentrating all development work on one new product at a time to catch up with competitors.

These nine good deeds, counteracting and repairing the nine deadly sins, were not, though, the real way in which the company was saved. They were, of course, important moves in themselves, but they also made a convincing contribution to the true cure by improving morale and changing attitudes. And, however lengthily it's described, this always boils down to two friendly words—"communication" and "involvement."

The double process had begun with that general meeting of employees. In fact, in the eight months it took to force through the concrete changes, the troubles left too little time to involve many people, but at least a regular newspaper was introduced to ensure that everybody was informed about what was going on.

That was being decided at the top level of the company, where the CEO had set out to weld his five senior executives into a team, with a weekly meeting as the main device. "Team" is one of those much overworked words in management: it suggests a cohesion and unity that you rarely get and may not really want all the time; effective management is the combined contribution of different individuals working along both independent and collaborative routes toward both individual and common objectives.

The CEO, recognizing this truth, made each man personally responsible for developing and implementing changes in his area, and personally accountable for achieving the objectives in a laid-down program. Those were only interim aims, but not until they had been achieved could the company move on to a proper set of objectives. The boss then set out to:

1. Double the sales turnover in real terms in five years.
2. Produce a profit on capital employed of more than 30 percent.
3. Reduce total waste, scrap, and customer returns to at most 5 percent of output.
4. Increase machine utilization (NB: *the current figures were not known,* so a target for improvement couldn't be set).
5. Improve the effectiveness of senior and supervisory management.

In the context of teamwork the last point should be first. As the corporate recovery proceeded, a significant difference in attitude appeared among the five senior executives and the six supervisors. Not only did attitudes differ, but a big gap also yawned in those vital twin areas of friendship—communications and involvement. This is the tender point in the corporate anatomy where the teamwork notion becomes bogus and dangerously weak. If the "top management team" is the *only* "team," yawning holes will open up beneath, and money will start to cascade through the holes. The junior managers are far more than cogs in a wheel; they are conduits of responsibility and implementation. In this particular company, which operated around the clock, the supervisors were wholly and solely responsible for the entire factory for sixteen hours a day.

The boss tried to bridge the gap by in-house meetings, but what had worked with the top five didn't work with the supervisors, because of the limited time available. So the supervisors were treated in a way commonly reserved for senior people alone: they were taken off for a weekend conference, along with their seniors, to examine at leisure the problems in everybody's mind and to start on the road to their solution.

The conference was organized as a training session—another of those dual-control devices. Not only does training impart useful knowledge—in itself it raises and creates morale and distills that curious liquid known as team spirit. For proof, you need only witness the bizarre way in which management students of all ages, strangers to each other, develop overpowering team loyalties and drives when playing management games on a training course.

You can see how much work the newly combined management-supervisor team still faced from that little lacuna mentioned—the fact that one of the targets, an increase in machine utilization, had to be left vague, for the simple reason that nobody knew what the current utilization was. It goes without saying that you can't adopt an intelligent program for improvement unless you know from what you're improving and to what you plan to improve. A team that's a real team will gain in cooperation and rise in contribution by combining to find facts, analyze faults, and cure the suitable cases for treatment. And in that process, as in the true story just told, the corporate terminal patient may pick up its bed and walk.

17. THE CORONA TORTURES

You can even recover from massive incompetence by mighty intelligence. Among the many disasters and near-disasters overcome by Toyota in its early development was the flop of the new Corona sedan, introduced in 1960—a technical "lemon" that was being clobbered all over Japan by the Datsun Bluebird. With the confidence of its customers and dealers sorely damaged, Toyota's task looked hopeless. As Seisi Kato records, "What the Corona needed was an entirely new image"; but changing a product image in the Corona's parlous situation is about as daunting a task as a salesman could face.

Kato thought "long and deep and landed on what proved to be a fantastic advertising idea." He commissioned a series of three television commercials. In his own words, "The first commercial featured a spectacular flying leap by a Corona. The car sped up onto a springboard and then literally took off through space on a twenty-five-meter flight. After landing, of course, the Corona calmly drove on as if its flight were nothing unusual.

"The second film showed a Corona being pushed off a drop of more than ten feet. The car fell and rolled over two or three times, its roof caving in and part of its hood being crushed. The shock value was terrific. Just as the viewer saw a brand-new car devastated before his eyes, the engine started up and the car drove away. The third commercial depicted Coronas grouped into teams, playing soccer. Quick turns, quick stops, and quick starts. The point was that the Corona could handle any kind of driving."

The "torture campaign" did exactly what was wanted—to destroy the idea that the Corona was a "delicate" car. After the commercials began to appear, its sales started to rise, and the model became a best seller. There was only one departure from strict truth in advertising in the tortures that turned the Corona corner—understandably, the driver didn't get into the car until *after* it had fallen off the cliff.

18. IT REALLY PAYS TO ADVERTISE

Why do managers in companies of many different kinds persist in the same error? There's no doubt of the truth that emerges so strongly from the Corona's tale—that it pays to advertise. But the truth is usually extolled, not by people like Kato, but by advertising agents or media owners—who are not exactly impartial witnesses for the defense.

Thus it's only natural, in a recession, for an advertising agency to urge one and all to promote, bang the big drum, and spend on marketing. "Reductions in expenditure by other advertisers," an agency once asserted, "create chances for the innovative marketer." Obviously true. You can't easily escape the cynical knowledge that no advertising means no advertising agency—but the agency happens to be perfectly right—and most clients get it perfectly wrong.

Consider the following facts. There's a study by the publishers McGraw-Hill (another self-interested party, certainly) which shows from the financial data of nearly five hundred companies that sales growth for those that didn't trim advertising expenditure in the 1974–75 downturn was about 12 percent higher than for companies that did cut back. The problem here is which came first? It's that chicken and that egg again. Were those companies encouraged to maintain their advertising because their sales were high—or was it the other way around?

Similar kinds of logical objection can be made to some 1976 figures from A. C. Nielsen showing that, across sixty-two product groups, 60 percent of brands with increased advertising budgets suffered only a minor sales setback, while 40 percent declined less than expected. The gains recorded ranged from 13 percent for health and beauty aids to 68 percent for food products. The implication that advertising helped is very strong, but the case is really clinched by what happens when commercial television is blacked out by a strike—as it was once in Britain.

At the time, the pundits jumped to the opposite conclusion: they burbled on about firms finding that they could get along fine (and much more cheaply) without TV. Later investigation by another advertising agency, D'Arcy-McManus & Masius, exposed the burble for what it was. Taking ninety-six advertised brands, the net loss of sales volume during the TV strike was 4.5 percent; in brand share, the net loss was 2.4 percent. The bigger the advertising cut, moreover, the steeper the fall. The thirty-six companies whose advertising dropped by over $150,000 lost 8.7 percent of sales volume when the commercials were off the air and waved good-bye to 6 percent of their market share. For sixty companies whose advertising drop was less than $150,000, the slippage was only 2 percent on sales and 0.3 percent in market share.

The defense rests. If everybody is cutting back, the brands that are usually advertised heavily will fall more than the market. What is true in recession applies just as forcefully in happy days. You reduce your share of marketing effort (in which "share of voice," or share of advertising, is a vital factor) at your peril. Some other Nielsen figures, drawn from the U.S., the U.K., Australia, and Germany, show that in three quarters of cases loss of market share follows on a reduction in share of marketing effort—yet companies persist in reducing it regardless.

A fundamental consideration here is that advertising is *cumulative.* It works just like memory—because, of course, the recollection of an advertising message *is* memory. Refresh your recollection of something you are trying to learn at regular intervals, and it will stick forever. Leave the memory alone for a while, and it will wither. According to three independent U.S. experiments, the primary effect of advertising on sales takes place within the first three to twelve months. The short-term effect of a week's TV advertising seems to build up brand share in that week and for up to four subsequent weeks. Then the effect starts to dwindle away.

Needless to say, this truth makes nonsense, not only of indiscriminate ad-slashing in recession, but of another time-hallowed practice of advertising companies: not doing any promotion in the summer. A meticulous study of the West German market by a Nielsen expert found not a particle of logic of any kind behind this universal abhorrence of the summer months, which cuts across all media. Radio and TV are equally affected, even though the radio audience *rises* in summer, while TV viewing *declines.*

The explanation lies in mental set. The advertisers are all fixated on the erroneous idea that all their target audience is on vacation, or in no mood to buy, or not paying attention to ads in the month of August (and in December as well). Because of the fixation, they allow the impact of their heavy spending in the favored months to wear off, meaning that much of the heavy spending after the summer merely returns their brand awareness to Square One.

The aim of advertising, as used by the greatest salesmen down the ages, is to develop long-term recognition and to reinforce consumer loyalties. Within that long-term aim, all manner of short-term switching is perfectly right and proper—though, even then, you have to be very careful that short-term decisions don't produce harmful long-term effects. For instance, transfer of budgets from advertising to promotions—reduced price offers and the like—can be counterproductive. A study by Nielsen thus found that consumer promotions often fail to attract new users and in the longer term can lose some regular purchasers, who do buy the brand on promotion—but then refuse to pay more for it. In sum, in recession and out, advertising is a most powerful weapon, but one which, like most management tools, deserves much more intelligent handling than it customarily gets.

In this case more than most, the mistakes made by the majority give opportunities that are seized by Supermanagers. That's one of the reasons why they stay at the top: they learn not only from their own mistakes, but from those made by others—and they exploit the latter for all they are worth, which is plenty.

To summarize some of the important points I've mentioned in Step Seven:

1. If you're not being critical about your business and yourself, you should be.

2. Supermanagement most proves its strength by its readiness to recognize and rectify its weaknesses.

3. If the wrong message is getting through to the public, it's your fault, not theirs.

4. If you Increase Productivity and Innovate in good times, you'll be far better placed in bad ones.

5. Always put the organization above the person—especially yourself: and never believe that anybody is indispensable—especially yourself.

6. Whenever people accept rejects or other malfunctions, they're accepting waste and inefficiency: you must not.

7. Get really good quality by really good methods and you get a really good company.

8. Use teams to solve problems: finding the facts, analyzing the faults—and curing the condition.

9. If you're making the same mistake as everybody else, stop it—and steal the free advantage you've been offered.

Step Eight: How to Manage the Future-Now

1. THE EXECUTION OF EXXON

Long-term visions of the future, even for the wealthiest company, are far easier formed then realized. No company in the world is richer than Exxon in terms of money (1982 sales: $9.7 billion), which means that no company is better placed to buy the best management, the best technology, or anything else. It can also easily afford to pay $1.2 billion for another company, which it did a few years back for a firm named Reliance Electric. This wasn't a step undertaken lightly; the rich management had decided to reduce Exxon's dependence on oil by building a conglomerate of other businesses, mostly with a high technological content.

Hence Exxon Enterprises, which ventured into activities as far apart as photovoltaic cells (for solar heating) to office automation.

For all the enterprise and the enterprises, for all the expensively purchased technology, the diversification policy proceeded to make not a cent. Reliance Electric enshrined the biggest, brightest, and highest idea—manufacturing a product far removed from Exxon's own areas of knowledge, "the alternating-current synthesizer," a gadget supposed to make all electric motors much more efficient.

But Reliance went wrong for two reasons that had nothing to do with the technology. Exxon paid far too much, after being outbargained by the other side, and it didn't allow for any complications arising from the fact that Reliance had just completed a big acquisition itself.

Both mistakes might have been overcome, in time, if the technology had worked—but it didn't. The *raison d'être* of the synthesizer was that it would be cheaper to make—but it wasn't.

So the superexpensive Reliance buy, with the hornet's nest of legal and other trials it landed on Exxon's head, had been made for a technological reason that disappeared beneath Exxon's feet. In no time at all, the financial damage of the Reliance deal totted up to $600 million. That represented the profits on an awful lot of oil.

2. HOW TO MAKE MIRACLES

Exxon can be blamed, and its management should blame itself, for the loss, but not for the cost they were willing to incur. Once you've embarked on a progressive modernization of any business, you can never get off the express train, and it's a harsh macroeconomic fact of our era that development projects large and small, technological and otherwise, have been getting more and more expensive.

Thus the premium on getting it right—buying the right machine or producing the improvement that the market truly wants—has become higher and higher. In concentrated companies, built around a concentrated product base, being right should be relatively straightforward. If the people you employ don't have a complete coverage of the technology, either through their own resources or those they can tap, new or extra technologists should be hired, fast. Similarly, any good company should be deeply and accurately informed about trends in market requirements. With excellent technical and customer information, managers should be able to make good decisions in a business which is, after all, the air they breathe.

The toughest problems come with new technologies—ones which you could possibly use, or ones which open up new markets that you could possibly enter to your great and abiding profit. Both avenues are mined with high explosive. Awful mistakes have been made by brilliant men and corporations haring off down technological blind alleys, or buying expensively into markets that either evaporate or turn out to be ruinously competitive. The first problem is often one of time lags—a new technology may promise huge future benefits, but the timing of that future is notoriously uncertain.

Not only that, but equal notoriety surrounds the tendency of technology to develop snags. Of the many technologies that appeared to be blossoming in the mid-sixties, most have still not produced any commercial payoff. One of the wonders then being touted was carbon fiber, which Rolls-Royce unwisely adopted for the RB-211 engine (the one which helped to bankrupt the company and its customer, Lockheed); the material had to be abandoned because it wouldn't bond satisfactorily to metal. Only now, in the eighties, is carbon fiber at long last coming into its own.

Technological forecasting, even with technologies that are well understood, is extremely hazardous, and the future can be missed by companies at every level of sophistication and wealth—including the kings of the market. RCA reigned supreme over the old vacuum-tube technology; in the rip-roaring semiconductor market that has replaced the tube, RCA is nowhere. Among the new giants making germanium-based semiconductors were names like Hughes and Transitron, but they proceeded to miss out on the next stage, the silicon device.

Among customers for that latest technology, NCR should have been first in the queue. Instead, it lagged so far behind in switching from electromechanical cash registers to electronic ones that only an amazing feat of tearing down and rebuilding the company (literally—whole plants were demolished) saved the day. That act of salvation amounts to Supermanagement, but in the meantime NCR had lost vital ground to the opposition.

At that, it did far, far better than a smaller competitor which, having made the same technological mistake as NCR, tried to make a Great Leap Forward into what was then the bravest new micro-electronic world, that of the 64K RAM (for Random Access Memory). Unfortunately, the marvel wasn't then available from any chip-maker in the whole wide world. At the last minute the rescue bid had to be redesigned around two 32K RAMs instead. The awful delays and expenses brought the new all-electronic register in late and at an impossibly uncompetitive price. The rescue product was the last nail in a $50 million coffin. Failure to update offerings and resources has become fatal in an era when market after market is becoming impossible to enter without expensive technology, and where in some markets (like office machinery) high technical so-phistication will be essential to keep abreast of the competition.

Spending so that the company can stay in the right markets with the right offerings is not a gamble—it's an insurance premium to the power of n. How much of a premium the company can afford to pay is another matter. Many companies set aside a fixed percent-age of sales revenue, which has the virtue that spending expands with the scale of the business. Other firms plan their research and development, cost it, and then decide whether they can afford to fi-nance the planned work—or, more important, whether they can af-ford not to.

Whatever way the spending is fixed, though, it must follow the general management rules. Each program must have a clear objec-tive, and the program mapped out must point right at that target. Nor do you, as Exxon did, venture with a bottomless purse into the bottomless pits of new technologies which are foreign to the man-agement in business sectors which are equally unfamiliar. Not only does this combine two high-risk areas, but it makes the essential controls and objectivity impossible to apply—and research, devel-opment, and exploitation are not areas which wither when managed properly.

On the contrary, controls and objectivity exercised by people who understand the business and what they want will make research and development more, not less, productive. The new president of General Electric says he has never taken a problem to the laboratories that they have been unable to solve. That sums up another vital part of nontechnological management's role in achieving technological results—simply, shortly, and sweetly, to ask for them.

3. THE MAN WHO GOT GOULD ELECTRONIC

The Supermanager doesn't seek technological results, though. He seeks them in the right markets. These days, that may mean major upheaval even after a great run of success. Consider the example of William T. Ylvisaker. Nobody could have blamed him for resting on his laurels in his mid-fifties. His company, Gould, Inc., was making batteries when Ylvisaker took over—and making them none too well—to the tune of $100 million of sales a year. One decade later, sales were $2 billion, thanks to a combination of aggressive buying and equally belligerent management. But the profit margins on Gould's largely traditional lines of business began to slip after 1977—and in 1980 profits actually fell (by 34 percent) for the first time under Ylvisaker's stewardship.

Out of the several strategies available to him, Ylvisaker took the boldest option—totally transforming the company into becoming primarily a high-technology electronics manufacturer, and doing so by selling off many of the fifty businesses he had acquired. As he told *Business Week,* "Of our four businesses—electrical, battery, industrial, and electronics—electronics has consistently shown the highest return on investment. Because we think electronics has by far the greatest growth opportunities in the 1980s and 1990s, that's where we have decided to concentrate our investment."

The bold bid for electronics strength—which took the company up to $1 billion of electronics sales in no time at all—has been described as a gamble. Whether the electronics bet is any riskier than sticking in Gould's older businesses is another matter. But gamblers need luck—and Ylvisaker seems to have it. In 1979 he made expensive bids for two leading semiconductor manufacturers, Mostek and Fairchild Camera. Both were lost to bigger, richer bidders shortly before the semiconductor market and manufacturers' profits went into a nose dive. Both could have been disasters for Gould—and Ylvisaker.

4. ADVENTURES OF IDEAS

Rule one in the great, rich sport of technology is "Race in the winnable races"—and the ones that are most worth winning. When Bill Ylvisaker decided on the dramatic shift to electronics, he couldn't guarantee success, but he could be absolutely sure that, if the Gould companies did their stuff in the chosen markets, the results would be spectacularly good and richly rewarding. The same effort devoted to Gould's traditional businesses could never have offered the hope of a similarly golden future.

This process of loading the dice in your favor, so that your throws have a better chance of paying off, doesn't merely consist of choosing markets or areas where good payoffs are possible. You must also select ideas that you can implement, turn into practical form. Ylvisaker had every reason to suppose that his conglomerate could successfully group together electronic businesses on a large enough scale and at a high enough level of technology. Win or lose, he was in a winnable game—and one where, although the ultimate risk (the failure of the whole company) was high, the intermediate risks were much lower.

Rule two, in fact, is "Never succumb to the illusion that, the greater the risk, the better the idea." When three self-made millionaires were once asked if their success had sprung from taking risks, they replied, as one man, "No." The only risk they took was that they might fail. Their ventures, as they thought and proved, involved ideas that were absolutely certain to pay off, as long as the execution was right. The success ratio of ideas depends critically on reducing and limiting the degree of risk, though, obviously, the riskiness rises with the length of the period you're considering.

The problem is not so much to generate ideas. Even in the

worst of businesses, ideas abound. If the business is a bad one, either the ideas are, too, or there's an effective mechanism for stifling any good notions at birth. But even in a good business, a huge proportion of the ideas generated wither on the vine—largely because they aren't any good. Although technical innovation is by no means the only area in which a manager needs ideas, it does provide a measurable and deeply depressing guide to the chances of successful thought.

One body set up specifically to foster patentable inventions looked at some 10,000 ideas from 1952 to 1979. Of those only seven turned out to be actual money-making hits—and only one of those seven made big-time loot. You could argue that such an outfit is less likely than a commercial company to adopt a rigorous approach to innovation. But the failure rate of all ideas in a company, of all the notions that are spilled out day by day, is very likely to be just as high. It will never be possible to come up only with good ideas; however, the manager who takes the future as seriously as he should can greatly improve the chances that schemes (which are ideas converted into plans) will earn their and his keep.

As Peter Drucker points out in *The Changing World of the Executive*, "Even the most competent management probably bats, at best, around 0.300 in the innovation area. Innovation is chancy. But surely there is a reason, other than luck, why some managements, a Procter & Gamble or a 3M, for instance, have done consistently so much better in product development and product introduction than most others. One reason is that all the businesses with a high batting average systematically appraise their innovation performance against expectations. Then one can improve. And then, above all, one can know what one is good at. Most businesses manage innovation by promise. The competent innovators manage by results."

Rule three is "Never confuse the really long-term 'blue-sky' idea with the more mundane and immediate variety." Most parts of an organization should be geared to continuous improvement by better ideas—whether it's a production line, an office, or the product itself. For instance, if a company isn't producing one or two successful extensions or developments in the existing line of business every year, not only is its research and development bad—very likely, so is the company.

Blue skies won't start shining above unless time is set aside for them. It seldom is. For instance, in a vast multinational, the directors are in theory supposed to think about little else but the future. In practice, in one such outfit, the top directors have forty-five meetings every year in all—the calendar doesn't allow any more. Since current matters obviously impinge on their deliberations, only about five meetings a year actually touch on the future at all. It probably pays to set aside at least one meeting each quarter when you talk *only* about the future—meaning up to fifteen years ahead.

Blue-sky ideas, however, require the same intense scrutiny as a little plan to buy a word processor. Every man or woman of ideas needs a sifting mechanism, an intellectual sieve to separate the good ideas from the bad, the winnable from the worthless, the practical from the impossible. Finding out the hard way—or "suck it and see"—can be very expensive. Here's a checklist that rests, not on sucking the candy, but on unwrapping it properly:

1. What assumptions does the idea rest on? (Be careful to ensure that you have subdivided the suggestion into any separate components.)

2. Are there any tests that can be applied to these assumptions before the project proceeds any further?

3. If it goes ahead, what are the likely financial results in the event of (a) acceptable success, (b) maximum possible success, (c) partial failure, (d) total failure?

4. What criteria do you intend to apply to establish the answer to the last question?

5. Is the trade-off between the maximum gain and the maximum loss acceptable?

6. How, if approved, is the project to be managed; and what are the weak points at which difficulty could be encountered? *If you can't answer question 6, don't proceed.*

7. What is the cutoff point at which you would want to abandon the whole thing if the results aren't up to scratch?

The seven questions shouldn't take long to answer. Unless you can answer them, you're in no position to move on any idea, however "good." Visions of the future must not be dreams—they must be applicable ideas which, when applied, will lead, if successful, to highly acceptable results.

5. THE TURNING OF TENNECO

Specific visions come within broad future landscapes. Thus the apotheosis of Levi Strauss came from the massive promotion of a specific product, blue jeans, within a broad worldwide trend—the growth of the jean-loving youth market. But did Levi Strauss spot the trend in advance? It ain't necessarily so. What actually happens, more often than not, can be seen in the transformation of Tenneco, once a dull and boring natural-gas pipeline company, into one of the better wonders of the conglomerate era. It's now a $15.2 billion group with interests, not only in oil and gas, but also in chemicals, tractors, car mufflers, nuclear warships, agriculture, and packaging—and with a spread around several countries as well as industries. Since many of these ventures have been great successes, you might think Tenneco a monument to the process of intelligent corporate planning. But you would be wrong.

The process began logically enough—natural-gas pipelines leading to oil and gas production, to refining, to petroleum by-products, to chemicals. Did anyone at Tenneco foresee a bright prospect for the car part and tractor businesses? Did its planners urge the diversifications into agriculture and land as sound investments in the future? No. All the above came in with a huge purchase made only for the sake of the oil. When it came to nuclear warships, Tenneco did take a view on the future—it seemed a good idea at the time to get in on government contracts. It wasn't. The purchase, Newport Mews, made only 3.1 percent on net assets employed in 1978. Then along came President Reagan, whose advent nobody could have forecast. In 1980 the company made 18.1 percent on its defense interests, and it confidently expected to do better still as defense spending boomed.

Diversification, having begun by accident, began to seem a brilliant strategy, because the oil and gas side appeared less and less promising. Back in 1972, Tenneco's U.S. oil and gas interests looked like a lemon, with returns below those in the rest of the company. Nobody foresaw the incredible oil-price revolution that started in 1973. The consequent great surge in the value of the U.S. holdings, thanks to the Arabs, completed the transformation of Tenneco. Its own management has powerfully helped along the process, though. Tenneco may have missed the economic future intellectually, but it seized its own future by intelligent and efficient management of the chances that came its way. It made the best of the best of all possible worlds—the actual one we live in.

6. THAT'S SHELL, THAT WILL BE

Still, it must help to get the future right, if you can. But can you? One of the main stumbling blocks that stops people planning is the distrust of any attempts, with or without crystal balls, to tell the future. They are right to stumble, wrong not to plan. Anybody who tries to manage without taking an intelligent look ahead will succeed only by sheer luck. But anybody who tries to put precise figures on an uncertain future will also be right only by a total stroke of good fortune.

Johan de Vries, a corporate planner with Shell, talking to a group of accountants, rubbed in the point by looking at forecasts of oil consumption in 1985 made in 1977. They ranged from over 70 million barrels a day (the Central Intelligence Agency) to under 60 million (the OECD). Now, actual consumption in 1980 was around 50 million—and nobody in 1980 expected much rise from that over the ensuing five years. As de Vries comments, "The difference between the current expectations and those of four years ago is comparable to total OPEC production!" He went on to point out that

if you agree that forecasting is an unrewarding activity, then planners cannot forecast, and should not try to forecast.

This will lead to a major change in planning philosophy in an organization. The planners will no longer draw up a picture of the future and hand it over to management as a reliable background against which strategies can be drawn up. Another part of the change in planning philosophy is that managers must be responsible for coping with uncertainty. Managers are in an uncertain world, and there are no planners who can remove that uncertainty; no planners who can provide a legitimate alibi for failure because they depicted an incorrect future. *The manager is responsible* for the business in an uncertain environment.

Intelligent planning, like intelligent budgeting, is designed to enable managers to react intelligently to anything that is at all likely to happen. Intelligent forecasting therefore has to take in the full range of likelihoods. Which means that when a manager asks, say, what the oil price is going to be in 1985 or 1986, or what the exchange rate for the dollar will be in six months' time, the only honest and useful answer is "We don't know."

At any rate, that is what the planners at Shell have been saying after a period in which forecasts have been going hideously awry all over the place. A business will end up the same way—all over the place—if it ties itself to erroneous forecasts. For instance, any company that makes a firm bet on exchange rates in an era of floating currencies can be crucified if the projections prove wrong (which is much more likely than not).

In an age when the dollar can bounce around like a yo-yo, good management means being prepared for any eventuality—so that, whatever happens, the company has a plan of action to follow. That is precisely what Shell has been trying to achieve—to think in terms, not of forecasts, but of "scenarios," descriptions of the possible futures.

In its crudest form (and the crudeness doesn't stop it from being a highly valuable technique), this approach is known as "best world, worst world." You write down what the worst possible circumstances are (a sales decline of 50 percent, say) and the best possible (a doubling of turnover, perhaps). Then you can work out (plan) how to cope with either set of circumstances.

The technique belongs to the same family as the tried and

trusty "fail-safe" method of appraising investment (or any other business commitment). The "worst world" question is "Am I prepared to take the consequences if the worst possible result occurs?" The other extreme is covered by "Is the best possible result worth the risk of the worst possible consequences?" If the answers are "No," "No," or even "Yes," "No," you don't proceed.

Similarly, as noted earlier, the right way to fix a price is, as part of the essential analysis, to ask the salespeople their best and worst estimates of the impact on sales of a price rise. A small trap is hidden here—that, given a range between best and worst, the unwary may be tempted to split the difference and work on that figure. There's no inherent reason why such a median should be more or less likely than either of the extremes.

You can see this very clearly in economic forecasting. When one group of planning and forecasting experts met in 1981, they formed a consensus in the above manner to arrive at a projected inflation rate for the U.S. of 9 percent. Then one of the assembled gurus suggested that the Reagan administration might head off in a different economic policy direction. So they tried again—and this time arrived at a 14 percent figure.

Any forecast is only as good as the assumptions behind it. The assumptions behind "worst world" may, on subjective asessment, seem far less probable than the "best world" bunch. In that case, you proceed on something nearer to the best world scenario, while being fully prepared for the worst one. Remember that events will determine what you can or must do, anyway. "We don't know" planning is merely preparing intellectually in advance for what will have to be done in actuality when the time or the event comes.

"We don't know" may seem like an abdication by the forecaster. But "you tell me" is an abdication by the manager. He is putting (or trying to put) his responsibility, which is to manage events, onto the shoulders of forecasters who are supposed to (but can't) tell him what those events will be. Facing him with a range of forecasts forces him to take the decision, and to that extent lets the forecasters off the hook—but not altogether.

The quality of their scenarios still makes the difference between poor and perfect planning. It's no easy trick to chart accurately an interrelated chain of events: "If the $ goes to X (or Y) what happens to U.S. inflation?"; "What do we do if?" is a hard question to answer at the best of times, and harder still at times like these, when the world is so full of "ifs." But don't get annoyed when forecasters say they "don't know." They really don't, do they?

7. THE SPERRY BOSS WHO WOULDN'T CUT BACK

Ascending from the general to the particular, to exploit the future, you must buy it. But it takes more than money to pay the bills. It takes guts. Thus, few manufacturing corporations are larger ($5.6 billion of sales) or in a higher degree of technology (computers, guidance and control, and fluid power equipment) than Sperry, which started with the famous gyroscopes, and whose Univac inaugurated the computer age. The chief executive in 1980, though, wasn't a technologist but an accountant, J. Paul Lyet, who had risen through the farm equipment side of the business. His pride and joy was an unbroken string of record earnings, quarter after quarter after quarter—a progression that in the recession of the Anxious Eighties finally came to an abrupt reverse.

The crux of the matter is that Lyet was absolutely prepared to see the proud accountancy record broken rather than cut back spending on research and development, even though that was rising by as much as 40 percent in a single quarter. As a nontechnologist, remember, Lyet wasn't in love with technology for its own sake. But he knew, as a businessman, that those successive quarters of rising profits had all rested on the product of R & D. The job of a manager in his position is to recognize this dependence and to be businesslike about technology—which means acquiring wisdom, hunch, and rules of your own.

When Lyet's board agreed to go into microcircuit production for Sperry's own purpose, the price tag, on a meticulously worked-out and costed plans, was $50 million. But Lyet told the corporate dignitaries that they had better understand the truth—they were really approving a $200 million project, because the company was letting itself in for that over the long run, and it had to pay the bill.

8. TECHNOLOGY'S MASTER KEY

What Lyet was doing is simply put. He was managing. No matter how rudimentary or sophisticated the technology may be, or how central to the main business or how peripheral (like, say, which cash register you use in a retail store), that technology has to be managed—and the better the management, naturally, the better the results. For a start, as with all management, knowlege is necessary. Without full and accurate information about what cash registers are available, what changes are under way, and what benefits can be obtained at what cost, you may easily end up like one large store chain—it put in brand-new electromechanical tills just in time to see them made totally obsolete by electronic terminals.

An infuriating thing—infuriating, that is, for those who believe in human perfectibility—is that the management of technologies seems to proceed almost wholly by trial and error, with the emphasis on the error. Here are some examples from a detailed study done by researcher Peter Senker. He looked at a highly specialized occupation—contract tool-making. Out of thirteen firms Senker studied, all were unlucky, save one, the only one actually to increase his sales. How?

The lucky man had bought advanced equipment (numerically controlled electrical discharge machines, if it matters), which cost five to eight times as much as a conventional profile grinder. The new equipment paid for itself in a couple of years, and the manager had since ordered four more of the new wonders. The result was by far the best productivity among the thirteen. "If all the firms had achieved the same sales per man," reported Senker, "they could have achieved the same sales, employing 30 percent less people." The point is not only that profitability would have been enhanced; shortage of labor (which they could have saved by the above investment) was the main reason cited by the Dirty Dozen for their dismal records of stagnant or falling output.

Here are the reasons they gave for not emulating their competitor (he sounds more and more like the wise one of the Three Little Pigs, who built his house of brick). The reactions are typical excuses for technological management ineptitude around the world.

1. The "Red China does not exist" syndrome. Just like the United States in pre-Nixonian diplomacy, you ignore inconvenient and unpleasant facts. One of Senker's firms just didn't like the new process at all, and thought (wrongly, of course) that its competitor would soon stop using the new-fangled equipment.

2. "A bird in the hand is worth any number in the bush." Another rival remarked, "If I had $150,000, I would not spend it on a wire eroder [i.e., the new process]. There's more to life than press tools." Much the same sentiment was expressed by the critic who noted that the single successful man, the Wise Little Pig, "aims to have the biggest trade shop in the country"; but, the speaker added, "I'd rather take the dog for a walk."

3. The third objection came from a firm that had actually installed one of the new machines—and didn't use the extra capacity. Since eight of Senker's thirteen made no effort to sell at all, that wasn't surprising. Technology and sales must go hand in hand but it's doubtful if the sales efforts of the five described as "active marketers" were up to much, judging by one of them. He visited his customers and sent them follow-up letters, but obviously disliked the whole business of selling.

The real truth of the matter, to quote Senker, is one that doesn't apply to these thirteen tool-makers, or rather to the twelve foolish pigs, but to most firms in all businesses: "The general attitude of owners and managers is to preserve existing methods of production unless the direct pressure to change is very great." That immediately lays down the Master Key in managing technology: continuous and direct pressure to change must be applied within the firm—otherwise, when it's applied from outside, by competition or financial squeeze, the pressure may come too late.

The corollaries of the Master Key are:

1. Take all innovation seriously and treat the idea with the utmost respect—as if it had been "invented here," by your people in your establishment.

2. Investment in the future, which is essential if you are to have any future, must be based on always having the best equipment, and the best product, that your money (however much or little that is) can buy.

3. Investment in new equipment and processes must be part and parcel of plans to enhance the firm's penetration of the market.

These maxims can make all the difference between life and death, growth and decline, all the way up and down the economic scale.

9. THE PRODUCT AND THE PRICE

But there's more, much more, to innovation even than that. You've taken a long, careful look into the future, and now you are thinking of launching a new product into the market, a precious innovation dear to the hearts of everybody in the company.

1. Do you price the product
   (a) above its competitors?
   (b) at the same price?
   (c) at a lower price?
2. Do you want the product to have
   (a) better performance than the competitors?
   (b) the same performance?
   (c) worse performance?
3. Will the product be
   (a) dramatically or very different from its competitors?
   (b) marginally different?
   (c) similar?

What should the answers be to give you the greatest chance of success?

10. *VIVE LA DIFFÉRENCE!*

There are no Tablets of the Law in business—only a quantity of experience which tells you where the bodies are buried, and how the winners won as much everlasting life as the marketplace will allow. Thanks to an analysis by J. H. Davidson of a hundred new grocery brands launched between 1960 and 1970, the answers to the above questions are quite clear. Half the hundred were winners, half losers. To have the best chance of being among the winners you evidently should offer a new product or service that is more expensive than its competitors, has better performance, and is dramatically or very different—in other words, all the (a) answers in the quiz.

If for some perverse reason you prefer to be a loser, then a very effective losing recipe is to combine worse performance with no other visible difference from the competition. Note that relative price is not a crucial ingredient of failure—or of success. A new marvel can succeed (or flop) at the same price, a lower price, or a higher one—although, in point of fact, almost every launch seems to be either similar in price or more expensive.

The reasons are obvious. People want to recover the horrible costs of new ventures as fast as possible. But Davidson's research shows that, as so often in management, the obvious can be obviously wrong. In Davidson's survey, those few products that did undercut the opposition were all successes. But it's no use being cheaper if the thing is actually worse. Nobody—but nobody—succeeded with a worse product. The customer may not always be right, but she (or he) isn't stupid.

On the contrary, the wisest course is to assume that the customers are extremely bright—so intelligent, in fact, that they won't be fobbed off with a "me-too" product. Among the failures, the largest numerical group are "me-toos," offerings that are to all intents and purposes identical to something already on the market. Most of the time, the paying customers will prefer the original to the imitation—and who can blame them?

Exactly the same arguments against me-too performance can be brought against me-too appearance. The great majority of the failures were only marginally different or similar to the competition, but dramatic or marked difference was part of the success recipe to almost as significant an extent as better performance. The table below, based on Davidson's work, deserves careful study. However, its conclusion is inescapable—the ideal strategy is to aim at a definitely distinctive offering with a better performance that will justify a somewhat higher price.

The latter has the additional virtue of signaling to the customers that your product actually is better. That's one trouble about a lower-price strategy—the signals don't immediately suggest better quality, etc. And if the extra quality, performance, and distinctiveness do exist, why are you charging *less*, you dummy? The classic error of this kind was the car that broke the auto industry's mold by being a transverse-engined wheels-at-the-corners box; a unique product, it was underpriced by its makers because they thought it wouldn't sell. Before many years had passed, it had sold a million units—but only then did the company start to make a profit from one of the most successful innovations in motoring history.

Table 11

SUCCESS AND FAILURE IN NEW BRANDS

	50 SUCCESSES	50 FAILURES
Price:		
Higher price than competitors	26	25
Same price	20	25
Lower price	4	-
	50	50
Performance:		
Better performance than competitors	37	10
Same performance	13	30
Worse performance	-	10
	50	50
Distinctiveness:		
Dramatically or very different from competitors	34	15
Marginally different	6	19
Similar	10	16
	50	50

The genesis of the car explains why the mistake was made. It came from the genius of one designer—not from any appreciation on the marketing side of the business of what the customers might want. More successful innovations start in the latter way than you might imagine. In a study of scientific instruments and component manufacture, one American researcher found that 100 percent of the major new product ideas—and 80 percent of the minor new product variations—in fact came directly from customers. But the tendency is to innovate rather by technology-push—especially in companies organized in the usual dumb way, where everybody, including the design people, operates in separate compartments.

The truly innovative company, on the contrary, uses innovation itself to break down the barriers. At Texas Instruments, great efforts went into ensuring that hierarchies and systems didn't obstruct the innovative urge. For instance, under the IDEA program (Identify, Define, Expose, Act) any young engineer could get $20,000 to $30,000 to test a new idea simply by convincing any one member of a large group of authorized technical staff that the notion was worth following up. One result was the speech-synthesizing Speak 'n' Spell Machine.

That machine couldn't be described as cheaper or dearer, better or worse, than anything else in the market. There simply wasn't anything else—either in home teaching machines for small children or in the use of artificial speech on such a scale. Making your own market is the best way of ensuring that an innovation will succeed. But such stunning innovation doesn't come easily. Usually, it comes through unremitting application and effort in an area which demands more of both than anything else in management—and much more of both than most companies ever provide. Those who do take the trouble never regret it.

11. THE CHICKEN FARM QUESTION

The questions on price are by no means the only ones that have to be answered. Try these, from the newsletter *New Product Development*. It found a novel approach to the problems that its title encompasses: the chicken farm method. It surveyed five consultancies in the U.S. to come up with the following twenty questions. Answer "Yes" or "No."

1. Has the product been in development for a year?
2. Does your company now make a similar product?
3. Does your company now sell to a related customer market?
4. Is R & D at least one third of the product budget?
5. Will the product be test-marketed for at least six months?
6. Will the ad budget be at least 5 percent of anticipated sales?
7. Will a recognized brand name be on the product?
8. Does the person in charge have a private secretary?
9. Would the company take a loss for the first year?
10. Does the company "need" the product more than it "wants" it?
11. Have three samples of advertising copy been developed?
12. Is the product really new, as opposed to improved?
13. Can the decision to buy it be made by only one person?
14. Is the product to be made in fewer than five versions?
15. Will the product not need service and repair?
16. Does the development team have a working code name?
17. Will the CEO see the project leader without an appointment?
18. Did the project leader make a go of the last two projects?
19. Will the product be on the market for more than X years?
20. Would the project leader quit and take the item with him if the company refused to back it?

A "Yes" score of eleven or more means that success with your new wonder is probable. If the score is between eight and ten, toss a coin—heads you go ahead with the thing, tails you don't—and don't cheat. If you answered "Yes" less than eight times, says the newsletter, "look into a chicken farm."

What if the score is less than six? Then, says the letter, "You couldn't run a chicken farm."

12. ALPHA, BETA, GAMMA, DELTA

You've scored eleven or more, so the project can proceed. But how do you find the venture in the first place? The first place is actually the most likely answer—your existing business. The consultancy firm Strategic Innovations won't touch a would-be customer who, say, makes a marvelous hi-fi turntable and asks for help in adding a pick-up arm and cartridge to its line. According to Fred Buggie, who runs the outfit, such a firm would know far more about its business than any consultant, and wouldn't really need any outside help in generating an obvious innovation of this variety.

But whatever its nature, no innovation can be any better than the combination of its economics, market appeal, and execution. And threefold success in this field demands intellectual and business rigor of the highest degree. The Strategic Innovations approach gives some idea of the demanding thoroughness which companies should, but seldom do, bring to bear.

Stage one is to form a clear, honest idea of what the true, real strengths and weaknesses of your business are. The hi-fi firm mentioned previously (a real-life case) has unrivaled skills at making precision components and building them into vibration-free rotating machinery. That definition might in itself suggest opportunities. By the same token, it rules out any question of going down-market in hi-fi to make cheaper, larger-volume products—not only would the firm's special strengths be redundant, but it happens to be appallingly (and in such a case fatally) weak at distribution.

Stage two: you've established what the firm is good (and bad) at. Now you set down all the targets you wish an innovation to achieve (return on investment, sales volume, share of market, etc.), plus the characteristics it should have (utilizing precision tooling skills, to take the hi-fi case above, and requiring only limited distribution, etc.).

This enables you to progress to Stage three—a process akin to brainstorming, a process which, like the roughly contemporary hula hoop, has lost popularity. That's because the unformed, crude notion is to assemble a number of participants and ask them to put or throw forward any ideas the stormers may think of, no matter how fatuous or farfetched, which is an excellent method of getting fatuous, farfetched ideas.

Lack of discipline is a very poor means to intellectual ends. Buggie's version of brainstorming, in contrast, is highly disciplined—as the following rules make clear:

1. Hold the session off premises.
2. Get yourself a *round* table.
3. Provide facilities for *visual exposition*: flip charts, blackboard, etc.
4. Tape-record the whole session.
5. Hold the session first thing in the morning, for a whole morning. Don't use Mondays.
6. Make sure the leader is skilled and experienced in running this kind of session.
7. The leader should have an aide—an assistant leader, or "facilitator."
8. Friends should not sit beside each other. The leader sits nearest the door. The facilitator sits opposite.
9. The number of participants (in addition to the leader and the facilitator) should be six (plus or minus one).
10. The leader must open the session by instructing the participants in how to behave—what is expected of them, and the rules of the game.

Even more important, however, is to select the right brainstormers. They must cover a broad spectrum. Invite the six brightest experts from, say, the sales department, observes Buggie, and there won't be six people in the room, but one salesman, six times.

Nor is it just the nature of their work that counts—the nature of the stormers is also vital. Buggie gives four basic types, which are easy to recognize. *Alphas* "are the sparks. They spew raw ideas out, one after the other, all over." *Betas* are "responders," who "react and develop and vary and build on the ideas of others."

That leaves *Gammas* and *Deltas*. Readers of Aldous Huxley's *Brave New World* will recall that all classes below Alphas were of progressively inferior intellectual material. Not so with Buggie's. Every innovating firm needs the Gamma people, who shake down and convert ideas to practical application, providing "the transition from concept to new product"; and you also need the Deltas, who come along a year later and make minor modifications and introduce refinements, which will constitute the next "new improved" model.

But you want only Alphas and Betas for the innovation session, and nobody else, because the purpose is to generate far more ideas than will actually be used. The reason is that wastage will be high—it arises as the ideas are tested for technical and economic feasibility. Nor is it enough to rely on internal resources of expertise. Strategic Innovations uses what it calls a "brain bank" of six experts to help in the innovation sessions, selecting each expert (they may be academics, they may be writers from the trade press, etc.) to represent one of "six potential sources of the solution to a task at hand."

Two general points arise here. First, the Alpha to Delta progression encapsulates the whole innovation process, including the vital necessity of consistently seeking innovations to improve the original one. Second, time and again in the sagas of successful businesses it is found that at crucial times the firms have brought in from outside, either temporarily or full-time, a supply of brilliant professional advice in the crucial area.

With the help of Buggie's experts, a short list emerges of new products worth investigating further. But the need for thoroughness is by no means over. The whole process must be repeated with the short-list candidates, even though they have already been screened once. The objective now is to settle on the project (it is now much more than a mere brainwave) which most closely fits the original criteria and promises the greatest benefits. Even then, the preliminaries are not complete—the launch must be planned with equal thoroughness and in meticulous detail, in an effort to eliminate the overruns and other calamities that are the sad and common experience of companies.

Innovators of any kind are best advised to plan costings, progress, and revenues to the most precise extent possible, taking exemplary care and using extreme caution at all times. Then, having arrived at (a) a money figure; (b) a time to be taken; and (c) a net cash flow forecast, double (a) and (b) and halve (c) if it's positive. If negative, double that, too. If the outcome still looks good, go ahead. If it doesn't, duck.

13. THE MISSING SIXTY-SIX

Before you can drive a business in the right innovative direction, you must find out which direction is correct—and how to get there. It's an obvious thought. But Supermanagement often means thinking the obvious, and acting on it.

That isn't what happened when a large U.S. multinational dispatched a small team to study the reasons for the employment of 463 more people in its British operation than in a similar plant in Germany. The report identified, as precisely as could ever be possible, where 397 of the differences arose (out of a total labor force of 1,191). Of the excess 397 pay envelopes, perhaps as many as half could have been eliminated by action within the power of the managers.

Another sixty-six of the additional employees in the plant could not be identified—that is, they were on the payroll, but there was no explanation for their additional presence. Confronted with this report, the local managers showed no interest at all in the 397 excess employees where the causes were known and, in part, curable. They concentrated all their attention and interest on something else—the missing sixty-six.

14. GET SET, GET UNREADY

Why? The managers in the case of the missing sixty-six seized on them, quite unconsciously, because the people who *weren't* there posed no threat to a set mental attitude—the notion that their factory was run as productively as possible, and that the comparisons with Germany could safely be ignored. On the other hand, the identified hundreds of surplus workers *did* pose a threat, and a very grave one, to their mental set, so the minds of the managers preferred not to see them at all.

Set is an enemy to innovation—but at the same time it is indispensable to any organized mental activity. People act all the time on what they imagine to be certainties because without assumed certainties, ranging from the trivial to the tremendous, any action would become impossible. The expert thinker, though, always keeps in mind the only universal certainty—that some of his certainties are nothing of the kind, and that the most dangerous of all are the certainties that by constant, often unquestioning, repetition have become set in concrete.

The dangers of set can be seen especially clearly in negotiations. A common fault in labor bargaining is to pay no attention to what the other side is actually saying because, on the management side, minds are set in the belief that the other side of the table is occupied by an obstructive bunch of left-wing morons who don't really speak for their members, while the aforementioned morons, for their part, regard management as lying, dishonest, incompetent boobies who are sitting on great hidden piles of money that rightfully belong to their underpaid members. Not surprisingly, the discussions create more misunderstandings than they clarify, and take far more time than they need.

Much better results follow when the negotiator takes the other side seriously, clears his mind of any set perceptions about them, and takes great pains to ensure that he has actually heard what *they* want him to hear—not what *he* wants to hear.

An excellent device is to repeat what you believe the other side to have said (for the sake of confirmation, not abuse) and get them to do likewise to ensure that each side has fully and correctly taken in the other side's meaning. It's the negotiating equivalent of another sound rule: never send off an angry memo or letter without submitting it first to somebody who is *not* emotionally involved. Emotion "sets" the mind so that it can see only what the emotion wants it to see.

Anger is only one of the mind-setters to be avoided. Another is the translation of something you *want* to be true into something that *is* true. The greatest obstacle to innovation is just three words long: Not Invented Here. Those who use the words, or think them, *want* it to be true that their ideas are the brightest and best, and that nobody else can come up with anything brighter or better. So the NIH-ers find all outside ideas not worth considering—because that's what they *want*. At the worst this reaction can become a dominating, paralyzing objection to any change—it *isn't* necessary, because it's not *wanted*.

Thus, the rich and powerful Volkswagen, having become Europe's biggest auto-maker by riding for year after year on the back of the Beetle, a great innovation in its time, refused to face up to the fact that, one day, the increasingly old-fashioned and technically inferior Beetle would scuttle off into history. The management didn't *want* to drop its miracle motor and so convinced itself that its no-change strategy *had* to be right.

That error almost brought the great company to its knees; only a bravura piece of Supermanagement, turning the company upside down inside a year, enabled VW to survive. The Beetle replacement, the Rabbit, became Europe's best-selling car and the key to VW's hopes of hanging on to the vital U.S. market in face of Japanese competition. But then VW's bosses did something that would be extraordinary were it not so common a manifestation of the mistaken human mind—they did exactly the same thing as before; failing to innovate, they let the Rabbit run too long.

This 1974 creation was overtaken by newer, more up-to-date competitive models and lost sales hugely in the U.S. (dropping from half a million in 1971 to around 50,000 in the first half of 1982). Adding indignity to injury, VW was even caught up at home by GM's Opel, to complete a process that all sprang from mental "set"—from the self-image of VW as an auto-maker whose models were impervious to fashion and obsolescence.

Exactly the same mental condition can produce disaster the other way around, when planning expansion. Once you accept and embrace some overriding objective, the game is up. The set company can then easily advance into catastrophe without knowing it—like the many firms, mostly American, which, seeing the continued development of the European Community, decided to proceed with plans that would make them, and nobody else, the leading pan-European force in their markets.

Because the European-minded men had their minds set on this concept, they noticed only the reinforcing factors, like the fast growth that the Continent enjoyed until the 1973 oil shock. They didn't notice the negative factors, or, if they did, ignored them—like the facts that European expansion on the grand scale would be extremely costly; that the ripeness of the multifaceted European market for pan-European coverage was unproven in many sectors; that the heavy investment on the Continent might be an excessive price for gains in European sales that could perhaps have been obtained, in many cases, by straight export expansion at far lower cost.

In any event, heavy and continuing losses in Europe in return for revenue gains that could never be quantified (and, anyway, were less than wonderful) dragged down the worldwide profits of outfit after outfit, until the disappearing point was reached: they quit, many of them. Some stuck it out, despite the losses. One of these heroes, as he hung in there, let the cat of "set" out of the bag. The cash-crunching venture, he said, was "something we *had* to try." Confronted with a mental set of this variety, one should always respond with another three-letter word: "Why?" "We *had* to" is among the most dangerous phrases in business. People almost never use it except when they were under no compulsion whatsoever—and it usually pops out in justification for a monumental shambles.

The purely voluntary decision that somebody is trying to cloak in compulsory clothing is a dead giveaway. The voluntary compulsion gives apparent respectability to a mind set that has prejudged what should have been the subject of careful, open-minded thought. Mind you, "set" applied to a rational objective can be a powerful force, making the manager continuously notice and seize the opportunities that will help him toward that objective. But the objective must be rational—and you can't be certain of that with a closed mind.

To demonstrate the point, only consider an everyday case of the "self-fulfilling prophecy" from the writer Mark Brown. Tell a person he's no good at something, or let him convince himself of that same fact, and he simply won't be any good—just as he was told. But it's irrational to seek poor performance. Tell him that he's good, and you greatly increase the chances that he will become so. The wrong preconceptions, as in the Case of the Missing Sixty-six, can make it impossible to think effectively—and that in turn makes effective management, of the present or the future, literally out of the question.

15. THE TRUCKS THAT WERE DIRTY

Effective management always means asking the right question. Take this real-life case. A company with a vast distribution fleet was worried by the bad effect on its image exerted by its vans. They were running around the country, each emblazoned with the company name, but covered with dirt—and dented, scratched, or scraped. The firm hired a design consultant to deal with the problem and much expensive head-scratching followed, to no good effect. Finally, a very cheap and foolproof solution dawned. What was it?

16. KING JOHN AND ROBIN HOOD

The human tendency to get "set" has especially embarrassing effects in the notion that problems have to be solved. Most organizations pour management time and funds into problem areas, even though (because they are problem areas) the time and money spent are very often notably unproductive. Consultant Michael G. Allen, when a top planner with General Electric, developed the firm conclusion, as noted earlier, that the strategic thought of other American corporate giants was generally poor to nonexistent. For a start, they would not simply chop out problem, or bad, businesses; instead they diverted funds from the good ones, and thus a "Robin Hood" strategy of "robbing the rich to feed the poor" enabled them to go on worrying at the "problem."

The correct policy is plainly King John's—taking money from the poor operations (by selling them, if necessary and possible) to provide the rich businesses with the capital they need to get richer still. Described in those terms, the mystifying matter of strategy, even at the level of mighty international giants like GE, comes down to simple basics. In fact, planning is nothing more than organized thought proceeding logically from sensible premises, or observations. You establish the latter, your starting points, by analysis—sifting and weighing all the information available about the business and its markets to establish, as far as possible, the objective truth.

The principle applies whether it's strategy or tactics that are being planned. Companies can't make sensible decisions until they know all they can about their problem. Sometimes analysis will show that actually there's no problem at all.

With the priceless ammunition of facts, *thinking* can begin. "Good thinking" is required not only to come to the answer, in fact, but to arrive at the right question to ask. For instance, suppose a company decides to follow Allen's recommended "King John" strategy. That means it must identify the poor who are to be robbed for the sake of the rich, who must also be identified. How?

At first sight, the answer might seem simple—just look at the current profitability. Think again. Strategy looks into the future, and the high profitability business could be a mere "cash cow," to be milked until the udder runs dry. In fact, in determining whether a business is strong, GE doesn't look at profit at all. It studies relative market share, price competitiveness, product quality, what knowledge of the customer and market resides in its business, effectiveness of the sales operation, where the business is located geographically (if your markets are in the south, and your plant is in the north, there's a heavy penalty to be carried), etc.

Thinkers can't escape from the necessity of homework, and of homework as thorough as that. Whether or not to buy another business, for instance, is not one question, but two. (1) Does the buy fit into a clear, well-planned strategy? (2) Does the company have clear and realistic criteria for buying another business?

Neither part can be answered without GE-style preparation. Before a company can even start to consider any actual deal, it has to establish a general framework by thinking about its own business and its objectives. If the criteria have been strictly enough defined, the proposed buy may be ruled out of court straightaway, which saves all further trouble.

Thinking, however, doesn't involve only orderly, logical, methodical mental work of the above variety. Many decisions "make themselves"; many brilliant moves are "hunches": the best managers are intuitive as well as intellectual; a whole raft of decisions can be based only on "informed judgment," which is merely another word for "guess." Also, it's well established that the mind can work at its most efficient when it's not focused at all—hence the injunction, when considering a problem, to "sleep on it," and the way in which sometimes the answer comes leaping unbidden into the head, even without sleep.

But the hunch answer will still obey the laws of logic. For example, have you found the answer to the delivery vehicle problem? The consultants simply took the company's name *off* the vehicles altogether. . . . A small proportion of the fleet was kept in livery (and in immaculate condition) for advertising-type reasons. But the solution was enormously less costly than any answer based on the question as originally phrased.

The objective was originally shaped as "For God's sake find some way of doing up our vehicles so they don't get banged about." As changed by the consultant, it became "Avoid damage to the company's image from having dirty, damaged vehicles running around with our name on." As with all properly phrased questions, this one immediately suggests the answer. By challenging the assumption with which you started, you start off new trains of thought which may be far more valuable than the original ones. Above all, you avoid being "set"—like a jelly, and acting like one.

17. THE PRICES THAT WEREN'T THERE

Try another problem that can't be solved by set minds. You run a discount grocery chain and have set yourself a fantastic target: 76.6 percent pre-tax on net capital employed—despite its discounts. How can you do it?

You have a brainwave: not to mark prices on the individual packages in the stores. If pricing can be eliminated, something like half the labor costs of the average supermarket will be saved. You can obviously communicate the prices to the customer very easily— by using placards. But what about the check-out girls? How will they know what to ring up?

18. THINKING ABOUT ORANGES

Mark Brown, consultant in matters of thinking, has various strategies for freeing mental processes from "set." One such technique, very appropriate in the case of a supermarket, is "oranges." Instead of asking (to quote an example of Brown's) how to make a manager better at delegating to his subordinates, you ask how to make an orange better at delegating to an orange, as follows.

Orange poor at delegation. *Why, if you are an orange, are you bad at delegation? Because I have a sticky skin. How do you avoid stickiness? Don't allow the orange to contact the task to be delegated, and/or wash the orange.* Being translated into practical terms, you allow certain specified tasks to be passed on automatically to the staff without having to be handled by the manager. The idea of washing the orange, however, might suggest rewarding the manager whenever he uses delegation, thus making him more aware of its importance.

Manager who is poor at delegating oranges. *Why would I be poor at delegating oranges? Because I like them too much. How do you stop me liking them too much? Make me eat so many that I become ill. Offer better-tasting fruits. Give me vitamin C—the essence of oranges, so that I don't feel I need them anymore.* You might, therefore, consider so overloading the manager that he becomes inefficient and more aware of his poor delegation. But the vitamin C idea is probably more interesting—discovering, say, what it is about the tasks that he so much likes doing himself, and then finding out the essence of these favored tasks in the areas where the manager should ideally be managing.

Manager who is poor at delegating to oranges. *Why am I bad at delegating to oranges? I don't believe oranges can do their job. What is an orange's job? To grow, to be ripe, to provide seeds and/or nutrition. How can I help this process? Plenty of sun, water, etc.* These ideas (you hope) will help make the manager more aware of his staff development responsibility.

Now see if you can solve the supermarket problem. How do you tell oranges the prices? They don't have them in their heads, because they can't read. Obviously, they have to be *told* the prices so that they can memorize them and ring up the right sums.

The obvious snags—what happens when prices change, and the limitations of the average memory capacity—can be solved with equal simplicity. A discount store carries a very limited range, which means big orders of individual items, which means that suppliers wanting big orders are in no position to refuse your conditions. You can even safely insist on no changes in prices, up or down, for three months. So every Monday the oranges (girls) have no more than twenty-odd new prices to memorize. She who learns fastest and best gets a prize. The story's a true one. The Supermanager who thought up the whole operation got a prize, too: $25 million when he cashed in.

The oranges idea may seem fanciful and irrelevant to practical life. But take a true-life example. In a corporate reshuffle, two executives exchanged jobs and thus also exchanged responsibility for a subordinate—a senior one, whose work impinged heavily on the superior's ability to perform well himself. The departed executive's very low opinion of the subordinate was fully communicated to the successor. The latter thus automatically regarded each of the subordinate's actions with suspicion; he never gave the man the benefit of the doubt; he felt that he had to take a tough, hard line with the fellow in all circumstances.

Whether or not the tough, unsympathetic line was the right one, the mental "set" effected by the preceding boss had precluded all other and better thoughts. In dealing with the harassed subordinate, the incoming manager had thoughtlessly accepted, from his predecessor, a wrong objective—how to get decent work out of this dreadful manager. The true object was something crucially different—to obtain effective operation of the department. Had it been approached that way, a more objective view might have been taken of the perfectly adequate and in some ways exceptional manager concerned. If he had been thought of as an orange, he would have been more intelligently judged.

Whether you use oranges to free your thought patterns from fixed ideas or not, the answer will most likely be a lemon if thought is not: (a) Deep—going right back to the heart and start of the matter; (b) Informed—based on all the accurate facts that you can gather; (c) Challenging—questioning every assumption and conclusion; (d) Emancipated—as free from preconceptions as you can make it.

Those four features produce the acronym DICE—a useful reminder that management thinkers can seldom deal with certainties. The role of their thought, though, is to limit the doubt and tilt the odds—as heavily as possible in their own favor. That way you can tilt the future in the same direction.

To summarize some of the important points I've mentioned in Step Eight:

1. If you want to achieve technological results, ask for what you want.

2. Race in the winnable races, and the ones most worth the winning.

3. The greater the "risk," usually, the worse the idea.

4. Develop as many blue-sky ideas as possible, but subject them to rigorous, down-to-earth scrutiny before giving any go-aheads.

5. Don't form a fixed view of the future—but do form views of the possible shapes of things to come.

6. Spare the innovation and ruin the company.

7. Take all innovation seriously and treat the idea with the utmost respect—as if it had been "invented here," by your people in your establishment.

8. Investment in the future must be based on always having the best equipment, and the best product, that your money (however much or little that is) can buy.

9. Investment in new equipment and processes must be part and parcel of plans to enhance the firm's penetration of the market.

10. To have the best chance of being among the winners you should offer a new product or service that is more expensive than its competitors, has better performance, and is dramatically or very different.

11. In any innovation, having arrived at (a) a money figure, (b) a time to be taken, and (c) a net cash flow forecast, double (a) and

(b) and halve (c) if it's positive: if negative, double that, too. If the outcome still looks good, go ahead. If it doesn't, duck.

12. Never let your mind get set—except on the objective of succeeding by exercising an open mind.

13. Make sure that your thinking is always Deep, Informed, Challenging, and Emancipated.

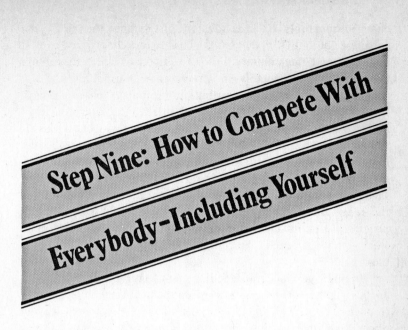

Step Nine: How to Compete With Everybody–Including Yourself

1. THE AROUND-THE-CORNER COMBATANTS

There's one common thread that binds together some of the most successful Japanese attacks on Western markets—and that isn't the Ministry of International Trade and Industry. The extent of MITI's influence can be seen from the fact that it tried to oppose Japanese expansion in cars and took little or no part in cameras and audio/video—doing nothing, in the latter case, to stop the wasteful duplication of effort by Sony and JVC, with two incompatible rival systems in video cassette recorders.

But how were the two Japanese companies in a position to initiate and lead the VCR boom, when the TV industry in every Western country had been dominated by rich giants (RCA, Zenith, Philips, Grundig, etc.) ever since TV began? When the technology

311

changed from tubes to semiconductors, first in radio, then in TV, the Japanese got in first. They used the change in technology to exploit markets where the mammoths didn't compete or which they didn't take too seriously—notably, in portables and transportables.

Having secured their distribution, technology base, and cash flow in exploiting this unconsidered market, the Japanese then moved swiftly upward until they were competing with enormous effect across the board. They've used variations of the same technique in industry after industry. In motor bikes, Honda started with tiny machines that Western makers like Harley-Davidson ignored. The saga ended with such overwhelming Japanese strength all through the range that only government protection could keep Harley-Davidson and its big bikes alive. In copiers it was the same story—slower, cheaper, and smaller machines broke the Xerox monopoly.

In machine tools, the Japanese manufacturer Fanuc (this time encouraged by MITI) concentrated on the next stage in technology (numerically controlled multipurpose machining centers), leaving the existing market to its competitors. It became the largest NC machine tool company in the world, with 80 percent of its home market and maybe 40 percent of the U.S. one. In adding machines, the Japanese piled into hand-held electronic calculators before existing suppliers had even begun to think about them. In watches, again, the new technology was used to swamp a Swiss industry that had for years seemed totally invulnerable—not so much on price, initially, but on the novelty, accuracy, and additional functions that made the digital watch definitely different.

In cameras, the German champions were comprehensively beaten by the use of mass production methods to offer cheaper high-precision 35-mm photography to the market—a strategy that became overwhelming when the Japanese seized on the single-lens reflex (an east European innovation) to leave the Germans hopelessly outmaneuvered. In this case, too, that common thread applied. The Japanese didn't tackle the Kings of the Market head-on—they probed for their weak spots, often technological, always the result of marketing rigidity, and they avoided confronting their mighty opponents at the point where they were strongest. In other words, they acted as good generals have always done. They recognized that they were in a war, and they fought their battles in the way in which military engagements have nearly always been won—not from the front, but around the corner.

2. GOING AROUND THE SIDE

From the time of the ancient Greeks to the First World War, out of thirty major conflicts and 280 campaigns, in only six, according to the military historian B. H. Liddell Hart, did decisive results follow from head-on assaults. I owe this fascinating information to an article in *The Journal of Business Strategy* by Philip Kotler and Ravi Singh, which discusses the application of military strategy to commercial competition—constantly making the analogy between war and business.

It's a comparison that's frequently heard these days, and for good reason. In the slowed-down phase of the world economic cycle, beginning in 1973, many companies found themselves in slow-growth markets; in these conditions, fast growth could be won only at somebody else's expense—in other words, by their defeat. Equally, the rarer companies in fast-growth markets could be sure that sooner or later, and probably sooner, their market would be attacked by eager invaders seeking for the only good territory around.

Offense on their part is mirrored by defense on the part of the occupying forces. So the military analogies make sense. Indeed, all the offensive strategies listed by the two authors have been used extensively and are still being vigorously employed: frontal attack, flanking, encirclement, bypass attack, and guerrilla warfare. However, on close examination the five ultimately boil down to just two—frontal and flanking.

Kotler and Singh themselves give the reasons why this should be so. A bypass attack means giving the archenemy a miss and attacking easier targets, by diversifying into unrelated products or finding new geographical areas where the enemy isn't represented.

They cite the strategy followed by Colgate-Palmolive when it recognized that Procter & Gamble was impregnable in the United States. Colgate took pains to maintain its lead over P & G in overseas markets, but diversified via a string of acquisitions, until in three quarters of its businesses it was either comfortably placed against the enemy or didn't compete against P & G at all. In other words, Colgate *didn't* attack—it kept clear. But a bypass can't properly be called an offensive strategy.

Guerrilla warfare can be offensive in both senses of the word: harassing the enemy by selective price cuts, trying to interrupt his supply lines, stealing his key employees, mounting short and sharp bursts of promotion. But as the authors warn, guerrilla war must ultimately be backed by a stronger attack if the aggressor hopes for victory; it isn't generally a winning strategy alone.

Encirclement is the very opposite: launching a grand offensive against the enemy on several fronts, forcing him to protect front, sides, and rear at the same time. In commercial terms, this means offering the market everything the opponent offers and more, so that the offer is one the customer has to accept—but you really do have to be better at every point. That is very unlikely to be the case. It is, in any event, difficult to distinguish between encirclement and a plain frontal attack—into which, as the authors say, an attempt at encirclement is likely to degenerate, anyway.

So that leaves just the two alternatives, frontal and flanking. Liddell Hart's depressing statistics on frontal assaults in war are matched in peacetime commerce. It is certainly possible to win by matching product for product, advertising for advertising, price for price, and so on—that being the purest example of the frontal genre. But the examples are seldom pure, and the citadel will be stormed successfully only by greatly superior strength. Kotler and Singh put the necessary advantage at three to one, and I believe them.

Thus IBM was well placed to launch a frontal attack on the personal computer market, because its strength advantage over any of the existing companies in that business, perhaps over all of them put together, was at least three to one. For most firms, success comes much more easily by finding an easier way around—that is, by a flanking operation.

In reality, most frontal attacks are modified in at least one crucial respect—pricing. The authors quote the way in which Helene Curtis rose from 1 percent of the U.S. shampoo market by making cheaper imitations of high-priced brands and saying so in its ads: "We do what theirs does for less than half the price."

But it's a moot point whether the Curtis attack was frontal or flanking—the competition's high price is a weak point in its defenses, its vulnerable flank, if you like. The point is not only moot, but irrelevant. The best strategy, call it flanking or anything else, is the one that wastes the least of your company's firepower in costly confrontation with the enemy and concentrates most (preferably all) of the expenditure on advancing your company's own attack.

That is why Digital Equipment founded its astonishing progress in computers on avoiding IBM altogether to become the most famous example of a "niche" strategy—going for a segment of a market. Seeing the huge market for computers dominated by so huge an opponent, DEC concentrated on making computers that were smaller than IBM's and which were aimed at the educational, industrial, scientific, and research and development markets, as far away as possible from the great enemy's business-use heartland.

The policy was a fabled success. By 1980, DEC had sales of $2.37 billion after a decade's growth in earnings per share (27 percent per annum) that was double IBM's. But DEC was missing more and more opportunities outside its rigidly preserved sales boundaries—simply for fear of treading on IBM's toes.

In fact, as it grew on and on to become the second largest computer maker, DEC just ran out of niches in which to hide. Unless it could compete vigorously and effectively against IBM and others in business computers and personal machines, it would lose out on the big growth areas, find its own specialist markets invaded—and tumble off its second-ranking perch. As it was, the long chain of earnings advances finally went into reverse as Supermanager Ken Olsen fought to revamp DEC's marketing and its machines to win its share of the office (and the market) of the future.

But DEC had lost a lot of time in the process. Had it only begun earlier, its bypass policy against IBM could quite easily have been turned into a flanking operation. Probably all successful onslaughts require a strong flanking element—a product attribute, or a marketing tactic, or some other proposition which differentiates the attacker and is difficult for the defender to counter. There's no escaping the general conclusion, though. Unless you have the vital three-to-one advantage, and even if you do—go around the side!

3. THE RIVAL WHO HADN'T A CHANCE

What do you do when somebody goes around *your* side? A solidly established and competitively sharp company was attacked on the flanks by a new venture launched by one of its own former employees. The company considered immediate, preemptive retaliation by launching its own project directly against this new enemy. The idea was eventually rejected, in favor of a less expensive but less formidable riposte, on the grounds that the opposition hadn't a chance. It didn't know what to do (it didn't), it would do it badly (it did), it would lose money (it did), and it would fail (it didn't).

The enemy who didn't know what to do learned how. What was done badly was eventually gotten right. The losses finally turned into profit, and the venture became a permanent thorn in the established company's too, too solid flesh. By not retaliating in full force and at once, it had given the enemy the one priceless asset he needed—time in which to learn. Always treat a challenge as serious. It probably is.

4. HEINZ'S BEST MEANS OF DEFENSE

Sometimes, but only sometimes, a "do-nothing" policy is right. In the article just quoted, authors Kotler and Singh tell another tale, of how Heinz let the rival Hunt's carry out a massive attack in the U.S. tomato ketchup market without too much counteroffensive. It just let Hunt's go on beating out its brains and its bank balance until the effort proved too costly, and the attacker gave up. The key was that people, as research went on showing, went on preferring the Heinz brand. As the authors say, though, "standing firm in the face of an attack . . . calls for great confidence in the ultimate superiority of the company's market offer."

Now compare the do-nothing tactics with the do-something response which Heinz adopted when attacked in a different country— the U.K.—by two assailants. Campbell's Soup went after the Heinz market with concentrated products, attacking the Heinz ready-in-the-can stuff. Gerber zeroed in on Heinz baby foods with products in jars as opposed to cans. In neither case did Heinz stand firm. It launched a preemptive product, just in case the market should swing violently to concentrated soups or baby food in jars.

It didn't. But Heinz had covered the possibility in the same way that a champion runner covers the leaders in the field to make certain that none of them can make a decisive break. What explains the different Heinz reactions? Nothing but difference. Hunt's was launching a frontal attack on a deeply established rival with much the same product. Campbell's and Gerber had more sense. They were trying to outflank Heinz by establishing different products with potential advantages.

The general rule is self-evident. You may well be able to brazen out a frontal assault. You neglect a flanking attack at your grave peril. The would-be flanker has by definition spotted a weak point in your defenses (or thinks he has). It is simple prudence, in those circumstances, to thank him for drawing the possible defect to your attention and to take prompt action to fill up the breach—with the aim of totally stultifying his attack.

That objective should give the philosophical observer of business food for worried thought. Since capitalism thrives on competition, in theory, shouldn't assaults on new competitors be deplored? The answer is that, if the attackers are repelled, either they weren't good enough, or the defender was. Survival of the fittest company produces better results than protection of the newcomer for its own sake. You need cut as well as thrust to achieve a healthy outcome.

On this law-of-the-jungle hypothesis, the duty and role of the established firm is to give the new enemy a run for its money. However, from the firm's point of view, its duty is only to itself. Is a counterattack in its own best interests?

The burden of proof should never be on the aggressors who want to hit back. It's the peacemakers who must prove their point, and prove it beyond a peradventure. That's because, as history shows time and again, the counterattack eventually gets launched anyway—but only after the attacked company has already lost large tracts of territory. The cost of counterattack is nearly always less in the early days, when, of course, the attacker may well be in his weakest and most extended condition.

But the decision—to counter or not to counter—must be based on just as rigorous an examination of the project as if it were a new idea that the company is considering voluntarily, instead of one forced upon its consciousness by external threat. There is, certainly, a bonus—the counterattack, if successful, will protect the existing profits, and this benefit can legitimately be counted in, as long as the counting is legitimate too.

But that bonus element will always have a hypothetical element, and enthusiasts will always be tempted to stretch the hypothesis to the limit, while taking an equally elastic view of the profits from the counterattack itself. Often, these aggressive/defensive moves are very expensive; it's because the attacker/defender tends to use two costly weapons at once—price and promotion. It is *never* smart to advertise heavily while selling at prices that undercut the competition.

It may *seem* smart—a quick way to boost or defend market share. But the evidence shows conclusively that high advertising expenditure allied with high prices (or, at the opposite extreme, low prices allied with low advertising) is what leads to the highest returns. The authors of a *Harvard Business Review* study on the subject found some exceptions: for instance, L'Eggs pantyhose and Timex watches were heavily advertised and relatively low-priced. But closer examination demonstrated that neither was competing in an established segment of the market, and that both helped to create altogether new markets.

By definition, that isn't true of the counterattacker, who must be operating in an established segment if he faces attack. He may not recognize that the threat is to his major market, of course. The mighty move slowly—thus, IBM doesn't seem to have realized that small computers might be a challenge to its larger machines until they were. By the time it woke up, its world market share was down from 60 percent to 40 percent. The personal computer it finally launched in 1981 was criticized as, among other things, too expensive. But in its pricing policy, as events proved, IBM was following the logic of its general market leadership, and was perfectly correct. You counterattack from strength to preserve strength, which cannot be done by weakening the whole market stance of the company.

5. THE BAD TERRITORY THAT WASN'T

It's no use producing an effective counter-strategy if you can't make it work effectively at the point of contact with the market. And that's the point—selling—where by far the most intensive training activity has taken place down the years. But much of it has misfired, partly because it's based on unexploded myths and indiscriminate use of two blunt instruments—the Carrot and the Stick.

Early on in the career of one Supermanager, he was a young but exceptionally successful salesman, so highly motivated and so methodically self-prepared (he even listened to lawyers in courtrooms to improve his verbal technique) that he rose swiftly to the top of his company's sales totem pole. For salesmen, the company followed a hard-nosed (not to be recommended) policy of using the Stick: the low man on the totem pole was automatically dropped off—fired.

In one case, though, the low man refused to accept his execution. He argued passionately that even the new young star couldn't do better on the low fellow's infertile territory in the South. The sales manager accepted the bet—and packed off both the hero and the recalcitrant victim to the latter's sales desert. Immediately the hero vastly increased the sales in the territory; but, unwilling to be the agent of the other man's expulsion, he also taught him how to sell, which the man hadn't truly known before. The pupil duly climbed to the very top of that totem pole from which he had nearly fallen, for keeps.

6. HOME TRUTHS ABOUT SALES

The selling weapon, though as effective as that case shows, has been neglected in recent years, during which much else in management has been revolutionized. "Sales" just hasn't been a fashionable function of management for a long time now—ever since "marketing" became the watchword of the modern firm, even the firm of quite small dimensions. But no company, however large, magnificent, and "marketing-oriented," can escape from one universal fact: that offense and defense, at the end of the day, rest on selling—and very often face-to-face selling, at that.

"Sales" was shunted so hastily to one side, not because marketing is White Man's Magic, but because it doesn't so obviously revolve around that direct, face-to-face confrontation. The duel is painful to many people, especially the inexperienced; and, largely because management minds have been closed to the subject, a whole mythology of selling has arisen which only intensifies the pain.

Closed minds have "closing" as one of their key pieces of mumbojumbo. It means "any behavior by the seller which invites or implies a commitment from the buyer." Very typically, the magic number of closes per call is five—that is, a "successful salesman" is supposed to "close" five times during each call on the suffering customers. Typical questions which the novice is trained to ask are "Would you prefer to take the red one or the green one?" or "Would you prefer the project to start in September or November?" (These are so-called alternative closes.)

According to some brilliant research described by H. Huthwaite in *Marketing* magazine, "closing" did improve selling success with low-value offerings, though not by much; but with high-value goods, "closing" made a significant difference—it *reduced* the percentage of success. Plainly, "closing" as such has nothing whatsoever to do with triumphs in selling—and it may be positively deadly.

Another mantra is *objections*. Apparently, one of the sovereign complaints of managers is that their sales troops don't know how to handle objections (i.e., reasons for not buying). But the Huthwaite research shows conclusively that, with an identical product, different salesmen met vastly more objections than others. In fact, objections have nothing to do with sales achievement itself, but a great deal to do with whether or not a particular salesman puts the customer off his feed.

Some relevant and productive know-how does apply. The later in the interview you discuss objections, the fewer the customer dredges up, and (much more important) the more sales are scored. But the customer who starts raising swarms of objections is not necessarily going to be a beast to sell to. The researches showed that over 40 percent of successful calls were made on customers high in "objecting [it doesn't say objectionable] behavior." In contrast, nice, easy customers who hardly objected at all accounted for only 15 percent of the successful calls.

The mystery again arises from the alchemy of face-to-face relationships. Objections are a form of reaction by the duelist; the low objectors were also low on all kinds of feedback or "supporting" behavior—that is, supportive to the striving salesman. These passive lumps are the customers who really do throw the salesman into confusion, and confusion is where they make all the mistakes in the traditional instruction book.

For instance, the poor souls stress features, not benefits. As every sales trainer knows, you never say, "My machine has a directly coupled fluid drive and double-dynamic hydro-pneumatic gears" or some such gobbledygook. You say rather that, because of the aforementioned wonder, the marvelous machine will give you three times the production at half the unit cost. But with the lumps, the "low reactors" who don't ask any questions, the frustrated, increasingly nervous salesman tends to fall back on ineffectively reciting his beloved features.

Much of sales training itself is stuffed with fallacies and irrelevant lore. For instance, the Huthwaite researchers found that for fifty-five years salesmen have been religiously taught to ask "open" rather than "closed" questions—that is, not "Would you like to buy a convertible car?" but "What kind of car would you like to buy?" Actually, the open or closed magic makes no difference, not a jot.

Then there's the standard practice of having acolytes in training watch while the others engage in "role-playing," the idea being that, although not involved themselves, the eager students will pick up education from seeing others make a shambles. Tests show that the results achieved by trainees are exactly the same whether they observe others or don't. The key to sales training, as to all training, is quite different: as common sense (the only invaluable and indispensable management technique) would lead you to expect, the key is how much time each individual spends being actively and personally coached.

The researchers threw up some golden rules for sales coaches to impart:

1. Don't confuse lack of response with hostility.
2. Ask a lot of questions (intelligent ones, preferably).
3. Don't talk too fast: gabbling gets you nowhere.
4. Stick to a planned and logical order of presentation.
5. Delay dealing with the person's arguments as long as possible.
6. Don't keep on repeating yourself.
7. Always keep in mind the crucial question "What's in it for him (or her)?"
8. Never take anything for granted, especially something you've always done.

The eight rules are golden, not just for selling, but for any occasion when the object is the same as in selling—to win friends, influence people, and force your way ahead of the competition, preferably for keeps.

7. THE SALES THAT SOLD THEMSELVES

But watch that "for keeps." In business, nothing is permanent unless you make it so. One day a pushy young Supermanager had to visit another business, which was far from being either young or pushy. It was old, somnolent, but apparently very successful; one of its main products was in constant and heavy demand. While concluding his routine transaction, the entrepreneur congratulated the senior executive with whom he was dealing on the obvious efficiency of his sales operation. "But we don't have one," replied that unwary man. "The orders just come in by mail."

The entrepreneur excused himself as soon as he decently could, went back to his office, and, after checking his intuition with some research, immediately set about launching a rival product. He knew that, if such heavy sales could be made without any effort, a properly organized, professional selling operation would make hay, whether the sun shone or not. And so it came to pass. The new product rapidly overtook the product that sold itself, and recouped all its launching costs in thirteen weeks flat.

8. FIVE SALES POINTS FROM OSAKA

No company can afford to neglect its selling operation—even if the pull of demand is so strong, as in the case of Irish Waterford crystal, that it is perennially oversold, with retail customers slavering for its output for months, even years, ahead.

That was once the case with the Jaguar car. Its creator, Sir William Lyons, used to pride himself on the year-long backlog of orders. This proved that the car was highly desired, true; but it also reflected the fact that it was underpriced (which artificially inflated demand) and that its sales organization and production performance were alike—weak. When Jaguar finally had to work hard for its sales, with the backlog gone and the factory working well below capacity, it didn't have the sales capacity for the job. In a key U.S.

market like Fairfield County, Connecticut, the small Jaguar representation was swamped by Mercedes-Benz—and so, inevitably, were its sales.

In the tough and toughening markets of the 1980s, with sales harder to come by for almost everybody, the sales side has begun to receive much more attention. Apart from the sheer need for volume, managers have become painfully conscious of the huge cost of maintaining a sales force. If that's, say, $30,000 a year per man, a single call on a customer can cost anything from $6.00 to $10.50—if not more.

This partly explains the rise of techniques like direct mail, coupon response, and telephone selling (the latter being the method used to unseat that foolish company which allowed its sales to sell themselves). But in many businesses the face-to-face salesman is still indispensable; and with only a few customers (like the big multiple store chains) looming larger and larger, the success or failure of the salesman could mean life or death.

That knowledge helps explain why, at the start of the 1980s, many multinationals were heavily revamping their sales organizations. Some parts of a company shouldn't be disturbed too often, but the sales side isn't one of them. Its environment changes all the time, and the organization must change to match; anyway, salesmen are restless, active, nervous people who mustn't be allowed to settle, or sink, into a rut.

Almost every organization will, at some time or other, in some part of its sales operation, have fallen into the soggy state that Seisi Kato once found in the Osaka dealership of Toyota. The future sales master of Toyota describes in his autobiography how half the directors, many of them holding sinecures, had already been superannuated; how the payroll was bloated—even though the sales outlets were few, and so were the salesmen.

In this fix, Kato turned for inspiration to Osaka's most famous business son, the electrical tycoon Konosuke Matsushita. With sales slumping, Matsushita had once taken over as head of sales himself. He had adopted the device of gathering all the sales managers in one hall and lecturing them, in order to achieve the single most important factor in selling: motivation. The Toyota man went one better.

Several times he brought together every employee, including even the office girls, to help generate the necessary "energization."

That apart, Kato adopted a five-part program which no sales effort worthy of the name should ever fail to emulate:

1. Achieve the optimum number of sales outlets. In some cases, this could mean a reduction—in most (as in Toyota's case), it means more.
2. Monitor the efficiency of sales activities and increase it—which will always be possible.
3. Never fail to reward merit, and never let a fault go unremarked.
4. Base promotions strictly on merit.
5. Delegate authority, but lead from the front.

On that last point, which contains an element of apparent contradiction, Kato describes how "I led the 'troops' myself, personally visiting fleet users and making the rounds of all sales outlets. If one laid out my strategy on a chessboard, I would have by no means been 'king'—sometimes I was a foraying rook, and at other times I bustled about as part of the fighting force like a bishop."

When a sales operation has gone soggy, there's no alternative to his personal gambit—and, indeed, Kato was able to leave Osaka for the head office quite soon: monthly sales had risen two and a half times within three months and nearly quadrupled inside a year. The remotivated managers he left behind would have failed in turn if they hadn't learned from Kato that sales are one battle you can win only from the front line.

But Sato learned something himself from Osaka: ". . . that the road to sales success is sincerity. To be a good sales manager, you must first be a good salesman, and you must demonstrate that skill as well as pay attention to each and every person who works for you, if you expect him to be a good salesman, too." In other words, effective selling demands communication *inside* the company as well as *outside*.

Two, if not three, birds can be killed with one stone by effective and continual training. The salespeople get their skills refurbished and sharpened; they are brought together with the superiors who should train them; and they should emerge motivated—or, in Kato's word, "energized." If those three objectives aren't met, you won't be as badly off and as vulnerable as that company which had no sales force at all. But you'll still end up in the Osaka mud.

9. THE OFFER ON THE TABLE

You seldom meet the market enemy face to face. But that's how you always meet the bargaining opponent—and that's where wonderful prizes can be won, or lost. Try these three questions from *Bargaining for Results* by John Winkler—all dealing with real-life adversary situations:

1. A trade union negotiator opens the first round of the annual wage bargaining. Other unions are getting about 2 percent above the inflation rate, with the top awards around 5 percent more. At the first meeting should he (a) submit a demand for inflation plus 2 percent; (b) ask the other side for its offer; (c) suggest he can work out ways of improving productivity so as to get inflation plus 10 percent; (d) say he will accept the going rate of settlement but they must guarantee no layoffs?

2. The management side say they are not prepared to formulate any offer yet, because the company is doing badly, and they must get increased productivity. They show the union negotiator evidence for this, and it's apparently true. He knows there are many areas where he can help increase efficiency and save costs. Does he (a) say he will discuss productivity only if they agree to a satisfactory wage settlement beforehand; (b) submit his demand for the inflation rate plus 7 percent with any productivity deal on top; (c) say he will not bargain without having an offer of theirs on the table first; (d) submit ideas for improving productivity one by one, with union members sharing the benefits each time?

3. A businessman has just named his price. What does he now

do or say in front of the customers? (a) Nothing at all; (b) add one more little benefit; (c) ask them for their opinion; (d) ask them for the business; (e) tell them his terms of business?

10. WINNING BY WORD POWER

The right answers to questions like that are indispensable. In an ideal world, bargaining confrontation would never be necessary—the offer would always be one the other side couldn't refuse. In the real world, few negotiators are in the luxurious position where they can ask for the moon, refuse to budge, and stick in there with re-laxed, infuriating persistence until they get what they want. For that to happen, the negotiator must not care whether he wins or not. The onus is thus entirely on the other side. If *they* care, the battle is lost (or won, if you're looking at it from your viewpoint).

That raises one valid point about all negotiation—basic sales-manship lays down that you should seek, at all times, to make the other side show its cards before you do. With that knowledge at hand, the answers to the three Winkler questions become obvious. In the first labor negotiation, you ask the other side for its offer *first*; once they are committed, you can counter with a much higher de-mand, in the happy knowledge that a floor has been established.

In the second negotiation, too, you try to get away with refusal to bargain—unless they put an offer on the table first. In the first case, the worst thing to do is to say you will accept, but they must guarantee no layoffs—you've given away everything before the ne-gotiation has even started. In the second case, the worst course is to submit ideas for improving productivity when you haven't even prised a pay offer out of the other side.

The third case is less cut and dried, because you've had to show your cards—by quoting a price. The best follow-up is to add one lit-tle goodie—it puts the other side slightly off balance and diverts at-tention from the price itself, that being the vital factor. As Winkler says, price is not "just another part of the presentation. . . . It requires a highly specialized approach all its own. It is the way you present price, as much as price itself, which gets you the result." What the bargainer seeks in all negotiation, though, is to retain as much initiative as possible (as with the extra goodie, above) and to avoid like the plague the apologetic or negative position—even when dealing, not from strength, but from weakness.

Sometimes, of course, you *will* be weak. There's a good story about the great lawyer F. E. Smith, Lord Birkenhead, which is re-told in the book *Trouble-shooting* by David Duckworth and Ian Blackshaw.

> In 1910, the defendants in a libel action, not liking the gloomy advice being given by their counsel, decided at the last minute to seek Smith's opinion. He was invited on the Friday (he was in Oxford) to consider the papers and give his Opinion at 9:15 the following Monday morning. He agreed, provided that a room was booked for him at the Savoy, stocked with a crate of champagne, a barrel of oysters and all the relevant papers. Precisely at 9:15 on the Monday, he delivered his written Opinion, which ran to all of 12 words: "There is no answer to this claim—settle for what you can."

Duckworth and Blackshaw say that the defendants were furious, especially in view of Smith's fee, not to mention the champagne and oysters. But the point is that sometimes you have to do just that—settle for what you can. In circumstances like these, the two authors advise, your object is to cause the other side to change a decision they have made in a way that's favorable to your side but one which still appeals to them. The other side's behavior, though, will be conditioned not by facts, but by assumptions. "Moreover, it is their assumptions that matter, not yours. . . ." Let's go back to the two labor negotiation examples. They were included with malice aforethought. Success in such confrontations is greatly assisted if you are capable of occupying the other party's shoes, thinking what they are thinking, assuming what they assume—and not making the fatal error of assuming that *they* share *your* assumptions.

The basis of all successful bargaining is realism. Here are some realistic principles culled from *Trouble-shooting:*

1. Be prepared to admit where you're wrong and to learn from the experience. A good negotiator gets better with each negotiation.
2. Trust completely the person put in charge of the negotiation—and make sure that the person really is good. Because success depends on face-to-face bargaining, the person chosen must possess sincerity (a basic rule of advocacy is that, if you aim to persuade, you should first seek to please). He must also possess (a) patience, (b) tact, (c) understanding, (d) a sense of humor, (e) humility—no gloating allowed, and (f) determination to close the deal successfully.
3. The better-informed negotiator has an advantage equal to the greater amount of his information.
4. Constantly seek for creative, unorthodox, unexpected solutions—not only because they could solve obdurate problems, but because they will get the other side off balance and maintain your initiative.
5. Insist on proper briefing and also debriefing of the chief negotiator. It may well be right for the boss to avoid getting sucked into a labor negotiation, but disaster will follow if the negotiator and his senior colleagues are not moving in step at all times.

It's a good idea, for a start, to write down a minimum or maximum for which you're prepared to settle. The success of the negotiation can then be measured, and its course directed, by an objective standard. In any adversary situation, lack of objective information and aims will land you in one of John Winkler's unhappiest categories: "You are being skinned, and you might not always realize it." Or, still worse, "I like you, and so does the rest of the world. Lend me $10, would you? If you have it left, that is. . . ."

11. THE TWO WHO GOT LUCKY

One successful deal may be all you need. Among innumerable examples is the case of Henry Ford I. He set up his company cannily enough—Ford and a now-forgotten coal dealer named Malcolmson shared 51 percent of the stock between them, but only Malcolmson actually put in any money, $7,000. It wasn't nearly enough. Hence the need for the other backers, with whose help the company finally started with $28,000 in cash and $21,000 in notes. Thirty days after starting up, Ford and his associates were down to their last $223.65; only their first auto sale (for $850 cash) saved them.

Just a year later, the directors had voted themselves $98,000 in dividends. They then sat back to enjoy their lush proceeds, which lasted until the First World War. Ford, who still had only 58 percent of the company, then produced his master deal. First he stopped paying dividends, ostensibly to finance investment in the company. It took a bitter courtroom wrangle before Ford paid up. Then he settled the dispute permanently by buying all the others out, using a borrowed $100 million. The key to the negotiation was Ford's threat to start up an entirely new company to build a better and cheaper car.

The backers may have thought their own deal wasn't bad—after all, each $100 investment was paid off with a cool quarter of a million. But Ford's $100 million bought total control of a company worth five times as much. . . . No wonder he danced a jig.

Two other jig dancers feature in a study on luck in the November 1981 issue of *Fortune* magazine, in which David Seligman told of men who made it big. One example is the lucky fellow Charles Lachman, who happened to be around when the Revlon cosmetics empire was started in 1932, agreed to put up $300, and then stayed there, with 30 percent of the stock, until he retired, ludicrously rich, in 1965—never having made any recognizable contribution to the company's fabulous growth. He told an author, Andrew Tobias, when asked what he did at the company, "I've got a rake, and I rake it in!"

The second case is that of William Fox, who started on his way to Twentieth Century-Fox by negotiating to buy a Brooklyn establishment that ran Kinetoscopes, machines that converted stills into movies. "When I went there, by appointment, there was a large crowd. When I went again a little later in the week, also by appointment, there was an even larger crowd. I thought it was a good thing, and . . . bought the establishment. I took charge of it on the following Monday, and only about two persons dropped in all day. I realized that someone had supplied the crowd on the two former occasions."

In both cases, though in very different ways, Fox and Lucky Lachman owed their triumphs to seeing and seizing an opportunity—the former got in on the ground floor of the cinema, the latter on that of the cosmetics industry. Their only luck lay in being right. That's no more lucky than being wrong is unlucky. Thereafter Lachman rode his success without allowing anybody or anything to budge him—and that must have taken enormous strength of character down the years. Fox mastered the infant film business, went on to open other Kinetoscope establishments, started producing his own films, and finally became a millionaire fifty times over in the 1920s. The date when he was conned in Brooklyn was 1903—so Fortunate Fox, no less than Fabulous Ford, truly earned his millions, not by luck, but by persistence, talent, and performance—the usual trio.

12. WHICH ROUTE FOR THE TOP?

Only a minority want the largest fortune, the best job, the highest salary, the greatest responsibility, the ultimate power—which is fortunate, since only a minority can have them. But even those who lack the driving competitive ambition which enslaves and enhances the career of the top-bound Supermanager share the need to make the most of those ambitions they possess. So it helps to know which routes are dead ends, or ends in themselves, and which are avenues opening out on to broader vistas beyond.

Despite the huge differences between countries, and between companies within countries, the answers come out broadly the same.

Go into legal, personnel, scientific, or manufacturing work (all vital areas on which the life of an organization depends in considerable measure) and that's where, by and large, you stay. Go into marketing (including sales) or finance, and you have probably three times the chance of becoming a chief executive, the apex of the pyramid known somewhat loosely as "general administration."

It follows that the sooner the corporate executive escapes out of his specialty and into general management, the better. Once typecast as a specialist, however highly regarded, you will rarely get the chance to play Hamlet (or clown), as the case may be. There's no obvious reason why this should be so, of course. Manufacturing management in particular looks like the most admirable preparation for general leadership you could want—dealing with live people, dead machines, deadlines, crises, critical customers and colleagues, plans, organization—you name it, the manufacturing manager knows about it all at firsthand. He is where it all ultimately happens, and that's his problem.

In most organizations, a great gulf is fixed between the theater of action and the high places where the script is written. The marketing and finance men help to create the plot, which the executants at the sharp end must eventually get on the stage. The manufacturing manager (like the store manager in a retail chain) gets little exposure to the overview. Because he isn't a member of the overseers' club, in other words, he isn't eligible for membership. This is probably as stupid as it sounds—and change could come from two directions.

First, more companies could come to recognize and reward production management's importance in an era when profits (and thus basic efficiency) are in short supply, and when quality and delivery (both wholly dependent on production) are the keys to successful marketing. As better people (perforce) are brought into manufacturing management, the vicious circle could be broken—at the moment the brightest and best will shun manufacturing, because it's a bad route to the top, thus ensuring that nobody will look to manufacturing management for promotion candidates—because it doesn't include the brightest and best.

The second possibility is that manufacturing, marketing, and fi-

nance—which are really Siamese triplets, impossible to separate—
will be more effectively fused. Any company that doesn't already
recognize the necessity of fusion is heading for big trouble, anyway.
You can't market well what you can't make properly, and you won't
make any money unless you do both—not in the highly competitive
world that stretches ahead into the next century. Not only should
the ambitious production man seek to muscle in on the marketing
man's act (and vice versa), but the company, and the way in which it
is organized, should positively encourage the process.

If general management is the path to the peak, then you want
managers with general experience—people who can produce budgets, run management accounts and read balance sheets, and launch
a product and plan a broad strategy, and run a factory, and mastermind the installation of a new product or means of production. But
the point remains: the self-seeking individual (and if he or she
doesn't look after their own interests, who will?) must seek a marketing and/or finance exposure if their career ambitions are to advance into membership of the General Management Club, where
the glittering prizes are kept.

It follows even more strongly that those ambitious people who
are prepared to job-hop will hop into better jobs if they have this
general aura. On the other hand, job-hopping is not the best summit
route—save for a very select few. According to the recruitment experts Heidrick and Struggles, barging your way in from outside
compares very poorly with climbing the ladder from within. Twice
as many chief executives get appointed from inside, according to
surveys across the major industrialized countries.

In the U.S., only 12.2 percent of bosses worked in their present
company for less than five years before reaching the top. In France,
a full 80 percent of chief executives are appointed from inside the
organization. The moral for the aspiring executive thus couldn't be
clearer—stay general and stay inside. Whether that's better for the
organization is another matter. But that is a fact of life.

Like most of life's facts, it could change. Job-hopping (or "executive mobility") may well be on the rise, because of changes both
in individuals and in organizations. The average chief executive of
today had 2.1 previous employers, against 1.5 a few years ago, while

since 1960 the turnover of the youngest corporate managers has quintupled. So times are changing, and it's probably truer now than it has ever been that the ambitious executive can carve his way to the top in any way he chooses. All that's needed are three things—the same three that the ostensibly lucky entrepreneur has always needed, too—persistence, talent, and performance.

13. THE FOUR LITTON DROP-OUTS

How well the PTP formula works, though, depends on the environment in which it is applied. Few if any Supermanagers spawned more carbon copies than the late Charles (Tex) Thornton, who had only one rival (ITT's Harold Geneen) for the title of America's most famous conglomerate king. The fame of Thornton's Litton Industries rested not only on its early supergrowth, but on the spectacular reverses at the start of the 1970s, which sent the stock price spiraling down from $91.55 to less than $3.00. By the end of 1981, however, the stock had only recovered to little more than half its former glory, even though, during its comeback from the nadir, earnings per share had risen by 17.4 percent annually (that was during a decade when ITT could manage only 3.8 percent).

But Litton's recovery figure is far outshone by the performance of another conglomerate over the 1970–80 decade, Teledyne, with 35.8 percent per annum. A third, United Technologies, with $12 billion of sales, has grown three times as large as Litton. Walter Kidde and City Investing have also mushroomed to great effect. The four conglomerates had one thing in common. As they grew, all were headed by four ex-protégés who had worked under Thornton at Litton—respectively, Henry Singleton, Harry Gray, Fred Sullivan, and George Scharffenberger. By 1980 the combined sales of Kidde and Teledyne came to handsomely more than those of their alma mater, while Teledyne earned much larger profits than Litton.

Plainly, Thornton not only picked men of high ability, but provided them with experience which they were able to turn to superb account later on. That raises several intriguing questions. First, why couldn't Litton hang on to its budding geniuses? Second, why did a company that could spawn and develop such great executive talent fail to perform in its own right? In other words, why did the Thornton Boys outperform the Big Daddy of the conglomerates—for year after year after year?

14. WHY THE MIGHTY TUMBLE

The outperforming of their business alma maters by one-time employees has obvious explanations, but the explanations are not excuses for the failure of an ITT or Litton to live up to its human and commercial potential. One reason is that such companies—rapacious, acquisitive conglomerates—attract men with a fair degree of rapacity themselves. So the best of them are likely to go for the biggest pot of gold in sight—and that won't be found in a group, however big and rich, which is controlled by other people. To cash in on their own value, they must move on; in fact an ex-ITT man, Michel Bergerac, pocketed no less than $1.5 million merely for signing up to run Revlon.

But if Bergerac was worth that much to Revlon, how much was he worth to ITT? Isn't the first job of a rapacious, acquisitive organization to retain those whose rapacity and so forth are the most highly developed? Or to have equally ferocious characters waiting to fill their shoes?

Second, the refugee can learn from his own mistakes (he gets a great deal of opportunity to make them from the plentiful operating experience in a company like ITT), and also from those made by the organization. Seeing at firsthand why the excellent, hard-driving management system doesn't produce excellent results, the refugee can eliminate the negative aspects and emphasize the positive ones, if he chooses to emulate the system in his new role. Moreover, if his system were to fall in turn, he wouldn't have the faults of a Litton or ITT to shelter behind. It would be his own responsibility, and he alone would have to carry the can.

But that only begs another big question. Are not the systems at a Litton or an ITT supposed to guarantee excellent performance by their very excellence? The answer is that no management system achieves anything by itself. It's like the finest rifle ever made—no use at all if aimed at the wrong target, or wrongly aimed at the right one, or not loaded with bullets.

It was inherently misleading when Harold S. Geneen, the architect of ITT, told a congressional committee that the giant had "a managerial process which has given ITT a capability unique in international industry." He described how the divisional managers were managed:

> Their own plans are what they run against, their own performance is what we monitor with them, and then we have this large central staff of about a thousand people who are there to aid and support them when they get into problems and can't meet their own predictions. So each of these people are essentially running their own companies with the support, the help, the monitoring, if you want to call it that, of the central staff, which is a large staff.

Such a system, with the pressure exerted on its inhabitants by the famous or infamous Geneen management inquisitions, provides a marvelous training ground. But it doesn't solve the question of who takes the big decisions—like the Rayonier pulp plant, which lost ITT a massive $600 million, or the failed purchases like the Levitt house-building business. The truth, according to a former executive of ITT, is that, far from planning its acquisitions, "We bought everything that came along, and sometimes we overpaid for the stuff."

As for the system, that could always be overridden by the man at the top. Geneen's successor told an interviewer that, under his own aegis, "if Sheraton wants to build more hotels in Latin America, for example, that's their job and their decision. Harold on the other hand—well, he'd have flown down to Rio and told them where to build the hotel and how big it should be." There's nothing unusual in that degree of interference. But the brilliant executive underling is a prisoner of the structure within a Litton or an ITT;

and that structure includes all the bad decisions on acquisitions and projects made in the past.

There's nothing that any manager, however great his genius, can do to offset a daft incursion into shipbuilding or a dopey investment in pulp production, where the losses are in nine figures. In the new place, though, the new man has to make his own decisions—good or bad.

For instance, Bergerac at Revlon uses the same inquisitorial method as ITT—one which, on humanistic grounds, has much to be said against it—a monthly session, starting at 10 A.M. and ending as late as midnight, at which the operating executives are put through the mill (or the grill). The annual budget rules the roost and is reported on by a monthly management letter which always starts with an "action alert." This is the section where the operating executive must pick out the trouble spots.

Bergerac told *Fortune* that "I try not to shoot the messenger. If someone has bad news, he—one—should know that he's got bad news; two—have a plan to correct it; and three—be prepared to do it within a reasonable time frame." But this impeccably logical system is successful only because of the uses made of it—to ensure that an 8.5 percent after-tax return is made on sales, say; or that the cost of goods made is reduced by 5 percent each year; or that the profits of companies purchased (mostly in the health-care field) do better under Revlon ownership than they did before.

Somewhere along the line, the superconglomerate that underperforms loses sight of the results and sees only the system, which then simply becomes a hideously expensive overhead, a drag on the whole corporation. Those former employees who then show their coaches a clean pair of heels do so because they are powered by the triple thrust of RIM—responsibility, investment, and motivation. The all-important job of those at the top is to change everything (including, and perhaps especially, the system) if those three forces are not effectively at work in the company. And you'll know the RIM-less company by its wretched results.

15. THE DIRECTORS WHO DON'T

You'll also know it by its rotten directors and their rotten processes. In theory, the summit of a company is the board, the place where vital decisions are taken in a dynamic, informed manner. In practice, what happens? The following quotes from company directors have a ring of truth: "It's like any sort of dinner party, isn't it? We discuss it, we try to persuade why or why not, and there is a group deal which emerges.... The chairman will summarize, or I will summarize, or I get fed up and push it a bit; what I think the group's saying, or he will say that. So that's how it's done...."

"It's frequently easier to get general agreement to spend, say, $10 million on something, than it is to spend $1,000 on something which everyone's familiar with. There is this danger, where everyone's got an idea of the color of the paintwork, but whether this type of plant is better than that type of plant, they're a lot less ready to comment on...."

"If it's a big issue, people are asked to give their opinions. Some directors don't like to give their opinions first, for fear of being contradicted by other directors with more influence later...."

"He picked up his papers at the airport when he arrived, and he tried to read them in the cab going to the plant, which was about three miles away.... The contribution he made was nil. He looked at his colleague, and if his colleague said, 'I agree,' he agreed...."

"In the end I suppose it doesn't matter whether they agree to go along with it or not, if there's a majority in favor, it's as good as done, anyway...."

"I can't ever remember recording a minority view, which shows that I must be soft or something, or I agree too easily, I see the other person's point of view."

As researcher Anne Spencer comments, "The board in practice proves to have no power—some members of the board have power, and, to sustain it, draw in the powerless people around them. Far from helping to form a genuine consensus, these directors are waiting to see what will happen, and throwing in their lot accordingly."

How these people behave, which the interviewer thinks probably arises from their own feelings of insecurity about their positions on the board, in itself justifies that insecurity; they aren't forming a real consensus; nor are they (on the board) making a real contribution; and if they aren't, then neither is the board of directors.

16. BUSINESS OF THE BOARD

The peak of most managers' ambitions is to arrive on the board of directors—any board being better than none. The peak is more easily scaled in many countries than in the U.S., where directorships are fewer and further between, and where the title of vice-president has to serve instead, as best it may, which is pretty well. That only makes the board directorship a rarer prize. But is it, or should it be, worth any more than a putty medal?

It obviously depends on the board. These committees (for they are nothing more or less, despite their dignity and privileges) vary all the way from complete ciphers, whose main function is to provide work for the secretaries, to bodies which really do try to take every decision and approve every action in the organization. In that they are bound to fail; but, setting aside that inevitability for the moment, what boards actually do should cast some light on whether the peak really is worth scaling.

Thanks to one exhaustive study of the subject, we know how often boards meet and what the assembled directors talk about when they do gather around. About half, which is no surprise, opt for the monthly meeting (i.e., twelve times a year). More frequent meetings are so uncommon that they aren't worth mentioning.

As for longer intervals, 14 percent of the boards surveyed met only once a quarter. Again, any longer frequencies were rare. "When needed" described the meetings of 7 percent of the sample, and in 15 percent of the cases "other answers" were given—meaning, perhaps, that the directors were never needed at all. Now, since the board is supposed to set the strategic direction for the company, while taking final responsibility for its tactical operation, it's natural to be amazed that the incidence of meetings is so variable—but the strategy role turns out to be a red herring.

For a start, the role is impossible to fulfill. Peter Drucker makes this emphatically clear in *The Changing World of the Executive*. As he says, "The board of directors cannot work out a company's strategy. This requires both full-time work and inside knowledge of a business, its markets, its products, its technologies." Of course, "it is the duty of a board to make sure that a company, and especially a large publicly owned one, has adequate strategies and that these strategies are tested against actual results." But does this actually happen?

Whatever boards are supposed to do in theory, the members in practice spend far more time discussing cash flow, market share, and profits than anything else. Four fifths of chief executives put this collection first, twice as high a figure as mentioned "capital investment." That came sixth on the list, followed by "future planning budgets" and "research and development." Yet, amazingly enough, over half the CEOs saw the role of the board as *generating* policy ("drawing on own/other expertise").

Ratifying decisions taken elsewhere, deciding whether to accept policy developed elsewhere, evaluating options coming from elsewhere—all these were poor also-rans. The defect is glaring. A group of people who meet only once a month and who spend their time talking mostly about cash flow, trading, and profits (and related matters) are not exactly in a position to generate much in the way of policy or provide much meaningful supervision of strategy.

For a start, how long are the meetings? The survey apparently didn't consider this question particularly important, but it is plainly crucial. The directors questioned listed fifteen subject areas that come up at their boards—and "other" was also a significant category. If only half those categories are discussed at a typical two-hour meeting, no more than fifteen minutes can be averaged per item. Extend the convocation to three hours and you still get just over twenty minutes of discussion.

As any veteran or neophyte of these affairs will tell you, even everybody's item one, the minutes of the last meeting, can eat up a quarter of an hour with no trouble at all. Any attempt at discussion in depth requires far more time. Say that the board has the typical six to eight members. If they average a five-minute contribution apiece, half an hour will pass like a summer breeze (though usually with far less pleasant results).

The clue to what actually happens comes in the survey's depiction of how the board makes those mighty decisions that it "generates": hardly any boards vote, hardly any let the chairman deliver the board decision, a few (15 percent, according to the chief executives asked) have what the chairman thinks is the most favored view put to them for decision. But in the overwhelming majority of cases a "general consensus view emerged which was obvious to all present." In other words, everybody falls comfortably into line and into step.

These boards are clearly not "generating" policy at all. For the most part, they are filling a "go/no-go/modify/why not?/why?" role: GNGMWNW. The consensus is easy to achieve because the detailed work and argument (if any) have taken place elsewhere. Thus it's an error to regard the seat at the boardroom table as the summit of ambition. It's rather like elevation to the British House of Lords—an honor, a nice thing to have.

The GNGMWNW role can be occupied in a very positive sense by a strong and effective group of people. But it isn't easy. Somebody has to ask and answer two questions. What do we want this particular board meeting to achieve today? And, afterward, what *did* this board meeting achieve? If the answers are "Nothing" and "Nothing" respectively, there's every point in admitting the truth.

Ask, then, what could this meeting have achieved that it didn't do? If that's a "Nothing" as well, then plainly the monthly meeting can be abandoned for one of the lower frequencies. To the nondirector, the boardroom may look like a career Everest. But companies and executives shouldn't climb it every month just because it's there; like everything else in the management of corporations and those who work in them, even the board, the summit of the organization, is only another mechanism, method, or mode, to be used or misused in the never-ending journey from Ambition to Zenith, or, to put it another way, from mere management to Supermanagement.

To summarize some of the important points I've mentioned in Step Nine:

1. In attacking, unless you have a three-to-one advantage—and even if you do—go around the side!

2. In defending, always treat an attack as serious—and always look for a counterattack as the best means of defense.

3. Don't attack with both price and promotion, or in any other way that undermines your own strength.

4. In selling against the competition, never take anything for granted, especially something you've always done.

5. Get the right number of sales outlets, maximize the efficiency of the selling, reward merit and note fault, promote on merit, delegate authority—but lead and energize from the front.

6. If you can, negotiate from strength; if you can't, settle for what you can.

7. You may make a lucky deal, but you won't make the most of it without Persistence, Talent, and Performance.

8. Employees need to be given Responsibility; to be backed with Investment; and to be provided with Motivation. Good people won't stay without them.

9. Don't try to manage from any board of directors—or any other kind of meeting.

Step Ten: How to Manage the New Industries

1. THE WRITING ON THE PAD

Supermanagement is always a combination of the old and the new.
But it has been tilted toward the new by two developments: one, the
rise of companies based exclusively on high, leading-edge technology, with information technology in the forefront; two, the soaring
growth of service industries, whose stock in trade is ideas and information. Neither by nature fits the old hierarchical habits—illustrated by a couple of stories from the past.

A dominant tycoon figure, famed for his imperious ways, hired
an executive for an important job. After the man had moved in, the
boss sent a handwriting specimen to a famous graphologist. On getting the report from this genius, the tycoon marched into his new
employee's office and fired him. The reason? "You're emotionally
unstable."

Another boss, equally overbearing, hired a man from the civil service. On his first day, a meeting was held to discuss a project that was going grievously awry in the south. Turning toward the brand-new employee, he said, "I suppose it would be grossly unfair to ask Hank, who's only just arrived, to go down there and live in a motel until this mess is sorted out?" Hank agreed that it would indeed be grossly unfair, and thought no more about it. The meeting continued. But as it ended, the tycoon, walking out with the company lawyer, said, "I want that man fired"—and he was.

The sequels to both stories perfectly point the contrast between the old management and the new—and provide the explanation of the latter's triumph. The first tycoon was fired himself, by his boardroom colleagues. The reason? Because he wouldn't treat them as colleagues. The second tycoon led his company into a sensational collapse. The reason? Because if he hired good people, they wouldn't stay in an atmosphere where they were not colleagues but dominated underlings. The only people who would stay in that atmosphere were no good. No-good people in a service industry (this was finance) are walking disasters. And disasters are what they produce.

2. IF THE CUCKOO WON'T SING

The main difference between those who Supermanage and those who don't is that the former know that looking after, working with, and working on behalf of other people is the essence of the new collegial style, or management by friends. The word "friends" is used here as the movie director Mel Brooks did when he called his children "those friends to whom we gave birth." Most of any manager's colleagues are wished upon him by accidents of fate as bizarre as birth. But in any organization worth joining, the accident becomes a working friendship.

You can control the accidents to some extent by how you recruit. Pick badly, and you always have a disaster on your hands. Bad appointments result not only in bad performance but in doing bad things to people—and, if they have become in any sense your friends, bad is made even worse. But even if the appointment isn't a disaster in itself, an environment which doesn't allow and/or compel the appointee to give of his best will risk disaster.

The friendly, noncompulsive atmosphere is the ideal—but, in truth and alas, it's not the only environment that can achieve results. Management has its Gulag Archipelagos, and the pressure that is part of any successful management operation can be applied in an acceptable or unacceptable manner.

For example, at a business run by another pocket tycoon, just as megalomaniacal as the handwriting buff and the swift sacker, "Board meetings were infrequent, papers were not circulated in advance. Nonexecutive directors had no chance to read often substantial documents until they were ushered into the boardroom as the meeting was due to begin. . . . An attempt to take papers away afterward produced an outcry," as reported by a witness. This monster held undated letters of resignation from each of his executive directors, and neither they nor anyone else in the company had any pension entitlement. People who displeased the peerless leader left with nothing.

The boss's entry in *Who's Who* gave "business" as the first of his very few interests, and he expected his managers to put in the same long hours that he worked himself. In some respects, their rewards were limited. Job titles varied at whim, and, said one senior executive, "Promotion wasn't a thing he readily indulged in." . . . "He wasn't difficult," declared another manager, "he was impossible."

To retain people, the boss issued them with shares which could only be traded at par—say, a dollar. The prospects of having later to trade in at par shares worth several tens of thousands of dollars was obviously, whatever the discomforts of life in the company, a golden shackle to deter any potential leaver.

But the old man wouldn't leave himself, either. As his reign wore on into his seventies, the one-time Supermanager made one nomination after another as his successor, but, "having appointed an heir apparent . . . repeatedly turned against his choice and sacked him or drove him out." When the board finally appointed the successor, the ex-dictator was "not on speaking terms with the choice, and publicly repudiated him."

In the circumstances, it was amazing that the business, with total domination from the top and no management development, survived at all. But in the process, its record as a progressive growth company disappeared entirely. Over the 1970s, after allowing for inflation, its earnings per share fell by 10.5 percent annually—Supermanagement had finally been turned sour by a man who had no friends.

Your own attitude along the gamut from Gulag to green fields can be tested by three statements. In which of them do you believe?

1. If the cuckoo won't sing, kill it.
2. If the cuckoo won't sing, make it sing.
3. If the cuckoo won't sing, let's wait until it does.

The statements comprise a form of haiku, a short Japanese poem, which dates back to the nineteenth century. The first philosophy is hire and fire—the price of nonperformance is dismissal. The second is the idea, basic to most Western companies, that you need to coerce people to get decent work out of unwilling troops. The third, according to author Mitz Moda, writing in *Technology Review,* is the secret of Japanese success: you act on the assumption that the troops are willing and, given half a chance, will work excellently without recourse to fear or coercion.

Management in Japan doesn't kill its cuckoos or try to force them to sing, and so, freed from anxiety and happy in their work, they warble like crazy. Maybe so, maybe not—although there are some interesting confirmatory figures on killed salesmen, the implications of which have an obvious bearing on executives generally.

If you kill cuckoos for not singing, you will have high job turnover—not to be encouraged, if only because you must do all that interviewing all over again. Far worse: the study concerned, conducted in 1,029 U.S. firms, showed no correlation whatsoever between sales performance and turnover of salesmen. The element and practice of dismissal, in other words, don't seem to have any effect, except to make the organization a nastier place in which to live. And in that environment, in this day and age, your cuckoos are much less likely to sing as well, say, as those of Soichiro Honda.

He and his partner, Takeo Fujisawa, were once addressed by a banker as follows: "I think you have an outstanding business going for you. I presume, of course, that you will eventually hand over the company to your sons." They replied as one man, "We have no such thought whatsoever." As Honda explained, with a rhetorical quote, "If the company belonged to the ... family, who would have the motivation to work for the company?"

The truly amazing Honda business career in motor bikes and cars really got under way only after a 1949 conversation between Honda and Fujisawa. Honda was then forty-two; and Fujisawa, four years younger, informed Honda, already known as a brilliant inventor, that "I will work with you as a businessman. But when we part I am not going to end up with a loss. I'm not talking only about money. What I mean is that when we part, I hope I will have gained a sense of satisfaction and achievement." A very Japanese wish, but a perfect expression of what business friendship means.

They never did part—retiring by mutual agreement on the same day twenty-two years later. You can get the flavor of their creation from a story about the initial buildup of Honda. It was based on a bike called "Dream Type D." The name arose when somebody, at a *sake* and sardine party to celebrate the prototype, remarked that it was "like a dream." At which point, Soichiro Honda yelled out, "That's it! Dream!" The story comes from an excellent book entitled *Honda Motor: The Men, the Management, the Machines,* by Tetsuo Sakiya.

Don't run away with the idea, though, that Honda, or any other Japanese businessman, is some kind of superhuman as well as a Supermanager. Honda made plenty of mistakes, even in his own triumphant field of technology, where he scored stunning success after stunning success. Most seriously, he obstinately insisted, against all contrary opinion in the company, that air-cooled engines, not water-cooled, held the future for cars. The cuckoos couldn't sing, because he wouldn't let them. Finally, Fujisawa resolved the issue at dinner with his long-time partner. Here's Sakiya's fascinating account of the proceedings:

> They had not seen each other for quite some time and Fujisawa's mind was made up: "If Mr. Honda refuses a water-cooled engine, this would mean he is following a path different from mine. If the two of us cannot go in the same direction, our teamwork will not function." At the dinner, Honda told Fujisawa, "The same thing can be achieved with an air-cooled engine, but I guess that's difficult for a man like you to understand." Fujisawa replied, "You can do one of two things. You can continue to serve as the president of our company, or you can join the engineers at Honda Motor. I think you should choose now."
>
> Honda looked unhappy to have to make such a decision, but replied, "I'm sure I should continue to be the president." "Then," said Fujisawa, "you will permit your engineers to work on water-cooled engines, too, won't you?" "I will," Honda agreed. Their conversation had lasted no more than a few minutes, after which the meeting turned into a party with both of them drinking *sake* and singing old folk songs together. The next day Honda went to the R & D center and told the engineers, "Okay, now you can work on water-cooled engines."

Although Honda was never seen to smile when anybody talked about water-cooling thereafter, it's a marvelous Supermanagement story. If you, the boss, can't give in when you're wrong, you can't be a fully effective leader, manager, partner—or friend—and you certainly can't manage the new industries.

3. THE MAZDA WORKERS WHO SOLD

The principles applied in the case of Honda's water-cooled engine, and exemplified in the cuckoo haiku, were familiar long ago to Western businessmen—whether they knew it or not. Collegial management is the essence of partnership; and that's how many of today's great businesses began—with two or more people getting together. When Hewlett met Packard the same alchemy took place as when Rolls met Royce—and, as everybody knows who has ever been in at such beginnings, everybody else in the business is a kind of partner.

The growth and the excitement simply don't allow for the limitations and demarcations of hierarchy. Usually, that comes later, when the business has grown so far and fast that it needs a corporate management structure. Sometimes, though, the business keeps that spirit of partnership when sales have soared into the millions, the tens of millions—even the hundreds of millions and beyond.

Increasingly, the preservation of partnership has become less a way of life, more a necessity, for companies in high-tech industries and the service businesses (some of which, like computer software, are high-tech themselves). Again, there's nothing unfamiliar about this aspect of service management. People in businesses like publishing (which more often than not start as partnerships) rarely work in any other mode. In publishing magazines, which happens to be my own business, I can't achieve anything without my partners: the editor who turns the concept into a finished product, the publisher who handles the practical matters, the advertising manager who generates the revenue, and many others. It's not a question of treating these people as equals—they *are* equals.

In this kind of business, the time when people have to be given orders is the time when they have to move on. Of course, some Supermanagers do emerge in these conditions. They do so by virtue of having better ideas, greater skills, stronger personalities, but all these attributes can become worthless if they can't practice the arts and crafts of collegial management. That is, in fact, one of the paradoxical secrets of Japanese success. Lifetime employment isn't a personnel policy, it's a cultural determinant, something which makes people behave in a particular way—as illustrated in a tale from Toyo Kogyo.

None of Japan's singing cuckoos have ever caroled more lustily than those employed at this company, which makes Mazda cars. It ran into one of the biggest brick walls in world industry when the 1973 quadrupling of oil prices hit the West amidships. The company had invested its future in the rotary engine. The rotary Mazda's appallingly high fuel consumption (8 m.p.g.) had a catastrophic impact on its sales. They crashed from 100,000 to a piddling 8,000 a year.

In a Western company the necessary reaction would have been redundancies and layoffs. Since, in a Japanese firm, these were unthinkable, the company turned to the cooperation of its employees. Factory workers by the thousand were shifted to the company's dealers to help in selling cars (the nonrotary ones). The workers and managers left behind at the plant met in small groups to find out how to improve productivity and tighten up quality control. Their efforts were a cardinal factor in nearly doubling productivity and converting a $44 million loss into $90 million profit.

Of course, other steps were taken. Working systems were improved, more automation was introduced, new models were developed and produced—including a rotary-engined sports car that picked up the flag dropped by the previous range. But the foundation of Mazda's miracle escape was that the cuckoos sang: management and work force were as one, equally willing to do anything to save the company—even to the extent of making door-to-door calls (the Japanese system) in the effort to sell cars. Many of the workers involved, when they returned to the factory one by one, did so with one piece of knowledge that most factory workers, even in successful firms, never have—they knew just what it takes to sell a car.

4. THE EAGLES WHO FLY HIGH

In the case of Mazda's singing cuckoos, it's hard to know which to admire more—the workers who went off and sold cars, or the managers who thought of sending them. Really, the two are inseparable. Good officers have good soldiers, and good soldiers make good officers better. Experts in recruitment are fond of listing the qualities to be sought in candidates: lists like (1) intellectual efficiency, (2) emotional maturity/stability, (3) human relations skill, (4) insight into self and others, and (5) ability to organize/direct. But none of these qualities is any use without the help of others—indeed, a couple of the above factors specifically stress work with other people.

The process known as "management development" (and, for that matter, management recruitment) must therefore keep those cuckoos in mind. One thing must follow if the object is to train managers who will neither kill birds that don't sing nor try to make them sing, but will rather patiently get them warbling for the love of it; that one necessity is that the managers themselves must be treated in the same cuckoo-loving way. What is true of workers is true of management: well and gently treated cuckoos—other things being equal—sing best. Which other things must be equal? You can see the answer to that from the answer to the following question.

What do you do with cuckoos who sing very well? The answer is, you turn them into eagles—highfliers. (As a rough definition, to justify the description, they should have reached general management by thirty-two and have arrived at a very senior management level by forty-one.) According to a management professor, Charles Margerison, they should fly high in stages, of which the first is obvious from the definition of high flying—and which also defines letting the cuckoo sing. You must give the cuckoo between the ages of twenty and thirty responsibility for a significant, personal part of the business.

That very first stage, like all its successors, must involve a position of leadership over others. As the eagle rises, stage by stage, he must get exposure to different aspects of the business in different functions. If the flier, at these stages, shows the necessary high need for achievement and the ability to work with and motivate others, you've got a candidate for the topmost eyrie.

"To work with and motivate others"—that's the essence of an effective relationship between colleagues, of a truly collegial management. It has to rest, if you're serious about developing his powers of flight, on one unbreakable rule. If you ask somebody to do something for you, accept what they do. Otherwise, don't ask. The only result of second-guessing and interference, before the event, is to weaken the authority and the will of the person involved.

This doesn't rule out the right to criticize. No management can function properly without a severe critic on the premises, and no manager can be fully effective who isn't a good critic himself, especially (and most severely) of himself. The criticism, of course, must cut both ways: the subordinate must be as free to challenge his boss as the latter is to complain, goad, and grumble when work is not up to his standards.

It probably won't be up to standard if the subordinates are not fully involved in, and informed about, everything that impinges on their business. Apart from anything else, their opinions on the matter in hand should be valuable—otherwise they shouldn't be in the job. Moreover, you want everybody to be committed to achievement, not just for themselves, but for the organization. If you shut bits of the company away from these people, the commitment, similarly, will be less than total; and the action, since it isn't based on complete knowledge, will similarly be less than complete.

The only way to obtain the collective, collegial style of management is to practice it. Every theory of management that has been promulgated in recent years, by no accident, revolves around the same central point of involvement: as enforced discipline has faded, so voluntary commitment for self-discipline has flourished. For instance, here is Max Taylor, a disciple of a consultant named Ralph Coverdale, writing in *Coverdale on Management* about taking over a new job (my italics):

1. Discover from your new staff how *they* tackle *their* own jobs. Get proposals from *them* on how working can be improved and what they would like to see done. Make sure that at least some of these are put into practice for the sake of morale, if for nothing else.

2. Discover the extent and the limits of *your* own authority.

3. Discover what is regarded as the essential purpose of *your* job.

4. Get clear success criteria. These should relate not only to the job's result, but to how *you* do it.

Whichever guru you turn to, every one will emphasize the you-and-them aspects of management, the inseparable dependence of colleagues on each other. There are plenty of companies in which these relationships are soured by hostility, insecurity, jealousy, and politics. Every atom of energy invested in these negative displays is energy lost to the real work of the organization. And in these hard times, organizations need all the management energy, and managers need all the friends, that they can get.

5. THE APPLE MAN WHO WAS <u>IT</u>

All industry and commerce—with no exceptions worth making—is being profoundly affected in its products, processes, and possibilities by new technology, mostly (but by no means entirely) microelectronic. That means one thing for sure: all businesses will have changes in management methods and style imposed upon them; changes many of which have just been discussed.

But the impact of change on one group of managements is and will be especially dramatic: the people who have the good fortune to be in the new industries, on whom everybody else depends technologically, and who include a whole new crop of Supermanagers, often super-rich as well. The frequently eccentric, maverick behavior of these new managements carries to its farthest point yet the nine-step formula for success, especially in the turbulent, explosive world of information technology. Theirs is a world of one-offs, not of archetypes—with one possible exception. If IT has produced a new breed of manager, then Steven Jobs is definitively It. Of all the gizmo-to-gold sagas of the Computer Age, Jobs has written the epic—whatever happens to his creation, Apple, in the tumultuous competition ahead. The Apple story isn't just that of Jobs, by any means. But he epitomizes, in a life-style that carries over from business to home and back again, the New Man, the Silicon Valley genus.

Seven years on, when Apple had become the quickest billion-dollar business in history, a journalist could still get a quote like the following on Jobs, from a friend: "He still prefers to drive over to my place on his motorbike and sit around drinking wine, talking about what we'll do when we grow up."

That was in 1983, when Jobs was twenty-eight, worth at least $150 million and facing the greatest challenge of his young, fabulously lucrative life: the onslaught of IBM, whose first anti-Apple product, the Personal Computer, has had such an electrifying effect on the market. In its bald facts, the story of Apple and Jobs reads like archetypal Hollywood hokum. Two men in their twenties start off in a garage in 1976 with $1,300 raised by selling a VW bus and a scientific calculator. Their first batch of fifty products is sold as kits for hobbyists to make their own computers. As demand increases, the two founders need more capacity and more management, for the jobs they held while moonlighting on their own business are no preparation for the big time—designing video games for Atari (Jobs) and working as an engineer for Hewlett-Packard (his partner, Stephen Wozniak).

As the fable continues, Jobs (jeans, sandals, long hair, and all) gets taken on at his third attempt by the PR king of Silicon Valley, Regis McKenna; McKenna introduces a venture capitalist, Don Valentine; and Valentine introduces Mike Markkula, a marketing man whose credentials include experience with Intel and Fairchild Semiconductor and (possibly even more important) a small personal fortune, some of which he invests in the fledgling company, becoming equal partner and president. As one writer put it, the partners "also did some market research and found that they had invented the personal computer."

After that epochal discovery, the first Apple II is shipped in 1977; sales hit $774,000; four years later, sales have multiplied 432 times. The story is the stuff of which myths are made—and in essence, the facts are quite correct. Apple did begin with what looked like (to quote another author) "a couple of zany computer freaks building computers in a California garage to the blare of pop music." But from an early date Jobs had the backing of two venture capital firms (one of them Rockefeller-owned); of Art Rock, who sat on the Intel board; and of Henry Singleton, chairman of the highly successful Teledyne conglomerate.

With that kind of backing, Jobs was able to capitalize on the critical invention, by another young genius, of VisiCalc, the financial software program available only on Apple II, which converted the latter from a domestic computer to a business machine—a development never envisaged in the original plans. True, with all this high professionalism going on, Jobs could still be highly eccentric. He resolved one stuck meeting by saying that if somebody didn't produce a decent name for the company in the next five minutes, it would be named after the apple he was eating.

The method may have been bizarre. But once McKenna had gotten brilliantly to work on the logo and the publicity, the name helped to position Apple perfectly as the friendly, lovable computer—an image which has been sedulously fostered by the technology and the marketing throughout a life story that owes far more to masterly professional cunning than to the revolution that's been styled "Computer Lib."

6. MOBILIZING THE MOBILE

The only parallel in history to the silicon chip is the internal-combustion engine. The explosion of entrepreneurs, of which Steve Jobs is the most conspicuous product, was prefigured by the rush of inventors as the Age of the Auto dawned. Just like that forerunner, the computer era is mutating fast as inventors run up against the hard rocks of business economics.

Thus Silicon Valley began with firms falling over each other in the pursuit of the better microcircuit. But as prices tumbled, and demand soared, the game became one in which only large companies could survive (and then not always with ease). The action has therefore moved on to products, led by personal computers—but here, too, the shake-out has started for exactly the same reasons that reduced Detroit from scads of competitors to only three. As the mass markets develop, the race goes to the business creators, not to the technological wizards.

But the difference is that the technology is developing so fast that new product fields (like video games or teleconferencing) are continually opening up. As the business opportunities proliferate, so do the career openings. The new manager has become highly mobile from an early age (Jobs, remember, was only twenty-one when he got going). It's not a question of how to keep them down on the ranch once they have seen Paree—it's how to keep them once they have seen the lure of a million bucks, or perhaps made it. Apple's 1980 public offering created 100 millionaires at one blow.

Plainly, one result has been to make the most successful electronic entrepreneurs into very special man-managers, able to handle their own kind. As Simon Caulkin wrote:

> Not surprisingly, the Valley's employment package is the most carefully thought out in the world. Extremely high pay ($36,000 for a fresh-minted Ph.D. at Intel) goes without saying. But other typical elements include preferential access to a company's own products (Apple); an eighteen-hour course, part of it taught by the chief executive, in "company culture" (Intel); sabbaticals (Rolm); Friday afternoon swimming-pool parties (Tandem); a variety of carnival gimmicks from free dentistry to company raffles (at AMD one winner picked up $240,000 last year); and high informality (general).

But more important ultimately than these, more important even than the "golden handcuffs" (the stock options that create those millionaires), is the changed emphasis in management—or, to put it another way, the increased stress. First, high performance alone has value; a high level of mediocrity isn't good enough in an industry where the challenges come so thick and fast. Second, that performance is certain to be firmly based on technology, on what is still called, though engines have precious little to do with it, "engineering."

Like the automobile era before it, led by engineers such as the first Henry Ford and Charles Kettering, the silicon century has elevated the engineer into the driving seat. The financier has his function still, and a vital one, but it is probably exercised outside the company, following principles that have no echo in the time-honored canyons of Wall Street. To quote Apple-backer Don Valentine

356

of Sequoia Capital Fund, "We're operating in areas of phenomenal ignorance. We're looking at businesses which two weeks ago didn't exist and about whose technology we haven't a clue."

Valentine's previous career was in marketing, with Fairchild and National Semiconductor, which rubs in another point. The boundaries between disciplines have become fluid. The engineers who last the course to found lasting companies are those who build in the marketing, financial, and other skills required, either by self-development or by import—as Jobs did, first with Markkula and now with his new president, John Sculley, whose battle honors have been won mostly in marketing Pepsi.

So the game is played with high technology, but it is won ultimately by marketing. The dialogue between the engineers and the marketers has to be continuous in a way that the formal rigidities of the classic corporation notoriously discouraged. The informal, open structure of the West Coast company, which mimics and maybe derives from California culture, isn't only the natural way to run companies in the information industry—it's the only way.

As stressed in earlier chapters, all the trends in management have been moving inexorably in this direction. High technology merely accentuates the trend. That's why a successful Japanese high-tech company like Canon, different in every external respect, works in ways so strikingly similar to an Apple. The Japanese tradition of collective, expert professional management fits beautifully into the necessities of matching wholly new products to new and rapidly evolving markets.

The description makes it appear as if success is inevitable. The reverse is true. At the end of 1981 there were perhaps a hundred firms making personal computers. On one prediction, only six or seven will be left with significant sales by 1984. This high rate of failure has been a fact of Silicon Valley for a long time. Venture capitalist Valentine has gotten well used to that fact, and doesn't mind:

"The trouble with the first-time entrepreneur is that he doesn't know what he doesn't know. After a failure, he *does* know what he doesn't know and can beat hell out of the people who have still to learn." That's number six of the nine attributes of management. In the high-pressure world of high-tech business, all nine are needed as nowhere else—and to the power of *n*.

7. THE STARS THAT STUMBLED

The proof that management has changed can be found without any effort by pondering three of the most formidable names in new industry: Xerox, Hewlett-Packard, and Digital Equipment. All three have in common phenomenal growth records and the achievement of an imposing worldwide scale. In 1982, Xerox had $8.5 billion of sales—more than General Foods, PepsiCo, or 3M. Hewlett-Packard had $4 billion—more than Burroughs or Bendix, and DEC wasn't far behind.

Yet all three had something else in common: the need, after relatively short corporate lives, for a drastic rethink led by new men. At Xerox, clobbered by Japanese competition in large tracts of the copier market, the future clearly lies in office products, once headed by what *Fortune* magazine called "one of the most unlikely people ever to work at Xerox." For a start, the unlikely thirty-eight-year-old Donald Massaro was a multimillionaire, thanks to the price Xerox paid for his flexible-disk memory company.

Whether or not Massaro is "a bull in the china shop" who is "crazy, and . . . won't take no for an answer," one thing is certain. He didn't operate as Xerox used to when developing advanced products. As an insider told one of those involved, "You'll know when you have a development program for a real product. One day, you'll dig a bottomless pit out front. Come sunup, the trailer trucks will start arriving with dollar bills and dumping them in. Your biggest problem will be traffic control." The system seems to have worked well in copiers and duplicators: "But in developing office systems—which change constantly and have much shorter life cycles—the company drowned us in cash and the controls that come with cash. Xerox put all its eggs in one basket, which got so expensive we couldn't afford to take risks or move quickly."

Massaro, typically for the new breed of entrepreneur, changed all that. He got independence for his division, rebuilt it entirely, settled a long-running and harmful dispute about whether to develop evolutionary products or go for something completely different, heavily intensified the sales effort—and turned an annual $50 million loss into a $5 million quarterly profit. With products like its latest electronic typewriters and its desk-top work station, Massaro's operation won the chance to cut a swath, not just through the market, but the whole method of operation and management in the Xerox Corporation. (Massaro, typically, broke away after a while to do his own thing again).

Over at Hewlett-Packard, the new man, John Young, is a less conspicuous break with the past in personal terms. In his fifties, Young filled an age niche that was opened less by H-P's failures than by the age of its brilliant founders, David Packard and William R. Hewlett, now both in their seventies. One measure of H-P's need for a new management approach is that two of the most successful new firms in IT are partial breakaways; both Tandem and Apple had ex-H-P founders.

Young's problem is not only to keep talent within the corporation, but to get out from under the competition in hot lines, like personal computers, where the conservatism of the two founders, the organizational overlaps within H-P itself, and the lack of marketing orientation in the company had held back its progress. The paradox is that H-P is the cynosure of high-tech companies, the one whose style has been most imitated up and down Silicon Valley. What Young is trying to do, as reported in *Business Week,* is preserve that H-P style (the "highly motivational" form of a small-division company made up of "organizations that people can run like a small business") while making these small divisions move, and thus move the whole corporation, in vigorous step.

The only difference between the problem faced at H-P and the upheaval at DEC is that the new man at the latter is the Old Man, founder Ken Olsen. Having previously handed over day-to-day operations, the fifty-seven-year-old Olsen had to move back to mastermind the recovery from an actual fall in net income, a previously unheard-of event at DEC. Like H-P, the corporation had become a partial victim of its own success. Its triumphs in minicomputers resulted in insufficient attention to the booming micromarket and (equally important) the different marketing approach needed to serve the latter.

The new products that DEC needed to become a convincing supplier in the office systems market were also inhibited by an out-of-date, bureaucratic organization structure. The governing principle by which Olsen set out to beat the bureaucracy was to dismiss HQ staff and decentralize decision-making to market-based groups. Like Xerox and H-P, DEC has the technology, for sure. But like them, it can only hope to succeed by harnessing that technology through radically revamped management—in DEC's case the fourth such shake-up since its foundation in 1957. Whether a company is in Palo Alto, California, Rochester, New York, or Maynard, Massachusetts, the situation is the same—high new tech hinges on high new management, and nothing less will do.

8. KNOWING ABOUT KNOWLEDGE

Is Steven Jobs truly typical of the new management? For a start, Silicon Valley is a California phenomenon, and the West Coast is a law unto itself. In the second place, the age of information technology wasn't born with Apple. It wasn't even born with Jobs in 1955. The new managers have been emerging in greater and greater numbers ever since the computer dawned; while Peter Drucker was writing presciently about the Knowledge Workers fifteen years ago.

You could meet the new managers in Boston in 1970, when Route 128 was the hottest spot in high-tech management. The characteristics of the breed were technical brilliance, verbal fluency, and a strong sense of the future. All those personal attributes translate readily into the pattern of the new management—technology, conceptualization, and vision are the watchwords.

In the first place, the tricks that can be played with technology are boundless, but the technology is tricky itself. As never before, the manager must manage technology. He needs the equipment to make rational choices, in the knowledge that the risks of error have become far greater, while the possibilities of error are also more substantial. You can't make such choices, against such a background, unless you can understand the technology.

That puts a premium on two types of people: the technologically expert person who can explain the consequences of his technology to the inexpert, and the manager, technologist or not, who can grasp the nontechnological consequences of scientific advance. In other words, the new manager must be able to form and convey in ordinary language concepts based on the advance in technology. That's where Jobs, the Apple computer, and (still more) the new Lisa and MacIntosh come in—bringing information technology down from the realms of the incomprehensible specialist into the reach of the competent layman.

Lisa needs only a twenty-minute workout before that layman can master her mysteries, or, rather, her nonmysteries. In this, the new computer represents the next logical advance in this particular technology—that of computing power made available for everyday purposes in small, convenient compass. The drawback of the computer has always been that it won't work in English, that a special breed of linguist was required to speak to the computer in a language it could understand.

The software packages like those that powered Apple's rise (especially VisiCalc) represented one huge step forward into intelligible computing. But the Lisa leap into virtual self-management, so that anybody could interact directly with the machine, was the obvious next step. And the obvious truth of the new management is that the next step forward in any product must be taken now—while the first step is still in progress, maybe at its very first moment.

The principle isn't new. In the auto industry, with its four-year lead times, managers have long needed to finalize plans for the next model before launching its predecessor. That became a trap for Detroit, making its managements prisoners of what they were already doing, when the real task was to find out what had to be done—in and for the future. Information technology managements can afford the luxury of conservatism even less. One after the other, the Seven Dwarfs in the famous old description of the industry (IBM and the

Seven Dwarfs) missed the next step—sticking to the main-frame macrobusiness where IBM was beating them hollow and missing the micromove. It represented the future and one which, technologically speaking, the Dwarfs were well equipped to exploit.

The pace of advance in information technology is so fast that the innovator can bank only on a short time before his innovation is replicated. The same is true of every branch of microelectronics. Sony's Akio Morita has said that, when his company introduced the revolutionary Walkman portable cassette player, it did so in the certain knowledge that competition would appear within six months; thus Sony had to be ready to go with the second stage in a planned program of updates and new features that would (and did) maintain its supremacy.

The need to think of the present in terms of the future, like the crucial importance of technology, and the basic essential of conceptualization, leaves no room for carelessness. The new breed of manager has to master his markets and his material resources, not just to win, but to have a chance of winning. Above all, he can't escape one single imperative—to THINK.

9. THE MAN WHO THOUGHT AT IBM

By no coincidence, the theme which Thomas Watson, Sr., the true founder of IBM, enjoined on his employees was enshrined in that one word—THINK. Objects bearing the word used to be ubiquitous at IBM. But the outward signs of common culture imposed by Watson have become much less conspicuous in the new age, whose new IBM men are epitomized by the man currently in Watson's chair, John Opel.

By comparison with Jobs of Apple, Opel is the man nobody knows. He is shy about where he lives, what car he drives (no motorbike here, presumably), what his personal life interests happen to be. But if Jobs is one variation, even one extreme, on the theme of the New Manager, Opel's version is just as legitimate. He's a self-confessed Corporation Man, one of the IBM-ers who still clings to white shirt, dark suit, and striped tie, the uniform that once, in the days of Tom Watson, Sr., was obligatory.

Opel is no technologist, but a business graduate whose first job was selling for IBM in his own home town, Jefferson City, Iowa. There were eighteen more jobs to come. While one involved manufacturing and another a crucial spell in the private office of Tom Watson, Jr., there's nothing on the record to indicate or apparently pave the way for this Supermanager's appointment to head up perhaps the most formidable technological powerhouse in the history of the world.

But that's the point. Information technology demands a new style of management—or, rather, a fresh and stronger emphasis on a tried and trusted principle, the Triple D, Divide, Decentralize, and Devolve. Rising up all those rungs on the ladder at IBM, Opel became convinced (just like many other Supermanagers today) that centralization was a bad and frustrating form of management. As Opel expressed it to *Time* magazine, "You have to have people free to act, or they become dependent. They don't have to be told, they have to be allowed."

The role of the nontechnological manager in the new world is thus to enable, to make possible, the release of technological energies. The more complex the range of technologies and possibilities, the more important the Triple D becomes. The Opel-type manager draws on all the strengths of the corporation that made him, and does so by the professionalism that knows its own strengths. "No matter what I had in my jurisdiction," Opel told *Time*, "I typically felt I was more competent to deal with it than anybody else. And that wasn't conceit, it was just simple laws of nature."

10. MAKING A MAMMOTH MIGHTY

Another simple law or force of nature seems to be IBM itself. No corporation has ever dominated so vital and profitable a business so comprehensively and for so long. Apart from its own might, the great corporation has spawned uncounted numbers of other companies in information technology as some of its fledglings have fled the nest—people like Gene Amdahl, whose large computers represented one of the few ways in which any competitor has found chinks in IBM's armor.

The sheer strength of that armor-plating can be seen in one staggering statistic. IBM's *profits* in 1982 were roughly the same as the *sales* of the industry's second runner, DEC (a long-time chink exploiter) and four times the expected 1983 sales of Apple, which opened up an even more conspicuous chink by fostering the personal computer. The competition has no more sapped IBM's market strength than the breakaways have weakened its collective executive ability. As those breakaways show, IBM cannot, in an individualistic Western culture, and in so hotly competitive an industry, rely absolutely on the lifetime careerism that cements the Japanese company. But IBM does display very similar characteristics to the Japanese, all the same—and by no accident.

The lifetime career is the norm, and during that career IBM-ers are still expected to follow corporate norms of many kinds. True, the compulsory dress of dark suit, white shirt, and striped tie that Opel still favors has been dropped, and so have other rules, such as teetotalism, favored by the IBM progenitor, Thomas Watson, Sr. While no angel in business ethics during his days with NCR (he was an expert at knocking out cash-register competition with underhand tactics), Watson laid down codes for his employees that added up to a whole corporate morality—and that still stands.

The current thirty-two-page code of business ethics, however, is only one part of a monumental system of values that is the real source of IBM's massive resilience. There's nothing miraculous about this corporate culture any more than there is about Japanese success in world markets. People policies, marketing tenacity, and technological effectiveness are the tripod on which IBM has always rested. Often, the corporation, for all its wealth in financial and technological resources, has not been first into the newest technology or its latest application. It was actually and famously beaten by a mile into the computer age by Univac. But just like the Japanese, the IBM-ers, once they spot a threat or an opportunity, have always reacted with a thoroughness and power that few competitors have been able to withstand.

The same reactive power drives IBM through its own worst mistakes, like the launch of the 360 computer series. Typically for IBM, the range didn't advance as far as technology would have allowed—but the step forward was far enough to land IBM in some very untypical messes in production and performance. They were cleared up, though, at considerable expense, and no competitor was allowed to benefit from IBM's momentary but monumental lapse.

In moments of need, the corporation can call on those people policies and marketing muscles to pull it through. People are treated like the lifetime employees they will probably be, with high pay and good perquisites, and continual training, excellent communications, and powerful motivational methods, an employment package that has successfully excluded unions from almost all IBM plants. They also have the total job security of a corporation that has never laid off workers, but they don't have job permanence—IBM-ers have been moved at the corporation's will ever since the days of the elder Watson, and they usually start on the sales side, which is the bedrock of IBM.

That same tenacity which Watson applied in the cash-register wars has seen attack after attack repelled by methods fair and maybe less fair—for instance, the alleged announcement by IBM of new machines that never see the light of day, but whose phantom existence spikes the guns of some competitive threat. There's a London department store which boasts about its prices "Never knowingly undersold." IBM's famous THINK slogan should have as its companion "Never knowingly outsold"—and it was this sheer selling strength that enabled IBM to breeze past Univac in computers, to override the 360 troubles, and to thunder so successfully into a personal computer market which its management hadn't taken seriously—let alone as a serious threat.

But small computers and other changes in information technology that had by-passed IBM were responsible for that fall in its market share, from 60 percent to 40 percent, over the 1970s. In any less rapidly growing industry that would have spelled disaster. In real, inflation-corrected terms, remember, IBM shareholders got no return on their investment for a decade—and that investment, remember, was in the world's most effective industrial giant. It did seem possible that IBM would go the way of nearly all corporate mammoths—stuck in its own bureaucratic mud.

The IBM executive, after all, is the Corporation Man personified: the faceless lifetime employee who may do everything (even dressing) the company way, who doesn't (as the company insists) call on customers in the afternoon if he's had a martini at lunch. Why has what would be a recipe for disaster in most companies not worked out that way? How was it that the 1970s turned out to be, not the prelude to IBM's comeuppance, but the preface to one of its most dynamic periods? The answers tell a great deal, not just about IBM, but about the new management that the new technologies have called into being.

11. THE IBM-ER WHO GOT PERSONAL

Before July 1980, hardly anybody outside IBM and the world of its watchers had heard of Philip Estridge. Today he ranks ahead of Apple's Jobs in the explosive world of personal computers, yet his fame is confined by and large to readers of the magazines, which identified him as the divisional vice-president who led a Boca Raton group of a dozen people to the Personal Computer triumph.

The sentence in itself contains a clue to the success—entrusting the project to a task force, given a clear, single objective (within a year, get ready an Apple-eating model that would be "user-friendly," in the industry phrase). Because of the short time scale, the task force not only had to work Trojan seventy-two-hour weeks but go outside IBM for virtually everything in the Personal Computer. The microprocessor (a sixteen-bit item with twice the power of the industry norm) came from Intel—a company in which IBM later bought a 12 percent stake for $250 million. The software came from a Seattle company, Microsoft, which was one of the earliest into the PC project—and (taking a leaf off Apple's tree) the PC was designed so that anybody else could write software or design equipment that could work with the IBM machine.

Uncovenanted expansion of its uses as users invented new programs has been a major factor in Apple's astonishing popularity. One member of the huge Apple fan club has apparently programmed his computer to activate a small motor that rocks the crib when his baby has colic. Not the most commercial of uses, perhaps, but a vital ingredient in the marketing mix for the personal computer. By doing likewise, IBM soared to 35 percent of the U.S. market in 1983 and has given Apple (right down to 24 percent) a very hard run for its money.

Nor is Estridge the only IBM executive to have been put in charge of small, discrete groups with specific tasks. The Boca Raton team that built the PC was one of seven independent business units set up by John Opel to operate within IBM—but to a large extent under their own steam.

The organizational method is one approach which is expected to prevent false starts like the 1970s launch of an IBM copier against Xerox—mismanaged technically and in marketing terms. With the "office of the future" attracting competition from every powerful technology-based company East and West, IBM can't afford its new venture executives to fare much less well than Philip Estridge—and he exceeded IBM's most optimistic projections by far.

12. MANAGERS WITH FOUR EYES

The new managers who can crack the big corporation code, you could say, have to be four-eyed. They need Independence, Identity, Iconoclasm, and Integrity—and the Personal Computer story at IBM strongly illustrates all four. The PC saga, though, isn't the only one inside this corporation. If it were, that particular IBM story could never have been written.

It's no paradox. Unless the culture of the corporation embraces the existence of task-oriented groups with the authority to shape their means to achieve their ends, the mechanism won't work. Many years before anybody dreamed of a personal computer, the great chemical company, Du Pont, tried setting up venture-based groups within a corporation whose culture was constructed entirely differently, built massively around the central fortress in Wilmington, Delaware. If Du Pont's groups achieved any wonders, they have been hidden from public sight. The truth at that time was that, although Du Pont prided itself on decentralization, every executive who mattered was in that one building, cheek by jowl with the top management which dominated the company.

IBM's centralization may have irritated and frustrated younger and newer managers like John Opel. But its structure was heavily influenced, not just by the huge disparity between markets like main-frame computers and typewriters, but by a geographical spread surpassed only by Coke. Because of the ardent nationalistic feelings aroused by computers, quite apart from practical considerations of control and closeness to markets, IBM has been forced to locate plants and research facilities overseas, to appoint and promote foreign nationals to run its overseas empire at a short arm's length from the U.S. center in Armonk, New York.

Just as the Japanese are now building plants abroad in an effort to blunt trade retaliation, so the IBM-ers for decades have adapted their policies to head off attacks on IBM—and very successfully. In most of its geographical markets, IBM has positions ranging from supremacy to near-monopoly. As evidence of its strategic success, it even has a strong market position (number two to Fujitsu, but fighting hard to regain its lead) in Japan—something which few Western manufacturers, in low or high technology, have contrived to achieve.

The political pressures have forced IBM in a direction which the new management demands and which the corporation might well have followed, anyway—but maybe later, possibly even too late for its own good. These days, with talent in such terrific demand everywhere, companies need to hire it wherever they can find it, and whatever language it speaks. Also, local companies should be built around local markets, which they won't serve well unless they have those four-eyed managers.

Independence, the first of the qualities required, isn't just something you give a manager, though. It's something he has to earn. The stand-alone command of the resources required for a task is worthless if it's entrusted to the unfit. IBM units abroad don't get assigned new production tasks (significantly, "missions" in IBM language) because of their managers' blue eyes, but as reward for their success in fulfilling earlier missions. Putting it around the other way, though, you won't get high-performing managers to perform at their peak unless they have not only independence, but the feeling of independence.

That implies *Identity*—not only a clear identification of the unit and the responsibilities of a clearly recognized boss, but also a clear aim, a practicable objective expressed in unambiguous terms, with a precise time scale and budgetary framework. The big corporation HQ customarily not only interferes with suboperations, thus undermining their essential independence, but surrounds them and their objectives with fuzziness.

For instance, new ventures are often budgeted on the same basis and in the same reporting framework as existing business. That's rubbish. In this way, the corporation loses clarity and blurs relationships between time and money (because the venture won't fit into the time scale of the usual quarterly reporting periods); the mistake also distracts attention from what the spending and the work are meant to be achieving—a strong and viable new business for the future.

Of course, deviations of this kind cause heart attacks in some financial vice-presidents' offices. That's exactly where *Iconoclasm* comes in. The new management is totally uninterested in how the corporation customarily does things. It has the Independence, remember, to go after the Identified objective in whatever way is deemed necessary—even if that fractures the corporate norms. If the Boca Raton group had not broken with IBM's traditions, going outside the company across the board for the Personal computer, the development could not have been completed within so short a time scale; and IBM, late into the market already by years, might have been fatally delayed. It also might have had a product with more glitches; the PC had only a handful, none of them serious.

But how can a corporation retain its cohesion when executives are free to fly off in their own directions? That's where *Integrity,* the fourth I, comes in. Whatever the corporation does, and whatever is done in its name, must reinforce the corporate image and strengthen its hand. Down the years, that's always been one of IBM's great strengths. The company's name has become one of the most powerful brands in history, probably the most powerful of all—so strong that customers feel safer with an IBM product than with a perfectly good, maybe better offering from a competitor.

Visually and commercially, the image must be kept whole—and there has to be a binding commitment. Old Tom Watson, with his hatred of losing a customer, set the theme, which evolved easily into the computer era—solving customers' problems. That was the magic ingredient that powered IBM past Univac at the dawn of the computer. The corporation's sales team and engineers brought the intimidating new machine into the ordinary lives of customer firms, making IBM one of the rare giants that have not slipped grievously when new technology (the computer replacing the punched-card machine in this case) breaks the market.

Apparently, the younger Watson was the catalyst in persuading his conservative father to plump for the new-fangled contraptions. In doing so, he demonstrated the force of what should be the fifth I—*Intelligence.*

13. THE FOUR-HEADED GIANT

Intelligence has many meanings, all of which are crucial to the new management. In any field where technology is moving fast, which means almost every field, the Supermanager needs to know what's happening and how to apply this knowledge—intelligently. What the information technology companies have done instinctively the others have had to adopt with conscious intelligence—witness the case of 3M and Lewis Lehr.

The conglomerate Lehr heads has one of the outstanding records in U.S. business—it's one of the stars chosen by Peters and

Waterman as an exemplar of success. Based on coated materials (like Scotch tape), 3M has been an apparent model of innovative success. It boasts that a quarter of current sales comes from products that didn't exist five years ago. Great stuff—although it means, of course, that three quarters of sales come from products that are *over* five years old, in many cases much older.

Lehr, in fact, came to feel strongly that 3M had spent too much of its time on just modifying products and had missed its chances—outstandingly so in the case of information technology, where 3M could and should have carved out strong positions in computers and telecommunications. For the 1980s that not only isn't good enough—it's potentially very dangerous. So in 1981 the 3M goliath was restructured by Lehr. He set up four business sectors, each built around a coherent core of technologies selected from the eighty-five distinctive ones within 3M's competence.

The four sectors are graphics, life sciences, electronics, and industrial and consumer goods, with a research laboratory for each, and at the center a 3M lab for basic research. Note that the principle of decentralization, a 3M article of faith since way back, hasn't been slung out of the window. The divisions retain their own labs, which are now held responsible for applied science in the product development and refinement cycle. In other words, the modifications and updatings of the products 3M already has, which are legion, are now clearly separate from the big issues of technology management: what technological leads to follow for the future; how to mesh together the resources 3M has and will develop; how to cross-fertilize technology between different parts of the business.

The corporation has a "technology czar" (a newly popular type of appointment in U.S. industry), Dr. Robert M. Adams. He explained to John Thackray that in the past 3M had grown by a process akin to spreading pancake batter. The big disadvantage of that, in the Age of Competition, is that each segment at the rim of the batter sees only a parochial and fragmented view of technology and the future. Adams claims that, two years later, he's already getting faster technological responses to market needs and more technology transfers.

3M's bosses know that it's going to need all the responses and

371

transfers it can develop. "We feel" says Adams, "that technological productivity may be the last frontier for productivity enhancement." Getting it, however, will be tough: "Other types of productivity problems are easy by comparison." Not getting it, however, will be tougher still. Those that stick with the batter process will simply get battered. Those that don't, win.

14. DOING WHAT COMES NATURALLY

There's a basic contradiction between the need of the big corporation to get dynamic, technology-based, entrepreneurial management and the fact that, simply, it is a big corporation. What's shown up in gross form by the failures of Exxon in diversifying out of its base business into information technology is the same syndrome that prevents giants, even in IT, from realizing their full technological and business potential. The center gets in the way of its parts—so that a Hewlett-Packard, for example, doesn't respond to the desire of a Stephen Wozniak to build personal computers.

How many other potential Apples have been lost, not just to big corporations, but to the American economy, nobody knows. Nor is it clear that the appointment of technology czars like 3M's Robert Adams will solve the problem in itself. That's another piece of corporate centralism, which can only work, if it works at all, at the periphery, where the individual businesses of which all corporations consist must battle against the competition and cope with the onrush of change.

The problem used to be much less severe before technology changed in nature. The gestation period (four years) and life cycle (seven years in its first version alone) that were typical of an automobile and its engine (and still are) are luxuries of the past in many industries. Canon took only two and a half years from scratch to develop its personal copier. Japanese manufacturers can take as little as fourteen months to bring out a new machine tool. Fall behind the pace of innovation and you may never recover your position—not just in products but in a whole crucial technology.

As an earlier chapter has pointed out, RCA, which was the Big Daddy of the vacuum tube, is nowhere worth mentioning in modern semiconductors. Nor are any other tube-makers. As for the germanium-based semiconductors that killed off the tube, where are leading makers like Hughes and Transitron in the silicon devices that formed the next and current wave of change? They, too, have been left behind—and note that the gap couldn't be closed, even though managements must have known it was there. For example, nobody in electronics could have failed to spot the signal importance of developments in solid-state physics.

Yet a great technology-based company like General Electric stayed out of the semiconductor game—apparently, notes Harvard Business School professor Robert Hayes, because change was too hectic.

> When things did settle down a little in semiconductors, they found that those companies that had gone through all the thrashing around, pursuing false leads and so on, somehow had the technological base that enabled them to move ahead much more rapidly than the companies that didn't get involved. And the technological base could not be bought. So now General Electric finds itself fifteen years later buying a semiconductor house because it lacks semiconductor experience. . . . The companies that wait for others to do all the work and then expect to be in a position to be able to choose the right technology, much less be able to implement it once it's chosen, are fooling themselves.

For companies with more vulnerable market positions and less financial might than GE (which means nearly everybody), a completely different approach is needed—as exemplified by Gould, Inc., and its current effort to transmute itself into a high-tech company. According to David Simpson, Gould's British-born president,

> Not too many years ago we were building test instruments that were completely stand-alone, function-dedicated products. If you wanted a different job done, you designed a new machine. Today you find with oscilloscopes, and in other types of

instruments, too, that you're really playing with the software to reconfigure the instrument's functions. Now, this software normally resides in read-only-memories (ROMs). So then you come to the realization that you need ROM capabilities to exploit this trend. That's how we decided to develop a stranglehold on our own silicon technology.

The problem is that you may simply need too many strangleholds—too many technologies may be relevant even with single product lines. Even companies as powerful and successful as the new Japanese high-tech stars have to come to terms with this reality. At Canon, for example, management knows full well that technology will power the future of the corporation, that it is the key to the future, as it was to the past. Optics and precision mechanics underpinned the growth of the 1950s. These two remained in the 1960s, to be joined by electronics, physics, and chemistry (the last needed for the copier business). In the 1970s, the classifications became broader: software, system technology, components, materials, communication. And in the 1980s? . . .

The company's president, Ryuzaburo Kaku, has no doubt of the dimensions of the answer. He plans to develop "at least ten very unique technologies—unique to Canon." The technological drive covers not only products, but also processes. Canon's predilection for building its own machines leaps out from any of its factories, and its plans include major ambitions in equipment for manufacturing microcircuits. However, Kaku is well aware that the developing, acutely competitive world market is akin to feudal Japan, in which the boundaries were continually changing. His conclusion is that "we must make our own power, but have a good diplomatic relationship"—which means that Canon will use its own technological successes as the bargaining counterweight in arranging exchanges of technology.

"Even today we have this kind of relationship," he says, making it clear that, without partnership, "we cannot survive." Nor can that survival (which in Japanese terms means success) be achieved without a huge increase in planned spending on R & D. Spending in the rest of the 1980s will at least double not only Canon's own existing level but also the going rate of competitors in office machinery and computers. Nor is there any lack of clarity about what the expenditure on R & D and on capital investment (another 10 percent of sales) will produce.

The key word now is not products, but systems—automation for the home, the factory, and the office, with Canon's stand-alone products serving as building blocks for these future systems. Kaku's thinking is that changes in technology provide the opportunity for outsiders to burst into markets—as Canon did in both calculators (only to suffer later in ruinous price-cutting wars) and typewriters, when electrics gave way to the electronic ones where Canon now competes. He is not interested in markets where there's "no chance for us to win—when technology changes, that's the time when we can win."

A case in current point is the camera side. The conventional equipment is the only mature product range in a portfolio which is otherwise on a series of growing curves. The business has been split into two: conventional and electronic imaging, where the obvious contender is Sony, which knew full well from the start that it couldn't bring its all-electronic, filmless camera to market without eliciting a strong response from Canon. The latter is working on technology which will enable six to seven hours' play on an ultra-compact cassette, and when that becomes reality, Canon "will enter very aggressively," with major impact, not just on photography, but on the whole video market.

The pattern is clear. The new managers have to manage their technology intensively, which means that it may not be theirs, but begged, borrowed, bought (preferably not stolen). "Not Invented Here" has evidently gone out of the window when even the mighty IBM, with its twenty-nine laboratories and $3 billion of spending, and with far-out technologies across the whole spectrum of electronics, turns to outside suppliers for a personal computer. But the equally pernicious "Invented Here But Not Used" has to be discarded, too—and there's no point in denying that technology transfer, within big corporations and between them, is among the most difficult arts of corporate management.

Or perhaps the truth is that corporate management makes it

difficult. When Steven Jobs and his software supremo, John Couch, saw Smalltalk, a revolutionary program devised at PARC (the Xerox Palo Alto Research Center), it was love at first sight. The most striking feature was a hand-held control ("the mouse") instead of a keyboard. Jobs hired one of Smalltalk's top developers, and used the Xerox technology in the product revolution ushered in by Lisa and its smaller stable-companion.

If you think about it, nothing is more natural than seeing what you want and using it; and nothing more unnatural than refusing to look, or seeing what you need and refusing to use it. Yet companies do that again and again, including some of the mightiest names of all. The tire companies unanimously, and with catastrophic results, tried to avoid following Michelin down the obviously better route of the steel radial tire. When NCR fell drastically behind the competition after the electronic cash register became technically possible, even after the supreme effort of corporate will mentioned earlier had forced NCR back into the game, it still couldn't regain all its old supremacy in the marketplace.

What the new management boils down to is doing what comes naturally. In fairness, in the old days, the natural tendency to defend and build on the established technology in the firm probably made sense. A company like 3M could stick to the technologies of coating and bonding, a firm like Canon to optics, precision mechanics, and their derivatives. But the logical roads that lead to information technology, which come from many directions, are taking managements a long, long way from their bases. They will never complete the journey successfully unless they're prepared to decentralize decisions, to change anything and everything if necessary, and to be proud only of their results.

15. THE CLIMB UP CANON'S MOUNT FUJI

The paradox is that all these themes of the new Supermanager are echoed and emphasized, not just among the hot-rod kids of Silicon

Valley, but in the most tradition-dominated industrial society of them all—Japan. A typical example is Ryuzaburo Kaku, the president of Canon. The fact that he has spent most of his career in what seem to be head-office finance jobs looks like another Western similarity; finance has long been a popular, common route to the top in the U.S. and Britain.

But the resemblance is only skin-deep; corporate accountancy to the Japanese, and in Japanese, means more nearly "controlling managers." Kaku's career is that of a businessman and manager, although he did start in cost accountancy, counting sales slips on an abacus. Bored beyond distraction, it is said, Kaku got the idea of seeing just how quickly he could get through this tiresome task, and discovered that finding ways of increasing efficiency made the boring not only better, but fascinating.

That was the start of a central conviction that "nothing is ever 100 percent," that efficiency must be increased—not only for its own sake, but for the knock-on effects on morale, dedication, and corporate capability. The conviction led Kaku from early in his career to suggest a profit center organization to recalcitrant superiors. They finally gave in, under the 1975 "embarrassment" of losing money and suspending the dividend; and the victory in this argument was presumably decisive in Kaku's elevation, on his predecessor's death, to his present job.

He makes no bones about his own performance in that role. Kaku is fifty-seven, short by Western standards, a practiced talker with touches of vivid humor, who smokes, blinks, and gestures as he expounds and expands on the Canon themes. He conveys a clear sense of the power he unquestionably wields: "In Japanese companies the president has the utmost or dominant power." There's no supervisory board of directors or individual shareholder breathing down his neck; he can even fix his own salary. As Kaku says, "Unless you are a man with good self-control, you tend to be a tyrant-type boss."

That Kaku is not. Objecting to the pure, naked capitalist with no corporate idealism, he says, "In that sense, I'm not a capitalist, nor a tyrant." In fact, the major change he made to correct the harsh fact that "Canon was a company with very poor management" was to decentralize power—to give authority to the product group heads. Their groups now operate as self-contained companies, with their own balance sheets, own R & D, own borrowings (from the core company), and own factories. The latter embody another Kaku reform. Before that, plants made a mix of unrelated products.

Throughout the company, the reform consisted fundamentally of pushing responsibility down the line, concentrating on strategic target-setting at the top, and leaving it to the lower levels to decide details of strategy and tactics, which feed back from the bottom for top approval. In other words, Canon operates the now standard American recipe for good organizational practice, but with far from standard success. Since 1975 sales have expanded by 385 percent and net profits by 1,233 percent, while the dividend is 158 percent higher than it was before the 1975 suspension.

The main purpose was to add to Canon's existing strengths (high-precision products and excellent personnel relations) two more: higher productivity (easy for a Westerner to understand) and an expansion of Canon's management philosophy (not so easy). Kaku's "premier company concept," though, is as real and important to him as the economic analysis of Canon's profit performance. That shows, going right back to 1950, how each major new product resulted in an upward burst in profits. "Ever since I worked in Canon, I saw this point. But the voice of the low man on the totem pole cannot be heard by the man at the top." After the "tragedy" of 1975 had propelled Kaku to the top, however, he achieved a most remarkable demonstration of the strength of his ideas.

The quintupling of sales and thirteenfold rise in net profits since then surely prove Kaku's point. The major innovations since 1973 have totaled seven—as many as in the previous twenty-three years. Kaku has reached his target ("a climb to the top of Mount Fuji") of making Canon a "premier" Japanese company in every respect—social, technological, and economic: "this is what I have done in the past."

For the future, he has started on a five-year second phase to achieve "premier" status on the world scene, "to get to the top of Mount Everest." Since that means, as noted, raising the proportion of R & D spending to sales to some 10 percent against 4 percent in

1982, Kaku has to accept that for those five years profits will be "more or less flat." After this comes the third phase, for which he is "dreaming that we can attain a similar growth rate" to the profits explosion of 1975–82.

Leaving aside (although you really shouldn't in Japan) the philosophical content and context of Kaku's extraordinary record, its elements are those which dominate the new management: setting a clear, strong overall corporate target; breaking that down into specific goals for specific businesses built around their markets; marshaling the resources of the firm (technological, design, financial, human, production) in support of the drive for the goals and the markets; animating the whole enterprise by a careful labor relations policy designed to maximize the motivational power of the overall strategy.

It's one thing to have a recipe, though—quite another to cook the dish. The quiet power and total confidence radiated by Kaku ("there is no limit to Canon") almost conceals the fact that to fulfill "the duty imposed on us," which "is to live for ever as a going concern," he took a high-risk route up Mount Fuji. The continuing risks are certainly no lower, as Kaku perhaps acknowledges when he says, "Maybe when you come back here in five years' time, Canon will be bankrupt. But I shan't be sitting here." One of his little jokes.

16. MASTERING AMERICAN MANAGEMENT

The ascent of those mountains by the premier Japanese companies, both in the older industries and in the new technologies, has been so rapid that many Americans have attributed it to magic—or machination. But there's no secret, no magic, no mystery—only the repetition, in Asia, of a process that astonished the world a long time ago—in the United States.

Relentless innovation, ceaseless invasion of world markets, steeply rising productivity, domination of new industries, seemingly unbeatable market power, apparently infinite management superiority—all these were characteristic of America, or the attitude of others to America, until the Eisenhower era. The Japanese are emulating the American takeoff, and over a much longer time scale than it appears. The amazing growth of a company like Canon, from world nonentity to international sales of $2.5 billion, may seem a typical product of the gee-whiz 1970s. The true parallel is the expansion of an American firm of Polaroid's generation; Canon covers much the same time span as Polaroid, but with vastly greater latter-day success.

The American company's sales got stuck at around $1.3 billion precisely because Polaroid did not, like Canon and other Japanese firms in older, maturing technologies, make a successful break into business machines, or find some other entry point into the new world of information technology. The Polaroid people, in the wake of Dr. Edwin Land's departure, are trying to pick up where that Supermanager left off, finding computer industry applications for their know-how. But they won't succeed in the new management unless they emulate the Japanese—and that means mastering, not Oriental mysteries, but American management at its very best.

Japan's success stems from Western-style objectives achieved predominantly by using and developing Western methods. It may be more comforting for those who could have done likewise, but didn't, to blame their failure on irrelevancies like MITI, national culture, Japan, Inc., bank money, protection, the cheap yen, dumping, etc, etc.). The reality is far more uncomfortable. The best Japanese have just managed the new industries more efficiently—much more.

The tables have been turned only where companies have let them be turned. Take Xerox. That there should be one Japanese copier firm is remarkable enough, given the original patent-protected power of Xerox. That there are several is again evidence, not just of competitive drive, but of a competitive courage that is either lacking in the West or, if it does exist, often lacks the same intelligent strategic effort.

James Abegglen, of the Boston Consulting Group, a thirty-year veteran of the Japanese internecine wars, recalls warning the chief executive of Xerox that it was worth giving away the 914 copier in

Japan, keeping the major profit, which comes from the consumables (paper, etc.), and keeping out the Japanese, who would otherwise go for the soft underbelly of the giant. The Xerox boss laughed; his successors are doing so on the other side of their faces. At Canon, Kaku now reckons to be ahead of Xerox in "one-year placements" of copiers and says, ominously enough for the Rochester, New York, giant that "we now have very unique technologies coming"— the age of the laser copier, for example, is about to dawn. Invented here or not invented here, Canon is determined to have the technology to meet its aims—"as a final stage, to be number one."

That is the starting point for the new management. Everybody can't be first, but those who don't try to win, and do all that is necessary for victory, will lose. In Japan, that urge runs right through the corporation, from top to bottom. "Let's upgrade our ability to meet more challenging targets," declares the challenging notice outside Canon's factory in Fukushima. Every identity card on every worker, from plant manager to guide, bears the initials ZD. It stands for "zero defects." Again, the temptation is to see this motivational zest as peculiarly Japanese, but it's the same rah-rah enthusiasm that used to offend European intellectuals as an expression of crude American materialism—and "zero defects" is, of course, an American management technique, first introduced in California.

Wherever you go in a star Japanese company in information technology or any new industry, the same striking fact leaps out— America was there before. But while the best Americans still practice the technique to near-perfection, most Americans have forgotten what they're supposed to be doing, and the Japanese have improved on what they have learned. Take quality. "Quality improvement will bring about lower cost of production," says one plant manager, echoing the pure doctrine of Frederick W. Deming, the American guru of statistical quality control. The Japanese have developed Deming's concept and his statistics to form production systems so rigorous that end-of-process defects are hardly worth enumerating.

Much the same is true even of management style. For all the hierarchy in Japanese companies, and for all the dominance of the president, the apparent behavior of Japanese high-tech managers bears most resemblance to the democratic, horizontal, participative style that is now the favored managerial mode in the West. It's hardly surprising—for group loyalty and group working are, of course, the Japanese norm. Not only does the lifetime career mean that every manager, having worked from the bottom to the top, knows everything (and everyone) on the same gamut. But an executive in any capacity—whether he's a scientist or an accountant or a salesman or a personnel man—is expected to be thoroughly familiar with every aspect of the business that his fellow managers are doing, including their experiences out in the marketplace.

This doesn't mean that the Japanese manager has no personal ambition. True, the competition for power, status, and success inside the Japanese company is concealed both by the layers of deeply innate Japanese politeness (it's a language in which swearing is next to impossible) and by reticence before outsiders. But the competition is still there and, so it is said, fierce. It works, however, through the group and the company. The object is not only for the executive to succeed but for the company to win—and winning means being best, which in turn means largest.

That's no different from the King of the Market philosophy that has long animated Western giants—although the best Japanese companies add another Western ingredient, the concept of the product life cycle. Firms like Canon didn't go into copiers, etc. for fun or to acquire "second or third legs," but because the camera had plainly become a mature product. To stay on a growth track, let alone become a "world premier" company, the firm had to have growth markets. The law of Japan's commercial jungle is survival. True survival to a Japanese is success, and the mistake of all too many American giants was not to see (a) that products had reached the maturing stage of the life cycle and (b) that only very important new markets, in which they could build a unique position, would fill the growth gap. Any American management professor could (and did) tell them so.

Any business historian could also have stressed the umbilical relationship between an end producer and his supplier—only think of the development of in-house supplies by companies like AT & T or IBM. But the long-term relationships that quality and reliability imply haven't been taken to their logical conclusion—except in Japan. Where a Western factory might have four vendors jockeying to supply an identical component, the Japanese have long-term relationships with single suppliers, regarded as part of the family. If that looks like one uniquely national feature, it isn't. The same principle has long been applied by efficient Westerners, who not only specify their requirements in exhaustive detail, but assist the supplier to meet the required standards—and, if need be, invest in that supplier.

IBM is doing just that by buying into Intel—while other investments (like that in Rolm, the private branch exchange, or PBX, company) are designed to strengthen IBM in areas of weakness. In modern conditions, even the strongest company can't be strong at all points—and Japanese companies have not only mastered the necessity of technology changes but, for the same reason, have incorporated the SWOT analysis (recommended earlier in this book) as one of the bases for American-style corporate planning. That is indispensable in the new industries—not because these are more plannable, but because of their very uncertainties.

Analyzing SWOT (Strengths, Weaknesses, Opportunities, and Threats) helps greatly to position the high-tech company as it pushes forward to meet its long-term objectives by following its medium-term, detailed course, allowing for contingencies as it proceeds. The basic procedures were pioneered by U.S. companies like General Electric. But too many of GE's imitators thought the plan, rather than its objectives, was the name of the game. That often trapped them in ill-conceived acquisitions and outmoded technologies. The real object of planning is to achieve the optimum supply, allocation, and application of resources to meet high but realistic targets, which a Canon planner rightly sums up as "to become rich by healthy growth."

You won't get that, however, without a healthy relationship between all the people in the company. The adversary relationship between management and work force that was allowed to grow up inside Western companies isn't the natural order of things—it's most unnatural. The IBM approach is no different from that of the Japanese high-tech leaders. In the common labor policies of leading-edge innovators, the critical elements include (1) carefully controlled numbers, (2) good, progressive pay, (3) good jobs, (4) excellent training, (5) promotion by assessed merit, (6) continuous and effective motivation programs, (7) constant communications, (8) highly accessible management, (9) social equality within the company, (10) growth and constant change in products and processes . . . and so on. Provide all that, and you don't need Japanese culture to get good labor relations and performance.

But none of this means that the Japanese are invincible or invulnerable. By definition, whatever they have done or are doing can be emulated, or has been pioneered, by companies in the U.S.— companies that have many natural advantages over an Asian country with restricted land area and domestic markets. At Canon, for example, president Kaku became convinced that without investing in overseas production and in vastly higher R & D, "there is no future for Canon." The same requirement applies to all industry in the IT era. Existing products, plants, and processes will not be enough without the plans and the planned spending to enhance and reinforce them.

Apart from anything else, the borders between industries are breaking down. Hence the new partnerships between not only IBM and Rolm but also L. M. Ericsson (Swedish, telecommunications) and Honeywell (computers), AT & T Olivetti (business machines), and Philips (Dutch, electronics). Just as departments within firms must learn to communicate rather than compete, so isolationism is impossible in tomorrow's industries—the manager needs to form partnerships, inside and outside the firm, as never before. The days have gone when one stand-alone product offered a golden key to an unlimited future. The new technologies offer future riches even greater than the phenomenal fortunes already created. But the evidence from Japan's successes, and from the equal triumphs of the best of the West, is that only excellence of all-around, commonsense, imaginative, competitive management will produce the necessary high-flying results.

To summarize some of the important points I've mentioned in Step Ten:

1. Hire well and you'll never have to fire.
2. If the cuckoo won't sing, help it to.
3. Always give in when you're wrong.
4. Never give in when you're right—except as a last resort.
5. If you want managers to manage well, manage them well.
6. Atmosphere doesn't Supermanage companies; professionalism does. That's why you need a collegial atmosphere—to get professionalism.
7. Get to know what it is you *don't* know as fast as you can.
8. Keep HQ staff numbers low, and the visibility of discrete, autonomous businesses high.
9. If you don't understand the new technology, get to understand its import and importance—at all costs.
10. Never take a step forward without working out what the one afterward will be.
11. Run your operation on the 3D principle: Divide, Decentralize, and Devolve.
12. Conscious or not, your company has a culture: marry it to your markets and aims. If your managers aren't four-eyed, with Independence, Identity, Iconoclasm, and Integrity, give them all four.
13. The fifth eye is Intelligence—all the relevant information and the wit to exploit it.
14. Manage technology naturally—by doing what comes naturally.
15. Don't look for the secrets of Japanese management: look for Japan's use of Western methods to achieve Western-style objectives—and copy that.

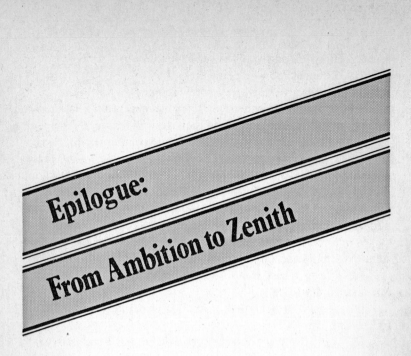

Epilogue:
From Ambition to Zenith

There's a vital reason why everyone should try to make the journey from Ambition to Zenith—from mere management to Supermanagement. Not so long ago, management was a specialized art, craft, or racket. The only people (almost all of them male) who needed management's arts and crafts worked in businesses, and those mostly of the larger variety. Even inside the corporations, management was the prerogative of an elite, a minority even of the men in the gray flannel suits. Not so today. Now the majority of white-collar occupations, male and female, demand some degree of management skill and knowledge—and not just in businesses alone.

In the proliferating bureaucracies; in the arts organizations; in the churches and the armed forces; in the public schools and the private clubs; in every place where two or three are gathered together in anybody's name, those with responsibility of any kind now have to understand and apply, in everyday practice, the principles of positive organization and execution which have been described in this book.

"Positive" is the basic word. Things have to be *made* to happen in the way you want them to happen. Without management, without the intervention of organized willpower, the desired result simply cannot be obtained.

In these bygone, good old days, you could safely leave the control and ordering of events to somebody else—the Man, the Boss. As for him, he was in a class of his own, relying mostly on instinct, personality, and authority. But today, instinct is not enough, personality must be coupled with intellect, and authority has fragmented. Inside every organization the number of bosses has multiplied enormously—and the big boss's work has been subdivided and parceled out, whether he knows it or not. That fact imposes powerful new demands on the person at the top—and on all those between that level and the bottom.

That's why he has to become a Supermanager—the boss of bosses. That's why the lesser leaders have to master the same know-how, the same ideas, and the same action routines that the Supermanager commands. The job is to manage yourself, and other people, brilliantly as you all move through the fast-changing late-twentieth-century landscape. Technology, innovation, marketing, organization, financial structure, productivity, futurology, turnarounds, etc., etc.—all the large words that used to belong exclusively to the large men in the large corporations now belong to almost everybody. To that extent, we're all bosses now.

There are exceptions—musicians and writers, painters and actors, and other solo performers. But "solo" is the giveaway. Move only a short distance from the solitary career, acquire only the slightest necessity to combine it with the careers of others, and you're in the world of management. That universe abounds with jargon and confusion, uncertainty and illusion—like most of human life. But the secrets of the Supermanager described here are not difficult to grasp. It's their application that sorts out the men from the boys—and the women from the girls.

The important trick is to forget the fear and self-doubt that so often come between the principle and the practice, that prevent people from utilizing the power of management to bend the world some of the way toward its wishes. This necessity to take events, and sometimes people, by the scruff of the neck is the reflection of a great tidal change—the coming and swelling of the Age of Complexity.

The difference between management and administration (which is what the bureaucrats used to do exclusively) is the difference between choice and rigidity. What makes today's society so complex, and management so essential, are the endless number of options and the increasing degrees of uncertainty. Take people. In days when they did what they were told, running the people side of an organization was almost entirely an administrative task. Nobody had to worry about the behavior of blue- or white-collar workers (as a whole host of management scientists do today) because behavior patterns were safe and predictable. Today, getting performance out of people has become a complex problem, and the choices of solution are innumerable. The men and the women can't be administered anymore.

They have to be managed.

Take technology. Time was when a printing business could be founded because the proprietor wanted to publish a little magazine close to his heart. There was only one cheap printing process, and competition was so local that the business could potter along for years without the boss even taking much interest in its affairs. But today the technology is diverse, expensive, fast-changing, electronically controlled; the competition is global; the market for print is far more various

387

and fragmented than anybody could have imagined at the end of World War II. The technology won't look after itself anymore.

It has to be managed.

Take markets. There was a time when a manufacturing company sold through only one chain of distribution and either used only one form of promotion or none at all. Today, amid a mass of possible outlets, and countless means of peddling his wares, the manufacturer has as many permutations and combinations as a chess player—and his competition may not even be in the same line of business. If many more people buy expensive cameras, or personal computers, or video recorders, fewer will buy hi-fi—because the products are competing for the same discretionary pound or dollar. Markets can't be taken for granted anymore.

They have to be managed.

Take competition, anyway. Two generations, even a generation, ago you knew where it would come from (home, seldom abroad) and how it would come. Market share and market segments meant nothing. In present (and future) conditions, competition can come from anywhere—possibly from right across the world—and precise information about competitive standing in the marketplace, defined as exactly as possible, may make all the difference between survival and sinking, let alone between success and failure. The competitive battle can't be waged by instinct anymore.

It has to be managed.

All the examples just mentioned, of course, are commercial. But the principles and the precepts are no different in organizations (in government or anywhere else) where the services, by and large, are not exchanged for money. They still *cost* money. There was a time when resources were more abundant, when administrators or bureaucrats could do their jobs without knowing or counting the cost. Today, when resources are limited, but needs are infinite, service organizations must be run with all the economic efficiency of profit-making enterprise—or else. They can't be taken for granted anymore.

They have to be managed.

All these activities and outfits can be managed only by individuals. True, they must act, more and more, in combination with others, but that, too, demands individual management skill. There's no escape; in the end, success is always an expression of the individual. His or her ambition, like any aspect of the human personality, can take many different forms; and it's also true that the realization of ambition, like any development of human life, depends heavily on hazard, on chance. But however generous the fates, the individual still has to harness his ambition to his means in order to reach his final potential and objective, his Zenith.

That's what Supermanagement means. For most people, negotiating the long distance from Ambition to Zenith is a once-in-a-lifetime journey—but it won't accomplish itself. It means competing with everybody, including yourself, to beat and raise your own best standards.

In other words, it has to be managed. The Supermanagers whose deeds have been depicted in this book have shown the way. The road and the destination are here for the taking.

Acknowledgments

This book grew originally out of my work editing and writing the *Company Director's Letter* and *Management Confidential*—both of which sprang from the fertile minds of Sylvester Stein and his associates at Stonehart Publications, Robert Troop, and the late Robert Pethick. To them and to their many thousands of management readers, I owe much firsthand experience in what practical managers want and need to know during the 1980s. My thinking has been influenced by Peter F. Drucker (above all), Kenichi Ohmae of McKinsey & Co., Tokyo, Thomas J. Peters, Philip Kohler, John Thackray, Tom Lester, and many others. I am in their debt.

    Management Today has been a prolific source of information and inspiration. I am grateful to its contributors whose articles on management themes have helped bring joy to my heart and knowledge to my store. The chapters draw for illustrative and other matter on many different published sources, some listed below, with my warm thanks.

    My deep and particular gratitude goes to my publisher, Truman Talley, for his major contributions and unstinting help. My thanks also go to Hilary Rubinstein, of A.P. Watt, who followed this book patiently through the many twists and

ACKNOWLEDGMENTS

turns that took it to its present form. William Armstrong, managing director of Sidgwick & Jackson, played an invaluable role in the book's genesis. Anne Leguen de Lacroix, Karen Gorman, Jane Morgan, Judith Yisowich, Liz Bowden, Helen Cooke, and my daughter, Jane Heller, have all given excellent and much valued assistance.

The sources on which I have drawn are acknowledged in the text. I should like to pay particular tribute to the editors of the *Harvard Business Review,* the *McKinsey Quarterly, Fortune, Time,* and *Business Week* for the high value of their publications. The November/December 1979 *Harvard Business Review* played a special role: the list of entrepreneurial qualities in Step One, Chapter One, appeared in an article by Geoffrey A. Timmons and inspired the shape of this book.

I must also thank the publishers for permission to quote from the following books: The British Institute of Management for extracts from *How to be Interviewed* by Mackenzie Davey and P. McDonnell and from *Time: The Essence* by Bruce Austin; David and Charles for an extract from *The Evolving Brain* by Tony Buzan; the Hamlyn Publishing Group Ltd. for an extract from *Fit for Life* by Donald Norfolk; Heinemann Educational Books for an extract from *Pricing: Principles and Practices* by Andre Gabor; State Mutual Book and Periodical Service for extracts from *Bargaining for Results* by John Winkler and from *Coverdale on Management* by Max Taylor; the London Business School for an extract from the 1979 Stockton Lecture delivered by A. S. C. Ehrenberg (published in the *London Business School Journal*); McGraw-Hill Book Company (UK) Limited for an extract from *Managing for Profit* edited by Patrick R. Mills (copyright 1982), published in association with the Institute of Chartered Accountants in England and Wales; Oyez Longman Publishing Ltd. for an extract from *Troubleshooting* by David Duckworth and Ian Blackshaw; Sanders and Sidney for an extract from a Sanders and Sidney pamphlet; the Toyota Motor Sales Company Ltd. for extracts from *My Years with Toyota* by Seisi Kato; Kondansha International for excerpts from *Honda Motor; The Men, The Management, The Machines* by Tetsuo Sakiya; Times Books for passages from *The Changing World of the Executive* by Peter F. Drucker; and Harper & Row for material from *In Search of Excellence* by Thomas J. Peters and Robert H. Waterman, Jr.

Selected Bibliography

BLANCHARD, KENNETH, and JOHNSON, SPENCER. *The One Minute Manager.* New York: William Morrow, 1982.
A one-idea book: but the idea—true delegation combined with management objectives—is a strong one.

CLEVELAND, HARLAN. *The Future Executive: A Guide for Tomorrow's Managers.* New York: Harper & Row, 1972.
Highly intelligent exploration of the demands that unprecedented change will make on management.

CROSBY, PHILLIP. *Quality Is Free: The Art of Making Quality Free.* New York: McGraw-Hill, 1979.
A valuable, practical, original American look at what has come to be regarded as a Japanese art.

DRUCKER, PETER F. *The Changing World of the Executive.* New York: Truman Talley Books • Times Books, 1982.
———. *The Effective Executive.* New York: Harper & Row, 1967.
———. *Management: Tasks, Practices, Responsibilities.* New York: Harper & Row, 1974.
Three of the best from the master of insights into the realities of effective management.

391

GELLERMAN, SAUL W. *Managers & Subordinates.* New York: Holt, Rinehart & Winston, 1976.

A practitioner's sound, hardheaded guide to the increasingly vital areas of people management.

HAMERMESH, RICHARD G., ed. *Strategic Management.* New York: John Wiley, 1983.

A collection of diverse practical insights into strategy from the fount of U.S. management—*Harvard Business Review.*

JAY, ANTONY. *Management and Machiavelli: An Inquiry into the Politics of Corporate Life.* Holt, Rinehart & Winston, 1968.

A clever application of Renaissance principles to the problem of modern management.

KATO, SEISI. *My Years with Toyota.* Tokyo: Toyota Motor Sales, 1981.

A brief but fascinating account of the hard truths behind the making of a Japanese myth.

KEPNER, CHARLES H., and TREGOE, BENJAMIN B. *The Rational Manager: A Systematic Approach to Problem Solving and Decision Making.* New York: McGraw-Hill, 1965.

A detailed step-by-step approach to sensible, planned decision making.

MCKINSEY & CO. *The Arts of Top Management: A McKinsey Anthology.* New York: McGraw-Hill, 1971.

Wide-ranging advice from the consultants who have been the most bountiful source of new ideas.

OHMAE, KENICHI. *The Mind of the Strategist: The Art of Japanese Business.* New York: McGraw-Hill, 1982.

An insider's expert view of how Japanese business has cracked its markets.

PASCALE, RICHARD T., and ATHOS, ANTHONY G. *The Art of Japanese Management.* New York: Simon & Schuster, 1981.

Where and how Japanese companies differ from—and most resemble—those elsewhere in the world.

PETERS, THOMAS J., and WATERMAN, JR., ROBERT H. *In Search of Excellence.* New York: Harper & Row, 1982.

The best account yet of the eight common factors shared by successful managements in substantial corporations.

SAKIYA, TETSUO. *Honda Motor: The Men, the Management, the Machines.* Tokyo: Kodansha, 1982.

An enlightening, engrossing account of an oddball Japanese entrepreneur who made motor management history.

SLOAN, ALFRED J. *My Years with General Motors.* New York: Doubleday, 1964.

A rare and rarely instructive self-told tale of the creation of a great industrial and commercial empire.

TOWNSEND, ROBERT O. *Further Up the Organization.* New York: Alfred A. Knopf, 1984.

An iconoclastic, stimulating, offbeat account of ways to unfetter bureaucratic straitjackets.

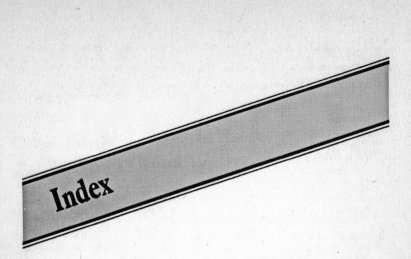

Index

INDEX

BIM Foundation, 37
Black & Decker, 82–83, 134, 135
Blackshaw, Ian, 328
BMW, 24, 179
board of directors, 338–41
Boeing, 138–41, 177, 178
Borman, Frank, 127
Boston Consulting Group, 60, 61, 86, 87, 380
brainstorming, 297–99
Branch, Ben, 106
branding, 196
Bray, John, 5–6
British Leyland, 179
Brooks, Mel, 344
Brown, Mark, 303, 307
Brown, Rosemary, 214
BTR, 64
budgetary control systems, 162
Buggie, Fred, 297–99
Burbridge, John L. 157–59
Burck, Charles G., 18
Bureau of the Budget, 50
Burger King, 149
Burroughs, 358
business: distinction between management and, 161–64
Business Segment Strategy Value (BSSV) ratings, 59
Business Week, 20, 51, 227, 234, 281, 359
buy-outs, 6–9, 12
buy response, 195
Buzan, Tony, 40–41
bypass attack, 313–14

Campbell's Soup, 317
"canary theory" of motivation, 242
Canon, 168, 202–4, 357, 372, 374–84
Carlson, Ed, 219
Carter, Jimmy, 269
Cary, Frank, 29
cash flow: negative, 106–7; ratio of current liabilities to, 96
Casio, 167
Caterpillar Tractor, 29, 84, 85, 177, 197, 199, 259
Cathay Pacific Airlines, 153–55
Caulkin, Simon, 356
CBS, 253
cellular production, 159
Central Intelligence Agency (CIA), 286
Chief Executive, The (magazine), 119
Chrysler Corporation, 97, 102–4
Churchill, Winston, 35, 72, 229
Citroën, 69
City Investing, 66, 334
Clausen, Tom, 233
clerical effectiveness, 114
"closing," 320–21
Coca-Cola, 50–51
Cole, Graham, 142–44
Colgate-Palmolive, 314

collegial management, 344–53; motivation in, 351–52
Columbia Pictures, 51
Commerce Department, 100
communication, 132–34, 247; clarity of, 15; in crises, 269–70; sales and, 325
competition: defense against, 316–19; internal, 29; Japanese, 166–67, 311–13, 358, 380, 382; management of, 389; strategies for, 313–16; turnarounds in face of, 203
competitor comparison survey, 196
Congress, U.S., 103
Connell, David, 109
Conoco, 187
consultants, 208–16; guidelines for successful use of, 213–16; innovation, 296–97; public relations, 242–46; reintroduction of management disciplines by, 208–10
continuity: as objective, 169–70; risk-taking vs., 50–51
Cooper, Kenneth H., 34
Corning Glass, 149
costs: constant, 104–7; fixed, 111–12; labor, 115–28; market position and, 179; reduction in, 112–15, 269–70; replacement, 100; waste and, 257–58, 265
Couch, John, 376
Coverdale, Ralph, 352
critical volume gain (CVG) or loss (CVL), 109–11
Crompton, 148–49
Crosby, Philip, 262
current liabilities: ratio of cash flow to, 96–98
Curtice, Harlow (Red), 20
Curtis, Helene, 315

Dana Corporation, 127, 230, 246–48
Dannon yogurt, 66
D'Arcy-McManus & Masius, 274
Datsun, 272
Davey, Mackenzie, 53, 56
Davidson, J. J., 293
decentralization, 246–47; in high-tech industries, 363
delegation: overcoming problems with, 307
Deloitte, Haskins & Sell, 109
DeLorean, John Z., 20
Delta Airlines, 177
Dembitz, John, 117
Deming, Frederick W., 381
Deming, W. Edwards, 262–64
Deming Prize for Application, 261
de Vries, Johan, 286–87
diet, 35–36
differentiation, 179; innovation and, 293–95; marketing and, 195
Digital Equipment Corporation, 4, 176–77, 228, 229, 315, 358–60, 364

Seacoast, 186
Securities and Exchange Commission, 46
security, 132
"self-fulfilling prophecy," 303
Seligman, David, 330
Senker, Peter, 290, 291
Sequoia Capital Fund, 357
served market share, 86
set. *See* mind set
setup: efficiency of, 130–31
Shana, Abraham, 248–49
Shell, 286–87
Shepherd, Mark, 176
Sheridan, Richard, 245
shoddy goods strategy, 83
Shorrock, J. E. T., 59
Siemens, 102
Silverman, Fred, 253
Simpson, David, 373–74
Singer, 232–34
Singh, Ravi, 313, 314, 316
Singleton, Henry, 334, 354
Smalltalk, 376
Smirnoff, 108
Smith, F. E., 328
Smith, J. Howard, 186
Smith, Peter, 156–57
Smith, Roger B., 20, 23, 24
Sony, 76, 77, 167, 311, 362
Spencer, Anne, 338
Sperry, 289
Squibb Pharmaceuticals, 66
Stanton, Michael, 133
statistical quality control, 260–64
stock control, 217–18
Strategic Innovations, 297, 299
Strategic Planning Institute, 107
strategy, 247; board of directors and, 339–40; competitive, 313–16; mistakes in, 251–52. *See also* goals; planning
stress interviews, 56–57
strikes, 145–48
success: criteria for measuring, 173–75
Sullivan, Fred, 334
Swannack, A. R., 122–23
SWOT analysis, 78–81, 383

Tandem, 356, 359
Tateishi, Takao, 166
taxes: inflation and, 100
Taylor, Max, 39, 352
teamwork, 14, 269–72
technology, 277–85; management of, 290–92, 388–89; markets for, 281–82; planning and, 282–85; snags in, 279; spending for, 280. *See also* information technology industry
Technology Review, 346
Teijin, 168
Teledyne, 334, 354
Tenneco, 285–86
Testing for Success, 174

Texas Instruments, 25, 176, 229, 240–42, 295
Textron, 4
Thackery, John, 25, 26, 66, 232, 233, 371
Thornton, Charles (Tex), 11, 334
3M, 29, 30, 176–78, 228–30, 358, 370–72, 376
time management, 38–40; organizational structure and, 71–73
Timex, 318
Tobias, Andrew, 330
top management: performance of, 334–37; routes to, 331–34
Toshiba, 166, 168, 203
Touche Ross, 106
Townsend, Robert, 213
Toyo Kogyo, 349–50
Toyota, 19, 24, 47–49, 167, 181–82, 272–73, 324
training, 247, 351; application of, 228–30; on-the-job, 227–28; in management courses, 224–27; quality control and, 263, 267; sales, 319–22, 325–26; teamwork and, 270
Transitron, 373
Travelodge, 3
Tregoe, Benjamin B., 222, 223
trends, 285–86; forecasts of, 190–93; identification of, 189–90
trust, 14
Twentieth Century-Fox, 330

underpricing, 108–11
unions, 141–44; negotiations with, 64–65, 301, 326; scapegoating of, 19; standing firm with, 144–45; strikes by, 145–48
United Airlines, 219
United Auto Workers (UAW), 19, 24, 103
United Scientific Holdings, 172–73, 175
United Technologies, 334
Univac, 364, 365

Valentine, Don, 354, 356–57
value-added scheme, 121–24
value analysis, 264–65, 268
values: instillation of, 227–28
Vanderbilt, Gloria, 190
Vickers da Costa, 173
visibility, 142, 247
VisiCalc, 354, 361
Volkswagen, 19, 23, 48, 49, 302

Wall Street Journal, 166
Wardle Lionel, 249–50
Washington Post, 52
Waste, 256–59, 265–66
Waterford crystal, 323
Waterman, Robert H., Jr., *xv*, 28–30, 175, 176, 178, 228, 370
Watson, Thomas, Jr., 370
Watson, Thomas, Sr., 29, 362–65, 370
Weinstock, Arnold, 3, 4

Catalog

If you are interested in a list of fine Paperback
books, covering a wide range of subjects
and interests, send your name and address,
requesting your free catalog, to:

McGraw-Hill Paperbacks
1221 Avenue of Americas
New York, N.Y. 10020